Critical Disaster Studies

CRITICAL STUDIES IN RISK AND DISASTER

Kim Fortun and Scott Gabriel Knowles, Series Editors

Critical Studies in Risk and Disaster explores how
environmental, technological, and health risks are
created, managed, and analyzed in different contexts.
Global in scope and drawing on perspectives from
multiple disciplines, volumes in the series examine
the ways that planning, science, and technology
are implicated in disasters. The series also engages
public policy formation—including analysis of science,
technology, and environmental policy as well as
welfare, conflict resolution, and economic policy
developments where relevant.

Critical Disaster Studies

Edited by

Jacob A. C. Remes

and

Andy Horowitz

PENN

UNIVERSITY OF PENNSYLVANIA PRESS

PHILADELPHIA

Published by
University of Pennsylvania Press
Philadelphia, Pennsylvania 19104-4112
www.upenn.edu/pennpress

Printed in the United States of America on acid-free paper
10 9 8 7 6 5 4 3 2 1

Library of Congress Cataloging-in-Publication Data

Names: Remes, Jacob A. C., 1980– editor. | Horowitz, Andy (Andrew Deutsch), editor.
Title: Critical disaster studies / edited by Jacob A.C. Remes and Andy Horowitz.
Other titles: Critical studies in risk and disaster. Description: 1st edition. |
Philadelphia : University of Pennsylvania Press, [2021] | Series: Critical studies
in risk and disaster | Includes bibliographical references and index.
Identifiers: LCCN 2021001911 | ISBN 9780812253245 (hardcover)
Subjects: LCSH: Disasters. | Disasters—Political aspects. | Disasters—Social aspects.
Classification: LCC HV553 .C76 2021 | DDC 363.34--dc23
LC record available at https://lccn.loc.gov/2021001911

CONTENTS

INTRODUCTION

PART I. KNOWING DISASTER

PART II. GOVERNING DISASTER

Introducing Critical Disaster Studies

Andy Horowitz and Jacob A. C. Remes

Scholars have come to accept the once controversial maxim that there is no such thing as a natural disaster. The causes and consequences of disaster are not defined by an autonomous natural order, nor are they inevitable. Rather, they are bound up in human history, shaped by human action and inaction.[1] The recognition of this truth does not close the book on the study of disaster, of course. It does, however, demand new books that take it as their premise, not their argument. This is such a book.

So here is a new idea: there is no such thing as a disaster.

There are floods and earthquakes, wars and famines, engineering failures and economic collapses, but to describe any of these things as a disaster represents an act of interpretation. The first principle of critical disaster studies is the insistence that "disaster" itself is an analytical conceit.

It is a conceit that suits our age. In the context of the climate crisis, the COVID-19 pandemic, and a seemingly endless barrage of spectacular human failures and devastating human suffering, disasters increasingly captivate observers.They offer lenses that can bring contemporary life into clearer focus.[2]

This book reflects the efforts of a group of scholars to consider a new generation of research on disasters and to chart a course for future study. We find common cause under the banner of "critical disaster studies," even as our individual research agendas span at least seven disciplines and four continents. The "critical" part of critical disaster studies signals a critique of dominant intellectual traditions. The questions we ask, and the kinds of answers we seek, distinguish our research from the applied work in the field of disaster risk reduction and much of traditional disaster studies in general.

Existing research often assumes the category of disaster as an objective given and aspires to a technical analysis of achievements and failures—while treating political and historical context as, at best, just another variable in the matrix.[3] Our approach is to do the opposite. We do not take disasters, as a thing in themselves, for granted. We find context essential. Therefore, although we often seek to understand one particular event, we do so by widening the frame to perceive the social surround.

This introductory chapter sets out three core principles of critical disaster studies, a foundation on which we hope future scholars will build: disasters are interpretive fictions, disasters are political, and disasters take place over time.

Disasters are interpretive fictions. As both events and ideas, disasters are socially constructed. Therefore, so are concepts that are closely associated with them, such as vulnerability, risk, and resilience.[4] These all demand interrogation because, as Pranathi Diwakar shows in Chapter 6, the question of who and what are imagined as vulnerable, at risk, or resilient has considerable political and material significance.

One of our central contributions is to demonstrate how much can be learned by bringing new tools of analysis to bear on events that have been studied mostly by people who think of themselves primarily as analysts of disaster. To be sure, we engage with the field of disaster studies, such as it is, gratefully calling on a century's worth of scholarship. Several chapters in this book—especially those by Scott Gabriel Knowles and Zachary Loeb (Chapter 1), Ryan Hagen (Chapter 2), and Kenneth Hewitt (Afterword)—describe some of the courses that tradition has taken. But we purposely have not situated ourselves in its mainstream or any of its various tributaries. The field has a set of venerable concerns, such as how to categorize different types of disaster, how humans behave under stress, and how communities rebuild from destruction.[5] Nonetheless, the scholars whose work comprises this book often came to the study of disasters as a way of trying to answer different, broader questions about power and inequality, community and trauma, nature and society, order and instability, and the cultural beliefs that shape people's uneven experiences of misfortune.

The breadth of the unified bibliography at the back of this volume demonstrates the disciplinary diversity that critical disaster studies brings together. As historians, we are attentive to how disasters exist in time; as geographers, we are attentive to how disasters exist in space; as anthropologists, we are attentive to how the meanings of disasters are constructed; and as political scientists, we are attentive to how those meanings are constructed within political systems and contexts. Taken together, this collection offers a vision of critical disaster studies less as a disciplinary destination than as an interdisciplinary intersection. Disasters, so-called, should not be set aside for study only by a single subfield. Rather, they present productive occasions for scholars across the humanities and social sciences to think together.

Disasters are political. As social constructs, disaster, vulnerability, risk, and resilience shape and are shaped by contests over power.

Managers and technocrats often herald the goals of disaster response and recovery as objective, quantifiable, or self-evident. In reality, the goals are subjective and usually contested. Take the basic concept of "restoring order"; it seems common sense until one recognizes that the existing order served some people much better than it served others, and its restoration therefore represents a power play par excellence. Critical disaster studies attends to the ways powerful people often use claims of technocratic expertise about vulnerability, risk, and resilience to maintain their power. So-called experts have politics and ideologies, just like everyone else. We can only understand their actions if we apprehend their motivations.[6]

We are especially wary of the easy technocratic solutionism that seeks engineering solutions to political questions.[7] Many of the chapters in this volume examine the governance of disaster and risk as a set of both practices and discourses. They demonstrate that policies that promise security for some often cause suffering for others. They demonstrate, too, how success is ideologically defined. Consider "resilience." This is a thoroughly political concept: it asserts the goals of a community's response to a disaster—conservative goals, to be sure, as "resilient" means a durable status quo—and also creates the conditions in which the community attempts to reach those goals. Technocratic plans promulgated in the name of "resilience" often reproduce existing inequalities, usually by design, and many such plans exacerbate them. Critical disaster scholars do not necessarily reject the goal of resilience, but we do caution against naive definitions of what the concept entails.[8]

At the same time, critical disaster studies takes seriously the actions and ideas of those usually not considered experts. Those closest to the trouble often have the sharpest perceptions of what went wrong and what can make it better. We privilege these lived, on-the-ground, and local experiences of disasters and the lay epistemologies produced by them.[9] Their visions of recovery are rarely narrow or technical. If resilience is to mean anything, it must be resistance; it is a political outcome, not a technocratic or biological one.[10]

Our scholarship is applied, but in a different way from the technocratic perspective that suffuses disaster studies.[11] Critical disaster studies does not aspire to bullet-pointed knowledge of best practices. Often the best approach we can take as scholars of disaster is to understand the politics and experiences of people who are most at risk and to join their efforts to build more just, equal, and safe communities.

In declaring that not just "natural disaster" but disaster itself is an analytical construct, we do not claim that how disaster is constructed or defined does not matter. On the contrary. The consequences of "disaster" as a belief are made real in the distribution of sympathy, material resources, and state power.[12] In many polities, a legal disaster declaration can authorize emergency action and facilitate funding. Denying that legal definition effectively inhibits government action or funding. The anticipation of disaster alone can give license for state and nonstate actions that might otherwise be absent, inform new modes of discourse and governance, and create new logics understood both by governors and the governed. To understand "disaster" as a discursive and political construction with material consequences thus heightens the need to study how the category is constructed and understood, as well as how it is instantiated by law, politics, and society.

But disaster, as a concept, is not just made in policy and politics; it is also made in personal and public imaginations. Critical disaster scholars therefore attend to how disasters are imagined and anticipated by authors and filmmakers, experts and policymakers, organizers and activists, and their various audiences.[13] Their ideas often conflict, and the disasters they anticipate often do not look like the ones that ultimately arrive. It is in their incompleteness, the disconnections and interstices among them, that the most powerful new ideas can emerge.

We write as the climate crisis is changing the way many people think about nature altogether. The Anthropocene idea, in particular—the claim that the relationship between humans and the natural world has fundamentally changed because humans now exert such power over the earth that it is measurable on geological scales—has unsettled a long-standing, if always fraught, philosophical division between the natural and the man-made. The Anthropocene idea also has prompted debates over the length and origins of our historical moment and the crises that seem to define it. While there is no consensus about the ultimate utility of the Anthropocene concept, we contribute to the broader discussion by working to show how terms like "nature" can serve technopolitical ends.[14] Because claims that certain kinds of inequality are "natural" often mask human responsibility for social arrangements, scholars must be skeptical of claims premised on an uncritical idea of nature. Moreover, as arguments over the length, and therefore the causes, of the Anthropocene crisis suggest, and as Dara Z. Strolovitch illustrates in a different context in Chapter 3, imagining "crisis" as acute or chronic is both analytically and politically meaningful.[15]

Disasters take place over time. We reject the notion that disasters are isolated events. Making sense of political and ideological contests demands seeing people in context.

The idea of disaster carries with it a theory of time and space that is often misleading. People commonly imagine disasters to be unexpected and sudden. Thus, seeing a problem as a disaster can make structural conditions appear contingent, widespread conditions appear local, and chronic conditions appear acute. In short, the disaster idea often obscures enduring social circumstances. Critical disaster studies aspires to peel away that veneer.[16]

Moreover, as historical processes, disasters not only reflect the social order; they can help to produce it. Scholars sometimes have been drawn to the study of disasters because they seem to offer a "window" onto—or to take one prominent example, an opportunity for an "autopsy" of—the fundamental structures of social life.[17] That can be a productive approach. Yet critical disaster studies also recognizes that "labeling something as a crisis," as Dara Z. Strolovitch writes, "is often itself part of a political process that makes it one by transforming it from an ongoing, taken-for-granted, and naturalized condition into an intervention-worthy policy problem." Disasters do not just reveal the world; as events and as ideas, they reorder it.

Ultimately, then, the goal of critical disaster studies is less to understand disasters per se than to understand the processes that create them as ideas, cause them as material facts, and define them as human experiences.

This book is organized into three sections. In the first, "Knowing Disaster," the chapters consider epistemology and definition. Scott Gabriel Knowles and Zachary Loeb follow an oil rig that came loose from its moorings during Hurricane Harvey in 2017 in order to trace how disaster scholarship can be a method to transverse scales of time and space, from immediate and contingent events to the Anthropocene. Ryan Hagen argues that disaster "is primarily a problem of knowledge"; as technologies of knowledge have changed, disasters, too, have changed from being understood and experienced as "acts of God" to "acts of man" to, finally, "acts of systems." Dara Z. Strolovitch, in the context of what became known as the American "mortgage crisis," considers how "disaster" (or "crisis") is defined and the political stakes of that definition.

Chapters in the book's second section, "Governing Disaster," explore how vulnerability, resilience, and risk are created—and therefore how disaster becomes a mode of governance. Claire Antone Payton shows how corruption physically cemented danger into the built environment of Port-au-Prince and so demonstrates how democratic governance is crucial to reducing vulnerability. Aaron Clark-Ginsberg's study of Sierra Leone shows the inadequacies of democracy's neoliberal substitute, community-based disaster risk management. Although intended to give local communities power over disaster preparedness, he argues, community-based disaster risk management in fact distracts from larger social and political root causes of vulnerability and piles more burdens onto already disadvantaged people. Likewise, Pranathi Diwakar shows how Indian elites wield the language of vulnerability and risk against slum dwellers in Chennai. Which risks are legible to the state in a disaster framework is a political question. Finally, Rebecca Elliott examines the history of the US National Flood Insurance Program to show how notions of market and governmental "success" and "failure" are contested, political, and contingent.

The book's third section, "Imagining Disaster," shows how existing studies of disaster often insidiously narrow our view. More capacious understandings are more useful, especially because whether they happen or not, anticipated or imagined future disasters become social facts in the present. Susan Scott Parrish posits the novel as a genre uniquely capable of communicating the inherently social and complex risks of disaster. Focusing on London's bubonic plague of 1665 and Hurricane Katrina in Mississippi in 2005, she argues that unlike the official and scientific assessments they complement, novels help readers to understand how disaster feels. Kerry Smith shows how the forecasted Tōkai earthquake became Japan's most anticipated disaster, even as other seismic disasters kept striking other parts of the country, and how its anticipation and predictability became articles of faith in Japanese culture and politics. Then, Chika Watanabe tells the story of a Japanese disaster education program that traveled to Chile. She makes the case for how incomplete translation—of programs, experiences, languages, and national imaginaries—can be generative and epistemologically productive. Taken together, these chapters demonstrate that while technocratic accounts of disaster and recovery perform a kind of certainty, that performance is premised on—and can even encourage—a blindness to the cultures, emotions, languages, and stories that give disasters their meaning. To be useful, scholarship on disaster must foreground the fact of its ideological construction.

Finally, in the book's Afterword, Kenneth Hewitt reflects critically on the scope of disaster studies itself, especially disaster risk reduction. He makes explicit the often unspoken assumptions of a field that has tended to exclude from its purview the deadliest forms of human catastrophe: famine, accident, and war. The climate crisis and other new forms of calamity ought not to distract us from the ways that destructive violence is, and has long been, a fact of modern life. Our reluctance to see famines and wars as disasters highlights, again, the ideology inherent in the definition of disaster.

*   *   *

This book was complete, we thought, when a novel coronavirus, SARS-CoV-2, began its spread around the world. The disease the virus causes, called COVID-19, has already killed millions of people. As we write these paragraphs, thousands more continue to die every day, and measures meant to slow the spread of the virus are severely disruptive. Economies are shuttered, as are borders. Much of the world's population has been ordered to stay at home.

We cannot know the future in which this book will be read, but we do know that the insights of critical disaster studies can help to make sense of a world in crisis. The problems presented by the pandemic cross the range of human knowledge—they are at once political, economic, cultural, environmental, medical, and more—and they demand the kind of interdisciplinary examination that this book models. The chapters that follow were mostly finished before COVID-19 appeared, but we believe the questions they raise are productive ones to ask about it nonetheless. We hope that future students and scholars put this book to good use.

Many chapters in this book demonstrate, for example, that the decision to declare a problem a "disaster" or a "crisis" is an act with material and ideological consequences. Thus, students of the pandemic should not take for granted that the COVID-19 pandemic was a disaster, but rather ask what made it so. For whom was it a disaster? What is at stake in calling it that? Critical scholars should scrutinize the contestable and contested lines between virus and disease, disease and pandemic, pandemic and disaster. They ought to ask how globalization, capitalism, nationalism, and other social and political processes shaped the various responses to and experiences of COVID-19. And they should examine how race, class, gender, and geography shaped the pandemic and its effects.[18] How did the pandemic and the responses to it variously replicate, aggravate, or rupture existing inequalities?

Questions about governance ought to remain a particular concern to students of the pandemic, as they are to the authors of this book. What role did borders play, both rhetorically and practically, as nations banned migration, immigration, and international travel?[19] Scholars should interrogate the mirrored gestures of incompetence and technocracy and consider how collective actions—from social distancing to rallies demanding quick "reopening"—changed the course and politics of the pandemic. How did people use the occasion of COVID-19 to contest and reimagine the relationships and mutual obligations of citizens and states; workers and employers; spouses, parents, and children; and neighbors to each other?

Students and scholars should ask, too, how people knew and imagined this global pandemic in which much was experienced in common but alone. Ideas and information about COVID-19 ranged across different languages and national experiences, so its students will need to consider the implications of necessarily incomplete translations. Scholars should examine how state-sponsored scientific priorities and local cultural beliefs informed medical knowledge of the disease. And they ought to ask what fiction can teach about the experiences of sickness, unemployment, isolation, fear, hope, and grief that other texts cannot.

Finally, we hope that this book will serve as a reminder that by defining certain experiences as exceptional and others as normal, conventional thinking about disaster has too often set limits on our social imaginations. At the heart of critical disaster studies are moral questions: Whose deaths ought to inspire outrage, and whose resignation? What kinds of suffering are a legitimate cost of the status quo, and what kinds of suffering ought to suggest that the status quo itself is illegitimate?[20] The pandemic only makes these enduring questions more urgent, as COVID-19 joins the climate crisis and other forms of precarity and collapse—manifest in the chasm between the rich and the poor, the resurgence of authoritarianism, and seemingly endless war—in defining the rough terrain of modern life. Understanding disaster is necessary for understanding the world. A critical disaster scholarship has never been more, well, critical.

PART I

Knowing Disaster

CHAPTER 1

The Voyage of the *Paragon*

Disaster as Method

Scott Gabriel Knowles and Zachary Loeb

When Hurricane Harvey made landfall at Aransas Pass, Texas, on August 26, 2017, it brought a twelve-foot storm surge up the Port Aransas ship channel that swept over Gulf Copper Harbor Island with tremendous force. This privately owned island at the mouth of the ship channel is a long-term "stacking" location for deepwater oil drilling rigs, and four were parked there when Harvey's wall of water and 100 mph winds arrived. One of these—the *Paragon DPDS1* (or *Paragon* for short)—broke loose, embarking on a brief and destructive voyage before coming to rest at the mouth of the channel. After six tense days, with ten thousand barrels of oil in the ship, a salvage plan was approved by the Coast Guard and the *Paragon* was towed back into the port of Corpus Christi.[1]

One might reasonably see the *Paragon* as a footnote to the most destructive hurricane season in American history; after all, the ship did not kill anyone or spill its oil, nor did it receive much media attention.[2] A more contextualized, comparative, and multiscalar approach to the voyage of the *Paragon*, however—what we might call a "critical disaster studies" approach—compels us to see this derelict drilling rig and its ignominious end as an opening to a much broader investigation.

Disasters are ordering mechanisms. They are not aberrant events, but rather reveal existing social orders and generate new ones. This observation links critical disaster studies to the broader tradition of critical theory, whose theorists have often been characterized by a fascination with the way that disasters reveal a society's true shape. At many important points critical theorists, especially from the first generation of such thinkers, placed greater emphasis on disaster as a theoretical framework than on disaster as a particular event, as can be seen in Walter Benjamin's famous evocation of the angel of history perceiving history as "one single catastrophe" piling wreckage at its feet, or Max Horkheimer's belief that "the whole of world history is just a fly caught in the flames."[3] Yet such theorists were also fully immersed in thinking through the calamities of their day (World War I, the rise of fascism, the experience of exile, the Holocaust, the dawn of the nuclear era) even as they lived through them; it was not only that these catastrophes were of historic import, but that these theorists thought history could best be understood through the lens of catastrophe.[4] Thus, from this theoretical legacy we can build on the idea that disasters operate as realms of sensemaking, conflict, memory, cultural practice, and imagination that define and bind societies over long stretches of time. Indeed, disasters are events *in time* but also function as phenomena linked *across time and space*, simultaneously exposing and provoking processes of institution making, environmental change, hazard formation, and risk-taking. Whereas Theodor Adorno observed that "the constantly enforced insistence that everybody should admit that everything will turn out well, places those who do not under suspicion of being defeatist and deserters," a critical disaster studies perspective dares to risk being cast under such suspicion by highlighting that all too often things do not "turn out well."[5]

These insights—which form a gathering consensus in critical disaster studies—distinguish today's scholarship from that of previous generations. The long-standing obeisance to disaster typologies defined by genres (natural, technological) or statistics (death counts, material losses) is now an object of analysis and critique, rather than a heuristic. The old "body and dollar count" definitions of a disaster do not answer what now are central questions of power, place, and historical change. Pressed to define "disaster" now, we look to more nuanced answers like "unwanted harm" or "material out of place," formulations that reject counting and naming as sufficient explanations of the social and environmental impacts of disaster. Disaster research today increasingly demands history, contextualization, and comparison.

A generation ago, the categories and questions of "disaster research" were articulated through the scholarly frameworks of disparate disciplines and subdisciplines: "disaster" sociology, anthropology and risk studies, geography, environmental and labor history, science and technology studies, to name a few. Each specialization took its own finely tuned sense of method:

preferred scale of analysis, the type and quantity of data to be collected or archive to be examined, the theoretical framework of power in society to be deployed. Oddly enough, one thing that often united these approaches was that they treated disaster as an epiphenomenon—a data-production catalyst useful for studying *something else*. The war was actually a way to understand presidential power; the earthquake was a way to think about urban planning. Disasters were often treated as separate events, with limited periods of background and aftermath. They faded with time, scary disruptions between long stretches of normal life.

Many researchers today, however, often working across methodological boundaries, no longer see disaster as a prop on the stage of broader historical inquiries. The disaster is now an object of study with as much complexity and causative power as any legislation, social movement, invention, or presidency. Reaching this point has meant the dissolution of old conceptual boundaries (yes, a war is a disaster) and some enhanced reflexivity (yes, a disaster is both an event and a process, shaper and shaped). Scholars have reached for new analytical language—"risk society," "vulnerability," "resilience"—while also being true to the task of contextualizing the conceptual and linguistic modes of the historical actors they study.[6]

Critical disaster studies thus must be especially attentive to questions of scale. Devastating events at one scale disappear on a longer timeline. Centuries-long, global environmental changes prove confounding in local measurements. Contexts of race and class, historical continuity and historical erasure, expertise and ignorance, each play a role in defining the social construction of a disaster. Consciousness of scale enables disaster researchers to think more precisely about the broader implications of their topic and evidentiary choices. It enables researchers to develop the most promising tactics for expanding the impact of their works.

"Scales," historian Gabrielle Hecht explains, "are emergent rather than eternal. But their situatedness and historicity do not detract from their reality. They do work in the world. They are performative. Scale is messy because it is both a category of analysis *and* a category of practice. . . . Scales have epistemological, political, and ethical consequences for both informants and scholars."[7] For Hecht, trying to explain the long history of uranium mining in Africa, the only hope is to find sources, or what she terms "interscalar vehicles," that can bear her across time and space, to explain historical action at a distance and on the timescale of the Anthropocene. Drawing on Hecht's

Figure 1.1. *Paragon DPDS1* on September 4, 2017, in the Aransas Pass near Corpus Christi, Texas. US Coast Guard photo by Petty Officer 2nd Class Cory J. Mendenhall.

theorizing of "scales," this chapter seeks to perform an "interscalar" analysis of the *Paragon's* voyage.

This chapter undertakes a Rashomonic experiment in disaster analysis as it narrates the *Paragon's* voyage three times, with each telling inhabiting a different spatiotemporal scale and a different causal chain. In doing so, we also document the heritage of multidisciplinary disaster scholarship that has borne us to this moment in time. The separation of the story in this way is artificial; all narrative structures order time and space according to the situation of the author. Our task is to critically illuminate three dominant trends in disaster analytics—disaster as "event," disaster in the context of "risk management," and "slow disaster"—treating each individually, separately, as a means of examining in turn the essential characteristics of each mode. Each framework relies on different types of evidence, produces sometimes conflicting modes of explanation and argumentation, and reveals divergent starting and ending points for disaster research. Furthermore, each framework focuses on particular sets of historical actors.

So now we return to the *Paragon*. Despite its rusting hull, the *Paragon* is sturdy enough to serve us as an intrepid "interscalar vehicle."

Scale 1: Disaster as Event

The temporal focus on the disaster as event bends scholarly work within a tight framing of time and place and shapes its policy applicability into a "focusing" mode. At the scale of "disaster as event," the voyage of the *Paragon*, if anyone outside of Port Aransas, Texas, notices it at all, begins when the ship breaks loose from the moorings of normalcy and ends once it has been successfully moored in normalcy again.

Such an analysis tends to focus on aberrant occurrences, on events that are deserving of particular attention insofar as they are breaks from the norm. Thus, what sets apart a heat wave, a flood, a nuclear power plant meltdown, a tsunami, a fire, or a ship coming unmoored is the extent to which these events disrupt the standard flow of everyday life. They transcend in various ways the normalization of traffic accidents or house fires. They overwhelm society's "ability to cope" and demand emergent reactions from average people, responders, bureaucrats, and elected officials. As the scholarship in this mode of disaster research demonstrates, these events present opportunities for specific sorts of quantitative information gathering: lives lost, damage in dollar value, lists of government agencies responding, relief efforts, amount of media coverage. And such a focus can capture the ways in which there are multiple events worthy of attention within the larger disastrous event; thus, the *Paragon* is an event within the larger event of Hurricane Harvey.

Hurricane Harvey was declared a "major disaster" by the United States Federal Emergency Management Agency (FEMA) on August 25, 2017, the day before it made landfall. The predictive and visual power of meteorology was on full display in the week leading up to the disaster declaration, as newscasters breathlessly conveyed threatening information to anxious audiences. Scientists might offer general assessments, and the public might harbor worry or premonitions of earthquakes or chemical spills, but hurricanes and other major storm systems now offer up a sort of "preview phase," allowing public officials like emergency managers and first responders time to make preparations, even as they urge the public to evacuate or batten down the hatches.

In the American context, this level of disaster declaration brings into play a precise series of actions described in the Robert T. Stafford Disaster Relief and Emergency Act (Stafford Act). Passed in 1988, the Stafford Act traces its lineage back to Cold War civil defense legislation geared toward allowing the president and the executive branch to direct the actions of the federal government in an extreme disaster event. Founded in the anticipation of war, this

FEMA-4332-DR, Texas Disaster Declaration as of 10/11/2017

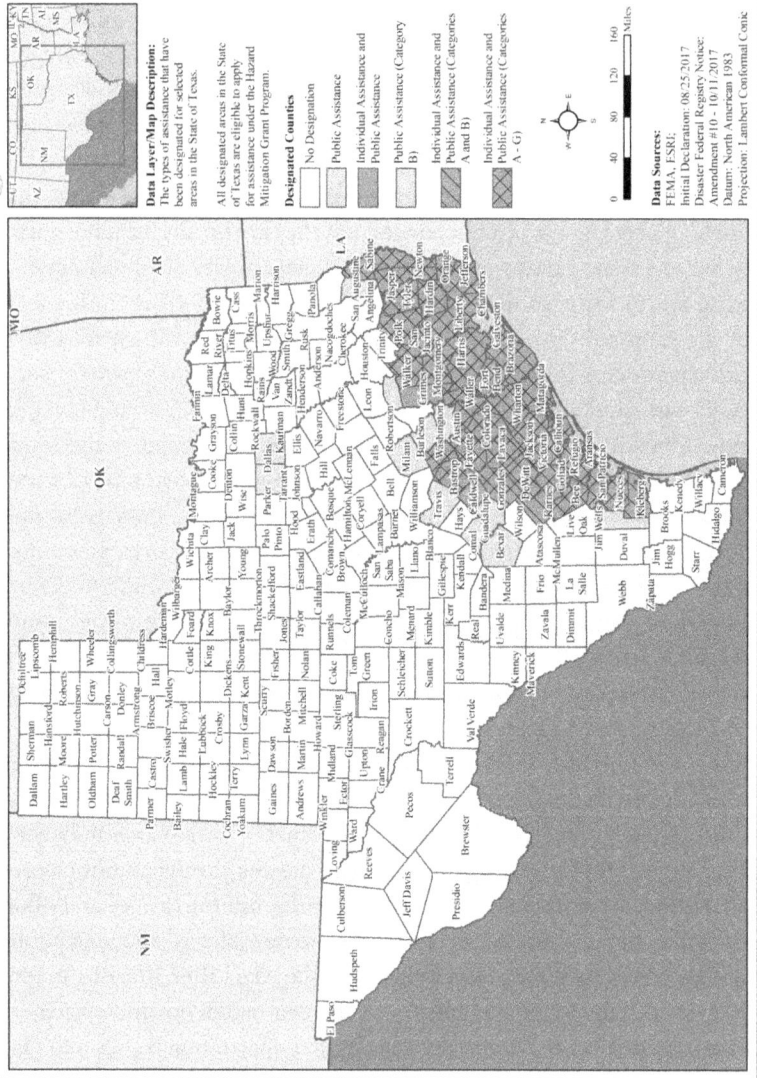

Figure 1.2. FEMA-4332-DR, Texas disaster declaration as of 10/11/2017, United States Federal Emergency Management Agency, https://www.fema.gov/disaster/4332.

legislation was reframed multiple times to encompass all types of disasters and to sharpen the tools of government, such that today it is not uncommon for major disasters to be declared even before an event occurs.

As Harvey bore down on Texas, the *Paragon* was ostensibly ready. Two standby tugs, the *Signet Enterprise* and the *Sabine Pass*, were deployed by the ship's owner to reinforce *Paragon*'s mooring system.[8] Yet amid the water and the winds, these preventative efforts proved insufficient. The *Paragon* broke free, smashing the tugs in the process, causing the 105-foot tugboat *Signet Enterprise* to sink, and requiring the Coast Guard to dispatch two MH-65 Dolphin helicopters to undertake a dangerous water rescue of the four crew members.[9] Free from its moorings, and having escaped the grip of the tugs, the *Paragon* drifted into the ship channel, destroying the dock of the University of Texas Marine Science Institute, then coming to an uncertain rest near the entrance to the port. Initially, the *Paragon* grounded on the northern side of the channel before the tide refloated it, sending it to run aground again on the southern side of the channel. Ultimately, the ship came to rest in a spot blocking the mouth of the channel, obstructing access to a port that generally moves $100 million worth of goods every day.[10]

When President Donald Trump visited Texas in the days following Harvey, Tony Hahn, the captain of the port and the incident commander for the unified command in Corpus Christi, told the president that the *Paragon* represented, "a major challenge for us."[11] In the days following President Trump's visit, Captain Hahn described "opening the port" as being "an important step in recovering from Hurricane Harvey."[12] Though the ship continued to block the channel, assurances were given that the ten thousand barrels of oil on board were not leaking into the surrounding water.[13]

The port was partially reopened on August 31, 2017, less than a week after the *Paragon*'s voyage, but the ship's continued presence kept passage through the channel limited.[14] Dangerous weather in the days following Harvey made salvage efforts perilous and forced the divers surveying the ship to put off their analyses.[15] It was not until September 4, 2017, that the *Paragon* was finally towed away and taken to the Gulf Marine Fabricators shipyard in Corpus Christi. Along with bestowing thanks on the particular individuals who had been instrumental in the effort, Captain Hahn described the recovery as "an incredibly complex effort achieved only through tremendous collaboration between the Port Authority, pilots, industry stakeholders, the salvage company and the Coast Guard."[16] With the *Paragon* no longer obstructing the channel, normal operations could finally resume.

The voyage of the *Paragon* did not compete with images of Houston's submerged highways for national media attention.[17] The *Paragon* did receive more attention from the local media, with reporters from the *San Antonio Express News* and the *Houston Chronicle* both describing the *Paragon*'s plight within larger accounts of Harvey's turmoil.[18] Insofar as the story of the *Paragon* captured the imagination of any onlookers, it was the global oil drilling and marine shipping press, in publications and forums like *World Maritime News*, *Offshore Energy Today*, G Captain, and *Professional Mariner*, which later bestowed its 2018 Samuel Plimsoll Award for Outstanding Service by an Organization to the Coast Guard's Texas air crews.[19] Among the commentators on the online forum G Captain, there seemed to be a recognition that things could have been much worse. One observed in astonishment: "All I can say is how on earth did such a large vessel come adrift but more so, how lucky the owners are that is [*sic*] did not roll on her side right in the middle of the channel? The Port of Corpus Christi might have ended closed for six months while the derrick was removed and the hull righted!"[20]

It was a dramatic situation to imagine, and it is fortunate that it did not come to pass. Still, such catastrophizing on the part of the commentator prompts a consideration of what would have needed to go wrong to turn the *Paragon* into a front-page story. The *Paragon*'s tale already involves crashes, sinking ships, and daring helicopter rescues. To earn prime-time coverage, what else would have been needed? Lives being lost? More lives being imperiled? A visual of oil leaking out of the ship's side into the water? Or was it simply that the *Paragon*'s story was not quite as spectacular as other destruction wrought by Harvey? The worst case scenario was avoided, but in a lesser storm, or on a slower news day, the voyage of the *Paragon* might have qualified as a significant story and raised public alarm. The *Paragon*, as an event, was not eventful enough to fit inside the media's Harvey frame, indicative of how media and official public accounts of an event frequently fail to capture the richer textures, the conflicts, and the open-ended mysteries of a disaster.

The power of the media, and of public agencies in official pronouncements and reports, to frame specific moments within a disaster event as worth more or less attention is crucial to the construction of the broader narratives emerging from disasters. "Headlining" at the event scale forces reality into a few pages, a few images, even just a few words and the names of heroes and victims. This process of media selection was crucial to the erasure of the *Paragon*'s voyage from the larger narrative of Hurricane Harvey. Likewise, scholars working on disasters often turn to media accounts as important sources in their historical work, and thus the choosing and framing functions of news media not only shape the event as it plays out for a broader public but also play a role in retrospective analyses of disaster events.[21]

The idea of disaster as an "event in time and in place" emerged as the dominant definition for the social sciences in the 1960s. This approach in the United States grew from sociology research early in the Cold War and was heavily dominated by funding from government agencies that sought to understand the ways that organizations and communities would react to the stress of nuclear attack. Key researchers here included Charles Fritz, Enrico Quarantelli, and Russell Dynes.[22] These were institution builders, and their immediate postdisaster casework became the default method of social science disaster research for the period from the 1960s to the 1990s. They went into the field, they conducted the interviews, and they modeled society under stress. It was a very vigorous period of research and theory formation (much of it undercutting civil defense assumptions, to no effect) with the nuclear disaster event at the core of a spatiotemporal disaster model.

The event scale of disaster analysis requires researchers to move away from the most conventional public sources and to zoom back and forth from scales of weeks and days into individual moments of activity that might be playing out simultaneously in different locations. This approach is epitomized by researchers who carry forward and refine the tradition of "rapid response" disaster research, capturing perishable data by placing themselves at the scene within hours or days of an event and even establishing relationships with victims and witnesses that may stretch forward in time for years beyond the event's seeming conclusion. James Kendra and Tricia Wachtendorf's account of the waterborne rescue of lower Manhattan on September 11, 2001, provides a paradigmatic example of this approach today, as does the work of Alice Fothergill and Lori Peek documenting the aftermath of Hurricane Katrina (2005) for a cohort of children. Such work can carry on for months or years, but its essential framings are established through observation of the disaster as it plays out in its immediacy. Scholars like Jennifer Henderson and Max Liboiron have recently challenged the research community to articulate its intentions in the disaster zone and to promote reciprocity and solidarity with disaster victims. Debates within the community over the ethical responsibilities of researchers present at the scene demonstrate the need for continuing reflexivity of researchers at the event scale.[23]

A consideration of a disaster as event also prompts a consideration of the way in which that occurrence may function as a "focusing event" in the polity.

Thomas Birkland's work, for example, explores the ways in which disaster events can exert an influence on public policy making; severe hurricanes can certainly serve this function. Looking back at a given event several years later may make it easier to assess just how much it served to prompt policy changes. Given the destructiveness of Hurricane Harvey (and the 2017 hurricane season more generally), it should not be surprising that these events drew attention from policymakers, though much of this attention seemed to be focused on ensuring that FEMA had the necessary resources for immediate response and recovery operations. As a case in point, Congressman Bill Shuster (R-PA), chairman of the House Committee on Transportation and Infrastructure, opened his committee's hearing "Emergency Response and Recovery: Central Takeaways from the Unprecedented 2017 Hurricane Season" by invoking the specter of how the 2017 hurricanes had "wreaked havoc" and "were nothing short of devastating" before shifting to praise for the federal agencies gathered to testify and highlighting the hearing as a step in ensuring that "these federal partners . . . have the tools necessary to help communities recover from disasters."[24] Insofar as the hurricanes of 2017 were focusing events for the committee, they stood in a line of similar focusing events, as Chairman Shuster couched the hearing in the work the committee had previously done in the aftermath of Hurricane Katrina and Superstorm Sandy. FEMA director Brock Long struck a similar tone in highlighting the "historic" nature of the 2017 hurricanes, but rather than use these "focusing events" to argue for policy change, Long largely asked for more funding.[25] Granted, while Hurricane Harvey may easily qualify as a "focusing event," it is unclear that the voyage of the *Paragon* achieved such a status. Corpus Christi, Port Aransas, and Coast Guard helicopter crews were mentioned in the hearing, but the *Paragon* was not. As a focusing event in this context, Harvey was a storm, part of a bad season, but not one that illuminated a broader set of environmental or industrial policy concerns.

For the event-focused analyst, questions about the *Paragon* abound. For example, why weren't there more established emergency preparedness protocols for keeping the *Paragon* in place during such a predictable weather event? Why did the ship's owners think two tugs would be sufficient to hold the *Paragon* in place, and what was their contingency plan in the case that the ship broke loose? In the lead-up to Harvey's making landfall, news outlets were tracking the storm, reporting in foreboding tones as the storm became a Category 3 and then became a Category 4, and noting that the governor of Texas, Greg Abbott, was warning that the storm was going to be a "very major disaster."[26] Thus, even before images of daring rescues and flooded highways could fill the airwaves, satellite images of the storm approaching the Texas coast had filled broadcasts. Many things can be said about Hurricane Harvey, including that its intensity was underestimated, but those responsible for preparing for the storm can hardly claim that they did not know it was coming.

There are also more specific questions that focus in on this particular event. How did local emergency managers coordinate with federal officials? Is six days in the ship channel a successful operation or a failure? Considering that there was no loss of life and no serious pollution, the operation seems to have been a success, albeit one that was delayed by the adverse weather conditions that continued in the aftermath of Harvey. And while the broader Harvey narrative points to struggles for control between Governor Abbott and local groups, Captain Hahn's comments suggest that the recovery operation was successful because of, not in spite of, cooperation. One can imagine a very different narrative of the event, focused on placing blame, had the story of the *Paragon* taken an even more catastrophic turn. The bleak irony, from a scholarly perspective, is that had the *Paragon*'s voyage been more catastrophic, there might have been a greater quantity of sources to sift through and more media coverage to analyze.

Further questions also linger. Whose responsibility is it to pay for the damage, especially when the owner of the rig is now gone and the *Paragon* has been "turned into razor blades" (as one online critic put it)? What new regulations might come about, even though the worst case—a voyage in which perhaps the *Paragon* ventured inland and spilled its petroleum—was avoided? To what extent can, or will, the *Paragon* specifically serve as a "focusing event" that will lead to future shifts in policy? Was the *Paragon*'s voyage suitably catastrophic to even merit being deemed a "focusing event"? These are the types of questions that would be crucial to seeing the interaction of the hurricane and the *Paragon* as a moment in which highly contingent social and political orders are revealed, new orders are constructed, and the role the media played in constructing and reifying those narratives is examined.

Importantly, the answers to many of these questions fit easily with the search for quantifiable data points that provide more context for the event. Answering these questions does not pull away from the event, but rather provides even more specificity about the event. Thus, the event becomes a data exercise: the eye of Harvey made landfall at about thirty miles northeast of Corpus Christi; wind speeds were so strong as to disable measuring equipment, though winds between 115 and 130 mph were reported; storm tides as high as twelve feet above ground level were recorded; as much as fifty inches of rain fell in some areas; thirty-nine people lost their lives and thousands were displaced; and the National Oceanographic and Atmospheric Administration (NOAA) estimated the cost of Harvey at $125 billion, making it the second most costly hurricane in the United States (Hurricane Katrina retains the woeful honor of commanding the number one position).[27] These are some of the quantifiable details of the large-scale disaster, but as the case of the *Paragon* makes clear, behind these data points are numerous stories about smaller-scale disastrous events.

By early 2018, when eighty-eight directly attributable deaths were known and the staggering $125 billion tally of Harvey's economic impact was coming together, the *Paragon*'s owner (Paragon Offshore PLC) had already declared bankruptcy and been acquired by a rival company. And given the *Paragon*'s deteriorated condition, so clear to see in the images from the salvage operation, some observers seemed surprised that it was still in the water at all. "Why on earth is [*sic*] that ship not been consigned to Alang already?" asked one commentator.[28] The question was prophetic. The *Paragon* was soon sold to be recycled, when its new owner, Borr Drilling, decided not to repair and modernize the ship.

As an event, the hurricane was over, and the *Paragon* was long gone.

Scale 2: The Scale of Risk Management

For risk managers, a single event is a data point, not an acceptable explanation of a phenomenon. The experience of disaster was for much of human history understood as a glimpse into the supernatural. Historians point to the 1755 Lisbon earthquake as a breaking point; coming as it did in the midst of the Enlightenment, the tragedy of Lisbon brought forth a raucous public argument in Europe about the will of God versus the workings of a mechanical nature. This was far from settled in the eighteenth century, but by the late nineteenth century the emergence of the insurance industry and the victory of the natural and physical sciences as the explanatory instruments of environmental understanding had pushed "act of God" aside as a viable explanation of disaster in industrializing nations. The engineering, science, and statistical culture of this era was marked perhaps most exceptionally by the invention of risk—that is to say, the transformation of uncertain occurrences into objects of study, statistical analyses, monetization, and prediction.[29] Alongside this revolution in risk came the development of the administrative, expert state. Management as a discrete set of skills took shape in the late nineteenth century as well. First taught in the United States at the Wharton School of the University of Pennsylvania, the combination of management, engineering, science, and risk led to a full revolution in human thinking about the possibilities for shaping the land toward profit and health. By the time the oil boom of the early twentieth century began, the interdisciplinary field of risk management was well formed as an expert discipline.

The *Paragon*'s genealogy spans the age of risk management. It was built by Scotts Shipbuilding and Engineering Company in 1979, in the port of Greenock, near Glasgow, Scotland. Oil drilling offshore has a long history, but for almost a century it was limited to shallow water. The discovery in the 1970s of oil deposits in deep water led to technological experimentation and to the rise of an entirely new sector of work in the petrochemical industry. The *Paragon*'s original name was *Pacnorse I*, and as the *Pacnorse* it drilled for oil in the Mediterranean Sea and later off the coast of Ireland in the "Celtic Tiger" days. The *Pacnorse* drilled off the coast of Newfoundland and Labrador at a time when the cod fishery (the economic basis of this region of Canada for four hundred years) was closing and being replaced by offshore oil and gas drilling. It was here that the *Pacnorse* was struck by an iceberg, yet still kept drilling. In 1996 the *Pacnorse I* was sold and renamed the *Peregrine II*, and then renamed again as the *Frontier Phoenix* in 2005. It drilled off the coast of Brazil, in the Caribbean, and in the Gulf of Mexico, the big time for offshore drilling rigs. In 2014 the rig was again sold and rechristened, now the *Noble Phoenix*, but that didn't last long; later that year it became the *Paragon DPDS1*. On May 30, 2017, the *Paragon* was brought to the facility at Gulf Copper Harbor Island, where it was expected to remain for between six months and a year.

By the time the *Paragon* broke loose from its moorings amid the waves and winds of Hurricane Harvey it had served thirty-eight years at sea and acted dutifully as an agent of a global petrochemical economy growing by leaps and bounds. The *Paragon*'s design, construction, and maintenance; the dangerous work of its crews; the profits of its many owners; the laws governing its movements; and its brush with fame in 2017 cannot be fully explained by a single event or port of call—the story is global and takes a generation to unspool. Its risky activities were measured and documented by experts of many backgrounds, reporting to private firms and public agencies charged with managing dangerous and profitable enterprises. We can think of the *Paragon* in this way, looking toward the network of environmental laws and regulations, technical codes and standards of safety, and financial entanglements that kept the rig "afloat." The *Paragon* is a prime case of risk management in motion.

In the scale of risk management, the key actors are the experts: the insurance firms, policymakers, planners, engineers, architects, generals, scientists (social and otherwise), and by the 1960s, emergency managers. For different types of disasters, from fire and earthquakes to chemical spills and war, the twentieth century was marked by quite remarkable achievements in disaster archiving and analysis—across time and space and across types. However, in general, disasters were viable as objects of study in intervals of decades; for governments and firms the timelines of disaster were defined predominantly by administrations and the life cycles of commercial ventures. For individuals and communities wrapped up in the age of risk management, the length of a mortgage or the life span of infrastructures defined the temporality. Though variability abounds, the time frame of risk management is generally in the ten- to fifty-year frame, and the spatial dimensions range from the city to the nation. Beyond those boundaries lie, once again, the anecdotes of individual events on one side and the mists of unknowability (hence unpredictability) on the other.

New disaster research tools were developing throughout the twentieth century in the service of risk management—especially a geographical approach through the work of scholars like Gilbert White, which saw change in the land and marine systems over periods of time that ran in measurable cycles. White was also an institution builder and a policy entrepreneur, who was instrumental in establishing floodplain management techniques as well as the National Flood Insurance Program in the late 1960s. An anthropological approach, seeking to unravel disparate cultural associations with risk, was made popular by Mary Douglas and appeared in her book *Risk and Culture* (1982). By the 1990s, after two decades of debate over the findings in these different disciplines, a consensus of sorts emerged: disaster is contextual, historically contingent, and reflexive. Ulrich Beck's pathbreaking *Risk Society* (1986), though not without its critics, crystallized thinking about the causality of disasters, particularly industrial disasters. In Beck, disaster was explained as a key feature of modernization, a product of science and technology, not an endogenous irritant or temporary visitor. In risk society, wealth creation and disaster production work together.

The next wave of social science disaster research, epitomized by Charles Perrow's *Normal Accidents* (1984) and Diane Vaughan's *The Challenger Launch*

Decision (1996), elaborated the ways that disaster can actually be *a production* of high technology systems. Books like Langdon Winner's *The Whale and the Reactor* (1986) and Kai Erikson's *A New Species of Trouble* (1994) worked in the same territory, while scholars including Kenneth Hewitt, Ben Wisner, Kathleen Tierney, Greg Bankof, and Dorothea Hilhorst (among many others) brought historical trajectories of social difference and income inequality, vulnerability, and colonialism to bear on the analysis.[30] An eternal, objective "science" of disaster was (for the most part) cast aside for a more highly nuanced and socially constructed approach. Identity was now in the mix; for the researchers as well as the actors under examination, disaster had become part of the social and the political, not just reflecting trends but driving them, creating inequalities in society while also revealing them. Historians like Ted Steinberg, Mike Davis, Carl Smith, and Christine Meisner Rosen developed narratives demonstrating the push and pull of real estate development, industrialization, professionalization, and intermittent disasters.[31] Revisionism for industrialization, urbanization, and nuclearism (Robert Jay Lifton, Lee Clarke) was at hand—and each was now documentable as a process over time productive of wealth, global security, and also environmental degradation and disaster.

Risk management requires comparison of data points across time and space. In this sense, the *Paragon* was one node of hazard along a vast and hazardous coastline. As costly as the storm proved to be, it was, in fact, a miss. It veered north of Corpus Christi's petrochemical facilities and missed the South Texas Project nuclear facility, and though it wreaked toxic havoc in Houston, it did not substantially flood the Houston ship channel—the nation's largest concentration of petrochemical facilities. Coastal Texas is a place ready made for disaster: it is hurricane prone; floods easily; and susceptible to hailstorms, destructive flash flooding, tornadoes, wildfires, and more recently, earthquakes. How many rigs like the *Paragon* are out there along that dangerous coast—how many working in the Gulf, how many in the ports, how many stacked like the *Paragon* was in 2017? Knowing these numbers, and their recent trajectories, might give us a sense of the ways that industrial infrastructures have grown over the century along the Texas coast; it is an urbanization narrative that gives us Galveston, Corpus Christi, Beaumont, Port Arthur, and Houston, the petrochemical cities of one of the world's wealthiest industrial geographies.

Within this narrative a host of different organizations and agencies appear as characters, monitoring and reporting on the measurable risks of the Gulf

Coast. These range from federal agencies like FEMA, NOAA, the Environmental Protection Agency (EPA), the US Army Corps of Engineers (USACE), and the Coast Guard to local government agencies such as municipal risk management divisions, the ports themselves, and local offices of emergency management; also involved are local citizens' groups such as the Port Aransas Conservancy (PAC) that seek to give voice to local concerns. Informational resources drawn from a variety of these sources (notably, FEMA, the USACE, NOAA, and others) were instrumental in the development of the "Aransas County Texas Multi-Jurisdictional Hazard Mitigation Action Plan," which was implemented over the summer of 2017.[32] Hurricanes and tropical storms were prominently featured in the assessment of risks outlined in the plan, which was submitted to FEMA for approval in November 2017, a risk assessment that Harvey had proven accurate only a few months earlier. This action plan is featured, and publicly available, on the city government website for Port Aransas under "Hazard Mitigation." It is an instrument of risk management, democratized.

While many disasters at the event scale are bounded by sovereign borders, commitment to and concern for building resilience and responding to disasters at the scale of risk management transcend such borders. The concept of resilience, initially a term of art in psychology and ecology, was applied to disaster risk reduction in the 1990s and now dominates this domain of risk management. The textbook definition of resilience usually reads something like the one on the website of the United Nations Office for Disaster Risk Reduction (UNISDR): "The ability of a system, community or society exposed to hazards to resist, absorb, accommodate, adapt to, transform and recover from the effects of a hazard in a timely and efficient manner, including through the preservation and restoration of its essential basic structures and functions through risk management." While the word "community" may seek to keep resilience locally bounded, the evocation of "system" and "society" demonstrates that there are reasons that concern with resilience is an international matter. In the age of globalization, a disaster striking one country can have effects that ripple throughout the world; furthermore, many disasters may begin in one nation, but the impacts will spread more broadly (spilled oil washes up on the shores of many countries; winds carry toxic air across borders). The UNISDR is also pivotal in setting standards by which resilience can be measured, such as the Hyogo Framework for Action 2005–2015. In this context the UNISDR, formed in December 1999, coordinates disaster reduction strategies across the UN. Such work involves a host of international organizations that are called upon in the wake of disaster, including the International Atomic Energy Agency, UN Office for the Coordination of Humanitarian Affairs, UN Framework Convention on Climate Change Secretariat, United Nations High Commissioner for Refugees, United Nations Children's Fund, World Health Organization, and World Bank.

Risk management describes a time frame that also aligns with the most consistently documented dimensions of human memory. In this sense it's worth considering that while the risk managers have been busily defining and managing risk, people have learned to tolerate the risky—either by choice or by having risk forced upon them. Here we could return to the *Paragon*. What are the imaginaries that the rig enabled over its life span? Did it inspire awe or anger (or both)? How is it an object of memory? This manner of exploring the cultural valence of disaster often includes memorials for the dead but also touches on the artwork, movies, music, folk objects, and myriad other markers of cultural meaning people attach to disasters. We need to know how people in Port Aransas remember the *Paragon*, perhaps as a symbol of rapid post-1960s industrialization on the coast. Was it an impressive sight on the skyline for the three years it was docked in town? What imaginative possibilities were created by this sublime piece of extractive technology? The *Paragon* was a talisman of economic progress, shared by some, but also a symbol of environmental injustice for those exposed to the regime of pollution it represented. We might call this process of cultural sensemaking around the *Paragon* the "normalization of risk," or we might better just say that it seems possible for people to adopt a dangerous piece of machinery into their daily lives, and for some to even mourn its disappearance; that attachment itself, perhaps, is a powerful way to manage the experience of living with risk.

Scale 3: The Slow Disaster of the *Paragon*

Let's shift the timescale and think about the voyage of the *Paragon* not as a discrete event, or as a chapter in the history of risk management, but as part of a long causal chain—less a moment in time than a process playing out over seasons, generations, even centuries.

The idea of a "slow disaster" is a way to think about disasters not as atomized events but as long-term processes linked across time. Sometimes the linkages are documentable through a written record; at other times the record recedes into the land, the archaeological record, or the atmosphere. The slow disaster stretches both back in time and forward across generations to

indeterminate points, punctuated by moments we have traditionally concep-
tualized as "disaster," but in fact claiming much more life, health, and wealth
across time than is generally calculated. The experience of atomic bombing
victims fits the concept well—as does the process of climate change, sea level
rise, and the intensification of coastal flooding. The slow disaster is the timescale at which technological systems decay and post-traumatic stress grinds
its victims; this is the scale at which deferred maintenance takes its steady toll,
often in ways hard to sense or monetize until a disaster occurs in "event time."

The slow disaster of pollution and climate change to which the *Paragon*
contributed for decades is far greater than the disaster event of which the *Paragon* was briefly a part in 2017. The fossil fuel of choice for the first century-
plus of industrialization was coal, but it was gradually supplanted by oil, the
literal liquidity of which made it easier to extract and transport, while this
less labor-intensive extraction meant that oil was less prone to be disrupted
by labor disputes than coal. While concerns about national oil reserves being
depleted were a feature of the early twentieth century, World War II and the
onset of the Cold War drew increased political attention to the need for oil
and the need to control access to it at home and abroad. Even as attention
shifted toward securing oil from the Middle East, technological advancements (in part spurred by the rise in energy prices in the 1970s) continued to
make previously inaccessible oil reserves available. The waters of the North
Sea, the Gulf of Mexico, and the coast of Brazil—all areas through which the
Paragon sailed—came to be home to offshore platforms drilling ever deeper.
While ships like the *Paragon* were once the cutting edge technologies of
extraction, by the time the ship was moored, further technological advances
in the pursuit of oil had made the *Paragon* something of a relic. The history
of oil extraction has been riddled with spectacular disasters (*Exxon Valdez,
Deepwater Horizon*), has fueled tragic disasters that have become normalized
(such as car crashes), and has particle by particle contributed to a colossal
slow disaster that now looms menacingly close.

The *Paragon* was an agent of the slow disaster of climate change and was
finally done in by a hurricane exacerbated by that very process. In the bank
accounts and lungs of its crews, in the memories of people who photographed
it, in the Coast Guard engineers who towed it ashore after the hurricane, the
Paragon lives. But its most lasting impact is in the atmosphere, where the
particular history of the ship becomes its particulate legacy.

Thus, even though the history of the *Paragon* may be punctuated by particular events described as disasters—being struck by an iceberg, blocking the

Port Aransas ship channel—the ship has been part of a long, slowly unfolding disaster. Taken as part of the larger story of Hurricane Harvey, the *Paragon* barely registers; similarly, taken as part of the larger story of fossil-fuel-driven anthropogenic climate change, the *Paragon* is but one contributor. Viewed as an event, the *Paragon* was a disaster averted by an adept government agency; the Coast Guard quickly reopened the ship channel. But viewed in the context of a slow disaster, the *Paragon* is one moment in a catastrophe that seems only to be gathering in intensity. Considered as a discrete event, this tale of the *Paragon* was ultimately a success, but considered as part of a slow disaster, it is a failure. To present the voyage of the *Paragon* as a single event, bounded on both sides by normalcy, is to overlook the ways in which events like Harvey reveal normalcy to be a myth.

By pushing the time frame back and considering the *Paragon* not only as a ship, but also as a particular kind of ship that has played a specific role in flows of capital and resources, we engage with the methods of the Anthropocene, a proposed geological era defined by human activity. As a slow disaster rubric, the Anthropocene forces analysis outside the normal periodizations and beyond the traditional focus on discrete events. In the Anthropocene, specific disaster events are mere data points in a planetary ecosystem that has been rapidly modified by human industrial activity. In this slow disaster mode of disaster studies, we are stretching geographical scales and timescales out past the normal frames of analysis—past the point where we have long runs of journals, media coverage, or reliable archives—to points where we may have to mix written sources with the histories of animals, plants, oceans, and geology to link the present disaster to a deep past. Even as the Anthropocene brings planetary changes down to a human timescale, it reveals that the tools we generally use to make sense of human timescales may be insufficient for understanding this strange new era. It is a pivot that involves an engagement not only with the disasters that have come before, but also with the disasters that are yet to come, and it involves a step toward seriously considering how disasters have been imagined throughout history. It is fair to say that the term "disaster" itself actually loses its conventional descriptive purchase when we study it in the "slow" frame. Invoking it in this way, one that unsettles the conventional focusing event, is not accidental, but strategic; it awakens the possibility for conceptual, and perhaps even ethical and legislative, breakthroughs.

A slow disaster telling of the voyage of the *Paragon* is, therefore, about much more than a ship. It is a story rooted in the emergence of carbon-based fuels, the development of capitalism, and the formation of the modern state.

In commenting on watching a sinking ship at the start of the second book of his *De Rerum Natura*, Lucretius remarked on the odd pleasure of watching the misfortunes of others from the safety of the shore. This is not to delight in schadenfreude, but because viewing the catastrophes of others may remind viewers of the calamities from which they have been spared. Treated as a singular event, the *Paragon* may inspire such a sentiment among readers who are relieved that they were not among the crew of the *Signet Enterprise*, waiting for Coast Guard rescue after the *Paragon* collided with the ship. Yet to see the *Paragon* through the lens of slow disaster is to be reminded that we are not watching the ship safely from shore—rather, we are all on the sinking ship. And we may not be rescued in time.

Conclusion

The voyage of the *Paragon* is about a particular event that occurred within the context of a larger event; it is also an account of risk management; and it is also a tale that needs to be understood within the context of a larger slow disaster. Each of these frameworks has drawn attention to a distinct set of historical actors: for the "event" the key actors are the victims, first responders, and political figures (the governor, the president), and for "risk management" the actors are insurance agents, FEMA, city planners, and environmentalists, while the shift to "slow disaster" poses more of a conundrum, pulling together geologists, social scientists, artists, and ostensibly every person who is a potential victim of industrialization and climate change. The range of historical actors is wide, yet they all have a place in this story. The point is not to suggest that one of these is the correct version, but to emphasize that to truly reckon with the *Paragon*'s voyage from a critical disaster studies perspective requires all three accounts.

On January 23, 2019, a meeting called by PAC drew more than two hundred people to the Port Aransas community center. At the meeting, John Donovan, one of the leaders of PAC, raised concerns about the Port of Corpus Christi's plans to develop a crude oil shipping terminal on Harbor Island. "The idea of building a mammoth super tanker port just a few hundred yards from our city's park has got people very concerned," he explained to a reporter. PAC was circulating a petition, calling on Governor Abbott not "to circumvent a fair and open evaluation of the best method for exporting large quantities of crude oil from Corpus Christi."[33] Among PAC's chief concerns were the "risks associated with locating [an] oil storage facility in [a] storm surge prone area."[34]

Considering that it was the twelve-foot storm surge brought up the Port Aransas ship channel by Hurricane Harvey that caused the *Paragon* to break loose from its mooring, it would seem that PAC has cause to be concerned about future storm surges. But when the next storm surge makes its way up the channel (and it is almost certainly a matter of "when," not "if"), the *Paragon* will no longer be there. It remains to be seen if the *Paragon*'s voyage was enough of a "focusing event" to ensure that the next time a hurricane bears down on Corpus Christi, ships will be more heavily secured. Regardless of the decision, a risk management decision connected to the disaster event of August 26, 2017, the *Paragon* has left its mark in the slow disaster of industrialization along the Gulf Coast and around the globe.

Ultimately, it is by booking passage on the *Paragon* that we have sought to sail through the seas connecting all three time scales. As a ship moving around the world, drilling for oil, the *Paragon*'s tale has ended—but as an interscalar vessel, the *Paragon* endures.

CHAPTER 2

Acts of God, Man, and System

Knowledge, Technology, and the Construction of Disaster

Ryan Hagen

> By nature, there are no castles in thunder-storms; yet, but
> say the word, and of this cottage I can make a Gibraltar
> by a few waves of this wand.
>   —Herman Melville, "The Lightning-Rod Man"

In the summer of 1868 a railway crash left thirty-three passengers dead in the Welsh countryside, the latest in a series of spectacular and gruesome accidents that plagued the Victorian rail system. Describing the crash, a writer in London's *Saturday Review* lamented: "We are, in the matter of railway traveling, always treading the unknown; experience is powerless. All that we know of the future is that it is full of dangers; but what these dangers are we cannot conjecture or anticipate."[1] In earlier years, railway accidents had been understood as "acts of God," providential or apparently arbitrary misfortunes that were duly cataloged in the press alongside "bizarre deaths from bolts of lightning, bites from pigs, falls from monuments and bedroom windows, slips into pits of new slaked lime and vats of ale-wort."[2] By the time of the Abergele disaster of 1868, this sense of arbitrariness was beginning to fade. The statistical revolution of the mid-1800s had underwritten new ways of understanding, predicting, and ultimately controlling technological misfortune.[3] Safety rules based on accident statistics had begun to successfully reduce fatalities in mines and factories. Such statistics were not yet available for the rapidly expanding rail system, however. The technology involved was still too novel, experimental, complex. With its precariously held balance of spectacular danger and revolutionary change, railway travel became an inescapable fact of Victorian social and economic life, transforming as it transfixed.[4]

It was this combination of ubiquity and uncanny instability that made accidents like Abergele so unsettling and so penetratingly personal. As the *Saturday Review* columnist continued: "Few of us know anything of mines and powder-mills and ships foundering at sea. These things are but as distant tales and personal histories to most people. But we all are railway travelers; these trains and collisions, the stations and engines, and all the rest of it, are not only household words, but part of our daily life."[5] The derailments and fiery collisions of the railway network produced new psychic and social traumas that would in time become more or less synonymous with modernity: loss of individual control in the face of awesome technological systems and the thrilling and terrifying destabilization of a previously familiar social order by a mechanized mass society. Indeed, today's medical and psychological understanding of post-traumatic stress disorder is rooted in the 1867 description of the debilitating but apparently nonphysical injuries suffered by the victims of railway accidents, a condition diagnosed at the time as "railway spine."[6]

In the years following Abergele, the British government moved to rationalize railway safety. The Regulation of Railways Act of 1871 required the reporting of railway accident statistics for the first time. Pamphlets about the human causes and remedies of rail disasters became increasingly popular. In 1877 British prime minister Benjamin Disraeli declared the struggle to tame the unstable railways "perhaps our greatest domestic question." The social production and control of technological risk as a preoccupation of government and public life had arrived.[7] It has yet to depart.

A century later, Anthony Giddens would describe anxiety associated with technological risk as a crisis of ontological security—an unsettling of what Giddens called the "confidence that most human beings have in the continuity of their self-identity and in the constancy of the surrounding social and material environments of action. A sense of the reliability of persons and things."[8] This sense of an unstable world would have been recognizable to the Victorians. Railway travel in the late-middle nineteenth century was reliable enough to become integral to daily life, yet unstable enough that a routine trip to the countryside or across the city entailed the risk of a sudden and irrevocable shattering of trust in the continuity of everyday action and the reliability of mechanical things.[9] The *Saturday Review* columnist emphasized the "peculiar form" of railway accidents, which seemed to regularly emerge from coincidences of failures "so exceptional that no human foresight could have guarded against . . . or even anticipated [them]." Again and again railway accidents "occurred under the precise but most unlikely conditions to do the most possible mischief," as if "to exhaust every conceivable, or even inconceivable, variety of the remotest and most unlikely danger."[10]

The trauma of Abergele is an indication that the conditions for what Charles Perrow would later term "normal accidents"—catastrophic failures of complex, tightly coupled systems that resulted from improbable alignments of smaller failures that on their own would not have been fatal—had begun to emerge in popular discourse a century before the advent of nuclear power and other complex technical systems more commonly associated with the concept.[11] The fundamental unknowability of the danger lurking beneath the surface of everyday life that Ulrich Beck made central to the risk society thesis had begun to take hold well before the horrors of Chernobyl and the other crises of contamination that he argued characterize the "new risks" of postmodernity.[12]

If we can see premonitions of postmodern crises in early modern events like the Abergele wreck, it is because the fundamental problem posed by disaster has been with us all along, though its manifestations change. The kinds of disasters we face, and the ways in which we understand, experience, anticipate, and repair them, are fundamentally shaped by the cultural and material contexts within which they erupt. Disaster is a problem of knowledge and is known by its consequences. It is, as the philosopher Susan Neiman described the problem of evil, "fundamentally a problem about the intelligibility of the world as a whole."[13] Over time, developments in the state of knowledge for understanding the world, along with innovations in technological tools for sensing, interpreting, and shaping it, change the nature and consequences of disaster. Evidence of this can be found in the long historical career of the discourse around disaster causation, which roughly speaking moved from the designation of disasters as "acts of God" in Enlightenment Europe, to "acts of man" amid the androcentric technological hubris of the mid-twentieth century, to the twenty-first-century sense that disasters are emergent effects of complex systems.

To trace the intellectual history of disaster, it is helpful to focus on representative moments—crises in which long-standing assumptions about sources of safety and danger are unsettled—and then examine what it was about these crises that threatened "our sense of the sense of the world."[14] This chapter examines three such moments: the Lisbon earthquake of 1755, the

Halifax explosion of 1917, and the landfall of Hurricane Maria on the island of Puerto Rico in 2017. Each of these moments is embedded in and accentuates broader transformations in scientific and cultural knowledge for understanding the world and developments in technologies for manipulating it.

Disaster is often treated as an alien incursion into everyday life, a force that stands outside society, striking out of the blue. In sociology, disaster has been roped off from mainstream research as an exotic phenomenon with few if any generalizable lessons for the study of society.[15] Disasters are sometimes dismissed as current events that only serve to distract serious scholars from analysis of the real structural and political forces at work in the world.[16] This chapter joins an emerging body of literature in critical disaster studies that interrogates these taken-for-granted ideas about the nature of catastrophe, asking, as Rebecca Elliott wrote of climate change, not what sociology can contribute to our understanding of disaster, but what understanding disaster can contribute to sociology.[17] It argues that disaster is primarily a problem of knowledge and technology that is inextricably embedded within the everyday sociomaterial reproduction of social life. Disasters are punctuations in this reproduction process, ruptures that may be triggered by environmental forces but are rooted in and emerge from the ongoing, moment-to-moment work of reenacting the social world.

Acts of God

The earthquake that decimated the Portuguese capital of Lisbon in 1755 is often considered the first modern disaster.[18] The massive quake, and the tsunami and firestorm that followed it, killed tens of thousands and laid waste to what was then the fourth-largest city in Europe and a major center in Atlantic trade. Eyewitness accounts of the destruction circulated widely around Europe in the aftermath, in the form of printed pamphlets that so captivated the popular imagination that even "central Europeans were beginning to convince themselves that they had also felt the earth shake."[19] This is one distinctly modern feature of the event: it marked the first time that the nascent mass press had been able to create an "illusion of proximity and unity among the people of different European nations."[20] Talk of the quake dominated newspapers in Germany for months afterward.[21] This coverage eventually included three essays published in 1756 in the Königsberg weekly paper by Immanuel Kant in which the philosopher, speculating on various natural explanations for earthquakes, sought to reassure his readers that the catastrophic shaking that felled Lisbon could not also strike Prussia.[22]

But spectacular accounts of catastrophic earthquakes had circulated in Europe before. In 1692, pamphlets carried accounts of a quake that destroyed Port Royal, Jamaica; in 1746 another earthquake and tsunami caused horrific damage in Lima and Callao, in what was then the Spanish Viceroyalty of Peru. These earlier quakes had widely been interpreted as acts of God, divine punishment for human moral transgression. This mode of explanation for misfortune, this theodicy, had been dominant in European thought since at least the fourteenth century, and responses to calamity were often moral-regulatory in nature. For example the city council of Strasbourg, responding to a minor earthquake there in 1357, issued a ban on the wearing of ostentatious gold jewelry and ordered a procession of penitents in the city streets; the Florentine senate in 1542 responded to a devastating earthquake with a strict denunciation of sodomy and blasphemy.[23] Witch trials were a widespread response to the slow-motion climatic disaster constituted by the Little Ice Age of the same period.[24]

What marked the Lisbon quake as a watershed moment in European modernity was that it posed major challenges to the dominant theodicy just as Enlightenment skepticism about the role of God in the natural world was coming to a head in the intellectual life of the continent. The quake struck in the morning of All Saints Day (November 1), in a city known for its piety and its prosperity. Lisbon had been both a gateway to lucrative overseas trade and the seat of the Inquisition. Questions over why such devastation should befall Lisbon, rather than Paris or London or any other European capital, fueled doubt about the divine meanings with which past disasters had been invested. Goethe, who was six years old when the quake struck, later recalled in his autobiography that Lisbon had moved his spirit "to its depths for the first time. . . . God, the creator of heaven and earth, whom the explanation of the first article of faith represented . . . as so wise and merciful, had proved himself to be in no wise fatherly in giving over righteous and unrighteous to destruction."[25] Voltaire, in his *Poéme sur le désastre de Lisbonne*, used the catastrophe as a decisive refutation of Leibnizian optimism, helping to cement the disaster as one that "shocked Western civilization more than any other event since the fall of Rome."[26]

The Portuguese state undertook efforts to counter claims that the Lisbon earthquake had been willed as divine punishment, perhaps out of pragmatic interest in self-preservation. The Portuguese monarch King José I charged one of his ministers, who became known by his later title as the Marquis of Pombal, to direct emergency relief and recovery from the quake, establishing the modern precedent for state responsibility over disaster recovery and prevention. Pombal, working to maintain order as the city recovered, pushed naturalist explanations for the tragedy, under the belief that "the more earthquakes were viewed as normal events, the easier it would be to incorporate them into a normal world—or to view the return to normalcy as a merely practical problem."[27] This secular vision was far from universally adopted, of course. Throughout this period theologians in Portugal and elsewhere in Europe continued to point to the earthquake as evidence of God's just wrath and as an omen portending further destruction. In Lisbon in particular, a Jesuit priest named Gabriel Malagrida preached that the quake had been punishment for Portuguese sins, and that the subsequent reconstruction of the city under Pombal's direction was an act of blasphemy for which divine retribution would eventually come. Rather than rebuild, Lisboans should repent, as tradition dictated. Malagrida was banished from the city as a public menace, then imprisoned, and ultimately put to death for heresy by the Inquisition at Pombal's behest in 1761.[28]

For Neiman, Pombal's defeat of Malagrida signaled "the end of a form of explanation" for catastrophes, a decisive "victory for the view that God's purposes have no public function . . . a shift in consciousness so profound that it often remains unnoticed."[29] This may be too tidy a conclusion. Beliefs and knowledge about the causes and significance of disaster were, in the early modern era, diverse and unsettled. Throughout the Renaissance and into the early Enlightenment, the resurgent philosophy of the Roman poet Lucretius supported one major undercurrent of resistance to the idea that God's hand was behind disaster,[30] proposing that instead catastrophes, whether they be earthquakes or plagues, could be explained by the chance motions of the atoms Lucretius envisioned making up the universe.[31] Regardless, the broadly accepted understanding of Lisbon as a point of departure into modernity, a crisis that "figured as the coming of age of the European mind," highlights the extent to which disaster is a problem of knowledge.[32] The quake inflicted such cultural and theological trauma because, in the moment when it struck, alternate explanations that challenged the dominant theodicy had already become thinkable. The material destruction of Lisbon and the anxiety it produced across Europe had made the previously dominant theodicy untenable.

Acts of Man

The Enlightenment's transfer of causal explanations for disaster from the transcendental to the material plane, the incorporation of horrific tragedies into the practical stream of normal problems in the world, was echoed in the opening decades of the industrial revolution, as society addressed the spectacular carnage that industrial technology could produce. Just as scientific-rational explanations for earthquakes and other extreme natural events were taming natural disaster, the development of probability science was also making possible new ways of understanding, predicting, and ultimately controlling technological misfortune. As the epidemiologist William Farr reported to the Fourth International Statistical Congress in 1860:

> Despite the accidents of conflagrations, the unstableness of
> winds, the uncertainties of life and the variations in men's minds
> and circumstances, on which fires, wrecks and deaths depend,
> they are subject to laws as invariable as gravitation and fluctuate
> to within certain limits, which the calculus of probabilities can
> determine beforehand. . . . Shall a system of fatalism be built
> upon this foundation? . . . No, for statistics has revealed also a law
> of variation. . . . Introduce a system of ventilation into unventi-
> lated mines, and you substitute one law of accidents for another.
> Therefore, these events are under control.[33]

The rationalizing impulse in taming catastrophe was not restricted to rail-road accidents, as discussed at the opening of this chapter. In this era the deployment of statistically and scientifically informed policies and technologies was advocated to curb other types of danger as well. On the European continent, the hygienists and Pasteurians were generating knowledge about the microbial causes of disease, replacing the notion of "spontaneous morbidity" with an understanding that human activity was producing, and could be used to control, the deadly illnesses that had been endemic in European cities. As Bruno Latour writes: "In 1871 and even in 1880 there was no connection between an infectious disease and a laboratory. To suggest one would have been as odd as to speak in the seventeenth century of a 'physics of the heavens'. . . . At the time, a disease was something idiosyncratic, which could be understood only on its own ground and in terms of circumstances."[34] The laboratory for Pasteur was an apparatus of control, in which "phenomena are finally made smaller than the group of men who can then dominate them."[35]

In the United States in this period, the problem of uncontrolled urban fire "challenged the notion of modernity itself as a sustainable urban condition," as conflagrations provoked a string of national traumas in the years surrounding the turn of the twentieth century.[36] As for railway accidents and communicable disease, a system of experts and institutions came into being around the problem. Organizations like the National Fire Protection Association, National Board of Fire Underwriters, and Underwriters Laboratory produced bodies of formal knowledge, trained experts, suggested policy, and developed technologies to combat the problem of urban fire, with enough success that by the early 1940s the "conflagration era" in American cities had been brought to an end.

Along with the growing promise of technical control, technological hazards achieved the potential to rival natural forces in their destructive power. Amid the devastation of the First World War, the Halifax munitions explosion of 1917 stood out as an early symbol of this parity. Set off by the collision of a Belgian relief vessel with a French munitioner carrying 450,000 pounds of TNT and 2,300 tons of picric acid out of Halifax harbor, the explosion obliterated large sections of the port city. The sociologist Samuel Prince's account of the blast and subsequent recovery of the city conjures earthquakes, tidal waves, firestorms, and tornadoes to describe the ferocity of the explosion: "It was an earthquake so violent that when the explosion occurred the old, rock-founded city shook as with palsy. The citadel trembled, the whole horizon seemed to move with the passing of the earth waves."[37]

Like the Lisbon earthquake, the Halifax explosion shocked the popular conscience. A new kind of "man-made" calamity had been proven possible. Prince used Halifax to lay out the case that "with the advent of the industrial age disaster grows more frequent every year."[38] In building his case, Prince recited a catalog of examples that indiscriminately intermixed dam breaks and the Halifax explosion with floods, tornadoes, and the San Francisco earthquake of 1906. If people in this period were beginning to see disaster increasingly as the result of human activity, they also saw rational social action as a solution, with mixed results. The technocratic reforms of the Progressive Era combined heroic efforts in the control of nature with efforts to alleviate social misfortune on a similar scale.[39]

By the 1930s, it was commonplace to talk about humanity's "conquest of nature." In the United States, the sociologist Lowell Carr wrote that while "nature is supposed to be most completely subdued," disasters still occurred only where human protections against the environment failed. "Not every windstorm, earth-tremor, or rush of water is a catastrophe," he wrote. "So long as the ship rides out the storm, so long as the city resists the earth-shocks, so long as the levees hold, there is no disaster."[40] This was the intellectual scene in which the geographer Gilbert F. White proposed, in his influential 1942 dissertation and later book *Human Adjustment to Floods*, that "floods are 'acts of God,' but flood losses are largely acts of man."[41] White's influence wrought such profound changes in the practical study and control of natural disasters that by the 1970s his work came to characterize the "dominant approach" against which radical scholars like Kenneth Hewitt levied criticisms that set the stage for critical disaster studies.[42]

If the Lisbon earthquake in the middle of the eighteenth century marked the turn away from understandings of disasters as acts of God, the decades around the middle of the twentieth century marked the height of the understanding of disasters as acts of man. As a controlling force in everyday affairs, the divine hand of heaven had been replaced, Lewis Mumford wrote mockingly, by the "divinity of the Control Room itself, with its Cybernetic Deity, giving His lightning-like decisions and His infallible answers: omniscience and omnipotence, triumphantly mated by science."[43]

And yet the Halifax explosion of 1917 also contained characteristics of a different sort of disaster, a type that preoccupies us a century later. That is to say, the Halifax explosion can be described as a normal accident within a global system: a French vessel in a British colonial possession, carrying explosives for use in a distant war fueled by imperialist competition, colliding with a Belgian vessel returning from a transatlantic relief mission.[44] The result was the unthinkably powerful release of energy on a provincial town in which "no one dreamed of danger save to loved ones far away."[45] Part of the trauma of the event was that it instantly brought the horrors of the front lines of the European theater to unsuspecting civilians half a world away. The Halifax explosion, historian Jacob Remes writes, stood "at the precipice of a new age of disaster, between the preaerial urban destruction of the American Civil War and the Spanish shelling of Valparaiso and the explosive horrors of twentieth-century total war."[46]

Thus the Halifax explosion can be seen as a prototypical example of a new class of risk that emerged with the Cold War's nuclear arms race and came into its own with globalization and the information revolution: the global systemic shock. This species of trouble is defined by its boundary-crossing peril and its concentration of extralocal forces.[47] A good model for thinking about global risk is the highly interconnected and tightly coupled, global system of sensors, vehicles, computers, personnel, and political actors that constituted the Cold War nuclear standoff between the Soviet Union and United States. Disequilibrium, disruption, or breakdown of the sociotechnical deterrence structure that prevented the outbreak of general nuclear war could have generated cataclysm far beyond the scale of nearly any "natural" event.

Though the Cold War has ended, the post–Cold War era nevertheless is replete with risks similarly rooted in complex, networked sociotechnical systems that amplify or otherwise surpass natural hazards. In public health, the mid-twentieth-century confidence that communicable disease could be eradicated by rational public health policy has been shattered by the emergence of novel emerging infectious diseases and the development of antibiotic-resistant pathogens.[48] Pollution from globally directed capitalist production has modified the atmosphere to such an extent that acid rain and ozone depletion were for a time threats to human safety on a planetary scale. Global warming from greenhouse gas emissions remains a grave long-term threat, one that will in the near term drive stronger and more dangerous meteorological disasters. The intensified exploitation of former wilderness areas exposes humans to new and exotic pathogens, and a densely interconnected global network of travel and trade provides new pathways to pandemic disease. To say, today, that disasters are "acts of man" seems almost comically hubristic; in the present we are more likely to understand disaster as the consequence of systems far beyond any individual or even institutional control.

Acts of Systems

The destruction wrought by Hurricane Maria on Puerto Rico in 2017 illustrates how even "natural" disasters can be understood as acts of complex systems today. Maria was an object of intense study as part of the global climate system. The intensity and timing of the storm's landfall on Puerto Rico were predicted several days in advance, thanks to a heterogeneous network of satellites, aircraft, radar stations, and instrument-laden buoys that fed data to be analyzed by powerful computers and experts in several centers in the United States and Europe. The storm's unusual strength was understood as a consequence of global climate change, a problem also made legible through the long-accumulating work of sensors, data, and experts. The level of precision provided by hurricane forecasts has been steadily improving in recent years, which has given people in harm's way increasing time to prepare. This in part explains why the death toll directly attributable to the force of the storm was so low. The vast majority of deaths from Maria came from the disruption of infrastructure systems, for example, prolonged interruptions in power, telecommunications, transportation, and food distribution. Systemic impacts were so central to the Maria disaster that the Federal Emergency Management Agency in its *2017 Hurricane Season After-Action Report* recommended an overhaul of the US National Response Framework to emphasize the fortification and resilience of "critical lifeline" infrastructure including food, communications, transportation, water, power, and medical treatment.[49]

The 2017 hurricane season marked the start of a string of disasters in the United States and around the world that seemed to combine forces of the climate system and human infrastructure systems. Hurricane Harvey in August of that year unleashed unprecedented flooding across southeast Texas, combining an unusually wet and slow-moving hurricane with largely unregulated urban development that had replaced thousands of acres of wetlands with impermeable surfaces. In California in November 2018, the failure of an electrical transmission line combined with unusually dry conditions to spark what became the Camp Fire, the deadliest wildfire in the state's history, as well as the largest in terms of acres burned. To prevent a repeat of that catastrophe, in October 2019 California utility companies began preemptively shutting off power to large parts of the state during periods of high wind, recognizing that their transmission lines were a primary source of wildfire risk in the state.

In the United States, deaths from infrastructure system failures now routinely exceed fatalities directly caused by natural hazards. In Puerto Rico, as few as 1 in 10 of the estimated 4,645 disaster deaths were directly attributed to the wind and water of Hurricane Maria itself, while as many as a third were caused by disruptions in medical infrastructure alone.[50] The case of Hurricane Irma, which struck Florida, Georgia, and North Carolina, again shows the extent of the problem. That storm caused 11 direct deaths from flooding, and 115 indirect deaths, from failures of medical care, heat deaths from failed air-conditioning systems, carbon monoxide poisoning from improperly installed portable power generators, and traffic fatalities from hazardous road conditions.[51] Failures in transportation infrastructure are often a significant cause of death after disasters; following Hurricane Harvey's landfall in Texas, for example, 21 out of 70 storm-related deaths resulted from people driving vehicles into floodwaters or being swept away by a current as they stepped out of their cars.[52] In a comprehensive study of fatalities from fifty-nine tropical cyclones between 1963 and 2012, indirect deaths outnumbered direct casualties in half of these storms. Tellingly, seven out of the ten storms with the highest numbers of indirect deaths occurred within the final ten years of the period.[53]

The COVID-19 pandemic is similarly understood as a catastrophe emerging from complex global infrastructure systems, the virus that causes the disease having jumped from bats to humans and spread through trade and travel networks from China to essentially every country on Earth within months of the first diagnosed infections in Wuhan. The first wave of the virus expressed its damage most acutely through the overwhelming of hospital systems first in Wuhan, then in Lombardy and New York City. The first efforts to combat the pandemic focused on shutting down economic activity, triggering a global recession which, while less directly lethal than the virus itself, nevertheless highlighted the extent to which everyday life depended on the rapid circulation of people and goods.

These eruptions occur against the background of a climate that is being warmed and destabilized by emissions of greenhouse gas produced as apparently unavoidable by-products of everyday life. Bruno Latour in his 2014 Yale Tanner Lecture described the experience of life in the time of anthropogenic climate change as "a strange new feeling of sliding along a Mobius strip." To illustrate the idea, Latour projected a photo he had taken through the window of his recent flight from Paris to the United States, showing in the foreground a jet engine and, in the background, arctic sea ice in melting and broken sheets. "In an earlier time I would have seen the ice, and then I would have seen the [engines] of the Boeing, with great pleasure but as separate things," he explained. "But now when you look at the ice *and* the Boeing itself, you feel that they are related, so that the distinction between the foreground and background is actually gone." Today, for the cost of a transatlantic plane ticket, it is possible to witness the melting of the Arctic ice cap while knowing that you are, at that moment, contributing to the destruction. "It is very difficult now to see the ice as just a spectacle in the new-old idea of a landscape," Latour continued. "There is no landscape any more, we are *in* it."[54]

The reflexivity Latour points to is a hallmark of Ulrich Beck's risk society thesis, with its central claim that today an unavoidable side effect of wealth production is the production of risk, and that inequality is as much a problem of the unequal distribution of those risks as of the unequal distribution of wealth.[55] These risks, rooted in technological and scientific triumphs, nevertheless cannot be adequately controlled through technoscientific means. The problem of global warming provides an excellent example: technological advancements led to a society capable of producing greenhouse gas emissions in sufficient quantities to warm the planet, along with the sophisticated instrumentation to detect the associated changes in the composition and temperature of the atmosphere, as well as techniques for computationally modeling future climatic states.[56] We have generated both an existential risk and the means to detect it and forecast its approach, but still a comprehensive solution exceeds our grasp. That is the fundamental terror of the risk society.

This idea that we are trapped in a landscape of our own making is more fully theorized by the geologist Peter Haff in his notion of the "technosphere," the globe-spanning, emergent system of all the people, technological artifacts, domesticated biological organisms, and physical infrastructure that comprise and support human civilization. It is a "matrix of technology" in which humans are "borne along by supervening dynamics from which they cannot simultaneously escape and survive."[57] The technosphere is so massive in scale that its effects register alongside those of the other "natural" planetary systems: the hydrosphere, lithosphere, atmosphere and biosphere.[58] The technosphere, then, is the engine driving the Anthropocene, a geological era in which collective human activity is measurably among the dominant forces durably shaping the surface of the planet.[59] Under the conditions of the Anthropocene, living within the technosphere, the commonplace distinction between "natural" and "man-made" disasters, while perhaps culturally salient, becomes theoretically untenable. Even when a disaster is triggered by "natural" geophysical forces, its consequences are felt most acutely by people within the technosphere. Disaster is immanent in the human social project. It is, as the historian William McNeill wrote, "the price we pay for being able to alter the natural balances and to transform the face of the earth through collective effort and the use of tools."[60] But this understanding of disaster as a failure of technical systems is not restricted to academic theorists. Pragmatic professionals view disaster this way too. Recall the FEMA 2017 after action report on the 2017 hurricane season and its emphasis on the resilience of supply chain systems. In the professional field of emergency management, the field most directly tasked with confronting disaster, definitions tend to revolve around problems of resource deprivation. A glossary published by the FEMA's Emergency Management

Institute, one of the field's premier training institutions, defines disaster as "an event that requires resources beyond the capability of a community and requires a multiple agency response."[61] The roots of this view of disaster as a disruption of resources lie in Cold War–era planning for nuclear warfare, as Stephen J. Collier and Andrew Lakoff have shown in their work on the history of what they call the "vital systems security" paradigm.[62]

The development of air power theory among US military strategists in the years between the world wars led to a view of nations as "industrial webs" that could be defeated in war by air strikes on key nodes in the production system. Industrial web theory guided the US strategic air campaign against the Axis powers in the Second World War, and following the war the defense establishment assumed that any future air attack on the United States would be based on the same logic. It therefore became imperative for the US government to conduct the same kind of analysis of its own industrial web for defensive purposes that it had conducted for offensive operations against Germany and Japan and ultimately planned for the Soviet Union and other nations.[63] The end result of this analysis, Collier and Lakoff write, was a "new understanding of cities in the nuclear age . . . as collections of vulnerable systems that had to be understood in their complex interrelationship."[64] The logic of nuclear warfare, in which any target could hypothetically be struck with almost no advanced warning and with devastating force, required a defensive posture that emphasized "the continuous functioning of critical systems in the event of disaster" and a shift toward the "imaginative enactment" of future disruptions as a way of preparing for low-probability, high-consequence events.[65]

This approach gradually drifted from a purely defense-planning context into general disaster preparedness policy and practice through the dual-use doctrine of US civil defense programs, which held that resources meant for defense against nuclear attack, which might never come, should also be used for response and recovery after devastating natural disasters, which occurred with relatively greater frequency.[66] By the 1990s, the drift of vital systems theory from strategic air power to general preparedness practice was epitomized by the presidential Commission on Critical Infrastructure Protection (CCIP), convened in July 1996 by the Bill Clinton administration. The problem the United States faced, according to the executive order establishing the commission, was that certain infrastructure systems had become "so vital that their incapacity or destruction would have a debilitating impact on the defense or economic security" of the country.[67] In a post–Cold War world, these threats could come from natural disasters, accidents, terrorists, or hackers exploiting cyber-vulnerabilities.

The commission's final report, issued in 1997, was quite explicit in its argument that modern social well-being was predicated on the flow of resources through infrastructure systems. "Life is good in America because things work," the report's first chapter begins. "When we flip the switch, the lights come on. When we turn the tap, clean water flows. When we pick up the phone, our call goes through. We are able to assume that things will work because our *infrastructures* are highly developed and highly effective."[68] The commission identified eight distinct but interdependent sectors of critical infrastructure: transportation, oil and gas, water, emergency services, government, banking and finance, electricity, and telecommunications. The trust engendered by the stability of these systems had allowed for efficiencies in production and service provision that were at the same time dependencies vulnerable to catastrophic disruption. The commission report noted that the market-driven proliferation of "just-in-time" supply chain practices meant that even minor infrastructure disruptions could produce debilitating effects.[69]

Complicating the problem of protecting this infrastructure, from a national security standpoint, was that a majority of it was not owned and controlled by the government but rather by private industry. The commission's definition of infrastructure emphasized this interconnectedness between organizations and between the government and corporate sector: "By infrastructure we mean more than just a collection of individual companies engaged in related activities; we mean a network of independent, mostly privately-owned, man-made systems and processes that function collaboratively and synergistically to produce and distribute a continuous flow of essential goods and services."[70] The interconnections between infrastructure systems and across national boundaries through global economic integration presented a "new geography" of risk that, the commission argued, resembled the Cold War's Soviet nuclear threat, only diffused through the channels of everyday commerce. In other words, "national defense is no longer the exclusive preserve of government, and economic security is no longer just about business."[71] Again as a reflection of the cultural context of the moment, the same report emphasizes the need to include the corporate sector in this effort: the neoliberalization of disaster preparedness by anticipatory osmosis, rather than through shock and postdisaster reform.

Conclusion: A Future Full of Dangers
Conjectured and Anticipated

A century and a half after the Abergele train wreck, and across the Atlantic, in New York's Times Square, the clocks ticked down to New Year's Day, January 1, 2000. Hundreds of thousands of people noisily awaited the annual ball drop that on this night would mark the turn of a new millennium. At the same time, four miles south, in a windowless room twenty-three stories above the streets of lower Manhattan, two hundred or so people held a different and strange new kind of vigil against the clock. They were gathered in the city's newly completed Emergency Operations Center (EOC). About 140 of them were government officials from an array of city, state, and federal agencies, along with representatives from utility companies and the banking sector. The gathering was unusual; in the course of the city's routine operations, the organizations represented here were rarely required to work directly together. But the possibility of a major emergency tied to the millennial turnover called for joint preparations. So they had been brought together under the auspices of the mayor's new Office of Emergency Management (OEM), which had been established in 1996 by mayor Rudy Giuliani to centralize command and control over the city's disjointed emergency response bureaucracy. The EOC was a physical manifestation of that effort. It was a hardened, permanent command post that would act as a central clearinghouse for information about potential and actual emergencies. The representatives who staffed it, working face to face, would expedite coordination between the sparsely connected network of agencies that handled public safety and operated the city's infrastructure. The EOC had been christened in June 1999 with an exercise simulating a biological weapons attack on the city. A few months later it was activated to monitor, prepare for, and respond to Hurricane Floyd, which made landfall on Long Island. Now the EOC staff watched the approach of a new year almost as if midnight itself were a hurricane churning up the coast. They monitored conditions, traded information, double-checked preparations and stockpiles, and stood by to coordinate the emergency responders if something went catastrophically wrong.

This scene, in turn, was being watched through a glass partition by some sixty journalists, who were on hand to capture the moment a millennial disaster crashed into the EOC through its screens, radios, and telephones, or else to record and transmit a reassuring ritual of government overseeing the stable continuity of society from one year into the next. To the observers in the press box the vigil in the EOC, with its preponderance of middle-aged men in uniform quietly talking and drinking coffee from Styrofoam cups, "more closely resembled a bland VFW mixer than a command center facing down a potentially apocalyptic crisis," one of the reporters wrote.[72]

There were several candidates for that potentially apocalyptic crisis. Foremost among them was the "Y2K bug," a time-accounting software flaw that, at midnight, 01/01/00, threatened to cripple the embedded computer systems that controlled everything from traffic signals to ATMs to nuclear power plants. In the worst-case scenario, the power grid would fail, factory equipment would malfunction, and passenger jets would fall out of the sky. The banking sector, which was heavily reliant on networked computers, was seen as especially vulnerable. That was why representatives from the financial services industry had been called to the EOC that night, the first time they had ever received such an invitation. Billions of dollars had been spent worldwide to upgrade computer systems against the Y2K bug in the years leading up to the millennium, and early tests suggested there would be no major problems. But a technological experiment on this scale had never been attempted before. The only way to know for sure that the fixes had worked would be to wait and watch as computer clocks around the world ticked over to 01/01/00.

The specter of a terrorist attack also stalked the room. In mid-December, a man linked to al-Qaeda had been arrested at the Canadian border with a cache of explosives, which he had allegedly planned to use in a strike against Los Angeles International Airport on New Year's Eve. Domestic terrorism too was a concern. In October, the Federal Bureau of Investigation had released a lengthy report warning that religious fringe groups, apocalyptic cults, militias, or lone wolf white supremacists might carry out violent attacks capitalizing on the symbolic significance of the millennial turnover. The threat of terrorism would have seemed particularly salient in the EOC. The complex was just across the street from the World Trade Center towers, where terrorists had set off a truck bomb that killed six people and injured a thousand more in 1993.

The clock ticked over to midnight. In Times Square, the ball dropped. Nothing happened. Applause broke out in the EOC. Jerome Hauer, director of the Office of Emergency Management, met the press: "The lights are on like we told you they would be," he said. "The water's flowing. This is the outcome we wanted. This is why you plan."[73]

None of the catastrophes anticipated for New Year's Eve on the turn of the millennium materialized that night. Yet those dangers, and the way they were prepared for, now look like prefigurations of the institutional encounters with risk and disaster that have become almost routine in the twenty-first century.

On the one hand, we have come a long way from the Abergele disaster that opened this chapter and the *Saturday Review* columnist's lament that all we know about the future is that it is full of danger, the nature of which we know nothing at all about. Today, discourse is full of detailed projections and predictions of future danger and plans to meet it. It is not clear this state of affairs is any better. As the case of the Y2K bug shows, even time itself in the twenty-first century can become a source of instability with the potential to upend things as fundamental as the water we drink and the lights that illuminate our homes and offices. In such an environment, only a relentless anticipation of the future can keep us safe from disasters wrought by complex systems beyond our understanding and control.

Our world seems increasingly dangerous and disaster ridden not because the world is more chaotic, but because it is more organized and therefore vulnerable to a wider array of disruption. More eloquently put by the playwright Friedrich Dürrenmatt, "the more human beings proceed by plan, the more effectively they may be hit by accident." The insight this chapter tries to convey is that our plans, not only in their execution but in their conception, are shaped by the technology available to us. Furthermore, these plans are shaped by the expertise with which we anticipate and interpret the accidents that threaten to unravel them.

In much of the existing sociological literature, risk and disaster are seen as resulting from deviation from formal design goals and normative standards or expectations. This chapter extends that idea to argue that technical systems produce risk not only by deviating from expectations, but by meeting them—because they shape our goals, normative standards, and expectations. We don't only expect the planes on which we fly not to crash; we construct a whole set of goals and routines dependent on the existence of a reliable, safe commercial aviation system. Scientific knowledge not only creates new risks in the ontological sense—the production of new techniques and devices that can cause harm through their failure, or indirectly through their unexpected absence—but in the epistemic sense as well. The expertise that produces nuclear power also produces a more general understanding of the dangers of radioactivity based on nuclear physics. It is central to the production of the interconnected set of cultural schemas we can recognize as the nuclear age.

Hints of this process are embedded within the etymology of the word "disaster" itself. Often translated as the state of being "under a bad star," the word originally denoted a state of being "abandoned by the stars and left to one's miserable fate among countless perils and calamities," Marie-Hélène Huet writes. "In French the form *désastré* (literally, 'disastered') came first; it was derived from the Italian *dis-astrato*, which designated the state of having been disowned by the stars that ensure a safe passage through life."[74] To be "disastered" in the contemporary sense is to find oneself bereft of agency because of an inability to access the material artifacts and cultural-cognitive frameworks with which we make sense of the world around us.

CHAPTER 3

When Does a Crisis Begin?

Race, Gender, and the Subprime Noncrisis of the Late 1990s

Dara Z. Strolovitch

Soon after Barack Obama won the 2008 presidential election, Rahm Emanuel, his then chief of staff, told a group of CEOs: "You never want a serious crisis to go to waste. . . . Things that we had postponed for too long, that were long-term, are now immediate and must be dealt with. This crisis provides the opportunity for us to do things that you could not do before."[1]

Emanuel's assertion that crises bring "long-term" problems to the fore reminds us that although we often assume that "crises" are material things, the contours of which we can identify, measure, and, distinguish from things that are *not* crises, many of the issues brought into relief by phenomena such as financial crises are not, in fact, new problems, unanticipated upheavals, discrete incidents, or isolated ruptures. They are often instead particular manifestations of long-standing conditions that have come to be understood as urgent problems that are amenable through—and therefore worthy of—state intervention and resources, frequently because they have become newly *salient* to new, and often relatively privileged, populations.[2] From this perspective, "crisis" is less a transparent descriptor of an event or phenomenon and better understood as itself made in and by political processes.

Among the circumstances that accompanied the financial crisis to which Emanuel referred, for example, were high rates of unemployment and sharply rising rates of home foreclosures. Both of these conditions, however, had long plagued low-income people, people of color, and unmarried women of all races. By some accounts, foreclosure rates had, in fact, been higher among African Americans, Latinos, Indigenous people, and female-headed households in the mid-1990s than they would be among whites and male-breadwinner households during what would come to be labeled a foreclosure crisis a decade later.[3] Similarly, rates of unemployment among women and within many communities of color had been as high during the economically booming 1990s as they would be among whites during the "Great Recession" of the early twenty-first century. Neither unemployment nor foreclosure among members of these marginalized groups was treated as a crisis by dominant political actors and institutions, nor was either one used to justify the mobilization of political attention, government action, and state resources to alleviate or resolve them.

Considering Emanuel's quip in this light reminds us that it is not inevitable that a "bad thing" will be defined and treated as bad, much less that it will be widely regarded as a crisis. It also calls into question the implication of his assertion that increased urgency is what makes a problem a crisis. Instead, as I show in this chapter (and as Jacob Remes and Andy Horowitz argue in their Introduction to this volume is similarly the case when it comes to "disaster"), labeling something a crisis is often itself part of a political process that makes it one by transforming it from an ongoing, taken-for-granted, and naturalized condition into an intervention-worthy policy problem.[4] In this light, Emanuel's remarks make visible the backdrop of persistent problems that *do* "go to waste" and invite us to consider the use of the term "crisis" as a way to describe some bad things, to question the absence of crisis as a designator for others, and to assess the political and distributional implications of these variations.[5]

I take up this invitation by exploring the political construction, deployment, and consequences of both "bad things" that come to be treated as crises as well as those that do not, which I call "noncrises." Elsewhere, I use a keyword approach from cultural studies to make a systematic analysis of print media and political documents, tracing the ways in which differently located political actors have deployed the term "crisis" and how this has changed over time.[6] Raymond Williams used the word "keyword" to capture a phenomenon that he encountered when he returned to England after serving in World War II and, as he described it, found that the meanings of words like "culture" had multiplied and "shifted" while he had been away, "forcing themselves" on his attention "because the problems of [their] meaning" seemed to be "inextricably bound up with the problems [they were] being used to discuss."[7] Crisis, I argue, is precisely such a word, one that has so permeated American politics and culture that both are unimaginable without it, but also one that has become so common that its use hardly registers as remarkable when we hear it. Scrutinizing its use cuts against its naturalized status by unsettling its "transparent meaning" and reveals that until the 1960s, dominant political actors deployed the term crisis sparingly and mainly as a designator for what I call "clear-cut crises": bad things such as wars, recessions, and conflicts in or with other countries. The use of "crisis" as a descriptor for a wider range of domestic problems originated in the late nineteenth and early twentieth centuries among abolitionists and racial justice advocates, who used it to try to transform public understandings of racism from something understood as natural, inevitable, and intractable and to cast it instead as a policy problem that faced a critical juncture at which the presence or absence of government intervention would make a difference. In the 1960s, dominant political actors appropriated this meaning—which I label "condition-as-crisis"—and brought it into mainstream political discourse. But while civil rights leaders had pioneered condition-as-crisis in an effort to justify using state intervention and resources to address the ongoing struggles of marginalized groups, dominant political actors redefined it to signal that the status quo was under threat and that state intervention was necessary to address bad things affecting privileged people. Using crisis language to identify some kinds of problems as urgent also normalized others. That is, this constitution of crisis also came to constitute its inverse, "noncrisis": bad things that have analogues that are treated as crises worthy of and remediable through government intervention but that are treated as natural, inevitable, immune to, and therefore as not warranting such intervention. In these ways, crises must be understood as phenomena similar to those the editors describe as disasters in their Introduction to this volume: as interpretive fictions, as political, and as problems that unfold over time. Like disasters, crises should also be understood, borrowing from Claire Payton's chapter in this volume, less as specific events "and more as the expression of larger social and historical contexts into which" they release their "powerful physical forces." That is, the processes through which some bad things come to be understood as crises while others do not are socially constructed, shaped by contests over power, and are longitudinally constituted, rather than discrete and isolated incidents. As Scott Knowles and Zachary Loeb put it their chapter in this volume, crises are not "aberrant events" but rather "ordering mechanisms" that both reveal "existing social orders" and "generate new ones."

In what follows, I apply this framework of crisis and noncrisis to a comparison of the ways in which economic reporters and dominant political actors addressed subprime mortgages and foreclosures during what came to be widely known as a "foreclosure crisis" from 2007 to 2008, comparing this attention with that devoted to these issues during what I label the "foreclosure noncrisis" of the late 1990s. Subprime lending was proliferating, and foreclosure rates were higher among people of color and unmarried women in the late 1990s than they would be among whites and male-breadwinner households during what would come to be labeled a crisis a decade later. But economic reporters and dominant political actors neither described nor treated these issues as problems worthy of and remediable through federal intervention during this earlier period. Instead—and in spite of increasing evidence to the contrary—they accepted lenders' claims that women and people of color did not qualify for better loans, thereby naturalizing both the extractive terms of subprime loans and the attendant high rates of foreclosure among these groups, treating them as normal and beyond the power of the federal government to remedy.

The 2007 Mortgage Crisis

There is no official starting date for what came to be known as the foreclosure crisis of the twenty-first century. Daniel Immergluck explains, however, that in late 2006 and early 2007, rates of foreclosure began to increase rapidly, particularly in Arizona, California, Florida, and Nevada, where rates had previously been quite low.[8] In early December 2006, two major subprime mortgage lenders, Sebring Capital and Ownit Solutions, failed, sending what the *Wall Street Journal* described as "shock waves" through the market.[9] Then, in the spring of 2007, New Century, one of the largest subprime lenders in the United States, went bankrupt.

By the fourth quarter of 2007, a "foreclosure crisis" was widely understood to be underway. The Mortgage Bankers Association issued a report early the following year estimating that 3.6 percent of all loans had been seriously delinquent (that is, more than ninety days late) or in foreclosure by the end 2007, and that an additional 0.9 percent were entering foreclosure, for an overall rate of 4.5 percent.[10] The comparable figures in 2005 had been that 2.1 percent of loans were seriously delinquent and 0.4 percent were entering foreclosure.[11] Much of this increase reflected high rates of default and foreclosure on houses financed through subprime mortgages, which lenders argued were necessary to extend loans to prospective borrowers with impaired credit records, and which typically carry higher—and often variable—interest rates than those of prime mortgages, ostensibly to "compensate the lender for accepting the greater risk in lending to such borrowers."[12] Many such loans had been bought at low "teaser" rates that adjusted upward when rates reset, often making them far more expensive than they had been when borrowers had originally bought their houses. So while 2.4 percent of homes financed through conventional mortgages were in foreclosure at the height of the crisis, this was the case for 17 percent of homes financed by subprime loans.[13]

The Seeds of Noncrisis, and of Crisis

The high interest rates and inflexible terms that would come to typify subprime mortgages had long been prohibited or mitigated by state and federal legislation. They were enabled, however, by a series of laws passed as part of the wave of federal deregulation in the 1980s, which together overrode state-level anti-usury laws; allowed variable interest rates and balloon payments; incentivized mortgage debt; and allowed investment banks to buy, pool, and resell mortgages.[14] This deregulatory wave came on the heels of a previous wave of important laws passed during the 1960s and 1970s, which were intended to address racial and gender discrimination in housing and lending.[15] The coincidence of these two waves of changes transformed women and people of color from credit outcasts to what appeared to lenders to be untapped pools of underserved borrowers.[16] In particular, it opened the door to lenders and legislators who claimed that relaxed protections were necessary to open credit markets to the borrowers covered by the antidiscrimination provisions.[17] Members of these groups, they argued, had credit histories that did not allow them to qualify for the conventional thirty-year, fixed-rate, self-amortizing loans that had dominated home lending—and which had been denied to women and people of color—since the federal government had intervened to stabilize the housing market during the Great Depression of the 1930s. Allowing for more flexibility in mortgage lending, they claimed, would advance fair lending and antidiscrimination by opening up the credit market to previously excluded and redlined groups.[18]

Rather than questioning such assertions, federal legislators and regulators ratified lenders' claims that the way to expand homeownership among women and people of color was to remove the guardrails that had helped and protected dominant groups. In this neoliberal logic, the deregulation and private market solutions that enabled subprime mortgage lending were themselves defined as the appropriate state action to resolve the histories of exclusion from credit and to increase rates of homeownership among formerly excluded groups. But because the federal government withdrew from regulating these new products, women and people of color, who had been systematically locked out of homeownership for decades—and by extension, locked out of its credit record *generating* function—were left with increased access to credit and homeownership but immersed in "a fractured, risky market without a legislative safety net" in which "new forms of lending disparities among women and people of color" were able to take hold.[19] Where they were once excluded, they were now, as Amy Castro Baker writes, "included but unprotected" by a system of what scholars including Louise Seamster, Raphaël Charron-Chénier, and Keeanga-Yamatta Taylor call "predatory inclusion."[20]

By 1993, concerns began to surface about abusive lending practices that had filled this legislative and regulatory vacuum. In response, Congress passed the 1994 Home Ownership and Equity Protection Act (HOEPA), which subjected a small subset of "high-cost" refinance loans to special disclosure requirements and restrictions and provided covered consumers with "enhanced remedies for violations."[21] Lenders soon found ways to evade HOEPA's narrowly defined triggers, however, by, for example, using adjustable-rate mortgages (ARMs) featuring low initial APRs that did not fall under the law's narrow definition of "high cost."[22] HOEPA consequently ended up covering fewer than 1 percent of all mortgages.[23] It also distinguished predatory mortgages from the more general practice of subprime lending, the legitimacy of which dominant political actors continued to affirm and to treat as the solution to inequalities in access to credit. The proportion of ARMs and refinance loans consequently increased substantially after HOEPA's passage, peaking at 14.5 percent of market share in 1997 before dipping to 10.3 percent in 1998, then expanding rapidly again during the first decade of the twenty-first century.[24]

The Subprime and Foreclosure Noncrises
of the Late 1990s

These increases in rates of subprime borrowing and in the disparity between rates of foreclosure on such loans and conforming ones are alarming on their own, but they also concealed troubling racial and gender patterns in both subprime lending and rates of foreclosure. By 1999, racial justice, antipoverty, and consumer advocates were decrying a practice they called "reverse redlining," in which majority-minority neighborhoods were targeted for expensive mortgages.[25] A 1999 study showed, for example, that by 1998 subprime loans accounted for only 22 percent of mortgages in majority white Chicago neighborhoods but 34 percent of mortgages in neighborhoods in which people of color comprised 50 percent or more of the residents, and several studies also showed that these disparities actually increased as incomes rose.[26] At the height of the housing "boom," more than one-third of borrowers who were well qualified for prime loans instead received subprime mortgages with fluctuating rates, a proportion that went up to almost 50 percent among women, African Americans, and Latinos.[27] In addition, and less often noted even by many scholars of and advocates for fair lending, were the gendered patterns in subprime lending, particularly the disproportionate shares of subprime mortgages sold to women, particularly to unmarried women, and especially particularly to unmarried women of color. A study of more than four million home loans published by the Consumer Federation on what would come to be understood as the eve of the foreclosure crisis, for example, found that women earning double the median income "were 46.4 percent more likely to have a subprime loan than their similarly situated male peers" and that unmarried female homeowners were overrepresented among subprime mortgage holders by 30 percent.[28] Effects were so exponentially worse for unmarried African American women that the report found they were 256 percent more likely to have a subprime mortgage "than white men with identical geographic and financial profiles."[29] That this inequitable access to mortgage financing was rooted in gendered discrimination was further evident in the fact that, as with racial disparities, these gender disparities widened rather than diminished as women's incomes rose.[30] A series of studies published in the late 1990s and early 2000s, some of which were conducted by the federal government itself, showed that these disparities in rates of subprime lending translated into disparities in foreclosures. In Baltimore, for example, subprime mortgages comprised 21 percent of home loans in 1998 but 45 percent of foreclosures, rising to 57 percent in majority Black neighborhoods.[31]

The sharp increase in foreclosures that began in 2007 took a disproportionate toll on African Americans and Latinos. Between 2007 and 2009, 7.9 percent of African American homeowners and 7.7 percent of Latino homeowners experienced a completed foreclosure, compared with 4.5 percent of white homeowners and 4.6 percent of Asian American homeowners.[32] A 2010 study from the Center for Responsible Lending estimated that

17 percent of Latino homeowners, 11 percent of African American home-owners, and 7 percent of white homeowners lost or were at imminent risk of losing their homes during this period.[33]

The disproportionately high rates of both subprime mortgages and fore-closure experienced by people of color, unmarried women, and unmarried Black women in particular in the midst of the broader meltdown is a clas-sic story about the politics of racial, gender, and economic inequality in the United States, a story in which hard times inflict disproportionate harm and suffering on members of marginalized groups. This narrative is not wrong, but it obscures as much as it reveals about the relationship between crisis and marginalization. Most germane is that longer-term data make clear that rates of foreclosure had reached levels among subprime mortgage holders, unmarried women, and people of color by the late 1990s that were similar to and even higher than those that would affect white male-breadwinner households when the crisis was declared in 2007.[34] So although the overall rate of 4.5 percent of loans that were seriously delinquent or in foreclosure in 2007 represented a significant increase over previous years, rates among African American, Indigenous, and Latino homeowners in 1996 were already 4.8 percent, 4.4 percent, and 5.4 percent respectively, while rates were 2.9 per-cent among whites and 3.7 percent among Asian Americans.[35] Another study estimated that 5.8 percent of homes with subprime mortgages were in fore-closure by 1998.[36] And as the dates of some of the foregoing studies suggest, policymakers knew about these racialized and gendered disparities by the late 1990s, and knew as well that subprime mortgages were being sold in discrim-inatory ways to people who were well qualified for conventional ones.

How to Semantically Mask a Crisis

Even a dedicated consumer of economic reporting in dominant news sources might have had little idea about these high rates of subprime mortgage lending and foreclosure among women and in communities of color during the 1990s, however. Instead, they likely would have perceived that subprime mortgage lending was a gift to "unworthy" borrowers and that rather than requiring federal intervention to resolve, it was itself the solution to racial discrimi-nation in mortgage lending. The same would likely have been true of those following policy deliberations in sources like party platforms, presidential addresses, and the *Congressional Record*. Even a more casual reader, however, would almost certainly have had a clear sense in 2007 that rates of foreclosure had risen exponentially; that subprime mortgages were partially to blame for this increase; and that dominant political actors believed that a resolution to these predicaments required, deserved, and could be achieved through federal intervention.

Both the discourse and the silences before 2007 were produced through several processes, of which three were most important. First, economic reporters and dominant political actors unquestioningly repeated and amplified lenders' assertions that the high interest rates and inflexible terms of subprime mortgages were necessary to extend mortgages to uncreditworthy and risky aspiring homeowners. Despite accumulating evidence to the contrary, reporters consistently depicted subprime mortgages as ones that made homeownership available to people whose credit they modified with an ever-expanding array of descriptors including "weak credit," "poor credit," "dicey credit," "tarnished credit," "rocky credit," "damaged credit," "questionable credit," "scuffed credit," and even "no credit at all." Of the 68 stories about subprime mortgages published in the *New York Times* (NYT) between 1995 and 2006, for example, a full 62 percent referenced one of these descriptors, as did approximately half (45 percent) of the 189 stories in the *Wall Street Journal* (WSJ).

Second, the naturalizing effects of such characterizations of subprime borrowers and borrowers experiencing foreclosure were enabled and reinforced by the ways in which dominant political actors and economic reporters simultaneously addressed and elided the racial and gender implications of and patterns evident in subprime mortgage lending and its attendant increases in foreclosures. On the one hand, they neither investigated the claims of lenders and legislators who argued that the relaxed lending standards associated with subprime mortgages were necessary to extend mortgage credit to previously excluded groups nor scrutinized their implications for these groups. On the other hand, stories that did examine the implications of subprime mortgage lending for women and people of color provided little legal or historical context for these implications, relying instead on raced and gendered assumptions and stereotypes to explain them. For example, less than a fifth (15 percent) of NYT articles about subprime mortgages during this period focused on their implications for people of color. Attention to race in articles about rising rates of foreclosure was even rarer. And even this scant attention to the implications of subprime mortgage lending and foreclosure for borrowers of color is extensive compared to that afforded to their gendered implications. Even though stories about subprime mortgage lending often featured or were framed around accounts about female home buyers, gender was almost never thematized as an axis along which these issues were playing out. Not a single story about subprime mortgage lending in the WSJ during this period focused on its implications for women or noted the gendered patterns in rates of subprime mortgage lending. The same was true of the NYT until March 2000, when that paper finally published one story in which women and the possibility of gender discrimination in mortgage lending featured as subjects. From 1965 to 2006, a mere 3.8 percent of stories about subprime mortgage lending in the NYT focused on its gendered implications. No story about rising rates of foreclosure in either paper addressed women or gender in even a cursory or incidental way.

A third—and quite literal—indication that subprime mortgages and rising rates of foreclosure among women and people of color were constituted as noncrises by dominant media and political actors during this period is that the term "crisis" scarcely appeared in conjunction with these issues before 2007. During the noncrisis period of 1995–2006, for example, the WSJ published only one article containing any of these terms, while the NYT published a mere three articles containing any of them during this period. Of these, only one referenced the potential implications of such a crisis for people of color, noting that "minority homeowners take out a disproportionate share of subprime loans." In stark contrast to the noncrisis period, 228 articles containing these terms appeared in the NYT and 307 in the WSJ in 2007 alone. That number would more than double again for the NYT in 2008, when it published 557 articles referencing a mortgage or foreclosure crisis. That same year, the WSJ used these terms in 536 separate stories. Consistent with the patterns in economic reporting, the terms "subprime crisis," "mortgage crisis," and "foreclosure crisis" were not used in party platforms, executive orders, or State of the Union addresses between 1995 and 2006. The term "subprime crisis" itself was never used by a member of Congress or witness at a hearing before 2007, while the latter two terms appeared in the transcripts and prepared testimony in a combined total of only 8 hearings. In 2007 alone, by contrast, these terms would appear in 177 hearings, tripling to 553 in 2008.

Perhaps most significantly, of the only eleven instances of the terms "mortgage crisis" or "foreclosure crisis" in oral or written testimony at congressional hearings between 1995 and 2006, all but two were spoken or written by consumer advocates or advocates for low-income people, who tried to frame the high foreclosure rates of the era as a crisis—that is, as a problem facing a critical juncture that was caused by, merited, and could be resolved through state intervention and resources. For example, Margot Saunders, counsel with the National Consumer Law Center, testified several times during this period about what she and her organization repeatedly called a "mortgage crisis for low-income homeowners." She also attributed the crisis to the legislative changes of the 1980s, including the "deregulation [that] has allowed a wide range of marginal players into the lending and loan brokering business" and to the fact that "many of the historic protections against unfair lending practices, such as state ceilings on interest rates and licensing requirements, were removed or eviscerated during the 1980s."[37]

It takes more than simply labeling something a crisis for it to be constituted as one, but it is nonetheless striking that the term crisis was used so infrequently to describe subprime mortgages and foreclosures when their calamitous rates seemed to be restricted to marginalized groups. It is all the more striking when compared with the term's widespread use to characterize the same practices and rates once evidence of their damaging effects began to extend beyond single women and people of color, as they began to threaten both white male-breadwinner-headed households and lenders themselves. Moreover, although advocates for marginalized groups tried to frame the situation in the late 1990s as a crisis, when dominant political actors used the terms "mortgage crisis" or "foreclosure crisis" during this period, it was typically to assert that no such crisis was imminent or in progress. In his prepared testimony at an August 2006 hearing, for example, Mortgage Bankers Association (MBA) researcher Michael Fratantoni maintained that although "some argue that default and foreclosure rates are at crisis levels and that a greater percentage of borrowers are losing their homes," MBA data "do not support this" characterization. "In fact," he asserted, "they tell quite a different story." Mortgage delinquencies and foreclosures, he declared, "are still caused by the same things that have historically caused [them]: 'life events,' such as job loss, illness, divorce, or some other unexpected challenge" or "by the inability to sell a house due to local market conditions after one of the above items has occurred."[38] Policymakers, too, downplayed the problems with both subprime mortgages and foreclosure rates, insisting that they were limited to the expected groups and therefore government concern or intervention was unwarranted. In December 2004, for example, a New York Federal Reserve report declared that "market fundamentals are sufficiently strong to explain the recent path of home prices and support our view that a bubble does not exist."[39] In other words, the Reserve characterized rising rates of foreclosure in ways that naturalized them as a noncrisis: they were natural and inevitable, affected a narrow band of borrowers, and were caused by *un*alarming conditions that were *un*remediable through, and therefore *un*warranting of, federal action. Rather than prompting state intervention, then, rising rates of foreclosure among women and people of color were particularized, treated as the perhaps unfortunate but nonetheless natural results of unremarkable conditions affecting groups one might predict would have trouble keeping up with their mortgages and would therefore, also predictably, face foreclosure at higher rates.

The Crisis Begins

As rates of foreclosure began to increase in 2007, and as their effects became more conspicuous, so, too, did attention to and alarm about them. The shift from noncrisis to crisis is apparent not only in the fact that economic reporters and dominant political actors began to use the term crisis to describe it, however. It is evident as well in the deindividualization of blame and the move to structural explanations for rising rates of foreclosure. Although economic reporters continued to refer to "easy," "bad," "poor," "weak," or "damaged" credit, the use of such frames declined, with only 12.3 percent of NYT stories about subprime mortgage lending in 2007 and 5 percent in 2008 using these terms (analogous declines are evident in WSJ coverage and in stories about rising rates of foreclosure). They also did not mince words in their assertions that part of what made the crisis a crisis was that it affected relatively privileged and "worthy" groups. A particularly revealing WSJ article, "Subprime Debacle Traps Even Very Credit-Worthy," stated bluntly that fair-lending advocates "have long alleged that minority and poor borrowers are often steered into subprime loans that carry excessively high interest rates and steep prepayment penalties." The growing use of subprime loans "by people with higher credit scores . . . suggests that such problems exist among a much wider swath of borrowers than previously thought and may have little to do with the ethnicity of borrowers."[40] An article published in that paper in August 2007 quoted a frustrated—and revealingly candid—would-be borrower who complained, "The market isn't discriminating between me and every deadbeat, zero-down borrower."[41]

Noncrisis in the Midst of Crisis

But even as economic reporters and dominant political actors treated the situation as a crisis, they continued to figure the situation as a noncrisis for women and people of color. This "noncrisis in the midst of crisis" is evident, for example, in the fact that race and gender figured almost not at all in coverage of the "crisis" itself. Only 4 of the 228 stories (1.8 percent) that used the terms "mortgage," "subprime," or "foreclosure" crisis in the NYT in 2007, for example, focused on the racialized patterns in foreclosures; one (0.4 percent) addressed gender. The analogous numbers for the 557 pieces in 2008 were 11 stories about race (2 percent) and 2 about gender (0.3 percent).

As had been the case in the previous era, the paucity of attention to these issues was exacerbated by the frames and tropes that were applied when they were addressed. For example, although economic reporters and dominant political actors were increasingly likely to attribute foreclosures to structural factors after 2007, they rarely extended these new understandings to women and people of color, who they instead continued to assume were unqualified for conventional loans and could not own homes but for subprime mortgages. These twinned presumptions were so deeply ingrained that few stories challenged them even in the face of disillusionment with subprime mortgage lending, and even in the face of a mounting pile of evidence that, for example, women were, on average, more creditworthy than men. The very first NYT story to refer directly to a "mortgage crisis," for example, stated that "poor and minority homeowners" "used easy credit to buy houses that are turning out to be too expensive for them now that mortgage rates are going up."[42]

And once again, the inadequate attention to the implications of subprime mortgage lending and rising rates of foreclosure for people of color was still vastly more extensive than that afforded to the gendered aspects of the crisis. One of only three NYT articles about the "crisis" to discuss anything having to do with gender was a December 2008 editorial titled "Mortgages and Minorities." As its title suggests, it focused on racial discrimination in mortgage lending, but it made one reference to "troubling gender differences" in rates of subprime mortgages. But while the story reported in detail about the racial disparities, noting, for example, that "a particularly striking analysis in 2006 by the National Community Reinvestment Coalition found that nearly 55 percent of loans to African-Americans, 40 percent of loans to Hispanics and 35 percent of loans to American Indians fell into the high-cost category, as opposed to about 23 percent for whites," regarding gender, it stated only that "there also were troubling gender differences. Women got less-favorable terms than men." Even some advocates for women participated in discourses that naturalized the noncrisis of the gendered inequalities made manifest by subprime mortgages. A 2007 NYT story about a 2006 Consumer Federation report showing that women paid higher interest rates in spite of having better credit than men included a quote from one of the report's authors stating that "the most likely reason for the disparity was that women were less familiar with the mortgage market than men and were therefore less likely to shop around for the best mortgage deal. 'There is some research indicating that women are, on the whole, less likely than men to bargain for major consumer purchases and credit transactions,' he said."[43]

In other words, even as subprime mortgages and foreclosures received more attention, and even as economic reporters and dominant political actors framed them as solvable problems facing critical junctures at which federal intervention would make a "decisive change," they continued to naturalize the associated racial and gender inequalities as outside both the crisis and the power of the federal government to remedy. It is therefore unsurprising that the federal policy response to the meltdown did little to help women and people of color.[44] Although initial calls for intervention had focused on appropriating federal funds to help homeowners refinance their mortgages and stay in their homes, in the end, federal intervention emphasized funds for banks and lenders. Interventions aimed at helping borrowers involved little in the way of financial aid and instead emphasized borrower education, raising standards for documentation, and the criminal prosecution of individual "bad apple" predatory lenders.[45] Federal interventions became somewhat more effective after 2010 but came too late to help members of the "vulnerable communities" who had been affected in the earlier stages of the crisis. As a consequence, as Immergluck explains, "the more effective responses benefitted households and communities impacted more heavily in the latter stages of the overall crisis" and the women and people of color who had been affected before 2007 "received effectively less assistance from the government than did middle-income homeowners."[46] Insults were added to injuries and disparities were compounded by the fact that many properties lost during the earlier period "were sold off by lenders to private investors," often at healthy profits.[47]

Because aid arrived too late to help the unmarried women and people of color who experienced foreclosure before 2007, both the wealth and rates of homeownership among these groups have also been slower to recover than those of their white and male counterparts.[48] A study by researchers at the Pew Research Center found, for example, that by 2016, homeownership among African Americans had fallen to 41.3 percent, down from a peak of 49.1 percent in 2004 and also lower than it was in 1994, when the rate was 42.3 percent. Although white households had experienced a decline from a peak of 76 percent in 2004, at 71.9 percent, rates were nonetheless higher in 2016 than they had been in 1994, when 70 percent of white households owned their own homes. Rates of homeownership among single parents (almost all of whom are women) declined from 51.3 percent in 2004 to 46.8 percent in 2016.[49]

There is also evidence that many of the racial and gender disparities in rates of foreclosure evident in the 1990s have persisted, due at least in part to ongoing and, by some measures, worsening discrimination in mortgage lending. Jacob Faber, for example, uses 2014 Home Mortgage Disclosure Act data to show that, even after controlling for a range of individual- and community-level characteristics, Asian Americans, Latinos, and African Americans continue to be approved for mortgages at lower rates than their white counterparts.[50] He shows further that Black and Latino borrowers continue to be significantly more likely to receive high-cost loans than white borrowers, and also that this disparity has actually *accelerated* in the years since the foreclosure crisis.

In addition, there has also been a resurgence in extractive practices such as contract-for-deed home sales, which are typically not protected by the laws covering homeowners who buy homes with traditional mortgages and under which borrowers make down payments and monthly payments but do not build equity or gain title to the home at purchase even though they are responsible for property taxes, insurance, and the maintenance and repair of properties that are often uninhabitable at time of purchase.[51]

In other words, the effects of subprime lending and foreclosures on marginalized groups were naturalized as outside of the crisis and beyond the power of the state to remedy. Whatever windows were opened by the subprime and foreclosure "crisis" ultimately provided few opportunities to address the kinds of ongoing and structural inequalities that had fueled and been fueled by it, and ending the crisis and returning to "normal" conditions meant a return to continued—and in some ways exacerbated—precrisis conditions of deeply entrenched inequality and high levels of subprime mortgages and rates of foreclosure among members of these groups.

Conclusion

I do not mean to equate the 1990s with 2007–2008; there were important differences between the two periods, including, as Immergluck argues, that "the overall scale of the subprime market was smaller on a national scale" during the earlier period, that the "first subprime boom did not cause major losses to the investment community," and that the foreclosures of that period were "both less severe and affected fewer neighborhoods and cities than did those in the late 2000s."[52] Similarly, in showing that rates of foreclosure during a period we came to view as a "foreclosure crisis" were, by some measures, no worse than rates during what remains framed as a time of booming rates of homeownership, my point is not to argue that the time of "crisis" was not, in fact, a "bad" one. And I certainly do not mean to suggest that those who were helped by the government programs intended to stem the tide of foreclosure were unworthy of such assistance, or even to suggest that the legislative and regulatory measures taken in the wake of the 2007 meltdown were adequate. I also understand that the increased attention to, alarm about, and calls for state intervention into these issues beginning in 2007 might seem proportional to the rates of foreclosure in each era.

But juxtaposing these two cases demonstrates that manifestations of conditions of vulnerability and harm, so often naturalized and treated as inevitable products of the normal social, economic, and political landscape when they affect marginalized populations, are likely to become regarded as crises—that is, as problems that can and must be resolved through state action—when they affect dominant groups or disrupt dominant institutions and processes. The result is not simply that such conditions are more likely to be called or to be "thought of" as crises, but also that whether or not a problem is labeled a crisis has significant implications for the kinds of solutions deemed appropriate to address it.

Coda

Revising this chapter in the spring and fall of 2020, it is hard not to think about the ways in which the COVID-19 pandemic has underscored the relationship between episodic hard times and the ongoing and quotidian hard times that structure the lives of marginalized groups. Because while the pandemic was quickly labeled and treated as a crisis, many dominant political actors have normalized the structural inequalities it has thrown into relief as noncrises, treating them as unfortunate but nonetheless natural and inevitable results of unremarkable conditions that are regarded as immune to, and therefore as not warranting, state intervention. For example, asked about the racialized health and economic disparities that have translated into disproportionate rates of infection and death among African Americans, Anthony Fauci stated:

> We have a particularly difficult problem of an exacerbation of a
> health disparity. We've known, literally forever, that diseases like
> diabetes, hypertension, obesity, and asthma are disproportion-
> ately afflicting the minority populations, particularly the African
> Americans. . . . Unfortunately, when you look at the predisposing
> conditions that lead to a bad outcome with coronavirus—the things
> that get people into ICUs that require intubation and often lead to
> death—they are just those very comorbidities that are, unfortunately,
> disproportionately prevalent in the African American population. . . .
> So we're very concerned about that. It's very sad. *There's nothing we
> can do about it right now, except to try and give them the best possible
> care to avoid those complications.*[53]

While Fauci framed these disparities as external to the crisis and beyond the power of the federal government to remedy, however, others are attempting to disrupt this boundary between crisis and noncrisis by trying to use the policy window that may be opened by the pandemic to address the ongoing and deeply entrenched inequalities that have been revealed and fueled by it so that returning to "normal" does not mean, as it so often does, returning to precrisis conditions of normalized injustice.

PART II

Governing Disaster

CHAPTER 4

Concrete Kleptocracy and Haiti's Culture of Building

Toward a New Temporality of Disaster

Claire Antone Payton

On the morning of January 12, 2010, Haiti's capital was a bustling Caribbean metropolis with more than three million inhabitants. By sunset, it had been transformed into the site of one of the deadliest disasters in history. Just before five in the afternoon, a nearby fault line erupted with a shallow magnitude 7.0 earthquake. In less than a minute, buildings across the metropolitan region collapsed. Between 100,000 and 316,000 people died—at least 1 out of every 30 people in the affected area. The vast majority of causalities were among those trapped in the rubble or killed by the blunt force trauma of concrete crashing down on them.

Scholarly explanations of the disaster generally incorporate one of two temporalities. Scientists, engineers, and architects tend to approach the earthquake as a singular physical event clearly defined in time and space. Their analyses focus on the interaction between sudden movements of the earth and the physical properties of the city on its surface. The disaster is framed as a series of technical failures: Port-au-Prince's structures were unable to withstand the lateral and horizontal forces generated by the seismic event. In some parts of the capital, unstable soil literally liquefied underneath the buildings. Top-heavy buildings toppled to one side. Thin and corroded steel reinforcement bars bent and twisted with the earth's spasms. Concrete block walls, untethered to corner support beams, tumbled to the ground. Increased pressure dissolved poor-quality concrete into rubble.[1]

The other temporality approaches the earthquake less as a specific event and more as the expression of larger social and historical contexts into which it released its powerful physical forces.[2] The earthquake manifested the violence, inequality, and precarity that Haitians have endured since the eighteenth century, when French Saint-Domingue was one of the most brutal slave colonies the world had ever seen. In 1804, Haitians ended thirteen years of civil war by defeating their enslavers and founding an independent state. But the new state was hamstrung by its colonial inheritance and the hostile powers that continued to surround it. With limited choices, its leaders perpetuated colonial modes of governance that maximized the extraction of wealth and resources from a vulnerable population. The population, in response, became distrustful of state power and sought to insulate itself by avoiding engagement with its institutions. In light of this history, the earthquake's destructive power can be read as a reflection of centuries of structural inequality and poverty that prevented the formation of strong government institutions that could have protected the citizenry through investment in public welfare, urban planning, regulation, and enforcement of zoning and building codes. This is what disaster studies pioneer Anthony Oliver-Smith called "Haiti's 500-Year Earthquake."[3]

Rather than seeing a binary, we can use the tension between these entwined temporalities to arrive at a fuller understanding of how disasters happen. The field of critical disaster studies is an invitation to theorize beyond the nature-culture dualism by using disasters to interrogate the mutuality of social and material life.[4] In this chapter, I sketch a history of concrete in Haiti to model what a hybrid analysis of disaster might look like in practice. Instead of focusing exclusively on either the *longue durée* of centuries or the forty-five terrifying seconds of the *evènman*, I create a middle temporality: the history of the city's material production.

This method combines extensive archival research on the material history of twentieth-century Port-au-Prince with the post-earthquake insights of engineers and architects. It narrows in on a building boom in the 1970s, the period during which the city's contemporary physical characteristics first began to emerge. I use architectural historian Howard Davis's concept of "the culture of building" as a point of departure. Davis defines the culture of building as the composite system of people, relationships, knowledge, rules, procedures, institutions, and habits that informs the building process in a particular social and historical context.[5]

This chapter picks up this theme by exploring how Port-au-Prince's construction industry imprinted the era's political and social dynamics on its urban topography. Then it analyzes the political economy of cement to show how the culture of building formed linkages between the physical city and the kleptocratic strategies of the Duvalier dictatorship that ruled Haiti from 1957 to 1986. This chapter provides a valuable case study of the historical roots of disaster in Haiti, but its implications extend beyond the shores of that Caribbean island. The analysis presented here illustrates how the built environment functions not as a passive backdrop to more dynamic social, political, and economic dramas, but rather as the very language through which those dramas are expressed. In any context, efforts to address the material dimensions of disaster preparedness or response must consider the social worlds of the materials in question. As suggested by the concept of a "culture of building," building materials are hardly the static objects they might seem at first glance. They are vehicles of complex social, political, and economic dynamics, histories, cultural norms, and personal aspiration. To be effective or enduring, disaster preparedness and response efforts must consider these context-specific factors as much as a given material's physical or logistical qualities.

The Social and Cultural Meanings of Concrete

When it was founded by French colonists in 1749, Port-au-Prince's buildings were erected in stone. This architectural style fell out of favor after the city was destroyed by an earthquake just two years later, in 1751. It was leveled again by an earthquake in 1770. Surviving colonial officials passed laws prohibiting the use of stone and bricks in reconstructing the city; buildings would be made of timber or adobe. But this style had its own risks. Wooden structures tended to catch fire. The city burned down several times during the Haitian Revolution and the tumultuous civil wars that followed independence in 1804. During the US occupation of Haiti (1915–1934), city officials established building codes discouraging wooden constructions as safety measures against the ever-present threat of catastrophic fire. At the same time, wood was becoming harder to build with for environmental reasons. Deforestation wrought by the international hardwood trade and the local charcoal industry had reduced the country's domestic supply of timber.

Modern concrete manufacturing techniques began to spread around the world at the beginning of the twentieth century. The first reinforced concrete structures in Port-au-Prince were high-profile, high-cost construction projects such as the Cathédrale Notre-Dame de L'Assomption, completed in 1914, and the National Palace, finished in 1920 under US military occupation.[6] By the 1940s, prestigious architects such as Albert Mangonès and Robert Baussan were designing concrete homes for elites in the international style, but the material remained an expensive imported luxury until 1954, when a French construction conglomerate opened up Haiti's first domestic cement manufacturing plant, Ciment d'Haiti.

The cement plant was part of a postwar economic boom that came to a grinding halt in 1957 with political turmoil that led to the election of François Duvalier. The new president built a brutal regime based on arbitrary violence and cult of personality. He declared himself president-for-life in 1964 and ruled until his death in 1971. The country declined precipitously by almost every metric during this period: the economy withered, human rights violations proliferated, and corruption thrived. Many who could afford to leave fled to the United States, Canada, or Europe. Thousands of professionals moved to the Congo by joining the United Nations missions there.[7] Airline statistics indicate that planes leaving the country in the late 1960s were fuller than those arriving, hinting at a net loss of economically mobile Haitians during the regime's darkest years. Those who stayed behind inhabited a world characterized by fear, censorship, and violence.

Construction was one of the many industries that atrophied during this period. Duvalier oversaw a few large state-funded projects, including the construction of an airport and a dam, and the development of a model city called Duvalierville that showcased modernist architecture in a kind of Haitian answer to Brasilia. But these modest state investments could not compensate for the era's massive exodus of people and capital. The cement plant languished at half capacity throughout the 1960s. Construction material suppliers laid off staff or closed altogether. Without the investments of middle-income and elite Haitians, there was little significant urban development.

François Duvalier was succeeded in office by his nineteen-year-old son, Jean-Claude Duvalier in 1971. Many Haitians experienced this as a watershed moment. The new administration knew it had an image problem and set about rebranding the dictatorship. It freed some of its political prisoners, relaxed press censorship, and started courting more foreign investment. The president appealed to expatriates by inviting politically unthreatening exiles to return home. The government took steps to encourage tourists to come admire the island's beaches and cultural vibrancy and bring wallets full of foreign cash. However, in time Jean-Claude Duvalier's government would reveal itself to be as morally bankrupt as his predecessor's. The dictatorship would ultimately implode in 1986, brought down by a nationwide grassroots democratic upswell that pushed the ruling family into exile.

But in 1971, the peaceful transition of power and the gestures of political and societal renewal allowed the population the opportunity to dream of reform. This sense of optimism generated explosive growth in Port-au-Prince's construction industry. As Haitians abroad returned home, many of them made sizable investments in land and housing. According to geographer Henri Godard, in the 1970s returning Haitians "wanted to be respected." Owning property was "one of the visible elements of their social ascension and their success."[8] Without reliable demographic statistics or information on remittances, it is impossible to quantify exactly how many people and how much money began to reenter Haiti after 1971, but the economic indicators are striking. Government statistics showed that the construction sector enjoyed 12 percent growth in 1971, 21 percent growth in 1972, and 25 percent growth in 1973.[9] Reports produced by the United Nations described a wave of building that stimulated a diverse array of economic activities, including the production of building materials including rebar, sand, rocks, and cement. They documented increased job opportunities in manual labor, engineering, and architecture.[10] The demand for cement tripled between 1968 and 1973. Ciment d'Haiti reached its productive capacity in 1972 and had to build new facilities to keep up with the country's rapidly growing demand. Cement, sand, and rebar are the main components in reinforced concrete, and the demand for all three indicates that the new urban extensions reshaping Port-au-Prince were built of concrete.

The sudden changes visible in macroeconomic indicators were also apparent in anxious cultural discourse. Commentary on the changing face of the city abounded in the newspapers and journals of the period. In 1973, author and editor Roger Gaillard described the recent flurry of construction activity as an "implosion of the capital" and complained that "the city is disintegrating. . . . [P]eople are building frantically, no matter where, no matter how."[11] Authors warned of cement shortages and black markets and bemoaned the lack of zoning and regulation. Others warned that the city's water supply and drainage system were compromised as new neighborhoods paved over sensitive environmental areas. Some regretted that the proliferation of reinforced concrete architecture was destroying the quaint tropical aesthetic of the city's older wooden buildings.

Yet for many participating in the construction boom, concrete offered an opportunity to forge a new identity specifically because it broke with the past. Concrete aesthetics made it possible to articulate an identity associated with internationalism, modernism, and futurity. The building technique commonly used in the countryside to make traditional-style houses is wattle and daub, in which a wooden frame is filled in with stones and a mixture of soil and lime.[12] Godard observed that concrete "offered a resident a sense of security and the opportunity to reject the shelters of his youth with a tin roof that periodically flew away."[13] It provided physical and symbolic distance between urban residents and the perceived indignities of rural life. Sturdier shelters were also practical; hurricanes and tropical storms sweeping through the Caribbean were regular facts of life. Port-au-Prince has been hit or brushed by a major storm eighteen times since 1950—far more often than it has been threatened by earthquakes.[14] Urban residents experienced small tremors from time to time, but a much more pressing and immediate concern was shelter that could protect them from dangerous weather.

Not everyone moving to Port-au-Prince in the 1970s could participate in the construction boom that was expanding the city's edges. The return of expatriates was one form of migration during this period; the other major one was rural-to-urban migration. Port-au-Prince, like cities throughout the global South, had become the destination for increasing numbers of farmers whose agricultural livelihoods were becoming undone by environmental decline, population pressure, and myopic government policies. As migrants arrived in Port-au-Prince, they tended to congregate in densely coiled, low-income neighborhoods encircling the city's downtown commercial core. Only the most well off in these communities could afford to build or rent a house with concrete walls and a tin roof; even the most basic concrete structure signified access to economic resources unavailable to most of the households. Others occupied houses ingeniously designed out of mud, straw, and reclaimed materials. Still others slept on the street.[15]

These different migration patterns produced distinct urban topographies. Low-income neighborhoods adapted to their increasing population by densifying. Shelters sprouted in previously interstitial spaces such as swampy shorelines and the courtyards and alleyways of the city's commercial core. This reflected the premium their residents placed on geographic proximity to economic opportunities. The city's poorest could afford neither the time nor the expense required to commute from the urban periphery. Meanwhile, new middle- and upper-income neighborhoods began spreading outward into the plains and mountains that surrounded the urban core. Their neighborhoods were far less dense and took up much more geographic space. A 1976 study of the city conducted by the United Nations and the Haitian Ministry of Public Works estimated that the wealthiest 10 percent of the population occupied 41 percent of the city's inhabited land. By contrast, 65 percent of the city's people—its poor majority—inhabited just 29 percent of its land.[16] From this, we see that while rural-to-urban migration was an important factor of urban transformation in this period, wealthier families' consumption of land had a far larger impact when considering the city in this period from a material and geographic perspective.

Concrete and Haiti's Culture of Building

Multiple engineers and scientists observed after the 2010 earthquake that one of the factors contributing to the disaster was poor-quality concrete, caused in part by inadequate use of cement. A 2011 analysis of samples taken from masonry blocks from damaged buildings of various ages revealed that the concrete had strengths ranging from 545 psi to 1,135 psi (pounds per square inch), all far below the minimum acceptable standard of 2,500 psi determined by the American Concrete Institute.[17] The assessment concluded that increasing the volume amount of cement used in the blocks from 1/30 to 1/6 and using better-quality aggregate doubled their compressive strength.[18]

But concrete is not just a question of ratios. The deficiencies detectable in Haitian construction express the health of Haiti's larger culture of building, which incorporates social, institutional, and economic relationships as well as built forms. The strength or weakness of those relationships shapes the quality of the buildings they produce. This incorporates all facets of construction, including engineering expertise, building codes, and the availability of credit. To analyze Haiti's culture of building more clearly, the rest of this chapter uses concrete as a window onto how the relationships that made up the culture of building in the 1970s became embedded in the built environment. Concrete was just one of the factors that contributed to the failure of the built environment in 2010, but its history models how the idea of the culture of building might be used to address disasters' dual temporalities.

Concrete is composed by mixing a paste of cement and water with aggregates such as rocks and sand. The chemical reaction between cement and water produces a unique material with dual properties. When wet, the mixture is malleable enough to be spread out or be poured into molds. When dry, the cement forms a strong adhesive that binds together the aggregates into a rock-like material. Its versatility makes it easy to work with and lowers the level of professional expertise required in masonry or carpentry. But concrete's ease of use is deceptive; though almost anyone can mix the ingredients, strong concrete requires a precise ratio of high-quality ingredients. Too much water results in a feeble concrete that is porous and prone to crack; too little water is not cost effective and is also prone to crack. Concrete is strengthened by embedding steel reinforcement bars, known as rebar, but ironically, rebar can also make concrete weaker over the long term. When exposed to the elements, rebar begins to corrode and expand, pushing outward on the encasing concrete and leading it to crack.[19]

Most concrete structures in Port-au-Prince were built under the supervision of independent small-time masons, known locally as "bosses." Bosses operated as foremen who oversaw laborers and mixed concrete and mortar on-site. They trained apprentices who worked under them to acquire construction expertise. Skilled construction work had been an organized trade since at least 1946, when a union had formed that aspired to provide consistent training and ensure standards. But by the mid-1960s unions had been either subjugated to or eliminated by the dictatorship, as were most other civil institutions. Those that remained operated as political organizations more than professional ones. Supervision and standards were hard to enforce, and there was little in the way of certifications or regulations.

Standards were also hard to enforce given Haiti's larger context of extreme material scarcity. One key example was the popular technique of using as little cement as possible. One builder, in a post-earthquake interview in 2010, acknowledged that his field could learn from technical errors they had made but reminded the interviewer that bosses were not the only ones contending with limited resources: "The problem is often caused by the owner. He tells us, 'Protect me for the cement.' . . . But instead of protecting him, this can kill him."[20] His observations reveal how poverty and scarcity can become technical problems, and how the structural integrity of buildings can reflect social issues.

Even more well-funded projects led by formally educated architects and engineers were influenced by the knowledge and training of those working under them. Mangonès, who made a career under the dictatorship designing elite villas and hotels as well as government buildings, reportedly asked at one point, "How can an architect function when workmen have no experience with precise drawing, fitting doors or windows, using T squares or levelers?" The difference in professionalization was a "problem we try to

solve. . . . We improvise. We do our best."[21] Even the most professionally exe-
cuted projects were embedded within the larger culture of building characterized by informality.

If pouring concrete decreased the skill required to build, improvising
with concrete was even easier when it was pressed into prefabricated concrete blocks, called concrete masonry units. Blocks were stackable and easy
to work with and therefore dramatically lowered the labor costs of building
a house. They could be purchased at retail hardware stores, but some bosses
rented or owned hand-cranked block presses to manufacture blocks on-site.
Blocks were appropriate for the financial realities of many Haitians because
they permitted intermittent construction. In a society with few credit options,
families could purchase blocks in small quantities, depending on what they
could afford at the time. Sometimes families cut costs further by doing the
labor themselves under the occasional supervision of a boss. Homes built in
this way often took years, or even decades, to reach completion. This model of
financing introduced its own vulnerabilities, however. Left exposed for long
periods, rebar becomes corroded and less earthquake resistant.

Some writers in the 1970s believed the ease of making concrete blocks
could be applied to the city's shortage of adequate housing. A 1973 article
in the Haitian newspaper *Le Nouvelliste* portrayed block presses as a tool of
community empowerment. The author described seeing "children and the
elderly alike digging at the earth, passing this soil through a sieve, and mixing it with a small amount of cement." They added water to the mixture and
poured it into a hand-cranked block press. "In less than three minutes, these
peasants created in front of our eyes the bricks that would soon serve to build
their homes."[22] The article envisioned a world in which the need for skilled
labor would be entirely removed from the process of concrete manufacturing.
Instead of raising the standard of living so that poor families could afford
concrete houses, the author imagined arriving at the same end by lowering
the quality of concrete—putting the buildings' inhabitants at much greater
risk of structural failure.

Concrete Kleptocracy

The absence of government oversight was partially a reflection of institutional
incapacity to provide services, but it was also a strategy of governance, what
political scientist Jean-Germain Gros calls "the politics of uncertainty."[23] The

weak, uneven, or inconsistent exercise of authority creates opportunities for the personalization of power that allow it be to more easily focused toward dictatorship's primary objective: longevity at all costs. For example, in the 1970s the wealthiest new neighborhoods in Port-au-Prince were built on a legally protected environmental reserve meant to safeguard a critical watershed. Journalists and the occasional renegade official warned that the city's water supply and drainage patterns were becoming compromised by rapid urban development, but there was never any serious effort on the part of the government to enforce environmental laws when it came to elites whose consent was critical to the regime's stability. Yet other dimensions of Haiti's culture of building were firmly under government control: namely, the distribution network of construction materials. It was through control over commodities like cement that the dictatorship exercised its greatest capacity for kleptocratic extraction—what I call its infrastructures of corruption.

Before an ordinary builder picked up an ordinary 42.5 kg bag of cement at a hardware store, the cement had passed through an elaborate supply chain organized through crony capitalism to maximize the amount of money that could be redirected to the ruling family, its inner circle, and their business partners. It started at the factory; when Ciment d'Haiti opened in 1954, it was granted a formal monopoly over both the production and importation of cement. Offering total market control and protection from competition was a common strategy used by many administrations to attract foreign industries, even if it meant much higher costs for the consumer. The price of such benefits was often a hefty sum paid to the president personally. In the case of the French-owned cement factory, the beneficiary was Duvalier's predecessor Paul Magloire. In the 1970s, journalists and even officials opened investigations into the company's practices, finding that, among other transgressions, management abused their domination of the market by selling low-quality cement at high prices domestically and selling higher-quality cement at lower prices abroad.

The strategies of extraction became more refined after the cement left the factory. The sole domestic buyer of the factory's output was the state monopoly office, the Régie du Tabac et Allumettes. The Régie had a monopoly on the distribution of cement, as well as dozens of other commodities, including flour, tomato paste, soap, and beer. After purchasing the factory's supply of cement at a fixed price, the Régie added a tax in the form of a "distribution commission" on each individual bag and then sold it on to wholesalers and retailers. The builder buying construction supplies at a hardware store in

1979 would have paid the equivalent of US$9.80 for a single standard bag of cement. (At the time, about 65 percent of urban households earned below 200 gourdes, or about $40, per month). About 15 percent of that went to paying the Régie's commission. The distribution commission was a regressive tax, since the burden of paying higher prices for basic goods was felt much more by lower-income families than by those with greater means.

To be fair, the price of most things was high in the 1970s. Rampant inflation and oil crises originating in conflicts in the Middle East created a decade of financial turmoil around the world. Monopolies, price controls, and taxes are not inherently corrupt. On rare occasions, the regime used its control over the economy to provide short-term protection to Haitian consumers, such as when the government temporarily refused to raise the price of cement in 1974 following a spike in the global price of oil. Used thoughtfully and with consideration for the concept of the public good, state-controlled financial instruments can ease the burden on consumers and redistribute wealth across societies. But the primary function of commodity controls in Haiti was to channel funds toward a system of crony capitalism and kleptocracy.

What set the Régie apart was that almost none of the revenue it collected was integrated into the public budget of the national government or reinvested in society. Taxes were transferred directly into personal accounts controlled by members of the Duvalier family. The Régie was, in the words of one American diplomat, "an untouchable instrument of personalist rule."[24] Its revenue was transferred into private accounts and used to pay for luxury cars, villas, and overseas shopping trips. It secured the loyalty of elites through cash payments and gifts. Jean-Claude was particularly fond of giving his favorites BMWs and Mercedes so they could drive from the elite peripheries in style and comfort. The money also ensured the compliance of the wider population by bankrolling a partisan paramilitary network commonly known as the Tonton Macoutes.

The Régie's accounts were among the regime's most closely guarded secrets. Without detailed receipts, it is impossible to know exactly the amount funneled from public to private hands. In 1969, the International Monetary Fund estimated that the office's annual income probably amounted to 50 million gourdes, the equivalent of US$68 million in 2019 currency, or approximately 40 percent of Haiti's entire national budget.[25] Combining statistics on Haiti's national cement production with information about the distribution commission collected on each bag of cement, I calculate that between 1968 and 1978 the Duvaliers collected 265 million gourdes from the sale of cement alone. Adjusted for inflation, this is the equivalent of approximately $39 million in 2019.

These kleptocratic pressures influenced builders' technical decisions both directly and indirectly. Through mechanisms like Ciment d'Haiti's monopoly and the Régie's distribution commission, infrastructures of corruption transferred as much surplus wealth as possible from the ordinary population into the hands of the ruling circle and its clients. With the cost of basic materials inflated to support this predatory system, Haiti's culture of building adapted by making do with less. Thus ordinary Haitians found themselves constructing their houses and other buildings with concrete that used less cement than was needed. Similarly, without state investment in professionalizing the industry, most construction projects developed under the supervision of bosses who possessed uneven qualifications and training at best. Some projects went up with hardly any professional supervision at all. These building strategies reflected the larger reality of a state that parasitically starved society and contributed to the overall degradation of economic, social, and political life. Even when the price of construction materials fluctuated, this pressurized environment meant that many builders continued to work as frugally as possible. The construction of the city unfolded within an economic environment in which builders were obligated to finance the predatory lifestyles of national leaders while simultaneously trying to finance their homes. As a result, they lived in buildings less likely to withstand seismic events.

Conclusion

The concept of the culture of building offers a holistic means of thinking through the earthquake's dual existence as both material event and amorphous historical process. Its emphasis on materiality opens a middle temporality that bridges the enduring inequalities first established by the violence of plantation slavery and the technical failure of the built environment in 2010. My analysis of Port-au-Prince's construction boom in the 1970s illustrates how the city's physical structures became suffused with the dynamics of extraction and neglect that have long characterized Haitians' relationship to the state. By focusing on construction, we can observe how political and economic vulnerabilities manifest as physical vulnerabilities of the built environment.

This brings us to a third temporality: the future. Considering Haiti's long-term vulnerability to seismic events, the expense of cement, and the expertise required to use it safely, it is easy to conclude that concrete is an inappropriate building material for Haiti. One group of architects asserted in a post-earthquake assessment that "the sustainability of concrete in Haiti seems almost impractical and irresponsible. The simple fact of knowing that concrete, reinforced or not, will not outlast any earthquake in the Caribbean, should be the first clue to completely deplete it from all future design proposals."[26] The authors suggested other possible building mediums, including a mixture of cob, soil, and rubble, and cob and bamboo.

But concrete has meanings that extend beyond its physical properties that cannot be transferred easily to other materials. It responded to middle-income and elite families' desire for social mobility and protection from what they perceived as a violent and unpredictable society. Concrete offered a means of participation in a global aesthetic of modernity and a way of inserting symbolic and physical distance between them and the stigmatized Haitian peasantry. Even an assessment of concrete's physical suitability for the region must consider that earthquakes are just one of the environmental hazards faced by Haitians. Concrete provides better protection than many other building materials from the quotidian risk of fire and the annual threat of hurricanes and tropical storms.

This helps explain how the immediate consequences of the earthquake were unevenly distributed across the city's extremely stratified society, pointing to extreme poverty endured by large portions of the population. By 2010, hundreds of thousands of families lived and worked in impoverished peripheries like Cité Soleil, where access to even the most modest concrete structure was a marker of status. Most households inhabited shelters built of flimsier, less rigid materials. The Cité Soleil area sustained much less damage than wealthier areas like downtown, Pétionville, or Delmas, where larger concrete structures were the norm.[27] Geography was partially responsible; Cité Soleil is located furthest from the epicenter of the earthquake. But the architecture of class and status also played a role. Simple houses built with concrete block walls and a corrugated tin roof, while still dangerous, were less likely to kill their inhabitants if they suddenly came crashing down. The earthquake's immediate impact was most keenly felt by Haiti's middle- and upper-income groups, whose wealth gave them access to the materials that would kill them. Even buildings designed by Albert Mangonès collapsed in the earthquake.

But concrete cannot simply be written off because it has been used unsafely in the past. Engineers and architects often use reinforced concrete in seismically active regions such as Japan or the Bay Area precisely because they believe it can be designed to withstand earthquakes. The issue is not the material itself but the health of a society's larger culture of building. Recommendations like using cob and bamboo are culturally tone-deaf. Construction is driven by aspiration. Until cob and bamboo become wildly popular architectural mediums in the world's wealthiest societies, they will remain stigmatized and unpopular in poorer societies like Haiti's, where there is a premium on symbols of wealth and modernization.

Concrete's structural issues are social issues. Advice about increasing the amount of cement used to make concrete, as found in the 2011 study of masonry blocks, fails to consider how building materials and practices have emerged in relationship to enduring social dynamics of structural violence, extraction, and inequity. Implementing meaningful change in Haiti's culture of building requires social, as well as engineering, solutions. Plans to build a safer urban future for Haiti must embrace a more holistic approach that incorporates the dual nature of disaster into efforts to create a healthier and safer culture of building.

CHAPTER 5

Risk Technopolitics in Freetown Slums

Why Community-Based Disaster Management Is No Silver Bullet

Aaron Clark-Ginsberg

"Always keep the latrine clean," reads the sign posted on a toilet in Kroo Bay, the largest slum of Freetown, the capital of Sierra Leone. The sign's message is a hopeful one, suggesting that slum dwellers can improve their health if they keep their latrines clean. However, the latrine itself is surrounded by polluted waterways of the Crocodile River, an "open sewer" of a river that delivers a continuously renewed source of risk: solid waste produced by Freetown's citizens living upstream from the slum.[1] As waste collects, it creates blockages that increase the chances for floods, which, in this slum located on a floodplain, have occurred every rainy season since 2008. This waste also contributes to other hazards, such as fecal sludge to diarrheal diseases including cholera and typhoid and heavy metals and other damaging chemicals to health problems, and the waste itself offers a source of food for disease-carrying vectors such as rats.[2] Keeping clean a local latrine does nothing to diminish these hazards, which stem from literal upstream behavior as well as figurative upstream policy. And waste-related hazards are but one of the risks Kroo Bay residents face; others include fires, indoor and outdoor air pollution, violence, building collapse, and what many identify as the biggest threat of all: eviction by the state on the grounds that Kroo Bay is too risky a settlement location (similar to Pranathi Diwakar's findings in this volume on framing Chennai slums as "at risk" to justify eviction).[3] Given the riskscape of the Bay, "always keep the latrines clean" may be good advice, but posting this message on a latrine does little to overcome the numerous and substantial risks that the Bay's residents face.

The latrine's messaging is emblematic of community-based disaster risk management (CBDRM), an approach to disaster risk reduction (DRR) that does not represent a viable strategy for addressing risks in Kroo Bay. CBDRM is part of a family of approaches, including community resilience and community-based disaster risk reduction, that emphasize local engagement in disaster risk management and emerged in the 1990s as an alternative to the top-down model of disaster management.[4] Instead of being mere recipients of risk services, communities are actively involved in all aspects of disaster management, from risk assessment to mitigation, preparedness, response, and recovery, with interventions tending to focus on making changes in how communities address risk. While community-focused interventions can reduce risk, the nature of Kroo Bay's riskscape means that CBDRM is not useful for meaningfully decreasing hazards or vulnerability for its residents. Hazards are created by forces outside of Kroo Bay, including citywide failures in waste management, land use planning, and natural resource management that increase waste and flood risk; national challenges in rural development that incentivize migration to cities, including to slums; and global governance problems such as failure to mitigate the risks of climate change.[5] Bay residents' vulnerability has a similarly macro-level origin and stems from issues such as limited access to basic health and educational services, social and political marginalization, corruption, and exploitative resource extraction; all of these together leave the slum's residents with few resources with which to mitigate risks or cope when crises occur.[6] To address the risks faced by Kroo Bay residents would require dealing with these issues through mostly macro-level interventions such as citywide waste management, national improvements in rural development, and global climate change mitigation.[7] Because CBDRM in Freetown has little impact at the macro level, it is, like risk reduction interventions enacted elsewhere, little more than a "cover-up, papering over the cracks of a façade."[8]

Why do organizations implement small, localized, and community-focused interventions like CBDRM in contexts such as Freetown, where risk reduction requires systemic change? It is not because they do not know to address the broader forces of hazards and vulnerability. The idea that disasters are the manifestation of inequitable distributions of power and resources is widely accepted in disaster research circles. The research tradition, now more than forty years old, that describes how global forces shape vulnerability is now orthodox.[9] Policymakers are similarly aware of the need to engage the broad forces shaping risk outside the community: the global compact for disaster risk reduction, the UN's 2015 Sendai Framework for Action, includes commitments to address underlying disaster risk drivers "local, national, regional, or global in scope."[10] Despite this, CBDRM remains "mainstreamed to the point of orthodoxy" in the international aid world, a silver bullet solution for addressing risk across any number of different contexts.[11]

In this chapter I examine why nongovernmental organizations (NGOs) implement CBDRM in situations where such approaches do little to reduce risk. To do so, I review the CBDRM interventions of one NGO, Concern Worldwide, working to reduce risk in the slums of Freetown. Drawing on data collected during a two-year, ten-country research project with the organization, including interviews and archival research in Freetown,[12] I examine Concern's CBDRM programs through the lens of technopolitics, "the strategic practice of designing or using technology to constitute, embody, or enact political goals."[13] The concept of technopolitics was developed by the science historian Gabrielle Hecht as a way to link technology with politics. Instead of existing in a space divorced from social or political concerns, technology, in this view, is intertwined with the political, used to advance the agendas of different groups of people in ways that may not always align with the surface goals for which the technology was designed.[14] This helps explain why CBDRM is implemented in situations where it is likely to not reduce risk; instead of being merely a way to reduce risk, CBDRM is a technology through which to pursue a multitude of goals. Its use becomes not contingent on whether it reduces risk, but on whether it advances the various goals of its users. In ascribing a politics to CBDRM, technopolitics also steps away from a deterministic view of CBDRM. Instead of having the same a priori blanket effect across time and space, the impact of a technology like CBDRM is socially imbedded, determined by the confluence of actors and how they use the technology to advance their agendas. The changes wrought by CBDRM create a "splintering disaster," redistributing risk and vulnerability in highly heterogeneous ways based on structures of power.[15] Thus, CBDRM is neither a silver bullet solution nor a failure but rather a technology whose use and impact is contingent on the social and political conditions under which it is deployed. Because of this, understanding CBDRM requires examining how it is used as a form of technopolitics, including the conditions that shape its failure and its success.

The Technopolitics of Community-Based
Disaster Management

Three structural conditions lead to a technopolitics of CBDRM that does little to address risk: separation between risk producers and affected populations, fluidity in responsibilities for risk management, and political and economic constraints. When communities at risk are not the ones producing the risks, CBDRM interventions fail to address the root causes that drive risk. CBDRM interventions focus on local communities as the site of their interventions, so they do not target risk producers when risks are produced outside of their intervention areas. Indeed, communities are rarely responsible for the risks that they experience.[16] The real drivers of risk—such as large development projects, corruption, land degradation, pollution, discrimination, neglected maintenance of critical infrastructure, and policy changes that reduce access to vital services—are mostly the products of actions of those elsewhere. But CBDRM leaves state authorities, large corporations, and the citizens in other regions and countries in positions of power, divorced from the consequences of the risks that they create. Because risks are produced elsewhere, focusing on how communities manage risk fails to address causes of risk creation and results in a continued accumulation of risk.

Instead of being imbedded in "social facts," risk management also operates in a fluid discursive environment, where its specific actions are highly open for interpretation. Described as "the universal acronym to mean whatever interpretation is chosen for it,"[17] DRR has numerous theoretical paradigms and belief structures[18] that manifest in different approaches to it.[19] Discursive fluidity is not static but can change based on the institutional environment surrounding a technology, with periods of consensus over meanings and processes ruptured by disagreement, uncertainty, and ambiguity.[20] Risk reduction is increasingly ambiguous. Framed as complex, it is "everyone's business,"[21] the emergent outcome of the combined actions of every element of society.[22] Such a framing means that there is little clarity about which specific activities to implement to reduce risk and who is responsible for such activities. As a result, risk management becomes a process of "muddl[ing] through,"making decisions not based on any sort of formal structure that can provide a check to power but by navigating and working within a web of institutions.[23]

Financial and political constraints also shape CBDRM. Financially, NGOs are beholden not just downward to those they serve but also upward to their donors, who have limited funds and increasingly demand interventions that are measurably efficient and sustainable.[24] CBDRM is attractive in this environment, since it frames communities as contributing to their own risk reduction (efficiency) and claims to empower communities and to promote local buy-in in a way that leads to continuation of activities post-intervention (sustainability).[25] Incentives to challenge broader forces are also stymied by the need to work in and with state systems, including in situations where informal state governance structures may be strong and state structures weak or even actively contributing to the creation of risk. To maintain operational presence, NGOs often must align their programs with the goals of their host state, and they may end up supporting host states even when states are producing risk.

Community-Based Disaster Management in the Kroo Bay, Freetown

Concern took a CBDRM approach in two of its programs designed to reduce risk in the Kroo Bay: the livelihood-focused 2009–2012 Peri and Urban Community Action for Food Security Programme, and a 2012–2014 program focused on strengthening health systems and responding to cholera outbreaks. Both programs operated across the slums of Freetown, and they involved activities such as establishing and training community disaster management committees (CDMCs) made up of slum residents and focused on localized risk management within the slums; linking CDMCs to the government's national disaster management body, the Office of National Security's Disaster Management Bureau (ONS-DMB); and establishing the Community Disaster Management and Emergency Response Team (CODMERT), a local NGO comprised of the CDMCs and designed to coordinate and scale CDMC activities across the slums. Concern also supported national-level risk management structures, for instance by assisting in the drafting of the government's national DRM policy and establishing a website for the ONS-DMB.

Although Concern's CBDRM programs were designed to create lasting changes in the riskscape of Kroo Bay, separation between risk producers and receivers, fluidity, and constraints all convened to create a technopolitics of CBDRM that did little to reduce risk for residents living in the slum. Risk producers and receivers were largely separate. Kroo Bay residents have little choice over whether to live in the slums. Freetown's population ballooned

during Sierra Leone's bloody 1991–2002 civil war, when many Sierra Leo-
neans fled the countryside to seek relative safety in the capital; having few
resources, they ended up settling in the slums, which grew dramatically
during this period. Freetown's population, including in its slums, has continued to grow since the war for economic reasons, as migrants move from
an economically depressed countryside for a chance to survive in the capital.

Risk-creating activities—including those that increased the frequency
and scale of hazards and that contributed to vulnerability—were the result
of decisions made by others living outside the Bay. Timber harvesting and
continued expansion of the settlements into the hills contributed to flooding
hazards, along with improper upstream solid waste disposal and decades-
long failures in municipal waste management (as of 2013, only 20 percent of
waste was disposed of through official channels).[26] Policy decisions such as
those related to health care, education, and livelihoods left Bay residents with
limited access to basic services, exacerbating vulnerability by giving them few
resources to mitigate risk or cope with disaster when it occurs.

DRR in Freetown also has high discursive fluidity. Many involved in
DRR in Freetown considered it a multistakeholder issue led by the state, yet
they tended to focus more narrowly on the role of the state, NGOs, and local
communities in reducing risk.[27] "We need to be working within government
structures," a Concern staff member stated. Concern program documents
described how working with the state was a way of "tackling the root causes
of poverty" and "ensuring sustainability of project/program impact and outcomes to the poor after Concern have left." A government official stated that
the government was the lead agency for risk reduction but also described
DRR as an "NGO issue" and a "new issue" to the country with weak legal
and regulatory structures and a federal disaster management policy yet to be
ratified. CODMERT similarly emphasized the importance of the state, but
echoing Concern's CBDRM approach, emphasized the importance of communities in risk reduction, describing how a "bottom up approach is better
than top down one."

DRR was also constrained, both politically and financially. Because the
government's disaster management policy was still unratified, the government authority responsible for disaster management, the Disaster Management Bureau, remained a unit of the much broader, security-focused Office
of National Security, and it controlled few resources with which to implement risk reduction. Instead, to implement risk reduction programs, it had
to "beg aid from donor partners," which was "not always forthcoming."[28]

The government's ability to enforce laws that could have prevented hazard creation was also constrained. People who dumped waste and or committed other environmentally destructive practices faced few legal repercussions, yet laws banned physical mitigation in Kroo Bay and the state repeatedly attempted to relocate slums. Concern also faced resource constraints, especially after the 2008 financial collapse, when the individual and institutional donations on which it relied decreased.

Regulatory constraints on physical mitigation and uneven law enforcement had a major influence on the ability to reduce risk. Representatives from Concern, CODMERT, CDMCs, and the government agreed that many illegal practices contributed to risk, including logging on government land, cooking with open flames, improper food handling, illegal dumping, unregulated construction, and illegal settlements. The state had tried to enforce laws, and on occasion had even resorted to extreme measures such as using the military to prevent deforestation around the main aquifer supplying water to the city, but its resources to enforce laws were limited, and many laws and regulations that would have reduced risk remained unenforced, resulting in a continued production of hazards outside the slum. CODMERT and CMDCs also worked to improve law enforcement by increasing rates of enforcement practices, particularly for smaller activities such as illegal dumping and cooking with open flames. However, many of their efforts were limited to work within the slums rather than at the broader municipal level, and offenders could easily escape by paying small bribes. Given this permissive regime, risk production continued unabated, with risk producers benefiting from the activities they were engaging in at the expense of risk receivers, the worst hit of whom were located in slums such as Kroo Bay.

While those involved in risk reduction agreed that the slums were risky places to live and that risk was a socially constructed outcome of human decisions, there was considerable disagreement about how agency and blame should be distributed for the construction of risk. For the state, settling in the slums was the ultimate contributor to risk. Government respondents argued that because residents were settling illegally in the slums, they were ultimately responsible for the risks that they experienced. To emphasize the illegality of slums was to shift focus away from the historical and economic factors that contributed to the production of hazards and vulnerability, including those driving migration to the slums. Instead of focusing on broader systemic changes needed to reduce risk, blaming risk on settlement justified slum resettlement programs and physical infrastructure construction bans.

In contrast to the state's focus on illegal settlement, Concern, CMDCs, CODMERT, and slum residents consider the *designation* of slums as illegal a major factor driving risk. They described proposed relocation areas as far from the city center and its jobs and feared that slum-dwellers' livelihoods would be crippled if they were resettled. CODMERT was active in opposing relocation and waged a letter-writing campaign against the state's resettlement efforts. While the government has not been able to implement its relocation plans, it has been able to maintain its physical infrastructure construction bans, which NGOs have been required to follow. Improving physical infrastructure—including by developing structures like floodwalls that can address immediate flood hazards and enhancing water supplies, drainage systems, electricity, and other infrastructure to address secondary hazards—could potentially transform risks that slum residents faced by reducing exposure, frequency, and severity of floods and by providing resources that slum residents could capitalize on to reduce vulnerability. Yet these interventions were not permitted. Partly because of this, Concern staff viewed their interventions as "firefighting," part of a "welfare state model" that might help stave off acute crisis but cannot resolve chronic disaster.

A certain level of ambiguity enabled these disagreements, reflecting the discursive fluidity of risk and resilience. As a Concern staff member put it, slums are a "policy no-man's land," not permitted to develop but not possible to destroy. Moreover, Sierra Leone has no standardized approach to determine what constitutes risk, to identify which specific activities should be implemented to reduce risk, or to determine if places like the slums are "too risky" for settlement. Such uncertainty can be seen in the statement a government official made about the provision of postdisaster support: "People expect aid post disaster and will even burn down their shacks for such aid. People don't understand what a disaster is and what the terminology is. They have a kitchen fire and describe it as a disaster. They misunderstand the terminology. An accident is not a disaster."

Concern voiced similar concerns, describing how "the [ONS-DMB] stated we must be careful to differentiate disaster and accident. . . . We are still in a debate with Disaster Management Department of the Office of National Security to really state whether it is a disaster or an accident. . . . The fear is that if we start giving support to few houses now, it will have to be perpetual."[29] For the government, any frustration with levels of postdisaster support was merely a reflection of people's confusion over the definition of disaster rather than a problem with the allocation of aid. The state further justified not providing support in order to avoid dependence. But government informants also described the difference between accidents and disasters as "a bit subjective. It is something we struggle against because it is contextual." DMC members also recognized uncertainties in how to reduce risk. Although opposing relocation, they acknowledged that many of the slums were highly risky. One described how the land that Kroo Bay was built on "is marshy so will not support these houses. 99% will not accept this but that is reality." Another described how Kroo Bay, because of its precarious position, is "not a habitable area, it is a high-risk area." However, they also thought the government based its risk reduction decisions less on specific rationales and more on overriding goals and concerns. For instance, a CDMC member hypothesized that the limited amount of postdisaster recovery aid "might be a strategy to discourage people from living in the area as support can encourage people to live in the area."

The combination of constraints and ambiguities made smaller scale and voluntary community-focused mitigation activities an attractive option for risk reduction. For instance, CODMERT, an organization comprised of slum residents funded partly from the personal contributions of its staff, helped organize efforts to clear waste from streams. Waste clearance is a highly effective, albeit short-term, strategy for reducing flood risk. It was also something feasible: it did not require broad systemic changes in waste management reform across the city, it did not require regulatory reform or challenge the state, and it did not disrupt or hinder any of the other power structures that create risk. Concern and the city supported CODMERT's waste removal efforts when funding was available, but funding was often limited. Concern also tried to encourage slum residents to remove waste on their own, but slum residents could not maintain such a massive and Sisyphean effort. CODMERT mounted sensitization campaigns across the slums, imploring residents to reduce risk with signage such as "don't build houses under hanging stones," "always clean your environment," and "stop open defecation." These campaigns placed primary responsibility on slum residents to reduce their own risk. But they were inexpensive, allowable under the regulatory environment, and, if residents could be convinced of their utility, sustainable and cost effective over the long term. Along with these formal efforts, many slum residents initiated their own forms of DRR, for instance by using tires to reduce erosion and protect their assets and property.

Like the government's ban on informal settlements, these forms of "do it yourself DRR" place responsibility on slum residents for disaster risk, but they do so with a sellable narrative of sustainability, progress, efficiency, and bottom-up empowerment. Indeed, communities and Concern constructed these responsibilities jointly during the participatory planning risk assessment process, in which, through a series of participatory exercises, community members developed risk maps, plans, and other documents to guide DRR interventions, with sections on what NGOs, the government, and communities could each do to reduce disaster risk. Although these exercises projected DRR as everyone's responsibility, including local communities', in reality local communities were solely responsible for their own well-being.

Resource constraints underlined many of these actions. Project funding is only available on a short-term grant cycle, after which programs are expected to be finalized and have contributed to positive transformational change. Transferring results of projects to local organizations and involving local end users throughout the project process, including through encouraging "voluntary" risk reduction and participatory methods, was a way of showing sustainability at community scale rather than at system scale.

Such structures of risk reduction created a highly individualistic and fragmented, "layered approach" to implementing activities whereby risk reduction would be a product of a multitude of diverse organizations spread over extended periods. DMCs were established by Concern and supported by Concern, the government, other NGOs, and local residents. Waste removal efforts were supported by everyone, when funding was available. A facility would be built by one organization and repaired by another. Scarce resources and the voluntary nature of DRR unencumbered by specific guidelines and regulations left actors to bargain for risk reduction; to receive support, they had to show not only that they were they "at risk," but also that they were working to reduce risk themselves and had the desire to do so. If risk reduction or management projects did not fit in funders' institutional or programmatic structures, activities would end and risks would be created anew. As a result, risk reduction activities were highly varied and changed over time and were dependent on whether people and communities had the ability to sell their needs to potential funders as politically feasible and economically justifiable.

The form of CBDRM Concern implemented was a compromise that managed to meet the needs of multiple stakeholders in a situation of limited resources and political constraints. Its power lay not in the ability to address the drivers and root causes of risk—which were being produced outside the intervention area and were politically challenging—but in its ability to conform to the multiple and conflicting needs of these stakeholders. It projected an image of community empowerment, value for money, and cooperation with the state; it provided slum residents with basic services that they desperately needed to survive; and it did so in a way that aligned with the legal structures of the state. The lack of firm ideas of what constitutes risk and who is responsible for addressing it creates a permissive environment that allows for risk reduction to take many different forms.

Conclusion

The use of CBDRM to manage risk in the slums of Freetown raises serious questions about the efficacy of community-based approaches in situations in which politics are challenging, resources are limited, framings are vague, and risks are being created elsewhere. Under these conditions, CBDRM does little to address risk. Instead it is at best a stopgap, a measure that can sometimes temporarily reduce catastrophe but in the process can also lay blame and responsibility on the victims of risk being created elsewhere.

A technopolitical orientation helps understand the politics of CBDRM. The use of CBDRM to address flooding in Kroo Bay is an example of community-based approaches being implemented because they fit the various political agendas of different stakeholders, not because they are the best for reducing risk. This orientation also demonstrates a need to develop a grounding of CBDRM in the realities of the context where it is employed. In situations where risk producers and receivers are not aligned, CBDRM might place responsibility on local populations to reduce risk on their own and provide cover for further risk creation. A technopolitical orientation realigns CBDRM toward theories of vulnerability in disaster studies. Vulnerability approaches understand risk as socially constructed and disaster as stemming from systems of power. Risk reduction, in this model, is about examining and reforming the conditions of power that produce risk. While having roots in the vulnerability perspective, CBDRM has become mainstreamed to the point of orthodoxy, a silver bullet solution that is often divorced from any sort of assessment of how community interventions affect political structures.

What does a more politically engaged form of disaster management look like? As this case study illustrates, rather than manage risk and its immediate causes locally, disaster management should address the underlying political and structural patterns that construct hazards and vulnerability. In some cases it may be possible to address the root causes of risk through localized interventions. In Dhaka, for instance, Concern helped homeless Bangladeshis gain government identity cards, reducing their "invisibility" in the structure of society and improving their ability to access resources and jobs. However, interventions like this may often require broader changes in patterns of consumption and relationships that allow for one group to benefit at the expense of another. Although there is increasing acknowledgment of the need to tackle complex drivers of risk, political and economic environments are still not conducive to more radical notions of disaster management. We instead see a technopolitics of disaster management that tends to essentialize individuals and communities as masters of their own safety, from NewOrleans, where residents are labeled "resilient" and subjected to continued shocks and stresses, to the Philippines, where the government banned settlement near the coast in the name of risk reduction following Typhoon Haiyan.[30] While such programs may be nondisruptive for those in positions of power and project an air of empowerment and sustainability, they are not effective for reducing risk and can be highly disruptive to vulnerable populations if they facilitate removal and reduction of services. Efforts instead need to focus on how risks are constructed and on disrupting the systems of power that create vulnerability and hazards.

CHAPTER 6

Spaces at Risk

Urban Politics and Slum Relocation in Chennai, India

Pranathi Diwakar

The cityscape itself often serves as a battleground for class war. The process of "world-class" city making regularly involves attacks on visual markers of urban poverty. Middle-class aspirations to refurbish the city are articulated through efforts to remove "eyesores," or aesthetically unpleasant markers of a less-than-global city. "Squatters" along waterfronts; street vendors occupying sidewalks; slums in parts of the city that might otherwise be developed to house malls, theaters, restaurants, residences—they all are deemed offensive to the new, aspirational, urban aesthetic. The slum, in particular, often comes under attack as the middle-class imagination constructs it as the perceived source of squalor, crime, and illegality within the city. As city planning prioritizes a vision of development comprising five-star hotels, restaurants, and malls, a direct result is slum evictions.

In India, this process, familiar globally, accelerated during the early 1990s. In 1991, the government of Prime Minister P. V. Narasimha Rao, under mounting global pressure, liberalized the Indian economy and thus integrated Indian cities into the global market for the first time since independence in 1947. India's newly liberalized economy supported the rise of the Indian middle class, which grew rapidly as a result of new economic opportunities within the private sector and the global economic order.[1] The mandates of Indian urban policy reflected the ascendance of the middle class, with a growing aspiration to fashion urban landscapes in the image of "world-class" or "global" cities, broadly characterized by an expectation of urban policy to alter the visual aesthetics of the city's built environment to match a modernist, Western aesthetic.[2]

In the quest for land upon which to build the markers of a certain urban modernity, Indian city governments repeatedly characterized the slum as dangerous and risky. But as the case of the southern Indian city of Chennai makes clear, there was a shift, over time, in understanding *for whom* the slum was risky. Moreover, another frame developed alongside the portrayal of slums as risky to justify slum relocation: namely, that slums were *at risk* and therefore in need of government intervention.

Most accounts of slum eviction across India paint a portrait of sharp and ceaseless conflict among slums, the middle class, and the state. The Indian constitution once ensured the right to shelter and housing for the urban poor, but in court cases in the mid-1980s, municipal governments began to characterize the slum resident as an "encroacher" and thus an illegitimate occupier of land and space within the city.[3] To delegitimize slum residents' claims to land and space, the slum first had to be reimagined as a source of "nuisance," a site that obstructs, damages, or harms the surrounding urban environment.[4] The simplistic equation of slums with nuisance, informality, and squalor found its resolution in urban policy, as evidenced by an alarming increase in slum evictions in cities such as Delhi, Mumbai, and Bangalore since the turn of the millennium.[5]

This history, however—and the easy, singular conflation of the slum with illegal occupation it reflects—does not capture the entire story. It cannot explain, for example, how sprawling slums have persisted in some cities despite middle-class demands for slum evictions. It does not account for the agency of slum residents in seeking their own political accommodations and in preventing the arbitrary removal of their settlements by winning the "right to stay put."[6] At the same time, the flat accounting does not reflect how accommodations provided by the government that allow slums to persist in their original locations might just as easily be revoked. The state itself performs "informality" by alternately and arbitrarily providing and revoking temporary accommodations to slum residents and to land developers and private contractors in the form of "exorbitant public subsidies that underwrite capital accumulation."[7] The arbitrary and ambivalent nature of government accommodations for slums keeps their residents in a state of near-permanent insecurity, thereby contributing to the same precariousness that marks the slums as illegitimate.

The history of Chennai demonstrates the richer reality. At the turn of the millennium, the government of Chennai began to relocate slum residents from their original locations in the city to rehousing colonies outside city limits. The government justified its systematic draining of slums to the urban periphery with the possibility of disaster-induced destruction. Slums thus were framed as particularly *at risk* in the event of disaster due to their physical, geographical, and socioeconomic vulnerability.

At the same time, the government continued, as it had done previously, to frame slums as *risky*. But in Chennai, where political parties rely heavily on slum votes, state actors have historically felt a need to present slum relocations as pro-poor. Thus, these officials configured slums as risky to their own residents because of hazards posed by their physical and built environment, as well as the limitations posed by the slum environment to residents' socioeconomic betterment. They also began to describe slums as risky to broader society due to the perceived threats of crime, filth, and nuisance generated by the discursive imagination of the slum within the city.

Then the aftermath of the 2004 Indian Ocean tsunami provided an opportunity for those who would reshape Chennai into a slumless global city. Following the 2004 tsunami, and in anticipation of other future disasters, rehabilitation and risk reduction committees were established in Chennai with an eye to long-term recovery and prevention. These long-term plans for recovery dovetailed with slum eradication agendas; the emerging primary modality of engaging with "risk reduction" was to evict slums from their locations in the city and relocate them to the urban periphery. As a result, the construction of slum relocation housing was fast-tracked and concrete complexes mushroomed on the outskirts of the city to house slum families evicted on the pretext of reducing the vulnerability of these residents to future disasters. The disaster rhetoric allowed the government to thread the needle between satisfying middle-class and business agendas while still relying on slum votes. The use of a disaster moment in Chennai captures a political turn away from a stridently pro-poor agenda to one encompassing a wider variety of political agendas.

The enactment of slum relocations on the pretext of disaster lends important insights into the construction of disaster by political agents and processes. The consequences of slum relocation in Chennai lay bare the contentious politics of invoking the disaster moment for a range of developmental agendas. The far-flung slum rehousing complexes severed slum residents' ties with the loci of their education, employment, and social networks, with the effect of ghettoizing these residents and exacerbating their conditions of poverty and disenfranchisement. During the monsoon season, the shoddily constructed rehousing complexes leak and flood because of their location on marshy wetlands, making these buildings unfit for habitation. The political wrangling of slum eviction produces an extenuated experience of disaster for relocated slum residents, some of whom did not even experience the effects of the tsunami touted as the reason for their eviction. In this context, the story of Chennai offers a keen lens to the very understanding of disasters as not just external, natural phenomena but politically opportune imaginaries to retain disparate vote-banks while using the language of vulnerability to portray marginal residents as "at risk" to produce stringently sanitized cityscapes.

The historical narrative that follows is based on some seventy policy documents and ten maps collected from central, state, and city-level governments. This corpus also includes reports by related international funding agencies and nongovernmental organizations (NGOs). I used informal conversations with relocated slum residents at a rehabilitation site in the summer of 2016 to substantiate these findings and corroborate my understanding of relocation's consequences with stories of their own experiences. I also used newspaper articles to confirm the execution of planned or announced government action and to study the effects of government action as reported in the media. I relied on targeted sampling of an English newspaper to supplement policy analysis. I used information from articles in *The Hindu*, which is the most popularly read English daily in Chennai. My use of NGO reports and conversations with slum dwellers was a supplement to my primary method of archival policy analysis.

1947–1980: From Relocation to Restoration

Indian cities experienced rapid growth well before the country's independence from British rule in 1947. Cities like Madras, Calcutta, and Bombay developed as ports and served as gatekeepers of colonial trade for over four hundred years before India's independence. Chennai was born from a plot of land granted to the British East India Company in 1639 by a local governor and was given the Anglicized moniker "Madras." In the late seventeenth century, Madras was consolidated into a bounded urban center. Within the city, a European-owned textile and railway carriage industry emerged, with a concomitant rise in employment opportunities. As a result, lower-caste migrants from surrounding villages began to migrate to the city, particularly to residential settlements surrounding industrial compounds. By 1933, there were 189 "hut" colonies in Madras that housed 202,910 people.[8] These hut colonies comprised the antecedents to modern-day "slums," and their existence points to the weight of the housing issue well before 1947. The British regime, however, had no comprehensive national or state-level strategy to address these nascent slums.

The emphasis on planning in early independent India brought the question of slums to the fore, articulated as a plan to tackle the national problem of an acute housing shortage. The arc of this chronological narrative follows the historical responses to the dilemma of what to do with slums: clear the houses away from near waterbodies and denser areas and relocate them elsewhere, or allow them to stay in the same location while upgrading the built environment and infrastructure of the area? The policy responses to this dilemma have oscillated over time, depending on various political, economic, and social pressures, but the two approaches can be broadly categorized as slum clearance and relocation, and in situ slum upgrading.

Shortly after independence, the national government formed a planning commission to address a host of socioeconomic issues that plagued the country. Of these issues, slums were highly prioritized on the planning agenda. The first (1951–1956) and second (1956–1961) national plans both considered slums problems to be solved, and national policy recommended slum relocation. In cities including Bombay and Calcutta, the slums that had formed over the decades prior to independence were razed and their residents relocated to the cities' peripheries. But slum relocation was exorbitantly expensive, and slum residents were too poor to pay any form of rent in compensation. Moreover, politicians in Tamil Nadu—of which Chennai is the capital city—whose ascent hinged upon promises of welfare for the poor and disenfranchised, worried that relocation disrupted residents' education, employment, and social networks. Thus, starting in the 1960s, Tamil Nadu slum management policy rapidly shifted away from slum relocation to favor minimal displacement of slum residents.[9]

State-level politics in Tamil Nadu mirrored national politics. The dovetailing of policy perspectives was evident in the bent of Tamil Nadu slum policies in the 1960s and 1970s, which preferred a restorative approach as the solution to the question of slums. The primary focus of the restorative approach was on slum improvement at site, so that slum residents would not have to be displaced. In situ slum improvement thus emphasized preserving the location of slums rather than shifting them outside the city. The restorative angle of this phase of slum policy ensured safeguards so that slum occupants were, for the most part, protected from eviction. If a site was slated for an improvement project, residents could file a declaration to be ensured a unit in the improved building, *at site*, once the work was completed. The operative focus for slum policy was thus on investing in rebuilding tenements and engaging in in situ redevelopment of slums.

At the same time, slums were also framed as risky to the residents themselves. The conditions in which slum residents lived were deemed unsatisfactory and "unfit for human habitation."[10] The volume of migration into Madras city was so high in this period that the imperative of slum policy under the Congress regime that dominated Tamil Nadu politics between 1954 and 1967 was to provide free, modernized housing with significant public investment for the poorest residents living in squalid conditions. In Tamil Nadu, Congress followed the national stance of the party in stressing nationalism articulated as modernization. The Congress campaign strategy involved courting low-income migrant and slum populations with the promise of modernizing and improving their living conditions. This modernization angle was reflected in the state government's emphasis on providing water taps, latrines, and electricity to slum areas.[11] The solution to the slum question was thus configured in the form of improving living conditions for slum residents at site as a welfare measure. The restorative in situ approach to slums hinged upon the framing that the built environment and social environment of slums were risky for their own residents; they thus needed to be modernized or improved to meet specific state standards of acceptable living conditions.

In 1967, a new era of Dravidian politics was born after the demise of the Congress Party in Tamil Nadu and the rise of the Dravida Munnetra Kazhagam, or DMK. This particular moment is significant because it represents a departure in national politics and regional politics in Tamil Nadu; the DMK positioned itself as the Tamil-speaking, Dravidian bulwark against the Hindi-speaking North. The DMK successfully maintained its power in the 1970s, dominating Tamil politics with its particular brand of welfare-based populism. The slum population was crucial to the DMK's success. A report from an official at the planning organization in Delhi stated, "It is understood that the Dravida Munnetra Kazhagam (DMK) came to political power with the massive support of urban slum dwellers."[12]

The establishment of the Tamil Nadu Slum Clearance Board (TNSCB) was the defining feature of this era's slum policy. The TNSCB was set up in 1970 in response to a series of fires that devastated slums across the city and rendered residents homeless overnight. The mandate of the TNSCB was to provide a statewide framework for tackling the problem of rapidly growing slums. The Tamil Nadu Slum Areas (Improvement and Clearance) Act was passed in 1971 to grant the board powers to frame and enact slum policies. The 1970s witnessed the continuation of slum welfare in the form of a restorative approach. Shifting slums away to the city's periphery was not an option for the DMK-controlled TNSCB due to the potential political fallout of antagonizing slum votes. The focus remained on improving slums in situ on the basis that their existing conditions were unsatisfactory for the residents or the public of its neighborhood. Indeed, the 1971 act defined slums by their risk: "[A slum is] any area that is or may be a source of danger to the health, safety or convenience of the public of that area or of its neighborhood, by reason of the area being low-lying insanitary, squalid, over crowded or otherwise."[13]

The TNSCB undertook an extensive audit in order to identify all slums in the city and instituted policy guidelines for slum improvement.[14] The guidelines reiterated the restorative focus of this policy era with increased financial commitments to increasing shelter stock. The TNSCB secretary articulated the motivation for slum management through reference to the misery of slum residents: "Cities like Bombay, Calcutta, Delhi and Madras have along with its credit of successful industrialization and urbanization also the problem of a sizeable portion of the urban population living in depressing conditions of poverty, misery spreading the cancer of insanitation, juvenile delinquency, crime and prostitution."[15]

The TNSCB developed as an organization with a focus on the welfare of slum residents, apparent in its motto: "God we shall see in the smile of the poor." The focus of the TNSCB in the 1970s remained on slum improvement at site, without shifting slums to far-flung areas. It displaced slum residents only as a last resort, since slum relocation would damage their networks of employment and education—and cause resentment that might hurt the DMK electorally. "Shifting the slums outside the city is practically impossible as the migrants who formed the slums on getting employment within the area will be thrown out of employment and the pressure on transportation will be increased," argued an executive engineer in a TNSCB report. "As a result, the slum dwellers are to be rehabilitated in the same areas where they live now."[16] Chennai slum policy in the 1960s and 1970s was characterized by a restorative approach to slums. Policy documents framed slums as risky to their residents and the surrounding area, and in need of modernization and upgrading. As a result, the preferred mode of dealing with slums was in situ slum improvement, with minimal displacement of slum residents.

But the entry of international financial institutions (IFIs) in the mid-1970s into development funding and assistance signaled a new era of slum policy. Understanding cities like Chennai as fairly new to the process of urbanization, the World Bank provided aid for urban planning and development, becoming involved in Tamil Nadu in 1975. Through various schemes, the World Bank provided conditional aid to government agencies involved in infrastructure development or mitigating urban poverty. In 1975, the World Bank offered $24 million in aid for slum improvement programs, inducing the government to spend less on providing housing free of cost. The World Bank urged the government to extract user costs from beneficiaries of slum improvement programs instead of providing these houses on the state's dime. A World Bank report on the cost recovery approach stated: "The policy impact of Madras Urban Development Project–1 (1971) could be understood as a shift of priorities in favor of slum improvement whose conception was at the same time considerably enhanced particularly through the introduction by the project of the concepts of security of tenure and cost recovery."[17]

As the World Bank worked to shift slum policy away from providing free housing toward the extraction of a betterment fee from beneficiaries, Tamil Nadu's DMK government offered tremendous resistance. It pushed back against a more aggressive national-level sites and services scheme that would displace entire slums to the urban periphery. The pro-poor agenda of the state government was most salient at this point in time, but the next phase of slum policy would slowly orient itself to concerns of other urban residents.

1980s and 1990s: The World Bank Era

As a combined effect of Indira Gandhi's declaration of a national emergency (1975–1977) and the subsequent opposition to the president's rule that followed, top DMK functionaries were imprisoned and met with harsh reprimand. At the same time, the DMK, riddled with corruption in its higher echelons, developed a reputation as a party of excesses.[18] The 1980s heralded a significant development in Tamil Nadu politics with the rise of the opposition party, ADMK (later renamed as the AIADMK), under the sensational leadership of film star M. G. Ramachandran, or MGR as he was popularly known. The MGR era was starkly different from that of the DMK, the latter of which had cultivated an image of the central government as distant and oppressive. The "MGR formula" diminished the state government's antagonism toward the center and advocated a policy of accommodation with national party politics.

This marked phase of accommodation with the center brought a new turn to Tamil Nadu's slum policy under the MGR regime, pivoting to a stance reflective of the national policy's receptivity to development aid from IFIs. Tamil Nadu slum policy in the 1980s met the demands of the World Bank to reduce state spending and increase user costs by levying higher rents from residents of redeveloped slums. The change in regime resulted in the weakening of TNSCB's political ties to the DMK, and it began to fall more in line with the World Bank's recommendations.[19]

The increased congruence of World Bank goals and TNSCB policies in the 1990s is attributable to a quantum leap in the size of loans being offered by the Bank. For the second urban master plan, developed in the late 1980s, the World Bank offered a loan of $300 million, as opposed to the $24 million provided for the first urban master plan of the 1970s. The raised corpus of funds for aid gave the Bank a sizable bargaining chip with which to push its agenda for reduced state spending and a heightened impetus for sites and services schemes. A change in political power from the DMK to the ADMK also resulted in lowered "inviolability," or protection against eviction, that slums had enjoyed under the DMK regime.[20] As a result, the funding for free-of-cost, low-income housing was massively cut in the second urban development plan despite a continued acute housing shortage among low-income groups.

By the 1990s, the nation and the world had turned to urban renewal for a diagnose-and-dissect approach to urban decay, remedied through land redevelopment programs. For India, this signaled an era of a hardening stance toward slums and marked the dying embers of the free-of-cost slum improvement programs in situ. Whereas the 1970s had witnessed massive public spending on free housing provision for slums, by the 1990s, slum improvement programs were largely paid for not by the state but through user fees in the form of rent.

Higher user costs for relocated slum residents were now accompanied by the entry of private players in the housing and infrastructure markets. The Indian economy liberalized in 1991; subsequently, consultations, construction bids, and environmental audits for urban development began to be outsourced to corporate developers and agents through public-private partnerships (PPPs). The PPP model is a method of engaging private participation, investment, and execution in projects that had previously been solely within the government's domain. The entry of private players galvanized the new user cost regime and effectively distanced the government from the decision to move away from free, in situ slum improvement to slum rehousing for a fee. The deployment of the PPP model was accelerated by the IFIs' shift to a more "selective approach to allocation of aid."[21] The new strategy allocated aid based on governments' commitment to reform, rather than merely allocating aid to improve the conditions and levels of poverty in developing countries, and the IFIs encouraged "good governance" reforms to incentivize reduced state spending and increase private involvement in development. The PPP approach began to be applied to the slum clearance and improvement schemes, but this shift to reduced state involvement was also accompanied by incentives for civil society actors such as NGOs and resident welfare associations (RWAs) to participate in reimagining the cityscape.

Political shifts in Tamil Nadu, changes in IFIs' lending practices, a liberalized economy, and higher user costs for relocated slum residents coincided with the growing importance of the Indian middle class in envisioning the city and its aesthetic. This phase of Tamil Nadu history was marked by the characterization of slums as *risky*, or essentially at odds with a new urban aesthetic. RWAs were largely composed of middle-class urban residents who took an antagonistic stance to slums, often invoking an environmental rhetoric. Newly empowered RWAs pushed to beautify their neighborhoods by building parks and playgrounds. These beautifications were often guarded by high walls and tall gates.[22] Like their counterparts in other Indian cities, middle-class RWAs in Chennai were often antagonistic to the "encroachment" of slums on their neighborhoods. RWA participants framed slums as risky and dangerous to neighboring middle-class neighborhoods. Pushpa Arabindoo shows how the development of a middle- and upper-class residential settlement in a southern Chennai neighborhood was predicated on a concerted RWA action that alleged that men of the fishing village or "slum" were defecating on the open beachfront, claiming that this was not only a public health hazard but a blot on an otherwise picturesque landscape.[23] In this way, the environmental discourse of restoring waterbodies is collapsed with an aesthetic anxiety over creating sanitized cityscapes, while framing the residents of slums as risky, messy, and illegal. Earlier, slums were framed in government policy documents as risky to their *own* residents, because of hazardous built environments and limited infrastructure, but by the 1990s slums began to be seen as risky to the wider urban public, particularly to the middle class.

But contrary to much of the "good governance" literature that depicts RWAs exclusively as instruments of the middle class in pursuing its class interests, often at the cost of low income counterparts, in Chennai, welfare associations abounded in lower-income areas in the city in the 1970s and 1980s.[24] These slum-based welfare associations emerged both spontaneously, in response to threats of eviction, and at the behest of political parties. As a result, many RWAs emerged in slums through the brokerage of local individuals affiliated with political parties. The success of associational groups such as RWAs in Chennai slums certainly presents a case that runs counter to the grain of much civil society literature, which traditionally posits RWAs as the preserve of middle-class neighborhoods.

Slum-based RWAs, which were closely connected with the DMK, were most robust in Chennai during the party's heyday in the 1970s and 1980s. Their numbers dropped off sharply in the early 1990s, as DMK lost its hold over the TNSCB and the board's community development (CD) wing worked to persuade slum residents to accept relocation.[25] Slum associations withered away in the face of a more authoritarian urban policy strategy to rid the city of squatters. Declining confrontational slum movements against eviction were replaced by the urban poor's co-optation of legal resources to make claims to land and property. In Tamil Nadu, the two major political parties compete to expand their base among urban constituencies such as slums, which no longer present confrontational approaches to slum eviction but still represent a constituency that must be courted by DMK and AIADMK functionaries. This situation of mutual dependency between political parties and slums in Chennai results in the need for presenting slum relocations as favorable to the slum residents.

2000–Present: Slums Are "At Risk"

By the turn of the millennium there appeared to be a conflict: nationally and internationally mandated urban policy emphasized slum removal and middle-class aesthetic preferences, but the pressures of Tamil electoral politics demanded attention to poor voters. This seeming conflict was reconciled by the mainstreaming of disaster policy. The framing of slums as "at risk" in their current locations, as well as being "risky" to themselves and the general public, became the mode through which the government presented slum relocation as a disaster welfare measure. Such a move allows the political interface between the government and the slum to remain intact, at least on the surface.

The restorative approach of in situ slum upgrading began to take a different tone by the early 2000s. By this juncture, a number of actors had emerged
on the horizon of urban planning in Chennai. Whereas in the 1970s the city
and national governments solely managed slum improvement and relocation
operations, by the late 1990s changes in development funding had led to a
new constellation of actors and institutions that made their impact felt in
slum policy. Among the primary movers of this arrangement were the private
developers, who began to approach urban planning bodies with construction
bids for constructing slum relocation colonies.[26]

Another major force in determining slum policy was the middle-class
environmental activists who began to articulate a vision for a "slum-free" city
as part of their environmental conservation efforts. For example, a call to
restore the Adyar River and clean its banks emerged from middle-class activist groups that characterized slums as part of the pollution affecting Chennai's waterways. "The river within Chennai city limits," an application before
the National Green Tribunal (NGT) from one such activist complained, "is
degraded due to unauthorized settlements and slums along the river banks
and its flood plains."[27] Indeed, environmental rating agencies, both private
and public, portrayed slums as part of the pollution problem. As middle-class
environmental groups increased their influence, slum residents lost their own
voice, as the number of welfare associations sharply declined. This meant that
middle-class understandings of slums as polluting—and thus that the only
way to solve the problem was to remove them from the site to be cleaned—
went unchallenged. The Adyar River cleanup plans slated six thousand families living in slums along the riverfront for resettlement to the outskirts of
the city. The report detailing the resettlement plan argued that in situ redevelopment would not be advised since it would "consolidate and worsen the
existing situation."[28]

Official slum policy began to bend to the interests of these powerful stakeholders in the 2000s. A year after the environmental agency called for slum
relocation, the Chennai city government commissioned sixty projects under
the Integrated Cooum River Ecorestoration Project to construct tenements
for 14,257 families outside the city boundaries. "The removal of encroachments is a critical activity without which many of the other activities cannot be initiated," the government order sanctioning the project read. "The
encroachments fall on the bank of the river where cleaning, creation of walk-
ways, cycle tracks, and parks are to be done."[29] In other words, slum dwellers
had to be relocated so the land could be put to better environmental use.

The combination of private construction interests lobbying for contracts and middle-class activism led to a boom of relocations. Between 2006 and 2011, the Tamil Nadu government commissioned 80,000 tenements at a cost of Rs. 30 billion, of which 46,650 were built or were under construction by 2010.[30] In contrast, the total number of *all* tenements built up until 2007 in Chennai's entire urban history was 81,038 settlements. In other words, the same number of slum rehousing tenements was built just within the five-year period between 2006 and 2011 as throughout the city's entire legacy up to that point in time.

This constellation of actors relies on portraying slum residents as essentially *risky*. Middle-class activists and private developers both articulate their demands for slum clearance and resettlement on the basis that slums are undesirably crowding an urban landscape that these stakeholders envision being used differently. They persistently aspire for and demand a "world-class city" with modern amenities such as green spaces and high-rises, and slums are imagined as eyesores. Consequently, in 2012 the slum clearance agency of Tamil Nadu initiated the Vision 2023 Scheme, which envisioned a "slum-free city" paired with a housing-for-all project; it relied completely on slum clearance instead of in situ slum redevelopment or improvement.[31] In this vision, slums—risky to the environment and to the city's aspirations to world-class greatness—would be removed and their residents rehoused far away and out of sight. The problem the proposal seemed to solve was not slum dwellers' demands for decent housing located close to their places of work and education or legal stability, but rather middle-class demands for sightliness.

But while Vision 2023 and similar projects drew strength from portraying slums as risky to others, in the context of Tamil Nadu politics, this middle-class politics would not have been enough. Postindependence Tamil Nadu has been characterized as practicing a sort of "machine-style politics," involving brokers and mediators to keep intact a system of voters and cadres through material inducements.[32] Charismatic Dravidian leaders have fashioned themselves in some way or form as being pro-poor in appealing to the public and thus constitute a political elite that remains attached to the slum as an important political constituency. But as the two major Dravidian parties—DMK and AIADMK—have alternated in state government, they have both abandoned their more radical claims made at inception, such as a separatist Tamil state or a militaristic attitude toward the central government. In fact, both parties have formed coalitions with national political parties such as the Congress and the Bharatiya Janata Party (BJP) at various points since the late 1990s. Furthermore, the political scenario in Tamil Nadu has undergone tremendous changes as a result of new political parties that have emerged since the 2000s with specifically caste-based agendas. Newer Tamil Nadu-based political parties have platforms that comprise the interests of poorer, lower-caste or Dalit voters, thus requiring the DMK and AIADMK to step up the expression of commitment to the poor and the Dalits. The concentration of the poor and the Dalits in slums obligates political actors to frame slum policies as pro-poor.

Thus slum relocation projects could not rely only on middle-class discourses of environmental protection or the aspiration to being a "world-class city." Rather, a decisive factor in promoting slum clearance was to describe slums as also *at risk*. In other words, slum clearance and the massive building projects of the twenty-first century have been enabled not only by imagining slums as risky to their immediate surroundings, but also by articulations that present slums are *vulnerable* to vagaries of the environment by way of their geographic precariousness. By presenting slums as at risk, slum clearance could be presented as pro-poor.

A crucial event for this reframing was the 2004 Indian Ocean tsunami, the most catastrophic disaster event of the early 2000s. The World Bank had incorporated emergency relief as part of its operations since its inception, with its name officially being the International Bank for *Reconstruction* and Development. However, the resources and planning devoted to disaster management had been considerably lacking until 1998, when the World Bank established the Hazard Risk Management team to streamline and monitor disaster-related investments.[33] The destruction caused by the 2004 Indian Ocean tsunami—which killed nearly a quarter million people in South and Southeast Asia and displaced nearly two million more—resulted in a greater preoccupation with mitigating poorer populations' vulnerability to disaster in development and planning realms. The tsunami marked a turning point not only in IFI priorities but also in the rhetoric around Chennai slums. The 12th Five-Year Plan of Tamil Nadu stated, "Disasters both natural and manmade are the biggest threats that humanity is facing today." The tone of urgency in dealing with the threats presented by disaster to the city's residents dovetailed with the concern that slums were metastasizing and blotting a "world-class" landscape.

Disaster policy mainstreaming, which was further emphasized by IFIs in the 2000s and embraced by Chennai's policymakers, implies that a focus on disaster management has pervaded all arenas of urban policy, particularly that of slum policy. Disaster mainstreaming within slum policies led to a coincidence of interests; slum clearance and relocation were presented as a way to reduce the geographic vulnerability of slums in their present locations along riverbanks or the oceanfront, which is, of course, what powerful actors wanted for reasons of waterfront development and producing modernized and "slum-free" urban aesthetics.

In Chennai, disaster mainstreaming has led to the emergence of stakeholders acting in concert and to a depiction of slums as at risk. The overlap of slum and disaster agendas is clearly evidenced by organizational correspondences. For example, the TNSCB chairman was appointed as the head of the Disaster Management Committee in the wake of the 2004 Indian Ocean tsunami. As a result, the contingent or executive orders from the government directed to disaster-affected slums focused on shifting slum tenure as an approach to mitigate their vulnerability to future disasters. The process of vulnerability mitigation is attributed to a new approach in disaster management that attempts to preempt the disaster by prevention and mitigation strategies, one of which is slum relocation: "There has been a paradigm shift in the focus of Disaster Management, from response-centric covering rescue, relief, rehabilitation, and reconstruction to laying greater emphasis on the other elements of disaster management cycle—prevention, mitigation, and preparedness—as a means to avert or soften the impact of future emergencies."[34]

This mode of disaster planning is predicated on reducing the geographical risks presented by settlement along precarious locations. Because, in this telling, people ought not to be living in dangerous locations to begin with, the solution is to move them: "People have continued to live and settle in disaster-prone areas, in spite of knowing about the risk and occurrence in the past may be due to certain cultural and historical reasons coupled with advantages of living in these areas. The risk gets amplified when the population increases, the area gets densified and activities increase thereby aggravating the situation and putting a large number of lives at risk. To cope with the disasters, preparedness and planning are the only ways."[35]

The framing of IFIs' disaster mainstreaming invoked again the language of "risk reduction" in the longer term, with future mitigation as the goal rather than spending in the short term on immediate relief efforts after a disaster event.[36] At the heart of the risk reduction narrative is the use of "vulnerability" or recognition that risk of disasters can be shared unequally and that risks may be exacerbated by the existence of certain preexisting physical hazards. The emphasis on long-term over short-term recovery funding is reflected in development agendas that privilege mitigating future risk. A spate of programs was initiated by executive order shortly after the 2004 disaster, including the Emergency Tsunami Rehabilitation Program (ETRP) and the Coastal Disaster Risk Reduction Program (CDRRP).[37] These programs advocated rehabilitation measures for slum residents as a way of reducing their future vulnerability to other disasters. Taking their cue from World Bank agenda setters, the focus of these programs was not on short-term recovery measures but rather on long-term rehabilitation in order to reduce vulnerability. To do this, slum residents would be shifted out of their current geographic locations—which were ostensibly precarious—and into slum relocation colonies built in the style of townships on the outskirts of the city. A government order in 2005 "envisage[d] the construction of about 130,000 concrete houses at an approximate cost of Rs. 1,50,000 each. Each house w[ould] have 300–325 sq. ft. of built-up spaces. The houses w[ould] have all disaster-resistant features." Crucially, these new disaster-resistant, concrete houses would not be built where old slum dwellings had been, but rather in new, more distant locations.[38]

In 2008, the TNSCB constructed thirteen thousand tenements in the peri-urban area of Okkiyam Thoraipakkam (OT) with funding assistance from the World Bank.[39] The case made in these executive orders was that despite being far away from the original location of the slum, these tenements would provide security against an ostensibly natural predilection to vulnerability that the geographic location created. The inner-city slum residents were being moved to OT, on the edge of the city limits, anywhere between fifteen and twenty-five kilometers away from their original inner-city neighborhoods.

In practice, the conditions of tenements built for slum relocation throw into question the actual benefits of the new tenements constructed on the outskirts of the city over the existing locations. For one, the executive orders declared a state of emergency precipitated by disaster, thus circumventing rules that prevent construction of housing in certain zones. Although existing rules banned the construction of new residences in wetlands, an executive order in 2005 waived those rules, replacing vulnerability to one hazard with vulnerability to another. "The Government after careful examination consider that in order to put the rehabilitation measures on a fast track, exempt the tsunami affected districts from obtaining prior permission from the Government to acquire wetlands for housing to rehabilitate the tsunami affected people, [which is] imperative," wrote the TNSCB chairman (and head of the disaster management committee). In other words, the order exempted tsunami slum rehousing colonies from needing to obtain prior permission to acquire wetlands.[40] As a result, the slum rehousing colony built in OT is located in wetlands that flood every monsoon season.

In addition, reports from NGOs and community audits show that the construction of OT slum resettlement colonies was supply driven. Private land developers and construction agencies approached the government, and the government awarded the contract to build OT slum tenements to the cheapest bidder.[41] This hints at a nexus of private developers operating in tandem with slum and disaster bureaucrats in developing a spate of slum relocation tenements before the need for alternate housing was even established. This is further clarified by an executive order that advocated relocation of Thideer Nagar slum residents to OT without even verifying whether or not they were equally affected by the tsunami: "Out of 1286 families [relocated to OT], only 1228 families are stated as tsunami-affected and the status of the remaining 58 families is yet to be verified." To compound the exodus, slum dwellers from North Chennai were also relocated to OT despite northern parts of the city being landlocked and far from any locations of geographic precariousness.[42]

Since the 2000s, the policies on slums have been moderated by two frames. The first frame perceives slums as risky, not just to the residents themselves, but to a wider public that comprises, among others, the middle-class residents of the city and private land and real estate developers. However, Chennai has witnessed the development of a new frame of slums as not just risky, but also at risk in their existing geographical locations. The latter frame emerged as a result of the World Bank's emphasis on disaster mainstreaming in urban policy and the development of a disaster regime comprising various policy actors, political parties, and stakeholders such as the middle-class and private developers. This new understanding of slums as simultaneously risky and at risk—together with changes in the economic and political conditions in Chennai and Tamil Nadu—led to the radical pivoting of the city's slum policy away from the in situ slum improvement of the 1960s toward an approach that prefers the relocation of slums to the urban periphery. The disaster regime has successfully created a paradoxical situation in which its supposed beneficiaries are adversely affected as a result of massive displacement and isolation on the fringes of the city. However, the deployment of slum relocation as a response to the disaster moment is premised on a need to present the relocation as pro-poor and a solution to the vulnerability of slums to future destruction.

Conclusion

The existing scholarship on slums and cities explains how aspirations to a world-class city have laid claim to Indian urban governance. Competing sets of stakeholders, like the middle-class and private land and real estate developers, have pushed the state to enact slum eviction and clearance by framing slums as risky, dangerous, illegal, and messy. However, as this chapter shows, the case of Chennai slums presents a different picture. Middle-class articulations of the slums as environmentally polluting, or illegally encroaching, have indeed fueled the drive to relocate slums. The government, acting in concert with IFIs and private developers, has created a regime that works toward a "world-class city" devoid of slums, as evidenced by Vision 2023's slum-free hope for Chennai. However, the political expediencies of Tamil politics necessitate at least a tokenistic framing of slum relocation as pro-poor. The cornerstone of Tamil politics has been a concern for its image, as represented in electoral campaigns, film, and the media as pro-poor. As a result, the framing of slums as at risk of disaster-induced destruction has become an additional modality through which political parties preserve their image as being for the "common man" while simultaneously appeasing other competing stakeholders in the electoral process.

Clearly, despite the framing of slum relocation as pro-poor, the actual relocation of slums to far-flung townships has been anything but beneficial to the displaced slum residents. Slum relocation has led to an extenuated experience of disaster, including by some who did not even experience the effects of the original event. Children and adolescents have experienced attenuation in their education, since the provision of infrastructure services has yet to follow the relocation of slum residents to many of these townships.[43] An official audit by the comptroller and auditor general of India found improper and shoddy construction that leads to flooding during the monsoon season, thus making residents more vulnerable to a different, more frequent disaster.[44] Slum relocation in the name of disaster prevention both depended on the diminished political power of slum residents and further decreased their remaining power.

The pro-poor framing of slum relocation on the pretext of natural disaster illustrates the potent capacity of disaster to motivate and justify a range of political agendas. The disaster framing in Chennai's case enabled policymakers and politicians to effectively "kill two birds with one stone" and reconcile disparate political claims. On the one hand, the anticipation of disaster and the portrayal of slums as at risk has enabled slum evictions on the basis of their residents' ostensible vulnerability in their original locations within the city's limits. The vulnerability framework provided by the disaster discourse has been crucial to politicians who want at once to produce sanitized cityscapes free of slums to satisfy developers and middle-class demands for a "world-class city," and to present slum evictions to slum residents, another important constituency, as pro-poor. On the other hand, enacting slum relocations as disaster prevention has enabled policymakers to appear to be acting in accordance with global demands for disaster risk reduction by funding bodies and regulatory authorities. The story of Chennai's spate of slum relocations encapsulates the incredible political power of disaster framing to manifest often contradictory and potentially controversial urban policies.

CHAPTER 7

Plan B

The Collapse of Public-Private Risk Sharing in the US National Flood Insurance Program

Rebecca Elliott

In a 2017 *Politico* op-ed, the Cato Institute, a libertarian think tank, offered its diagnosis of the problems facing the politically embattled US National Flood Insurance Program (NFIP). At the time, this public, federal program of flood insurance owed $24 billion to the US Treasury (at the time of writing, its debt hovers around $20 billion). The fifty-year-old program was plunged into fiscal disarray by the damage following Hurricane Katrina in 2005 and had been unable in the years since then to work its way back into the black. The reason, according to Cato, was that the NFIP was undercharging for insurance, offering unduly subsidized coverage that kept flood insurance affordable but also meant the program never had enough money to cover the expected costs of its liabilities. "The optimal solution," the authors wrote, "would be for the government to get out of the flood insurance business entirely and leave it to the private market, which would endeavor to accurately measure risk and charge a price for its insurance that covers the expected costs." Given the unusual politics around flood insurance—a rare issue that forges bipartisan solidarities between floodplain Democrats and Republicans—the authors acknowledged that full privatization "may not be politically feasible now." But Congress could take smaller steps "that allow private insurers to compete with the NFIP on a level playing field and introduce a modicum of market discipline on the market."[1]

The Cato Institute is one voice in a growing chorus of actors calling for the privatization, partial or complete, of the NFIP. Cato made the argument on libertarian grounds: here was an example of irresponsible and unnecessary government interference in a domain that private markets could more efficiently, and fairly, organize. Insurance industry interests have also lobbied for privatization measures that would allow them to underwrite flood risk where it is profitable to do so, and recent rule changes have led a handful of primary insurers to take beginning steps in offering private flood insurance lines.[2] Others have not argued for privatization per se but have argued that the NFIP should emulate certain practices of private insurers. Environmentalists, for instance, have argued that the NFIP ought to incorporate private industry techniques for mapping flood risk, in particular bringing climate science to bear on assessing future risks.[3] This might help the program to achieve one of its long-standing, but largely unmet, objectives: discouraging people from moving into and building—or rebuilding—in hazardous floodplains. And in the context of urban climate governance, public officials are also interested in the promises of private (re)insurance, particularly its capacity to provide new forms of financing (e.g., catastrophe bonds) that will support the recovery and operation of public services and infrastructure in the wake of disasters.[4] In brief, we are at a moment of ferment around the adequacy and future of the NFIP, and of public risk-sharing systems more generally. Private insurance appears to many to be a solution to public failures and a better way to organize a societal response to future risks and disasters.

This chapter excavates a neglected facet of the NFIP's history: it *was* a largely private program at its start. The NFIP began in 1968 as a pool of private insurance underwriters, with the state as a financial backstop. Congressional records, records of the Federal Emergency Management Agency, the Department of Housing and Urban Development, and other government agencies show that policymakers never really intended to have the federal government underwriting flood risk. Rather, this public-private risk-sharing partnership fell apart in less than ten years because private profit making could not be reconciled with public goals.

Distinctions between government or market "function" versus "failure" are not self-evident. Instead, they are *made* conspicuous and meaningful through political claims-making and institutional arrangements. The NFIP is not and has never been categorically public *or* private; elements of both have always been present, in different combinations. Yet today, conventional accounts of "failure" in the NFIP blame the government rather than the private actors, markets, or industries that are implicated in its operation.

A Tale of Two Parts: Authorizing the National
Flood Insurance Program

How did the federal government get into the flood insurance business? There is a kind of irony to this outcome, given an observed American ideological preference, across policy domains, for market-based forms of social provision. In 1968, after almost two decades of false starts, Congress established the NFIP to solve several public policy problems at once. First, the costs of both avoiding and recovering from flood losses had become expensive for the federal government. Flood experts at the time identified a "levee effect," wherein the federal government paid for the construction of structural flood protection, only to have people move into these seemingly "safe" areas, where they would suffer losses in the event that a catastrophic flood overwhelmed the defenses—losses that the federal government was then often called upon to address.[5] Flood insurance would mitigate these costs in a few ways. First, in the event of a loss, policyholders would have "prefunded" their own recovery through paying annual premiums, rather than turning to the government for aid (at the time, often in the form of subsidized loans). Second, an actuarial system of flood insurance, that is, one in which premiums were indexed to the risk, would economically incentivize risk-avoiding and risk-reducing decision-making on the part of individuals and local authorities, shifting development and habitation away from "uneconomical" uses of the floodplain.[6] It would be a "nonstructural" form of floodplain management, one that used market techniques of economizing hazards and pricing risk to influence the behavior of individual private actors in pursuit of the collective objectives of more prudent land use and reduced flood losses.

At the time, however, the private insurance market in the United States was not interested in underwriting flood risk. The extraordinary Great Mississippi Flood of 1927 prompted the several dozen private insurance companies that had been writing flood policies to exit the flood risk market by 1929. That catastrophe had demonstrated that flood risks were often concentrated in specific regions, putting significant financial strain on any insurer in the position of owing claims. The industry had also come to believe that the technical challenges associated with estimating flood risk with sufficient precision, combined with the commercial challenges of getting people to buy what would likely be an expensive product, made flood risk effectively uninsurable.[7]

A federal insurance program, however, could operate on geographic and time scales that the private market could not. Providing insurance, its proponents pointed out, would make flood, by definition, insurable, correcting a market failure. Under a federal program, no risks would be too bad to be covered. Such a program could create a national risk pool in a "workable program of protection for property owners in disaster areas," in the words of President Lyndon Johnson when he signed a bill mandating that the Department of Housing and Urban Development further study the feasibility of a flood insurance program (Pub. L. No. 83-339, passed in the wake of Hurricane Betsy).[8] HUD convened a task force to produce its report, headed up by Marion Clawson, an economist and president of Resources for the Future (a think tank focused on environmental, energy, and natural resources issues). That report, entitled *Insurance and Other Programs for Financial Assistance to Flood Victims* and delivered to Congress in 1966, sketched out four alternatives for a flood insurance program, each with a distinct configuration of private and public participation. Ultimately, the HUD report settled on a private industry program, "with major federal help" as the "likely and desirable program."[9] The primary responsibilities of the federal agency would be to engage in flood risk assessment through mapping and classifying the nation's flood zones, to set insurance premiums, and to provide backstop financial support against excessive losses. The private insurance industry would provide initial capital for the program (predicted to be $75 to $100 million) and sell and service policies thereafter, bearing risk up to a to-be-determined "excessive loss point." The program would benefit from the "extensive organization of the private insurance industry, and the greater financial strength of the Federal government to cope with the unusual hazards."[10]

The private market would participate in this version of a flood insurance program by forming a "pool" of member companies that would work with the government to run the program. In a 1967 report, the US Senate Committee on Banking and Currency suggested that the pool, with the companies as risk bearers, would sell and service policies as they already did against other perils, sharing in the aggregate profits or losses of the pool's operation for a particular accounting period and being jointly liable for the payment of claims by insolvent members. Member insurance companies would be allowed to charge "rates deemed adequate to cover all costs," including the administrative costs of writing the policies.[11]

If the insurance industry was "unable or unwilling to participate" as outlined, there was another acceptable—but much less desirable to Congress— configuration: an "essentially Federal flood insurance program might be developed, which the private industry would operate and manage" without bearing the risks of flood losses.[12] Under this arrangement, the federal government would provide all the capital and take on all the risks, with the private insurance companies "to serve, in effect, as fiscal agents for the Federal Government."[13] The flood insurance program would need appropriations from Congress and a line of borrowing with the Treasury, to pay claims if or when especially severe floods depleted the fund. Though the HUD report deemed a full-risk-bearing arrangement to be less desirable than a risk-sharing one, this option at least leveraged the "existing manpower and administrative structure of the industry," as well as private agents' experience selling and servicing policies. The report cautioned, however, that "such arrangements have also been criticized on many grounds," including private interests not coinciding with public interests, distorting the program, as well as overly generous contract terms with the private industry, leading to unwarranted profits.[14] Ultimately, the report concluded, "The exact terms of any government-industry relationships, in [both alternatives], would have to be developed by negotiation, and would have to do with the willingness of the industry to participate and with the fairness of the general idea."[15]

Shortly thereafter, HUD began developing draft legislation to establish a flood insurance program, in close consultation with representatives from the private insurance industry. The legislation up for debate on the floors of the two chambers of Congress in 1967 authorized HUD to establish a flood insurance program according to the recommendations that came out of the 1966 report: namely, a private program with federal backup.[16] Should such a program—part A of the proposed National Flood Insurance Act—fail, the legislation also authorized HUD to move on to the next-preferred arrangement, part B, a federal program with private administration. However, advocates of the legislation in Congress, who came from both sides of the aisle, were sanguine about the prospects of private participation, based largely on conversations they had had—both formally, through congressional hearings, and informally—with representatives of insurance companies and trade associations. Virtually all the private property insurance trade associations, including the American Insurance Association, the American Mutual Insurance Alliance, the National Association of Independent Insurers, the National Association of Mutual Insurance Companies, the National Association of Insurance Agents, and the National Association of Mutual Insurance Agents, submitted enthusiastic and favorable testimony. The legislation also received support from the Proposed Association of Flood Insurers, a group representing several insurance companies from these same trade associations, which proposed to commit risk capital to the industry pool that would be formed under the legislation.[17] Senator Wallace F. Bennett (R-UT), one of the bill's cosponsors, said during floor debate: "The insurance industry has participated throughout the development of this bill and the industry's suggestions have had a major influence on this proposal,"[18] noting later that the bill was "difficult" to write "because we are trying to write a pattern for cooperation and joint participation of private industry with the Federal Government."[19] Nevertheless, he was able to conclude that "there is not one shred of evidence that industry will not cooperate in a reasonable program."[20]

In the words of Senator Harrison A. Williams (D-NJ), who led the legislative effort in the Senate, "both the insurance industry and the Government have agreed that the joint approach under part A would be preferable to the Government approach under part B. All efforts will be directed to making certain that the joint program under part A works out."[21] Bennett also asserted that options with less private involvement should only be "last resort measures."[22] In the House floor debate, Representative Wright Patman (D-TX) described part B as a "remote possibility."[23] In earlier hearings on the proposed legislation, Under Secretary Robert C. Wood of HUD was asked if the federal government would end up in the flood insurance business in its own name, given the possibility of part B becoming reality. Wood replied: "Our expectation is at this time that it will not occur, and certainly the intention of the Secretary is that it is not to happen."[24]

In hearings on the proposed legislation, as well as during floor debates in both the House and the Senate, many members of Congress expressed the hopeful expectation that the federal flood program might even eventually be *fully* privatized. Senator Thomas J. Dodd (D-CT) characterized the vision of the bill thus: "The Government role in providing flood insurance shall gradually be phased out, and that the private companies will eventually provide this service by themselves."[25] Senator Ralph Yarborough (D-TX) criticized private insurers for failing to get into the flood business and expressed his expectation that the government, through this program, might jump-start a private market for flood insurance. "Once we have established a Federal flood insurance program," he argued, "the private sector of the economy will respond as before and begin to compete for that business."[26] From the hearing and debate transcripts, it is clear that the legislation had robust bipartisan support. But it did have its critics. Senator Roman Hruska (R-NE) expressed skepticism that the federal burden could ever be minimized, because once a federal program "of this kind started, very seldom is it reversed." "If it is," the senator continued, "it is only after disastrous and catastrophic raids upon the Federal Treasury happen to a degree so scandalous that we are forced to do it. We should not invite that kind of situation here."[27] Williams attempted to reassure Hruska by insisting that part A of the legislation would work. Senator Spessard Holland (D-FL) agreed. "The private insurance industry does not want the Government to go on its own into this matter," he asserted. "Private insurance industry will go a long way, as far as it can safely go, to cooperate with the Government in this field."[28]

However, no formal agreement had been made that committed the private insurance industry to any form or extent of participation in the federal flood program. During the Senate floor debate, Senator Allen J. Ellender (D-LA) asked for clarification about "the proportionate share of risk that is assumed by the Government in comparison with that which is assumed by the privately owned insurance companies." Williams replied: "The percentages are not in the bill. We have provided for the Sec. of HUD to negotiate this matter with the insurance companies. They have been talking, and they are waiting for our legislation. But we do give latitude to the Secretary to establish these relationships." Ellender then asked why there were no limitations set in the bill, asking whether the federal government might end up "assum[ing] a greater percentage of the losses than would the privately owned insurance companies." Bennett answered that he believed insurance companies would assume liabilities up to $50 million, but the actual proportion, relative to the federal government, would have to be worked out in negotiation.[29] With these expectations for a successful public-private risk-sharing partnership in place, the National Flood Insurance Act passed in 1967. The National Flood Insurance Law of 1967 ultimately became part of the Housing and Urban Development Act of 1968 (Pub. L. No. 90-448), which established the NFIP and the Federal Insurance Administration (FIA) under the purview of HUD.

From Part A to Part B

With the passage of the National Flood Insurance Law, HUD began work to get the NFIP up and running in 1968. The FIA within HUD was the designated administrator of the NFIP and would manage relations with the new National Flood Insurers Association (NFIA), the private industry pool that would supply risk capital, share losses, and issue and service policies.

The NFIA was ultimately composed of eighty-nine companies that together pledged $42 million in capital.[30] The NFIP, taking the form outlined in part A of the authorizing legislation, began selling policies in 1969. Fairbanks, Alaska, and Metairie, Louisiana, were the first communities enrolled in the program.[31]

The early years of the NFIP's operation were challenging ones. The federal government and private insurers had agreed to share the risk, but it was not clear how, in the practical administration of the program, to share the authority and responsibility. Tensions quickly developed between the federal government and the NFIA as they negotiated and struggled over the boundaries of their respective purviews.[32] The federal government believed it had the authority to review and approve the NFIA's overhead operating budget; the NFIA refused to accede until threatened with the loss of its involvement with the program. HUD also believed that the NFIA was derelict in its duty to market flood insurance, leading to unacceptably slow take-up of flood insurance. In Senate Subcommittee on Housing and Urban Affairs hearings about a series of floods in 1972, George K. Bernstein, then federal insurance administrator, testified that so few affected individuals had flood insurance because of "the failure of local agents to actively market flood insurance," which was, he believed, the private market's responsibility.[33] In August 1972, the FIA within HUD sent letters to every state insurance commissioner, requesting that they require every licensed insurer to formally advise existing and potential policyholders about flood insurance.[34]

In 1977, disputes over the costs of the program surfaced, revealing additional disjuncture between public and private interests. The General Accounting Office (GAO, now the Government Accountability Office) criticized the NFIA for failing to generate and share accurate data related to program costs, such that "the government was unable to properly calculate the Association's share of expenses reimbursable under the program, and the amount of the operating allowance to be retained under the program could not be properly determined."[35] During Federal Insurance Administrator Robert Hunter's tenure in the 1970s, he found that the NFIA refused requests for competitive bids. Instead, "non-competitive bids for servicing flood insurance policies had largely been granted by the NFIA's executive committee to the very companies on NFIA's executive committee . . . and were very expensive." It was a clear case of "self-dealing," he argued, and taxpayers shouldered the extra expense.[36] The potential for waste and undue profits in the public-private partnership belied expectations of greater efficiency and cost savings.

One of the biggest areas of disagreement related to the interpretation of the flood insurance policy itself, particularly related to the servicing of claims. To the government, flood insurance policyholders were citizens and voters—constituents who expected to receive sufficient funds to rebuild their properties when they flooded. Akin to the logic governing other government (social) insurance programs, people had paid in; they should get money out if and when they needed it. The government was therefore inclined to respond rather favorably and generously to claims. For the NFIA insurers, however, flood insurance policyholders were also often customers of their own private property insurance lines (e.g., for wind). The insurers were inclined to be more conservative with their claims payouts. According to Hunter, "[NFIA] Insurers would not pay because they feared that if they paid claims under the flood program that were similar to those they sought to deny under their privately written homeowners' policies with similar policy language, they would have to pay the homeowners' policy claims as well."[37] The desire of private insurers in the NFIA to protect their other lines of business introduced obstacles to the government's objective of providing sufficient financial protection to floodplain occupants.

The initial HUD-NFIA contract was set to expire on December 31, 1977. In anticipation of this deadline, in late 1976, contentious negotiations between HUD and the NFIA took place to clarify both entities' roles in and authority over the NFIP. In the course of these negotiations, it became clear that the two held discordant interpretations of the scope of the NFIA's "operational responsibility." The NFIA considered its sphere of responsibility and authority to be more broadly defined than did HUD and objected to HUD's attempts to increase its role in the operations of the program. In July 1977, HUD then proposed new and stronger regulations to formalize and enhance its authority over the management and operations of the NFIP. The NFIA resisted these.[38] The following month, the NFIA issued a "termination notice" for the arrangement with HUD in order to highlight the seriousness of the disagreements between the NFIA and the government on issues of authority, financial control, and other operating matters.[39] Then, secretary of HUD Patricia Harris said: "Joint negotiations broke down when it finally became clear that we were not going to be able to agree on terms by which NFIA could spend government funds. NFIA wants the right to expend funds without prior approval of the Federal Government and nobody has that right."[40]

Secretary Harris also undertook a cost comparison with a potential part B version of the program: full federal risk bearing and underwriting, with private administration. The FIA within HUD found that HUD could manage the program directly, contracting out the administration, for almost $15 million *less* than under the NFIA agreement. It appeared that the state had been spending more to involve the private market in risk sharing than it would have bearing the risk alone.

In November 1977, Harris informed Congress that she intended to make the NFIP a fully government operation. The projected savings that could be realized by converting the NFIP to "part B," which Harris was empowered to do under the terms of the authorizing legislation, would be put toward further reducing premiums for policyholders. The NFIA sought a temporary restraining order to prevent HUD from initiating part B, but the courts sided with Harris. HUD and the NFIA officially parted ways effective December 31, 1977. Private companies could continue to work as "servicing contractors" to sell policies, train insurance agents, and service claims on behalf of the state, but the NFIP, now run as authorized under part B of the 1968 legislation, deposited premium checks in the Flood Insurance Fund in the US Treasury. Claims made were made against the United States. The Department of Justice handled any litigation resulting from disputed claims. Now, under part B of the NFIP, "a policyholder could have no doubt that he or she was dealing with the federal government."[41] Despite all promises and expectations to the contrary, the NFIP directly issued all flood insurance policies.

After conservative Republican Ronald Reagan became president in 1981, however, his administration soon reopened conversations about private industry involvement in the NFIP.[42] The result, in 1983, was another reconfiguration of public and private participation: the "Write-Your-Own" (WYO) program, which remains in effect today. Under the WYO program, private insurance companies act as "fiscal agents" of the federal government; they sell and service policies and receive a commission on each policy. The Federal Emergency Management Agency (FEMA), which had been created in 1979 to coordinate federal disaster response, became the federal agency responsible for the NFIP. "Write-Your-Own" refers to the fact that participating insurance companies could write flood insurance policies on their own "paper" or policy forms. Participating companies sell flood insurance from their offices and agents, often alongside their other insurance products.[43] However, unlike the arrangement with the NFIA, the private companies do not take on any of the financial risk; the federal government bears responsibility for paying claims. With the WYO, "the 'real' insurer (the entity holding all risk of loss) is the federal government—but the federal government designed the WYO program to virtually eliminate any interaction of the federal government with policyholders."[44] Within a few years, over 90 percent of NFIP policies were issued by WYO companies.

Public and Private "Failures" and Reconfigurations in the Life of the NFIP

Today, observers of the NFIP often discuss the program in terms of public failure, as the Cato Institute's op-ed illustrates. Members of Congress have failed to charge actuarial rates for flood insurance, they argue. The program has failed to repay its debts to the Treasury; the federal government has failed to enforce land use regulations that are a supposed condition of accessing flood insurance; and this "nonstructural" floodplain management strategy, ultimately, has failed to stem flood losses. For some, these failures provide the justification for a turn to private markets and the capitalist discipline they might provide. The history provided here offers up a number of less remarked upon "failures" that have also shaped the course of the NFIP: the failure of the private market first to underwrite flood risk at all and then to underwrite it efficiently, with government support; the failure of the private industry to achieve public ends; the failure to reach agreement on authority and oversight; and a certain failure of imagination that the NFIP might really one day have to operate as a part B rather than a part A program. These failures implicate both public and private actors. But whose failures matter and, more fundamentally, what constitutes a failure to begin with, are a product of political claims-making and institutional arrangements. There are multiple, competing ways to make sense of the NFIP's history.

First, though the NFIP has long been narrated as a failure in many respects, it has persisted. Policymakers have not yet declined to reauthorize its operation (a sunset clause in the initial legislation requires congressional reauthorization of the program every five years). In other words, there seem to be functional elements to this program, which may go unstated, but which have thus far ostensibly justified its continued existence. If we ask, "what does the NFIP 'succeed' at doing," we might bring into view the fact that by keeping insurance coverage broadly affordable for American families, it forms part of a larger policy infrastructure that has supported a post–World War II vision of mass homeownership. This has also worked to buttress the real estate, home building, and housing finance industries, important sectors of the US economy and powerful political interests, which have benefited from the continued (re)development of floodplain areas. For local communities, many of which finance their public services and infrastructure via property taxes, these developments have sustained the possibility of continued, if unevenly felt, growth and prosperity. This is not to say that this particular political economy is itself altogether functional or fair, given the way it inequitably distributes the benefits and burdens of homeownership. The point is rather that, when viewed within that larger political economy, the NFIP's debt might start to look more like a relatively small cost (in the scheme of the national budget) for providing things that American policymakers have, through a variety of other programs and policies, worked affirmatively to protect and promote. For those who are committed to expanding and securing home-ownership, as well as to local real estate development, the NFIP's financial obligations may seem less a debt than an investment.

Second, the NFIP's history can be read instead as largely the product of private industry failures, failures that have not been politicized to the same extent, historically or in recent contestation over flood insurance reform. These failures have been less conspicuous, perhaps, but they have been documented. For instance, the GAO has consistently called for closer oversight of WYO practices in order to ensure that payments made to private insurers are "reasonable." There is evidence that those insurers are pocketing a great deal more than they spend administering the program, and that they do not effectively market the policies to improve insurance take-up rates, driving up costs and making the NFIP less fiscally sound. More than one-third of premiums collected by the NFIP go the WYO participating companies as a commission, which bear no risk. This reflects the incorporation of a 50 percent "loading factor" for the costs of doing business. By contrast, 20–30 percent loading costs are not uncommon for private lines of insurance—even as private insurers also pay for rate making and product development and need to hold sufficient capital and ensure returns to shareholders.[45] In the GAO's view, FEMA "cannot be assured that the WYO program is achieving its intended goals in the most cost-effective manner."[46] Yet the WYO structure does not itself typically come under scrutiny for reform.

Narratives of blame and failure do political and economic work. Sustained perceptions of government failure create and expand opportunities for new forms of private profit making. The reinsurance industry has in recent years

signed on to flood insurance reform efforts that would allow further privatization of the program, if not its outright dismantling, in favor of what they
define as a more "actuarially fair" arrangement in which each new disaster
would lead to revised risk reassessments and, in turn, justify higher rates.[47]
Reinsurers are eager to offer their services of risk modeling as well as their
commercial products—at least in markets where this is profitable—as well
as to sell reinsurance policies to the federal government. In early 2017, with
the authorization of Congress, FEMA announced that it had for the first time
secured more than $1 billion in private reinsurance, from a group of twenty-
five reinsurance companies. Insurance and reinsurance companies stand to
benefit from accounts that position them as technically sophisticated and
financially prudent, as they offer to fix the problems of flood insurance for
individual customers and the federal government alike.

Policymakers in the 1960s took it on faith that private insurers would want
and be able to participate in flood insurance in ways that also achieved the public policy objectives of such a program, leaving the particularities of the relevant arrangements largely unspecified. Going forward, a number of questions
loom about this intersection of public and private: Which risks will the private
market take on, and how will the government manage the risks to homes that
are privately uninsurable? Who will be responsible for assessing and mapping
flood risk, in order to price insurance, and according to what standards? Will
private insurance close or enlarge existing "protection gaps" in coverage? How
will private flood insurance interface with disaster aid and other forms of
relief? We see these potential problems of private markets already manifesting
in the context of other perils, like wildfire. In the wake of the November 2018
California wildfires, private insurers dropped policies, hollowed out coverage
conditions, and raised premiums, putting financial protection out of reach for
many who need it and sharpening inequalities between those who can afford
to buy their way into private networks of risk sharing and those who cannot.
Markets need states to function, and these are the market-making arrangements that should preoccupy publics and policymakers.[48]

The contemporary politics of flood insurance in the United States emphasizes government failures to do what it "ought" to do, and the centering of
the public sector in narratives of blame shapes the demands that are made on
the program. But the history of the NFIP offers up less-told stories, about the
complex relationship between public and private actors and objectives, that
if told more frequently or at higher volume might give rise to different criticisms and demands. I am not suggesting that this alternative view of function

versus failure is more accurate or legitimate. I outline these issues instead to illustrate that interpretations of what the NFIP does or does not do well are unavoidably premised on normative understandings of the appropriate roles of government, markets, and individual citizens in providing for physical and financial security in the face of disasters—understandings that vary across stakeholders and can change over time.

PART III

Imagining Disaster

CHAPTER 8

Mediating Disaster, or A History of the Novel

Susan Scott Parrish

In Jesmyn Ward's *Salvage the Bones*, the 2011 novel about a coastal Mississippi family in the days leading up to and including Hurricane Katrina's landfall on August 29, 2005, there is a scene in which the family watches their television for news about the approaching storm. The Batistes' black-and-white TV gets its signal not through a cable line or satellite dish, but in the old-tech mode, using its antenna to pick up broadcast radio waves. Seeing only static on the screen, the teenage daughter (who is also our narrator) splays the antenna outward like a "wishbone" until the picture and sound partly come through. The local Mississippi weatherwoman is talking with the news anchor and showing him the storm's progress on the station's interactive screen. Because the Batistes' TV is old, though, it makes the "map look like concrete, and the storm, an oil stain." The station's latest technology of data gathering, representation, and transmission is also compromised in the auditory register, for the Batistes can only pick up parts of the news team's sentences. The anchorman asks: "'Does anyone . . . idea of where . . . projection of storm?'" The weatherwoman answers: "'. . . unclear,'" and then adds, "'. . . prepare as well as they can for the storm. Katrina is on the . . . if it does not weaken . . . moving northwest, they should also prepare . . . .'"[1]

Ward inserts this scene not only because it captures the experience of a poor family coping with old technology, and trying, through this means, to access expert information as well as they can, but also because it gets her readers to think about how assessment and communication during disaster are fraught with various kinds of epistemological and social static. At first, we think that Ward is drawing our attention to the fact that meteorological data and state-generated directives are not equally clear, comprehensible, and actionable for *all* Gulf Coast citizens—that she is making us think about the economic and spatial underpinnings of the reception of knowledge and how the further you get from what Bruno Latour calls "centres of calculation," the less the knowledge made in that center makes sense.[2] But then, as we pay attention to the odd dialogue, we realize that Ward breaks up these statements to get us to attend to their inherent incompleteness: the experts' "projection of [the] storm" is, despite high-tech sensors and interactive screens, essentially "unclear." This whole anticipatory situation, both in the Batistes' house and at the TV station, is more "wishbone" than clear data stream.

I have begun with this scene from *Salvage the Bones* to introduce the central concern of this chapter, which is disaster communication—specifically, how novels can communicate knowledge about disaster after the fact while also teaching publics how to read future disasters for their inevitable complexity. Ward's novel provides my central example of how the novel genre represents an underappreciated resource for a critical public engagement with disaster. Novels do not merely entertain or only offer leisurely diversion from real life. Novels ask readers to inhabit a world, over a period of days or weeks, *as if it is real*. They ask readers to think as if they are other people, who certainly live in different bodies and very likely in a different condition, and who will certainly undergo some kind of crisis. They put readers in an experimental frame of mind, wondering: How will these conditions play out? Novels often make readers inhabit multiple characters' perspectives and produce a complex kind of knowledge out of this cognitive flexibility. Novelists wanting to represent disaster rely on the feature inherent in almost all narrative—a vexed turning point—but they scale that feature up. By doing so, the reader is asked not only to identify with an individual's crisis but to see (through lengthy narrative immersion) how that crisis is situated within a larger set of social and material problems. This capacity of the novel needs to be recognized. Novels are—and have long been—one of our best tools for getting a public to linger thoughtfully over how disasters feel and thus have a motivation to ask the more challenging abstract questions: Why did this disaster occur, and how could it have been prevented?[3] Scholars and professionals who take an exclusively technocratic or material or top-down approach to disaster management and disaster pedagogy should consider incorporating novels into their research, their teaching, and their public-facing work.

Scholars in the field of disaster studies have for many years been concerned with what they see as a problematic gap between official and experiential knowledge. Lars Clausen suggested in 1992 that there was a dangerous social and communicative separation between the "problem-solvers and problem-laymen," between those experts the state charges with addressing disasters and those with a more direct, bodily experience of them.[4] Claude Gilbert, writing in 1998, defined disaster as not only a "consequence of socio-structural risks" but also a "disorder triggered by communication problems."[5] Writing about the slow disaster of climate change, J. C. Gaillard has coined the term "climate gap" to draw attention to the ways that scientific and policy communities' adaptation planning neglects the "everyday concerns of vulnerable communities" and, in so doing, renders their own directives unheeded because unfeasible.[6] R. Dean Hardy and his colleagues have proposed the concept of a "racialized climate gap" in which the gap between the "palpability of race in everyday life and the absence of race in colorblind planning" undermines the usefulness or uptake of this planning. In particular, they argue, "local knowledge, [which is] often related through storytelling and 'everyday talk'" is little considered by the "technocratic approaches to climate change"; what results is a "disrupted knowledge network."[7] Whether in response to an unfolding disaster or in planning to mitigate future disasters, the goal is to create a knowledge network that operates in multiple directions with the smallest possible gaps in awareness and concern. Given that such networks might be only partially face to face and thus must extend through print and screen media, it is crucial to ask: How do various media modulate variant kinds of experience, knowledge, and discursive habits? Do certain media offer unique ways of bridging what I call the "disaster gap"?[8]

Disaster communication does not only involve technocratic experts, on the one hand, and lay people afflicted by or especially vulnerable to disaster, on the other. Because disasters are always to some extent the result of broad social structures, which cause an uneven distribution of risk, it is important to consider how a society communicates with itself in broader terms, beyond the expert/immediate victim polarity. It is important to think about how overlapping and conflicting publics do or might become aware of the "riskscape" in which they all variously live.[9]

To that end, communications and media theorists have debated the interrelationship among disaster, communication, and the health of a given society's public sphere. Some scholars argue that disasters bring out the power of the ordinary citizen to produce transformative knowledge. For example, Pantti and Wahl-Jorgensen, in a survey of the British coverage of man-made disasters in the second half of the twentieth century, found that while most of the time "ordinary people . . . tend to be represented as apolitical and passive spectators to a political drama over which they do not have any influence," disasters can by contrast allow non-elites to act as the "'primary definers' of the story of blame and accountability" as they "direct criticism at power holders in society," forming a "disaster citizenship" in which there is a "democratized systemic critique of complex social processes."[10] Other scholars and critics argue, on the contrary, that disaster coverage and the intense mass audiences it produces represent a deterioration of the modern public sphere. Many have taken the growing affinity—over the twentieth and twenty-first centuries—of mass media for disaster as a symptom that news has turned into mere spectacle. Jürgen Habermas argued in 1962 that the "critical publicity" that print had made possible for some two hundred years was being "supplanted by manipulative publicity," by news as a "staged display" that invited identification rather than deliberation. Disasters, in particular, he argued, had become more prominent, constituting "immediate reward news" that was "dressed up" as entertainment.[11] There is also a recognition that when large-scale disasters destabilize vast "imagined communities" (made up of strangers who have only a mediated relation to each other), the media coverage typically functions like a virtual ritual intended to cohere a public potentially divided by the political inequities implicit in the disaster.[12] The scholarly controversy surrounds whether such rituals reinforce an untenable status quo by their meaning monopoly that forestalls critical thought, *or* whether these mediated rituals of recovery can bring out in the open new kinds of witnesses.

Rob Nixon and Timothy Morton have recently urged us to consider how we might learn to perceive disasters, or disastrous planetary conditions, that do not manifest in a temporally and geographically limited event. Nixon points out that disasters that are slow to unfold or have invisible or lingering effects, or may be dispersed across space, are overlooked by the media, which crave fast, concentrated, and visually striking events to satisfy their attention-deficit audiences.[13] These audiences cannot deliberate (to use Habermas's term) about a disaster because they may not perceive it at all, or they may only perceive one stage or one visible aspect of a much broader and longer, diffuse "event." In a related way, Timothy Morton has argued that because our environmental challenges today—global warming, for example—are only detectable in their grand, distributed scope through "our advanced technology and measuring instruments" and through "statistical causality" but not as typically through direct bodily experience, we as a species have a new epistemological challenge: we need to learn how to recognize the inherent reality of these "hyperobjects" that our bodies cannot sense in full and that are only detectable through sophisticated mediation.[14] Moreover, this mediation—as our opening example of the weather expert attested—is not in itself perfect or perfectly predictive. Both Nixon and Morton then are urging us to invent forms of representation that make what is not directly perceptible, and never in fact fully knowable, feel as real as it is.

"Disaster gaps" can thus assume many forms. In order to bridge these gaps as well as possible, we need media that can linger long enough to trace indirect, slow, or structural causes and effects; that can turn the invisible into a sensed or credited reality; that can describe the outer world of matter and how it interacts with the inner world of thought and emotion and bodily response; that can be flexible enough to host a variety of knowledge modes and a multilogue of witnesses, including typically obscured witnesses; that can acknowledge the powers of both human and nonhuman actors in producing or alleviating danger; that refuse to foreclose these complex detective and deliberative processes for the sake of quick and flimsy social "repair"; that can draw out the shortening span of human attention; and thus, finally, can produce a healthy "disaster citizenship." The novel, I propose, is potentially one such media form. It can help readers imagine, and inhabit over time, others' material and psychological experience of risk and disaster. It can model a network that is diverse in knowledge, discourse, and even species. And it can take the closed history of a past event and open it up again, inviting the reader's own, in-the-moment vicarious modeling of outcomes.

To be sure, the novel's capacities on this front are under attack. The South Asian writer Amitav Ghosh has recently issued a pessimistic assessment of how well novels have, and can, represent disaster in his 2016 book, *The Great Derangement: Climate Change and the Unthinkable*. Ghosh asserts that though climate change represents a planetary existential crisis, it and its attendant disasters have not been addressed in what he calls "serious fiction," but only in what he takes to be fringe genres like sci-fi and fantasy. To explain why "catastrophism [has been] exiled to the margins" of the novel, he looks to the nineteenth-century realist tradition (represented by the likes of Jane Austen and Gustave Flaubert) and claims that, as the novel was defining its protocols in this time period, there was a "banishing of the improbable and the insertion of the everyday." In other words, the novel, as it initially made a bid with its reader for believability (i.e., practiced mimesis), favored "everyday" experience over and against the catastrophic (which he associated with the "improbable").[15] The nineteenth-century novel did this, Ghosh argues, because its writers and readers were immersed in a world newly governed by the sciences and institutions of *probability*.[16] Along with this inheritance of a normalizing everyday-ness, Ghosh adds, the novel is incapable of thinking through climate change in our own day because it focuses on the individual (rather than the collective) and the human (rather than the interaction of living species and nonhuman things), and scales down the universe to a local or national setting. The novel's unwavering habit, then, of making the world within its pages believable by banishing disaster has, given the threats posed by climate change, been "carried to the point of derangement."[17] Ghosh thus continues a long critical tradition, which includes the likes of Karl Marx, Georg Lukacs, and Michel Foucault, that has judged the realist novel to be a mystifying organ of Western bourgeois ideology and modern power.[18] The realist novel, this tradition asserts, is essentially complicit in harmful epistemologies that have baleful social consequences.

This critical tradition—and Ghosh in particular—keep us from seeing how the novel *can* make disaster "thinkable," and has done so, in fact, for three centuries. While I agree with Ghosh's urgent call to attend to our current modes of mediated, collective thinking about catastrophe, I do not share his pessimism about the novel form, nor do I agree with the literary historiography upon which it is based. Most egregious are his contentions that (1) disasters, being inherently improbable, do not coincide with the everyday; (2) the novel only knows how to make risk-saturated worlds seem *normal*; and (3) the novel necessarily scales down life to the human individual.

Disasters, as I have already explained, are often diffuse, slow, structural, or cyclical; they are not, in other words, actually walled off from everyday experience or the aforementioned "everyday concerns of vulnerable communities." For masses of people today, who for reasons of income, employment, sex, race, geography, or colonial history (or a combination thereof) are chronically exposed to hazards, probability and disaster are not at the opposite ends of a pole, but instead are at the same end of that pole. To appreciate how a population put disproportionately under risk endures it, understanding their everyday experience is crucial to that analysis. Second, a key twentieth-century aesthetic theory, from Russian writer Victor Shklovsky, argued that what art does is not normalize the world but rather "defamiliarize" what has become bland through cognitive routine. Shklovsky summarized the problem thus: "And so life is reckoned as nothing. Habitualization devours work, clothes, furniture, one's wife, and the fear of war." Therefore, he theorized, "art exists that one may recover the sensation of life; it exists to make one feel things, to make the stone stony."[19] Disasters have the capacity to do some of this defamiliarization themselves (as one's cityscape is covered in water, for example, or a well-known forest is reduced to char). In the case of disaster then, a novel could make use of that environmental defamiliarization to make readers consider in a new way a landscape they think they know. Moreover, disasters represent an especially destabilizing meeting of outer and inner world and hence have been fertile ground for novelists who want to explore how consciousness operates by making it operate under duress. Third, novelists have long acknowledged other life forces beyond the human.

A very brief history of the novel, then, can show not a banishing but rather a long and eager *hosting* of disaster. Indeed, one could argue that the novel learned how to operate *through* narrating disasters. As early as the sixteenth century, the word "catastrophe" indicated the "change or revolution which produces the conclusion or final event of a dramatic piece"; in other words, it indicated the alignment in the English imagination between narrative structure and situational reversals in the actual world.[20] Moreover, at that time the word "novel" referred to printed news ballads and tales. As Lennard J. Davis explains, these printed journalistic ballads were published to "inform the literate and illiterate lower classes of public events such as earthquakes, wars, murders, freaks of nature, and supernatural happenings."[21] The new technology of print made possible "the rapid and relatively instantaneous publication of matters of public interest," which, importantly, usurped royal and ecclesiastical channels. Because novelty and recentness was a premium, and because early modern cosmology made room for wonders and accidents, the early "novel" kept close company with that which was unexpected. What mattered was that an emerging, non-elite public could feel perceptually close in time and space to remarkable events. Expectations about facticity escalated in the later seventeenth century with the institutionalization of Baconian empiricism, including its emphasis on direct investigation aided by technologies like microscopy and telescopy, its dissemination in print of its findings, and the general popularity of the interconnected natural history and travel genres. Preternatural wonders became new facts. Meanwhile, the printed spiritual autobiography promised close readerly access to a true human interior, or what we would now call subjectivity. Internal, infinitesimal, and distant environments—all previously blocked from visibility—were made newly present and tangible through print. Print's ability to embody the elusive introduced the possibility that *only* in print would life feel thoroughly real.[22] The developing novel genre responded by incorporating these modern empirical energies and forms.

Catastrophism, then, was by no means "exiled to the margins" of the emerging genre. At the novel's beginning, readers could not yet have expected to find the calming experience of a "normal" probabilistic world contained in its pages. By contrast, because the Anglophone novel was born as part of a process by which previously inaccessible wonders were brought close for public scrutiny and pleasure, it contains at its core the power to persuade a mass public of novel material developments and to link these with individual characters' internal responses. Moreover, even as it came in the eighteenth century to embrace and avow the make-believe, or fictionality, the novel could retain the moral and cognitive weight of its early association with empiricism. Novels did not shape readers to credulity, but rather initiated them into an experimental milieu in which they decided what to credit.[23]

Daniel Defoe, for example—positioned by literary historians as one of the major Anglophone inventors of the novel form—helped experiment the novel into being *through disaster*, whether that was a tempest hitting London in *The Storm* (1704), a shipwreck off of the coast of South America in *Robinson Crusoe* (1719), or London's experience of the 1665 bubonic plague in *A Journal of the Plague Year* (1722). In his 1722 novel, we see Defoe moving away from the strictly journalistic compilation of others' accounts (as he does in *The Storm*) to a form that is more recognizably fictional. In particular, he invents an all-seeing ambulatory narrator (and supposed author) "H.F.," who allows Defoe, while tacitly in the genre of a "true history," to make a fifty-year-old, sprawling disaster seem as if it is suspensefully and coherently unfolding in real time right before the readers' eyes. H.F. claims to do so in order to "give the reader due ideas of the horror that everywhere presented itself."[24] The signal technique by which H.F. achieves this transfer of reality across time is by moving from the public streetscape to the private scenes of misery, from environment to psyche, and from data to sentiment, freely. Doors and windows represent those all-important barriers to both disease and information communication. It is H.F.'s ability to carry his readers *through* these apertures that helps them, in 1722, know this 1665 pandemic extensively and intimately. This capacity to help readers move across epistemic and affective registers while experiencing their motion *as if it is real* is a great achievement of the text. It is, too, a particular talent of the novel.

Working on the big, external, and environmental scale, H.F. repeatedly surveys the city amid unpredictable disease progression. Typical sentences include the following: "We perceived . . . the distemper to draw our way, viz., by the parishes of Clerkenwell, Cripplegate, Shoreditch, and Bishopsgate" and

"Cripplegate parish alone buried eight hundred and eighty-six" by "the second week in August."[25] One critic has called the novel "topographic" because it conveys the reader perpetually around the diseased cityscape: "pushing forward, pulling back, circling around . . . stalling, stopping, shifting sideways."[26] Moreover, H.F. reproduces within his text bills of mortality, orders by the Lord Mayor for the shutting up of houses, and other official documentation in order to give the reader a sense of what we might now call the biopolitical management of the crisis. Alternating with this topographic, demographic, or biopolitical mode, H.F. periodically investigates more singular, private scenes of misery by breeching the boundaries of the quarantine. To be precise, he assumes the perspective of various characters—doctors, watchmen, surviving family members—who penetrate these boundaries dividing public from private. By doing so, Defoe shows that a signal feature of this epidemic disaster is the turning inside out of spaces of refuge so that the most domestic spaces become the most exposed. While the fleeing king, court and Parliament experience nothing of this pandemic, and while the officials tallying deaths do not employ H.F.'s common-going ear and hence underestimate mortalities, H.F., the waftingly present man, never singular or apart but rather always "among," improves on the investigative powers of officialdom. H.F. tells the reader, "I know so many that perished [alone], and so exactly where, that I believe I could go to the very place and dig their bones up still." And "it was for want of people conversing one with another in this time of calamity" that no one knew "all the extraordinary cases that occurred in different families."[27] Living in a year of uncertainty, in which the latency of disease signs made knowing danger difficult, H.F. nevertheless presents himself as a universal witness to calamity. The ruling elites abandoned the people, and the municipal authorities, while capable, nonetheless lacked a common ear. This narrator, moving as he does "among" households, perpetually crossing public-private boundaries, constitutes himself and his *Journal* as a superior kind of disaster medium.

By extension, as Defoe is working out this new genre of the novel, he comes to understand—by representing this 1665 disaster—that the novel can be a key means by which the public knows itself and its risk environment. He does not make this world normal to achieve believability, but makes the true horror—the true but mostly hidden everyday experience of a strange, plagued city over a nine-month period—open for vicarious experience fifty years later. Following Defoe's early lead, Anglophone novelists continued to develop the novel's capacity to dwell over time in complex disasters: registering their complex causes and how they variously affect human perception and feeling. If we construe the centuries-long duration of US slavery, for example, as a slow disaster whose consequences are still being felt today, consider how a novel like *Uncle Tom's Cabin* (1851) surveyed the behaviors, mentalities, and experiences of a host of geographically, racially, and economically diverse participants in plantation life, offering readers not only a sentimental case for abolition but an analytically rigorous, virtual survey of the everyday world of a catastrophic institution that had been normalized. Even novels that have worked on the scale of the single family, or small community, tap into deep Western traditions of allegory, to encourage readers to scale up their inferences by seeing how a small group can stand for a big complex society. William Faulkner practiced this, for example, in his 1930 novel *As I Lay Dying*, a story he began writing the day of the 1929 stock market crash, two years after the Great Mississippi Flood of 1927, and a dozen years after World War I. As the reader encounters the members of the Bundren family, whose histories, subjectivities, and sensations the novel serially explores, she or he is asked to inhabit the outflow of these economic, environmental, and geopolitical catastrophes on the small, daily scale while inferring how the Bundrens represent a much larger region. The novel, in sum, has never banished disaster; on the contrary, it has been deeply curious to know what riskscapes feel like both materially and psychologically and to make its readers vicariously inhabit such experiences.

Salvage the Bones

I have so far proposed a series of conditions that need to be fulfilled by meaningful disaster communication and have argued, through Defoe, that the novel originated as a form capable of meeting these conditions. Now I demonstrate how the novel is still thriving as a disaster medium by examining Ward's 2011 *Salvage the Bones*. I also have in mind that if my reader is a teacher in the social sciences, she or he might feel encouraged to include a novel in any number of courses dealing with disaster. What follows would ideally work as a primer on interpreting contemporary disaster fiction in the classroom—and an implicit case for why this would be pedagogically useful.

Ward, an African American native of Delisle, Mississippi, a town in one of three coastal Mississippi counties hardest hit by Katrina, lived through the storm. As she explains, she and her family left her grandmother's flooding house, "were refused shelter by a white family, and took refuge in trucks in an open field." A few years after the hurricane, Ward chose to write about Katrina because she felt "dissatisfied with the way it had receded from public consciousness." As she attests, in order to do justice to her family's and her town's experiences, she summoned a combination of "narrative ruthlessness" and "hypnotiz[ing]" language.[28] In other words, she refused to grant her characters more shelter than she had witnessed being accessible to members of her community in late August 2005. What makes Ward's style distinct, though, is that she combines this unsparing, into-the-storm linear emplotment with a slow-paced, sense-driven, dilated form of description that is indeed hypnotizing. The reader must navigate the tension between the relentless approach of the storm, coming daily closer, and the deeply paused sensory world her language suspends one in.

One way to approach the novel is to compare its narrative and descriptive work to a piece of nonfiction prose, say, the National Hurricane Center's *Tropical Cyclone Report* about Katrina, especially the sections on coastal Mississippi, revised for the last time in 2011, the year Ward's novel was published. One might ask, calling to mind our earlier discussion of the "disaster gap": How does a reader know this disaster after reading the NHC's report, and how does a reader know it after reading *Salvage the Bones*? Can Ward's novel productively complement narratives produced by officialdom? How? The report begins: "Katrina was an extraordinarily powerful and deadly hurricane that carved a wide swath of catastrophic damage and inflicted large loss of life." True to this opening line, the most complex "character" in the report is Katrina the storm, the tropospheric phenomenon, its life out in the ocean, including its "complex genesis" in various Atlantic systems and how it dissipated and organized, received its name, and developed "an inner core." The authors go on to tell of Katrina's career on land in many parts of the Gulf, including its final act of touching down at the mouth of the Pearl River at the Louisiana/Mississippi border on August 29: how it brought a storm surge as high as 27.8 feet along about twenty miles of the Mississippi coast, which penetrated at least six miles inland. In the section "Casualty and Damage Statistics," we are told that 238 people died here and that "Katrina struck the Mississippi coastline with such ferocity that entire coastal communities were obliterated."[29]

It is hard for a humanist *not* to read various terms—"depression," "inner core," "ferocity," and "inflicted"—as describing the life history of a disturbed and aggressive person. Alternately, as an all-consuming supreme actor moving across the water, Katrina the "character" fits comfortably into multiple religions' typologies for their divinities. Even if one hears none of this personification or deification in the report's prose, one nonetheless must note that it is *Katrina's* evolution and career and agency that is primary in this story told by the NHC, and that the humans in its path are minor, aggregated players. The affordance of such a form of narration is that the workings of the troposphere can be appreciated in all their contingency and complexity. The limitation, however, is that "Katrina" does it all: carves, inflicts, destroys. There is no acknowledgment of how, and in what way, human action has primed these coastal Mississippi communities for "obliterat[ion]." And, of course, these "communities" remain an abstraction.

In Jesmyn Ward's novel, the central character, the one whose genesis, inner core, and career we follow, is her teenage, human narrator Esch. Unlike the authors of the report who zero in on Katrina, however, Ward places Esch within a thicker social network of actors: human, animal, mythical, and meteorological.[30] These actors are a father and brothers and family friends, but also her brother's pit bull China and China's litter of puppies, the mythical character she reads about (Medea), and memories of her mother, who died in childbirth. Katrina is also one of these actors, but one who only makes glancing appearances until the second to last day of the novel's action. In those first ten days, Ward's narrator Esch pulls us in close to her physical and emotional turbulence by making us vicariously feel her secret, new pregnancy. We watch Esch try to understand what being pregnant means, and what sustaining love requires, as she remembers her own mother, as she watches China deal with her pups, as she watches her brother care for his dog and her father begin to prepare the house for hurricane season. When Katrina makes landfall, we watch Esch incorporate Katrina into this network and make sense of the storm in relation to other potent, destructive mothers (against whom she ultimately defines herself).

The diurnal structure of the novel, combined with its densely descriptive language, immerses us in Esch's everyday experience before that experience is affected by disaster. We vicariously inhabit, through Esch's focalization, the "everyday concerns of [one] vulnerable communit[y]": how Esch copes with a new pregnancy without any female or professional health advice; how her brother tries to keep his fighting dog and her litter (who are also his livelihood) alive; how her other brother tries to win a basketball scholarship; how her father, who works at a scrapyard and has been a heavy drinker since his wife's death, salvages materials and resolves to prepare for the coming hurricane; and how the whole Batiste family struggles seemingly outside a cash economy and outside any state protections. Esch helps us feel the "palpability of race in everyday life" to a small extent through a scene or two of interracial contest but to a much greater extent through the intraracial culture of music, sport, food, talk, survival strategies, and the horizon of opportunities in Bois Sauvage.

We also come to know this rural family in its relation to the nonhuman world. Our understanding of the particular mesh of materiality in which the Batistes live is crucial to our appreciating their responses to the storm. Her father, lying under his truck trying to fix it for hauling, is part of that machine: "Daddy is a voice billowing from the bottom of the car like smoke." This truck "bulks over him like the rest of the detritus in the yard," as in "refrigerators rusted so that they look like devilled eggs sprinkled with paprika." Later, the father gets his hand badly "clenched" in a tractor-pulled wire so that "what was Daddy's middle, ring, and pinkie finger on his left hand are sheared off clean as fallen tree trunks." When she sees her father's bandaged hand in the hospital emergency room, "it looked like a webworm moth nest wound tight in a pecan tree."[31] These examples show how little the human is an isolated, controlling species in Esch's felt experience of Bois Sauvage. The human voice is a kind of machine exhaust, and the human hand is redesigned by machine power; these cyborgian forms themselves morph again into botanical and zoological ones: eggs, trees, insects. The human, to thrive, has to operate as best it can within the generative and degenerative powers of these other elements.

We see how "official knowledge" filters into their own decisions. In other words, we watch the Batistes respond to the "disaster gap." As the opening example showed, meteorological predictions about the course and force of Katrina were necessarily inexact. Compounding the issue of imprecise forecasts was the issue of the Batistes' old technology of reception: their antenna TV could only pick up fragmentary parts of the already incomplete information. Their old communications technology is part and parcel of the salvaged machine-scape in which they live, which is in turn an index of their limited economic resources. Class, Ward suggests, affects not only one's reception of (necessarily partial) expert knowledge but also one's ability to respond to that knowledge.

Added to this issue of the material underpinnings of a knowledge network is the issue of social trust. Her brother's friend, responding to news warnings of an approaching storm, suggests: "News don't know what they talking about." He makes this judgment by extrapolating out from how faulty the news media's social knowledge is: "Everytime somebody in Bois Sauvage get arrested, they always get the story wrong." Esch's brother counters: "That's journalists. Weatherman's a *scientist*." But, this brother adds, "There ain't even a tropical depression yet." The father ends the discussion by saying: "News is right: every week it's a new storm. . . . I can feel them coming."[32] We see in this scene how each of these three men takes up news-mediated meteorological prediction based on his own trust or mistrust of media and of science and his own experience of past hurricane seasons. The knowledge circuit is not an untroubled flow from storm to sensors to human message output to human message uptake to material response. There is socially inflected deliberation and materially vulnerable transmission all along the circuit.

Vicariously living with this family as the storm approaches gives the reader a means of understanding the nature of the choices people in Bois Sauvage actually have, and how they respond in something like real time. With no vehicle in operation and no money, the Batistes cannot evacuate. They can only use at-hand materials to reinforce their home against the storm. They call upon past experience, dating back to Hurricane Camille in 1969, to plan for looming circumstance. They attempt to incorporate mediated official predictions. On the day the hurricane strikes, the Batistes have gathered in their main house. They board up windows, assuming it is wind they need to defend themselves against, rather than water. But water begins to come through the ground floor: "*Why are my shorts wet?*" Esch wonders, "*Is it [the fetus] gone? Am I bleeding? . . . I stand. The floor underneath me is dark.*" In these moments, Esch interprets the material world from within the sensorium of her own body; she thinks she is bleeding out rather than that the Gulf Coast has surged and produced flooding all the way inland. Soon she sees that a lake has "swallowed the whole yard and is opening its jaw under the house."[33] The family ascends to the second story, then to the attic, then out onto the roof (a situation in fact typical of many residents of Harrison County responding to the storm and its twenty-some-foot surge). Once on the roof, they see that part of the deceased grandparents' empty house is still above water. If they venture off the edge of their roof, jump onto a "spreading oak tree," work their way along its branches, and jump again to this house, they might survive. These are their choices: to stay on the roof or make this dangerous crossing. They decide to cross. Soon enough, amid the crossing, when China the dog and Esch plunge into the water at the same time, her brother has to choose: Who is family? Whom do I save? How do I define love? He chooses his human sister over his canine familiar. All five Batistes survive, while the animal, mechanical, structural, and botanical world that has supported them is, at least temporarily, destroyed.

One of the reasons Ward wrote the novel, along with Katrina's slipping out of "public consciousness" in the years after the disaster, was that she was "angry at the people who blamed survivors for staying and for choosing to return to the Mississippi Gulf Coast after the storm."[34] This blame comes from the presumption that coastal inhabitants had clear and actionable choices and that they perversely chose not to act rationally. Watching the Batistes live through the ten days leading up to Katrina's landfall, we are given a sense of their lives as a negotiation of necessities, with almost no room for maneuvering. Slowly coming to inhabit this everyday world of necessity, we see what their choices amount to: these involve deciding who or what can be inside their extremely tight economy of care.

In conclusion, *Salvage the Bones* makes the Mississippi theater of Katrina thinkable. It takes that past-tense and passive-voice abstraction from the NHC's report—that "entire coastal communities were obliterated"—and opens up a slowly unfolding, historically informed, and complex situation. If, according to Shklovsky, "habitualization devours" our ability to closely perceive the world around us, then Ward's art exists to make the storm stormy—in its material and social and affective registers. It makes readers see how a character inhabits multiple riskscapes simultaneously—whether they involve reproductive health, occupational, or environmental vulnerability. It takes witnesses who, during Katrina coverage, were seen on TV screens from the distance of helicopter cameras, and brings them to what feels as close as one's own mind and body. As we hear Esch comparing China, Medea, and Katrina as maternal models, we see a human figuring out her condition by considering other life-forms and setting herself within deep time. We watch humans make decisions not at some Cartesian cognitive remove from matter, but by placing human chances within a vector of forces. We hear not only Esch's voice, but those of her family and community, as well as the transmitted voices of virtual authority, all of whom give us some room not only for identification but also for deliberation. Finally, by Ward's combination of dilated description and compulsive linear directionality, the reader, drawn on by slow suspense, extends her powers of attention. Given that *Salvage the Bones* was both the winner of the National Book Award in 2011 and a national best seller, it earned a wide readership and one that will endure. Ward's novel has contributed in a positive way to what Mervi Katriina Pantti and Karin Wahl-Jorgensen call our "disaster citizenship." By getting readers to feel how someone else's everyday riskscape allows for disaster, it makes possible "democratized systemic critique of complex social processes."[35]

The scientists who wrote the official Katrina report did not know the disaster the way a novelist can, which is the way we all must. That report only measured the meteorological component of Katrina, whereas a novel can move from meteorology to zoology to history to psychology, and if it's good, keep the reader nimbly moving between and connecting these registers. Disaster scholars and managers need to cultivate a similar capacity and flexibility of attention if they want to address the "disaster gap." The technocratic view of disasters fails to adequately understand what is disastrous about them; therefore, it offers weak protection, a flimsy guide to mitigating or forestalling its harms, and a mode of analysis that lacks sufficient explanatory power. The novel, by contrast, is capacious: it is a genre that attends to the chronic, the grinding, the cyclically traumatic across a group of people, and so is by definition social and political. In other words, novels engender critical disasters studies' understanding of what a disaster is.

CHAPTER 9

The Tōkai Earthquake and
Changing Lexicons of Risk

Kerry Smith

Two of the central tenets of Japan's disaster prevention strategy over the last forty years have been that a major and potentially devastating earthquake would soon strike Japan's Tōkai district, and that scientists would know ahead of time when that earthquake was imminent.[1] Both of these beliefs were woven into a remarkable piece of legislation, the 1978 Large-Scale Earthquakes Countermeasures Act (LECA) (Daikibō jishin taisaku tokubetsu sōchihō), and subsequently had a powerful influence on popular conceptions of the nature of the risks Japan faced, the role the earth sciences might play in mitigating those risks, and how resources to protect against an earthquake disaster were allocated. The government has directed more of its seismic retrofitting and other disaster-prevention funding to the Tōkai District than to anywhere else in the country. Funding for seismology in Japan and for research into earthquake prediction in particular has for many years also skewed heavily toward projects tied one way or another to the prospects of a Tōkai earthquake.[2] Most visibly for average Japanese, the country's annual Disaster Prevention Day exercises have since 1978 featured elaborate scenarios in which a team of seismologists "predicts" that the Tōkai earthquake is about to occur, prompting the prime minister to issue a mock declaration of emergency and sending citizens to gather their emergency gear and wait for an earthquake that—thankfully—has not yet come.

In the forty years since the Tōkai earthquake took center stage in Japan's anti-disaster planning efforts, neither of its central tenets has held up all that well. Japan has suffered through a number of catastrophic earthquakes since 1978—the 1995 Hanshin-Awaji earthquake, which killed more than six thousand people, the 2011 Great Eastern Japan earthquake, which left some twenty thousand dead or missing, and the 2016 Kumamoto earthquakes (fifty killed)—but none of them occurred within or in close proximity to the Tōkai region. The fault movements responsible for those events were not directly related to the ones government experts had been so closely monitoring since the late 1970s, and the communities devastated in those earthquakes had not been eligible for the disaster prevention programs and other investments in hazard reduction that were commonplace in Shizuoka, Gifu, and the other prefectures designated as at risk because of the Tōkai earthquake threat. The government's and its scientific establishment's unflinching focus on that one region has in retrospect come to seem misguided.

The assumption that diligent monitoring would allow Japanese seismologists to issue reliable warnings days or hours before the Tōkai earthquake struck has proven to be even more problematic. In the late 1970s, enthusiasm for short-term earthquake prediction was widespread in the earth sciences, not just among scientists in Japan but also among those in the United States, the USSR, and China. Researchers were excited by news of apparently successful cases of prediction and filled with growing confidence that the field would soon have the capacity to systematically identify earthquake precursors. As discussed later, scientists and policymakers in Japan may have embraced prediction's potential earlier and more enthusiastically than their counterparts elsewhere, but it seemed only a matter of time before other countries would follow suit.

We now know, of course, that they did not. Despite the sense that breakthroughs were just around the corner, none appeared, and by the end of the 1980s most researchers outside of Japan were stepping well back from their earlier expressions of confidence in prediction's future.[3] In Japan, however, the passage of the LECA and the subsequent hardening of a monitoring and research infrastructure focused on the detection of earthquake precursors meant that short-term prediction remained in the mainstream of earth sciences research programs and research budgets long after it had been relegated to sideshow status elsewhere. The Japanese government has only just begun to acknowledge that short-term earthquake prediction appears to be impossible.[4] That admission had been sought by critics of Japan's prediction research regime for years but was fiercely resisted until late in 2017, when a spokesman for the committee charged with reviewing the country's preparedness for another earthquake disaster stated unequivocally that "there was at present no scientific method to forecast when, where, or at what magnitude an earthquake will occur."[5] It is not yet clear what impact, if any, this admission will have on the LECA and the assurances it offered.

This chapter is an attempt to show how the idea of a Tōkai earthquake—by which I mean the consensus that one was likely, a common definition of the hazards associated with it, and some degree of belief in its predictability—came to be. Highlighting how those conclusions were reached, and by whom, brings us closer to an explanation for Japan's unusual research and disaster-prevention policy trajectories over the past several decades. It is also an opportunity to take up a version of Deborah Lupton's intriguing question, "How are risks constructed as social facts?," in three different contexts.[6] The first focuses on the scientists who "discovered" the Tōkai earthquake and explained what it was to the public; the second looks at the role of expert knowledge and imagination in helping people picture a disaster that hadn't happened yet. The third and final section explores the entanglement between short-term earthquake prediction and the search for solutions to the Tōkai earthquake.

As particular as these contexts might be to developments unique to Japan in the 1960s and 1970s, Japanese earth scientists were active participants in a global scientific community at this point and regularly consulted with and were consulted by their counterparts in the United States and elsewhere. Japan was also just one of the places where fears of future catastrophes were taking shape alongside the growth of government-funded "big science" and the emergence of experts and institutions devoted to disaster mitigation. In Japan the focus was on earthquakes, and on one earthquake in particular, but as Lee Clarke, Scott Knowles, and other scholars have shown, the anticipation of future disasters and the belief that experts would be able to manage their worst effects are among the defining features of the latter half of the twentieth century.[7]

Discovering the Tōkai Earthquake

The phrase "Tōkai earthquake" as shorthand for a specific very large seismic event didn't come into common use until late in the 1970s. Scientists and the media before then would have been more likely to refer to an event off the Tōkai coast as the "Enshūnada earthquake," after the region of the Pacific where such an event was expected to originate, and where its potential to do harm would be greatest. Prior to 1976, there was no consensus in the field that an earthquake off that particular segment of the Japanese coastline was necessarily more worrisome than any of the others scientists might imagine happening soon.[8] No reasonable seismologist would suggest that there was nothing to be worried about—this was Japan, after all—but here too it wasn't until fairly late in the 1970s that there was widespread agreement that the Tōkai district was indeed at risk in ways that other parts of Japan were not.

One reason experts would not have ruled out the possibility of a major earthquake off the coast of the Tōkai district was that many had occurred there in the past. Historical records revealed evidence from as early as the seventh century of communities damaged by offshore earthquakes not just in the Tōkai region, but extending further along the Pacific coast into the Kansai district and Shikoku island as well. Many of the most destructive earthquakes in Japan's more recent history—including the Hōei (1707, M8.4), Ansei-Tōkai (1854, M8.4), Ansei-Nankai (1854, M8.4), Tōnankai (1944, M8.1), and Nankaidō (1946, M8.1) earthquakes—had originated deep beneath the ocean floor along a rough line that ran for many hundreds of kilometers, all in the vicinity of the Nankai Trough.[9]

The Japanese earth sciences community had been quick to embrace plate tectonics and its implications for the study of earthquakes, and by the early 1970s they understood that the Nankai Trough was the product of the ongoing subduction of the Philippine plate beneath the Eurasian continental plate.[10] They also realized that the frequent massive earthquakes in the area were themselves products of the subduction process.[11] The movement of the Philippine plate under Japan at the edge of the continental plate was inexorable but not always smooth; scientists pictured parts of the former "stuck" beneath the latter, locked in place until that segment of the subduction zone ruptured, releasing all its stored energy at once. Plate tectonics gave scientists insights into why the earthquakes originating in those boundary zones were often very large, and why they tended to happen with some regularity.

In mid-1973 Andō Masataka, a graduate student in geophysics at the University of Tokyo (Tōdai), added an important layer to the field's understanding of seismicity along the Nankai Trough, which was to show that the fault region along the trough appeared to be made up of "four parts, A, B, C and D from west to east, which are more or less decoupled mechanically from each other." Andō's dissertation research suggested that each of these four segments could rupture independently of the others, and that they could also slip together in blocks.[12] In 1707, according to Andō, all four segments moved more or less simultaneously, resulting in the massive Hōei earthquake. In

1854 the A-B and C-D segments ruptured separately from each other, but as in 1707 all the energy that had accumulated along those four segments appears to have been released. In 1944 and 1946, however, Andō showed that only three of the four segments had behaved as expected. Where segment D's earthquake should have been, assuming that the previous patterns were still relevant, there was only a worrying "seismic gap."[13] If previous patterns held, then at some point in the relatively near term Japan could expect an earthquake somewhere along segment D. Andō suggested that it would be a powerful and potentially destructive one when it happened.[14] At the time, his colleagues were skeptical and pushed back against the likelihood of an earthquake like the one Andō was describing.[15] No alarms were raised, and public interest was minimal.

The discovery that transformed the Enshūnada earthquake from a relatively minor threat into something potentially catastrophic built directly on Andō's work. In 1976 Ishibashi Katsuhiko was just a few years behind Andō at Tōdai. His own research had little directly to do with the Nankai Trough, and his initial interest in the discussions around Andō's findings was casual at best. It nevertheless occurred to Ishibashi that many of the inconsistencies in Andō's analyses of how the trough's different segments worked could be resolved with a relatively minor adjustment to his assumptions about how the fault zone behaved. Andō had categorically stated that the faulting sector did not extend into Suruga Bay, that its boundaries were well offshore. On a hunch, Ishibashi started poring over historical records from communities along the bay looking for reports of damage around the time of the powerful earthquakes in 1707, 1854, and the more recent ones in the 1940s. What he discovered, to his and apparently everyone else's surprise, was convincing evidence that the fault zone had indeed extended well into Suruga Bay in 1707 and 1854. The scale of the damage described in those local records was too extensive to have been caused by anything but a large-scale rupture extending into the bay. What that meant, in turn, was that there were good reasons to think that an Enshūnada earthquake would not be nearly as benign as originally hoped. If the "missing" segment ruptured in ways that mimicked earlier patterns, then the number of cities and towns in Shizuoka Prefecture and points north and east that would be at risk of sustaining catastrophic damage was much higher than previously thought. A magnitude 8 earthquake within Suruga Bay would leave tremendous devastation in its wake.

Much as Andō had done, Ishibashi shared his findings first with his advisers and a handful of senior scientists, and only after they agreed that he might be on to something did he begin to present his work to the field's other gate-keepers. The Coordinating Committee on Earthquake Prediction (CCEP) reviewed his conclusions in May 1976, and again in August.[16] The field as a whole had the opportunity to hear from him at the Japanese Seismological Society's annual conference in October. In each of those encounters, and in others that followed, Ishibashi's methods and findings held up well under scrutiny. His conclusions seemed sound.

Ishibashi also reached out to a broader audience. In September he appeared before a packed auditorium in Numazu City, where he spoke publicly about his discovery and its implications; other appearances followed.[17] At first, only media outlets in Shizuoka were interested in the story, but by October Ishibashi's warning was national news. By early November he had been on television a half dozen times and had at least that many magazine and newspaper articles in the pipeline for publication.[18] One aspect of the potential quake that Andō had not emphasized but Ishibashi and other scientists did was its timing, and that too would have made it a more pressing topic for many. At his lecture in Numazu, Ishibashi said, "It wouldn't be a surprise at all if it were to happen within the next 2–3 years, but it could just as well be 20 or 30 years from now."[19] In other settings he remarked that it wouldn't be a surprise if it happened tomorrow. His mentor, Asada Toshi, used similar language to express the same idea during Diet testimony in October. In both instances, and especially in Asada's case, the media emphasized the likelihood of it happening sooner rather than later. A phrase attributed to Asada, "It wouldn't be at all strange if it happened tomorrow," entered the public lexicon for discussing a Tōkai earthquake almost as soon as it left his lips. Papers the next morning reported what Asada had said, some at length; the *Asahi* called it a "shocking assessment."[20]

By the end of 1976, then, Andō's observation that there was a seismic gap where an Enshūnada earthquake ought to have been, and Ishibashi's discovery that the "missing" earthquake had more implications for the coast than originally thought, had both been vetted by other Japanese earth scientists. The fact that both Andō and Ishibashi were products of Japan's most prestigious university, Tōdai, almost certainly helped give their ideas credibility, but so too did the process of subjecting their work to review through channels that other scientists policed. Had either of the young researchers gone directly to the media with their concerns before that process was nearly complete, for example, their findings would almost certainly have been subject to the field's leaders' almost instinctive reaction to claims that risked ratcheting up public anxiety, which would have been to downplay their significance.[21] Instead, what happened in this instance is that the public learned about the possibility of a powerful Tōkai earthquake in the very near future at about the same time that the earth sciences community was coming to the conclusion that worrying about it might be an appropriate response.

Making the Disaster Legible

Part of explaining to the public and to policymakers that a Tōkai earthquake would be a disaster was making the hazards associated with it legible to them. Andō and others had mapped out where the seismic intensity would be most severe in the event of an Enshūnanda earthquake, for example, and how high the tsunami that accompanied it might be at different points along the coast.[22] Ishibashi's discovery meant that those estimates would have to be modified, but this was work that Japanese earth scientists already knew how to do well.

Echoes of the precision and objectivity of the seismologists' perspective on how the Tōkai earthquake would be experienced are also evident as damage and casualty studies for specific locales began to surface. Such reports estimated the number of deaths and injuries that experts calculated would result from the earthquake, the scale of the property damage, long-term economic impacts, and so on. The Tokyo Metropolitan Fire Department had been using metrics like these since the early 1960s to model possible catastrophes in the capital city.[23] It was therefore not much of a conceptual leap to begin using the same methods and categories to describe the harm the Tōkai earthquake could do in Shizuoka's major cities and elsewhere in the region. In an early 1978 appeal to legislators for help protecting his prefecture against the coming quake, for example, Governor Yamamoto Keizaburō of Shizuoka shared what he said were experts' recent estimates of how much damage an M8-class Tōkai earthquake would do. He had been told, he said, to expect that one hundred thousand homes would be flattened, and that a fifth of the prefecture's population (or around six hundred thousand people) would be harmed in one way or another as a direct result of the earthquake. Sixteen thousand citizens would be badly injured and another ten thousand killed. In light of these facts, what he needed legislators to also understand, Yamamoto pleaded with his audience, was that those estimates reflected only the initial effects of the earthquake. None of the secondary hazards had been factored in. "Fires were not included, and neither was tsunami damage. The Shinkansen, expressways and the like—none of that was included. . . . Please, I ask you to fix in your minds that the damage will be widespread and severe."[24]

In the lead-up to the government's decision to respond to Yamamoto's pleas for help and do something about the looming threat to the nation, ideas about what a Tōkai earthquake would be like came in at least two other formats of interest to us. In one, the mainstream media provided a steady stream of often richly detailed depictions of the hypothetical destruction of one or more Japanese cities. Tokyo was the usual target, but its vulnerabilities were easily translated to other locales. The *Yomiuri* newspaper's fourteen-part "Magunichūdo (Magnitude) 7.5" article series in 1970, for example, highlighted the many ways that the city's new infrastructure and sophistication created new hazards on top of old ones.[25] NHK contributed *Prepare for an Earthquake: Your Disaster-Prevention Countermeasures* the following year.[26] Part disaster preparedness primer, *Prepare* also turns to fiction to tell the stories of two families before, during, and after an earthquake that devastates Tokyo. Through their experiences, readers run a gauntlet of hazards—fire, floods, collapsing buildings, explosions—each described in vivid detail, but are never directly confronted with the death of any of the individuals at the center of the narratives. A reader could decide that everyone in both families survived in the end, or that none of them did. Leaving open the possibility of survival is in keeping with some of the broader messages of works like *Prepare*, which called attention both to potential hazards and to the steps that society might take to mitigate some of their worst effects.[27]

On an even more speculative front, Komatsu Sakyō's novel *Japan Sinks* (*Nihon Chinbotsu*) was a best seller when it came out in 1973; the (first) movie based on the book was released later that same year, and it too was a big success.[28] *Japan Sinks* predates the national focus on the Tōkai earthquake, it did not focus on events in that district, and it is unlikely that many people mistook the story's premise—that changes in the mantle's convection patterns would cause the whole country to disappear beneath the waves, but not before it suffered violent earthquakes, tsunamis, volcanic eruptions, and so on—for anything other than the pseudoscientific plot device that it was. That said, the book and the film both relied on already familiar scenarios in their depictions of what powerful earthquakes would do to modern Japanese cities. By familiar I mean that the earthquake hazards *Japan Sinks* chose to highlight were more or less the same as the ones that government experts and the press had at that point been warning city dwellers about for years: massive fires in crowded residential areas, showers of broken glass and debris falling from swaying skyscrapers, flooded subway lines; the list goes on. In other words, *Japan Sinks* destroyed Tokyo (and ultimately other cities as well) in ways that closely echoed official narratives of how such an event might unfold. The film's state-of-the-art special effects showed audiences for the first time what it might be like to witness the effects of a powerful earthquake in an urban setting, but it did so using a vocabulary that already had a long history in 1973. That same vocabulary and the same scenarios were also central to portrayals—official and otherwise—of what the country could expect when the Tōkai earthquake finally arrived.

One final category of ideas for thinking about a Tōkai disaster came from two actual earthquakes. The first was the M6.5 San Fernando earthquake of February 9, 1971. Japanese survey teams had good news and bad news when they returned with their reports on that event. They noted, for example, that building standards in Japan were generally more rigorous than those in California, and that Japanese highways and bridges subject to the same forces that had been so destructive in Los Angeles would likely have been left intact.[29] But they were also quick to emphasize that however good Japanese engineering might be, an earthquake as powerful as the one that had rocked LA would still have done serious, widespread damage. Southern California's relatively firm surface geology, the good coordination and communication among the different medical and rescue efforts that followed the event, and LA's sprawl had all helped keep casualties to a minimum, but none of those factors were necessarily relevant to city dwellers in Japan.[30] The more experts and average citizens alike learned about what had happened in LA, the more reasons they had to worry about their own circumstances.

The second earthquake was closer to home. The January 14, 1978, Izu-Oshima earthquake originated under the ocean floor roughly ten kilometers off the eastern shore of the Izu Peninsula. It was a powerful (M7), shallow earthquake. The landslides, train derailments, and building collapses it caused left more than two dozen dead and hundreds injured. It also highlighted uncomfortable realities about the state's ability to prepare for and respond to major seismic events. The Japan Meteorological Agency (JMA) had been monitoring unusual seismic activity offshore and had cautioned about the possibility of an earthquake at some point. Those warnings were muted, in part because there was no way for the JMA's experts to know for sure that they were observing precursors to a major rupture. More important, seismologists were at the time working on the assumption that any earthquake to come out of that fault structure would be M6 at most. There were good reasons to believe this would be so, and since an M6 earthquake in that area would likely not cause significant damage on the peninsula or elsewhere along the coast, the JMA's announcement that morning stated merely: "A moderately large earthquake, capable of giving rise to slight damage, may occur shortly."[31] Residents of the islands near the ongoing seismic activity took notice, but very few people in Izu or elsewhere in Shizuoka appeared to have done so.[32] Had they been better prepared, it is possible that the number of deaths and injuries would have been reduced.

Before the Izu-Oshima earthquake, little progress had been made toward a comprehensive earthquake disaster law for the Tōkai district. The pace picked up significantly afterward, and it wouldn't be going too far out on a limb to suggest that the LECA came when it did, and looked like it did, at least in part because of the congruities between the shortfalls in the government's capabilities that the earthquake highlighted and the problems the new law was supposed to address. There is also Governor Yamamoto's role to consider, and how the January earthquake provided him with a platform he might not have had otherwise. He was quick to turn invitations to the Diet to talk about the last earthquake in his prefecture into an opportunity to remind his audiences of the larger threat still waiting in the wings, and to lobby for the new law.

Predicting the Tōkai Earthquake

Part of what made Japan's policy response to the threat of a Tōkai earthquake disaster so unusual is that it took the successful short-term prediction of that event as a given. The most significant interventions the LECA authorized—the mandatory evacuation of public spaces, restrictions on road and rail traffic, emergency price and banking controls, and so on—were all designed to go into effect only after scientists agreed that an earthquake was imminent. This section points out some of the factors that brought together short-term prediction and the nation's response to a Tōkai earthquake.

For most of the twentieth century, Japanese seismology had avoided providing any formal institutional support to research into earthquake prediction. So had seismologists just about everywhere else; there was nothing unusual about the reluctance of the field's leaders in Japan to allocate attention or resources to prediction.[33] Attitudes in Japan began to shift in the early 1960s with the formation of a working group of prominent scientists and the production of a "blueprint" for earthquake prediction research.[34] The latter explained why the time was ripe to take a close look at earthquake prediction, not because the group were sure it could be done but because they were no longer certain that it could not. A better grasp on earthquake mechanisms and access to better instrumentation were among the factors that led the blueprint's authors to propose an initial ten-year research project, the purpose of which would be to determine whether or not earthquake prediction was worth pursuing in earnest. In other words, at the end of that initial ten years of work, the seismologists involved expected to know whether more research and effort could in theory allow them to one day predict earthquakes, or whether they should focus their efforts elsewhere. What they did not do was promise that in ten years they'd be able to predict earthquakes.

Ishibashi Katsuhiko's warning about a Tōkai earthquake came just over a decade after the blueprint's release. By then attitudes toward prediction were far more optimistic than they had been in 1965. This was not just the case in Japan. In the United States, the Soviet Union, and elsewhere mainstream scientists spoke of earthquake prediction as almost within reach; scientists in the People's Republic of China went one better and pointed to the evacuation warning issued shortly before the 1975 Haicheng earthquake—no doubt saving many lives—as an example of prediction in practice.[35] Enthusiasm for short-term earthquake prediction among scientists worldwide was arguably at its peak just as the implications of the next Tōkai earthquake were coming into focus in Japan.

There, research into earthquake prediction had morphed into a semi-official undertaking involving the nation's universities, a conglomeration of government agencies, and funding to keep the project afloat. In 1969, the Coordinating Committee for Earthquake Prediction (CCEP) (Jishin yochi renrakukai) was set up to encourage researchers to share information and resources and to help steer funding where it was needed most. The CCEP also involved itself in designating parts of Japan known to have had powerful earthquakes in the past, and believed to be capable of producing ones in the near future, for different degrees of enhanced seismological surveillance. By 1978 it had identified eight zones as places to be monitored especially closely. The Tōkai district was one of them.[36] The logic behind the monitoring was that among scientists doing earthquake prediction research, it was widely believed that measurable physical changes in the earth's crust would precede a major seismic event. Those changes could take many different forms. They might become legible as deformations at the surface, as increased stress or pressure at different locations in the crust, in the detection of unusual levels of radon in groundwater, and so on. There was no single marker that

scientists agreed was the equivalent of the smoking gun of short-term prediction, but many did think that the lead-up to an event as violent and powerful
as a major earthquake must be accompanied by precursory signs. Monitoring
areas known to have produced major earthquakes in the past gave seismologists a chance to watch for anomalous developments; if they were lucky they
might spot the changes before the earthquake they foretold actually occurred.
If they were less lucky, and the earthquake happened before they had been
able to spot any precursory signals, they could still review the monitoring
data after the fact, hopefully spot the anomaly, and thus come away with a
much better sense of what to be on the lookout for in the future.

In the six months or so between the Izu-Oshima earthquake and the passage of the LECA, many of the leading figures in prediction research met
with the legislative committees considering how to respond to the Tōkai
earthquake threat. On balance, the scientists who knew the field best offered
what can only be described as quite conservative assessments of short-term
prediction's capabilities (at least in their on-the-record statements). There
were gradations of optimism within that cohort, naturally, but Asada Toshi's
comments before legislators in April 1978 capture some of the nuances of
the explanations he and his colleagues provided that spring. In the following
quotation, he was responding to a question about the network of instruments
monitoring the Tōkai district and whether it would provide sufficient warning before an earthquake. "For the Tōkai area, it depends entirely on how
it unfolds," Asada replied. "If through chance a sufficiently large precursory
sign appears over a sufficiently wide area, then I think it might be possible
to say that something would happen in 10 hours or so with a good degree of
accuracy." "But this is our first time doing this," he went on to say, "and we
don't know what to expect, so we have to make every possible preparation.
We also need to expand the network beyond the Tōkai district and get all the
experience we can there as well."[37]

He and his colleagues were generally consistent in suggesting to legislators that a short-term prediction might be possible, but only under exactly the
right circumstances and even then only if they were very, very lucky. Government spokesmen for the Land Agency and the Japan Meteorological Agency
had historically also been reasonably cautious in their public statements
about prediction's prospects, but their position changed once discussions of
the LECA were under way in the Diet in 1978. The shift was in some ways a
subtle one, in that the agency technocrats never directly contradicted what
the scientists had been saying about the limits to prediction's capabilities;

legislators were never forced to choose between one set of experts' conclusions and another's. Agency spokesmen avoided the appearance of disagreement with their university colleagues by focusing their much more optimistic assessments of what prediction could accomplish on scenarios that Asada and the other scientists had never taken up in their appearances before legislative committees in the Diet.

What officials like the Land Agency's director Sakurauchi Yoshio and the JMA's Suehiro Shigeshi did was to suggest that even if scientists were still a long way away from being able to predict most earthquakes, the Tōkai earthquake was different in at least two important ways. First, there seemed to be general agreement that a Tōkai earthquake could be an immensely powerful one, quite possibly an M8-level event. Second, the district was already home to networks of instrumentation thought to be sensitive enough to detect the sort of surface deformations or other anomalies that would surely precede an M8 event. The historical record implied that the only other part of Japan where an earthquake of such power was likely to originate was under the sea-floor off Japan's northeast coast, where regular monitoring was difficult if not impossible. In other words, Sakurauchi, Suehiro, and their fellow technocrats argued that because the Tōkai earthquake was likely to be an M8-class event, and because the precursory signs that would appear in the lead-up to such an event were detectable with existing instrumentation, they were confident they that would be able to provide the short-term prediction the Large-Scale Earthquake Countermeasures Act (LECA) required. At the same time, they avoided entirely questions about the predictability of other potentially destructive earthquakes in Japan, since the conditions that allowed them to speak with such confidence about the Tōkai district were relevant nowhere else. Variations on this argument were repeated over and over again in response to legislators' questions as the LECA made its way through parliament. Not everyone was convinced by the assurances Suehiro and others offered—representatives from the Japan Communist Party were among the act's most consistent and astute critics—but with the support of the ruling Liberal Democratic Party behind it the act had passed both houses of parliament by early June 1978.

The gap between what earth scientists like Asada were saying and what technocrats like Suehiro were suggesting may not have seemed that wide to legislators, but the differences were actually quite significant. Under the LECA, the main mechanisms for mitigating harm from a Tōkai earthquake relied on scientists' ability to warn the government that one was imminent. The act made it possible for the prime minister to order a wide range of preemptive interventions—evacuations of public buildings, the closure of highways, and prohibitions on travel by rail, for example—but none of these steps could be taken unless the scientists appointed to monitor anomalous developments in the region concluded that the earthquake they had all been waiting for was about to take place. One of the scientists who later led the committee tasked with assessing the data from the Tōkai district suggested that he, Asada, and the other university scientists hadn't known about the assurances Suehiro and the other technocrats offered legislators in 1978, and that he himself was shocked when he realized much later how wide the disconnect was between what legislators had come to believe about prediction and what he (and his colleagues) knew to be true. By then, it was far too late to revisit the act's premises.[38]

Over the next forty years, the official position of the Japanese government was that a destructive Tōkai earthquake could happen at any time, and that scientists would alert the nation before it did. The district's residents, and indeed the nation as a whole, were regularly reminded to be ready for the disaster to come and for the warnings that would precede it. Both premises—that a Tōkai earthquake was likely to occur soon and that it could be predicted before it struck—were targets of intense criticism from within the Japanese earth sciences community beginning in the early 1990s. Neither position has been entirely abandoned by policymakers. In late 2017, Japan's Central Disaster Management Council (Chūō bōsai kaigi) did acknowledge that "there was at present no scientific method to forecast when, where, or at what magnitude an earthquake will occur."[39] The LECA remains in force despite this admission, and officials have not entirely ruled out the possibility that scientists might still get lucky and issue a warning of some kind. As more time has passed since the last major event along the Nankai Trough, government agencies have begun to argue that the real threat is no longer confined to the Tōkai district. It consists instead, they say, of a future Nankai Trough mega-earthquake, involving not just one segment of that fault zone but several, and possibly all of them at once. The slow disaster that was the Tōkai earthquake hasn't ended so much as it has been reimagined on an even larger scale.

Conclusion

One argument to be made about how the Tōkai earthquake disaster was "constructed as social fact," to again borrow Lupton's phrase, is that it was the product of unique circumstances, a one-off event, and therefore not so useful for thinking about anticipatory modes of preparedness anywhere else. Had Ishibashi's discovery not been followed as quickly as it was by the Izu-Oshima earthquake, for example, would the Tōkai earthquake have taken on the salience it did after 1978? Would Shizuoka's residents have endured forty years of worry and Disaster Prevention Day drills had enthusiasm for short-term earthquake prediction not peaked when it did and provided a way forward for policymakers? So much about the process that made this disaster Japan's most legible and present, for so long, seems idiosyncratic to that moment in the country's history.

A more productive approach to thinking about the construction of the Tōkai earthquake disaster, on the other hand, would be to point out some of the ways that it reflects processes that up to this point have largely been discussed only in Western contexts. Japan's pursuit of short-term earthquake prediction is one example. To the extent that deterministic earthquake prediction research in Japan is touched on at all in the English-language scholarship, it tends to focus on Japanese scientists' anachronistic attachment to it long after almost all of prediction's earlier proponents had given up. Less often acknowledged is the role new government funding mechanisms for research and the advent of "big science" in the 1950s and 1960s played in shaping Japanese research agendas, including those in the earth sciences. The state's ability to channel scientists and their work toward projects it deemed politically expedient in that era is perhaps best demonstrated by Japan's headlong rush to begin its own nuclear energy program, but seismologists too found themselves emphasizing the immediate, practical benefits of their research in order to win government funding.[40] There are potentially interesting commonalities here as well with the rise of Cold War funding programs for science in the West.[41]

Similarly, and thanks to Scott Knowles, we know a good deal about the rise of disaster science and "disaster experts" in the United States and the contexts in which they emerged.[42] Knowledge production related to disasters and disaster prevention in Japan, and the institutionalization of expertise in those fields, look a lot like the processes that Knowles described. In Japan, the experts and expressions of expertise came into their own by the end of the 1960s, just in time to help shape the public's understanding of what a Tōkai earthquake disaster was. I wouldn't want to suggest that disaster experts in the United States and Japan played identical roles or that they arose simultaneously, but here too there are intriguing institutional and epistemological parallels to think about. Japanese scientists and policymakers drew on

American studies of the potential economic and social implications of earthquake prediction, for example, and the mid-1970s burst of enthusiasm in the United States for research into short-term prediction was fueled in part by developments in Japan around the same time. As unique as the circumstances surrounding the Tōkai earthquake were, scientists and experts in Japan were hardly the only ones for whom the capacity to imagine, and possibly predict, future disasters was becoming an increasingly pressing concern.

Finally, a word about the Large-Scale Earthquake Countermeasures Act. Some of its provisions—its presumption that short-term earthquake prediction worked, its convoluted distribution of responsibility, its focus on "just-in-time" disaster prevention, and so on—are unlikely to find direct counterparts elsewhere. If we were to step back a bit and consider the broader functions that the act performed in 1978, however, then it's hard not to be struck by the resemblance between it and what Lee Clarke has called "fantasy documents."[43] Clarke argues that "symbolic plans" like those that describe how a massive oil spill will be contained, or how residents downwind of a nuclear power plant will all be safely evacuated in the event of an accident, come about when organizations and experts are compelled to demonstrate their ability to "control things that are, most likely, outside the range of their expertise."[44] A dynamic quite similar to the ones Clarke describes played out as policymakers and scientists in Japan faced a choice between admitting there was nothing much they could do to prevent a Tōkai earthquake disaster and claiming that they did in fact have the knowledge and tools necessary to defend against it. The act, much like the examples Clarke provides, shows how technocrats and their institutions in Japan sought to resolve the tension between uncertainty and risk.

CHAPTER 10

Translating Disaster Knowledge from Japan to Chile

A Proposal for Incompleteness

Chika Watanabe

The sprawling complex of experts engaged in disaster risk reduction (DRR) has for years emphasized the importance of international "disaster coopera- tion." A central focus has been an effort to work transnationally to improve disaster education, as underscored in the 2005 Hyogo Framework for Action and the 2015 Sendai Framework for DRR.[1] The Japanese government in par- ticular has taken an active role in promoting disaster cooperation through educational activities, both for children and adults, tasking the Japan Interna- tional Cooperation Agency (JICA), a government agency devoted to human resource development, with responsibility for this goal.[2]

Since its establishment in 2007, JICA's Disaster Reduction Learning Cen- ter (DRLC) in Kobe has offered many DRR-related training courses—and has hosted, in particular, a number of DRR officials and experts from Chile, building on a relationship between Japanese and Chilean seismologists that dates to the 1960s.[3] Indeed, the Japanese government's 2012 *Country Assis- tance Policy for Chile* lists DRR as the primary objective of Japan's cooperation with Chile.[4] Given the long and active history of Japan and Chile's relation- ship, it is an exemplary case of disaster cooperation.

But how does disaster cooperation actually work? What are the processes of translation that make possible the travel of particular disaster-related knowledge and techniques from one country to another? In this chapter, which is based on participant observation and interviews with key informants in both Japan and Chile conducted over the course of field trips lasting one to two months every year (a total of approximately six months), I suggest that incompleteness—whether a shortage of information or contextual knowledge, misunderstandings, or miscommunication—is not an impediment to cross-cultural translation, but an important part of it. Translations do not happen *despite* incompleteness; rather, they happen through gaps, slippages, and excesses.[5] This is not a new idea for anthropologists, science and technology studies (STS) scholars, and others in allied disciplines, but it can offer useful insights for disaster studies scholars and practitioners, who often aspire, in contrast, for certainty and totality. Specifically, what I call the labor of half-translations proves to be an important process in disaster cooperation because it creates spaces for people across different countries to take ownership of the tool in question, making the preparedness activities more relevant and effective in a given context.

In a world of DRR and international cooperation wherein terms such as "coherence," "harmonization," and "standardization" are ubiquitous, the attention to half-translations might seem misplaced. Nevertheless, my ethnography illustrates how effective incompleteness can be in encouraging people from different countries to make DRR and disaster education techniques their own. This is work that requires effort and is not without risks, but I propose the argument as a provocation to fundamentally change the epistemological assumptions behind much DRR scholarship and policy. On the one hand, an aspiration for total knowledge and a confidence in our control of the world to mitigate disaster risks characterize dominant areas of DRR work such as disaster risk science, engineering, and policy making. Brian Wynne's observations continue to hold true: scientific knowledge and conventional risk assessment methods, when turned into policies, proceed as if there were no uncertainties or areas of ignorance, or that they could be eliminated with better implementation of scientific and managerial instruments.[6] Much DRR scholarship and policy making still predominantly focuses on better calculating and controlling risks "to narrow the supposed uncertainties and gain more precise definition of it."[7] For example, many DRR policymakers and practitioners rely on the International Organization for Standardization (ISO)'s standards, such as ISO 31000, *Risk Management—Principles and Guidelines*, to create universal guidelines for risk assessments, the building of resilient cities, and other measures.[8] The expectation from the implementation of ISOs is precision in the definition of terms and a codified standard that everyone would follow, regardless of disciplinary, cultural, political, economic, or environmental differences.[9] Conversely, policymakers and scientists alike state that barriers to effective risk assessments arise from a lack of common standards across disciplines.[10] Observers of disaster cooperation also point to standardization or "the alignment of goals and methods" as key to better outcomes in disaster response.[11]

But is this kind of enforced coherence and universalization necessary to reduce disaster risks and build resilience across different countries? In his study of intergovernmental coordination in disaster response, Daniel Aldrich examines how the failure of coordination could be overcome through greater standardization, for example. However, he ends his article with the interesting but unexamined conclusion that sometimes local practices might clash against standardization efforts, and policymakers would need to ensure that local needs are not ignored in those instances.[12] But how would this negotiation be possible? The focus on coherence, standards, and totalizing and generalizable knowledge does not allow for an understanding of these local divergences, and more generally, what is produced in the frictions or failures of coordination. Friction is seen as a problem to resolve, rather than a site of cultural rearticulation and innovation. There is no tool here to help us understand both global coordination and local practices in the same analytical frame.

Science-based approaches, in and of themselves, need not be based on epistemologies of fixity. Again, as Brian Wynne stated all those years ago, indeterminacies are in fact central to scientific knowledge. "Contingent social behaviour" and "open-ended situational forces" are always already at play in science, as well as in risk analyses and engineering.[13] The problem emerges when policymakers and others mobilize science as if it were a complete and static knowledge, showing surprise when things go wrong. There are scholars of disaster who follow Wynne and reject totalizing approaches to knowledge; instead, they attend to affective and embodied experiences of uncertainty in decision-making around disaster risks,[14] or the contingent relationality between different forms of knowledge rather than essentialist categories such as "local knowledge."[15] These approaches enable an understanding and appreciation of the co-emergence of multiple forms of knowledge from the ground up.

I follow Wynne and others in proposing that we pay attention to the generative capacity of incompleteness because it is in these slippages that global coordination and attention to local practices could be considered at the same time. In other words, incompleteness is where cross-cultural encounters can produce something new, whether that is across different societies or different forms of knowledge such as "lay" and "scientific." More fundamentally, the focus on incompleteness is a call to shift the epistemological assumptions of DRR policies and studies dominated by static understandings of knowledge. Incompleteness is not antithetical to science, engineering, or policy-making efforts. Rather, the proposition here is that incompleteness is always already present in these domains, but instead of treating it as a problem to fix, we should examine its role in the social production of DRR knowledge and practices on the ground. Moving away from the never-ending work of minimizing uncertainties, failures, and gaps to create a more "complete" knowledge base and toward an understanding of what different actors do with these openings means that we can create room for multiple strategies of resilience to emerge. People are already innovating in spaces and moments of incompleteness; it is high time that DRR scholars pay attention to this labor.

The Ethnographic Starting Point

On May 25, 2018, more than five hundred students between the ages of nine and eleven gathered at a sporting arena in the south-central port city of Talcahuano in Chile. They came from fifty schools around Talcahuano and the surrounding areas of Bio Bio region to participate in the *caravana escolar de la seguridad* (school caravan about security). They were there to learn various skills in disaster preparedness through playful, fun activities: first aid using dummies, what to do in the case of a tsunami using a game, and other tips for surviving the first seventy-two hours of a disaster. There were twenty booths at the event, each with a hands-on activity, staffed by adults from organizations such as the Chilean Red Cross and some led by primary school students who had participated in past caravanas.

The organizer of the caravana, the head of the disaster risk management department (Departamento de Gestión Integral del Riesgo de Desastres, DGIRD) of Talcahuano city, Nicolás, emphasized throughout the months leading up to the event that the caravana was not to be an exhibition event. Those putting on the booths should not simply display their knowledge and cutting-edge techniques.[16] They needed to design participatory activities. Nicolás had adopted this method of building community-based disaster preparedness skills among and through children from the activities of a Japanese nonprofit organization called Plus Arts.[17] He had been to Japan several times to attend JICA's training courses on DRR. During his first visit in 2012, he heard a presentation by the founder of Plus Arts, Nagata Hirokazu, and he was taken by it. Nagata-san's[18] presentation about Iza! Kaeru Caravan, the event on which the Talcahuano caravanas have been based, left a strong impression on Nicolás.[19] He went on to organize the first caravana in July 2014. Since then, Nicolás had organized several caravanas of various scales across Talcahuano and nearby regions.

Given the success and thorough planning of these events in Talcahuano, I was surprised when Nicolás told me that when he first learned about Iza! Kaeru Caravan, he did not actually see it in practice.[20] What he saw was a PowerPoint presentation and an in-class workshop that Nagata-san organized during one day of the month-long JICA training course. When Nicolás returned to Talcahuano, he emailed the Japanese official he knew at the JICA office in Santiago to ask for Nagata-san's contact information because he wanted his help to design the first caravana. But according to Nicolás, the JICA official never replied. Whatever the reasons, Nicolás did not get more information than the rough summary he heard during his course in Japan, and he had to invent much of the first caravana that he organized.

The detail that interests me most in this story is the incompleteness—how the lack of a "full picture" played a central role in the translation of Plus Arts's Iza! Kaeru Caravan into Nicolás's caravana. The insufficient information in the JICA training course forced Nicolás to improvise and experiment with different methods. In April 2018, he commented to me that it was probably a good thing that he did not see the actual Iza! Kaeru Caravan when he first heard about it. "If I'd seen it in person, it would have been easy for me to just replicate what I saw," he said.[21] Indeed, while a couple of the activities and the design motifs were similar to the Iza! Kaeru Caravan in Japan, Nicolás and his collaborators had created their own activities. At the latest iteration in 2018, Nicolás had set up a "feedback booth," where he had a former radio host interview the students and teachers to conduct an informal kind of evaluation.

It might be helpful to compare Nicolás's predicament with the work of the Chilean architect Alejandro Aravena, who won the prestigious Pritzker Architecture Prize in 2016.[22] One of his signature works is the Quinta Monroy social housing project in Iquique, a city in the far north of the country. It is based on the concept of "incremental housing": instead of building mediocre row houses or small detached houses using the small budget, he built "half a good house" with the same amount of money.[23] Aravena's firm provided a half-formed house with two rooms, which was handed over to families, who gradually built the rest of the house using their savings. These families were able to change their homes to suit their needs and tastes. This approach was in tune with the usual practice of *auto-construcción* among poor families in Chile, and with wider, long-standing policies and practices of progressive housing or incremental construction in Latin America, to establish land tenure and housing gradually and build extensions over time to match changing desires and extending families.[24]

I see resonances between this incremental housing design and the process of incomplete translation in the Chile-Japan disaster cooperation case. It is impossible to give a fully complete translation of Japanese approaches in the JICA courses, given their short-term nature. Rather than try to see these discrepancies as gaps to fill, both phenomena show that the incompleteness is their strength. Nagata-san from Plus Arts would agree; during a public talk in Kobe in July 2017, he explained an idea: the art of incompleteness (*fukanzen no susume*). He argued that, in designing a community-oriented activity, we need to create surplus space (*yochi*) so that other people have to provide input to complete the activity. That way, the activity or thing becomes everyone's. Leaving what cannot be explained as things unsaid or unformed allows partial connections, different worlds overlapping without one being subsumed within the other.[25] If that is the case, and if a desired outcome of JICA training courses is that participants innovate on what they learn, the emphasis should be on leaving some things unsaid rather than fully explained.

Yet half-translations are forms of labor, because the incompleteness could pose problems on its own; a half-formed house without electricity or plumbing would not be desirable.[26] There is a particular precision required of incompleteness. In the case of Iza! Kaeru Caravan, Nicolás might not have had the "full picture" from his training in Japan, but he had grasped the key value of participation in the involvement of different actors and in the design of the child-friendly activities. Nevertheless, he overlooked issues of socioeconomic differences and politics, an omission that I also observed in the JICA trainings. In this sense, something crucial might be missing, making the translation invalid. Moreover, although the aim of the caravanas was for the children who participated to take back what they learned to their families, this communication of knowledge from municipal projects to ordinary families was still missing. There is a lot more research to be done to address these questions; this chapter is inevitably incomplete. Yet I take Nicolás's experience and perspective seriously as a potentially new way of thinking about disaster cooperation that turns attention to the productivity of incompleteness.

Understanding Disaster Cooperation Through Translation

Despite the fact that disaster cooperation is touted among policymakers and practitioners, little is known about the everyday mechanisms and processes through which DRR-related knowledge travels from country to country. On the one hand, there is an emphasis on standardization and consistency between national and international policies. For example, a ministerial roundtable for the 2015 Sendai Framework hosted discussions about "aligning goals, targets and indicators across frameworks or at the very least ensuring that no contradiction exists across them."[27] Similarly, the European Union's policies on disaster education are "characterized by a high degree of standardization."[28] This is not unusual given that in international cooperation more widely, standardization is a common goal among development and humanitarian actors.[29]

On the other hand, scholars and practitioners alike have been attentive to the problems of standardized measures, especially in global, multicultural contexts. Anthropologists and historians of disaster have shed light on the existence of "cultures of disaster"—that is, cultural reservoirs in a particular place based on experiences of different kinds of hazards that have been handed down through generations to mitigate disasters, or not.[30] Standardized policies do not create spaces for these various cultures of disaster to inform practice. At the same time, "cultures" do not only exist among local inhabitants or victims of disasters, but also emerge in the interactions between local people, state actors, nongovernmental actors, medical personnel, the media, researchers, and others who weave through any particular disaster-affected place.[31] The attention to cultures in DRR is not simply an academic issue, as practitioners also ask how to account for cultural differences, diverse understandings of "rationality," and cross-cultural communication.[32]

Amid various cultures of practice, translations *are* important to enable communication across different people and forms of knowledge. Scholars have addressed the significance of bridging gaps between, for instance, scientists and community actors,[33] between global DRR policies and national governments,[34] and among people of different cultural and linguistic backgrounds.[35] Thus, while standardization is not necessarily useful or possible when taking into account cultural differences, effective communication is important. What many of these analyses downplay, however, is the valuable role that incompleteness plays in translations. According to Alev Bulut and Turgay Kurultay's study of search and rescue missions after the 1999 Marmara earthquake in

Turkey, interpreters helped ease communication between the rescue workers and local people. But this was not necessarily based on accurate or complete translations. One of the interpreters explained the presence of the German Red Cross to local inhabitants "as members of Alman Kızılayı, the German 'Red Crescent' (Red Crescent being the Turkish first aid organization) . . . [because] this 'domestication' saved time and guaranteed cultural acceptability."[36] The authors explain that these strategies of obfuscation facilitated efficient communication in situations where cultural and religious differences could prove difficult.[37] This value of incompleteness—or, to be more precise, the careful labor of half-translations—is not foregrounded in their article, but I suggest that it is a key component of translations in international cooperation.

To understand the role of incompleteness in translations, it is helpful to draw on STS analyses that have shown how translations are not only linguistic practices but processes of relationality that assemble diverse human and nonhuman actors to hold a form of knowledge together.[38] Translations always leave "gaps, misunderstandings, and omissions."[39] Translation is "necessarily faithless appropriation"; thus, it always leads to new formulations of the world.[40] On one level, as Walter Benjamin stated, a "real translation . . . does not cover the original, does not block its light."[41] The aim of the translation is not only to convey meaning but also to evoke the manner of expression, and thus the translation might not be wholly grammatically correct. But in that movement from one language to another, "the foreign tongue" should always affect the translation, inevitably changing both in the process.[42] Thus, on another level, more than an equivalence of meanings, translation is "a poetic expansion of its [language's] semiotic, political, and material effects."[43] It is neither entirely of the original nor of the translation's language.

Translation, therefore, is not the production of isomorphism between words or knowledge across worlds, nor is it the creation of a wholly new language. It is a "partial connection" that is "neither singular nor plural, neither one nor many, a circuit of connections that joins parts."[44] This is a useful way to think about disaster cooperation, and the matter of incompleteness in the travel of techniques from Japan to Chile more specifically, because the concepts and knowledge that are translated across countries are evidently not singular, unified things; but neither are they entirely different from each other. As Nicolás and his adaptation of Iza! Kaeru Caravan showed, the DRR method of using child-friendly games in Japan and Chile appeared similar and different at the same time. The notion that "one is too few, but two are too many" helps us get out of the "problems of cultural difference" in which moments of encounter are reduced to radical sameness or radical difference, both of which are two sides of the same coin of seeing "wholes" pit against other wholes.[45]

The "cooperation" that happens around disaster preparedness is not the dissemination or imposition of universal DRR methods, nor is it rebuffed by "local" cultures of disaster. Rather, the processes of translation of particular disaster preparedness tools partially connect different societies and relations, one implicated in the other. The incompleteness of this work is not a shortcoming in disaster cooperation but a generative characteristic of the translation process. In this new epistemological framing of DRR, the challenge for disaster cooperation actors is not how to give the most accurate information about a particular approach—it is how to create the kind of incompleteness, a way of holding back, that inspires actions that are new and old, innovative and situated, at the same time.

How, specifically, to hold back in a way that is generative, is a central question here. What decisions do particular actors make in the labor of half-translations, in ways that convey certain meanings and leave others untranslated? What are the consequences of these selective translations?

Bōsai, DRR, and la Gestión del Riesgo de Desastres

Behind the labor of half-translations that I discuss in this chapter are three different contexts. First, as one JICA official explained to me, one of the most fundamental aims of all training courses is that participants understand the Japanese concept of bōsai.[46] Bōsai is often translated as DRR, but this is also incomplete. On the one hand, the concept of DRR circulates in a world governed by risk.[47] Unlike uncertainties, risk is the rationalization of problems projected into the future so that they can be organizationally managed.[48] Most important, scholars have shown that risk is not a condition that exists out there in the world, but the product of "a particular type of calculative act: the weighing of the relative magnitude of a potential loss due to a hazard against the probability of this hazard actually occurring."[49] In the realm of disaster management, it is a calculation of the interactions between hazard, exposure, and vulnerability that defines disaster risks. The notion of risk, especially environmental risk, has become a logic of displacement against particular populations, of government, and of securitization around the world.[50] The understanding of disaster risk, however, is not universal, and different actors will determine it in various ways depending on their social, political, and economic positions.[51]

In Japan, the most common term used to refer to disaster preparedness efforts is bōsai, and this is usually translated as DRR.[52] From one perspective, bōsai is not entirely different from DRR in its link to risk thinking. Anthropologist Kimura Shūhei has argued that various legal, technological, and other mechanisms developed in Japan to construct Japanese citizens as subjects who can respond properly to disaster risks—that is, who can become actors of bōsai.[53] In his historical account of "risk-alization" (risuku-ka), as he calls it, the political and legal concept of bōsai in Japan was solidified after the devastating Isewan typhoon of 1959 in the form of the 1961 Disaster Response Basic Law. Even though the law emerged in the wake of a typhoon, it was earthquakes and fires that were emphasized in the text, setting the tone for subsequent bōsai policies and approaches. From the 1960s to the 1980s, with various earthquakes hitting the country, the science of prediction became prominent, and it has culminated today around the imminent Nankai megathrust earthquake. In the 1990s, Kimura explains, the predictive sciences were able to increasingly visualize disaster risks such as on hazard maps, which citizens could directly access. Individuals in Japan have been increasingly mobilized as active participants in the mitigation of disaster risks.

In this sense, bōsai and DRR are both mechanisms that reorganize societies and people around conceptions of risk. Yet bōsai and DRR are only partially connected. For example, disaster risk and preparedness in Euro-American contexts, on which conceptions of DRR are based, first emerged in relation to civil defense in the face of potential armed nuclear attacks in the context of the Cold War.[54] This is not the case with bōsai in Japan, where disaster preparedness activities emerged from the state's mobilization of neighborhood associations or "community councils" (chōnaikai) in the early twentieth century to tackle disaster-related issues, and eventually during the Second World War to prepare for air raids and mobilize citizens for war efforts.[55] These government-fostered initiatives at the community level have continued with the "autonomous organizations for disaster reduction" (jishu bōsai soshiki) that have grown in particular in Kobe since the 1995 earthquake.[56]

Furthermore, the approaches to bōsai that participants encounter in the JICA training courses derive primarily from specific experiences in Kobe. As one Japanese DRR expert delivering part of the JICA training course explained, the message conveyed in the courses is more about Hyogo prefecture's (where the city of Kobe is) experiences rather than a national Japanese approach to bōsai.[57] One of the main lessons from the 1995 earthquake that bōsai-related government officials and experts in Kobe promote is the fact that 80 percent of survivors were helped by neighbors and not by the government or professionals such as firefighters. Consequently, their message is the importance of self-help (*jijo*) and mutual help (*kyōjo*) among neighbors, when public help (*kōjo*) is limited.

The other relevant term here is *la gestión del riesgo de desastres* (literally, management of disaster risks) in Chile. On February 27, 2010, an earthquake of magnitude 8.8 and subsequent tsunamis devastated the coastal regions of Chile. Over 520 people died and more than 220,000 houses were destroyed.[58] In Talcahuano, 33 people died, more than 50,000 more were affected, and more than 13,000 houses were damaged. Many basic services like water and electricity were also disrupted.[59] In 2011, United Nations Development Programme (UNDP) officials from the Chile office visited Talcahuano and selected it as one of the pilot cities for creating a municipal-level DRR office. With additional funds from the European Civil Protection and Humanitarian Aid Operations (ECHO), the country's first municipal-level department for gestión del riesgo, DGIRD, was established, and Nicolás was appointed as the head of office. Three more staff members were involved in the early years, developing together a number of community-based DRR activities and emergency response systems. JICA also sent some Japan Overseas Cooperation Volunteers (JOCV) to assist the office, with the last volunteer, a woman in her late twenties, being posted in Talcahuano from 2016 to 2018. As of the winter of 2019, there were only Nicolás and one more staffer working on DRR projects, and an additional staff member responsible for emergency response.

In many ways, given this history, the gestión del riesgo de desastres in Talcahuano seems to be an almost literal translation of international conceptions of DRR. Nevertheless, a number of particularities need to be taken into account. First, all of the current and former staff members of the DGIRD have trained in Japan through JICA's training courses. Nicolás has gone to Kobe multiple times over the past few years to attend trainings on noninfrastructural DRR methods. He has put particular effort into the caravanas, based on Plus Arts's activities, and other educational activities for children. The other current staffer, Gabriela, focuses on other community-based activities with neighborhood associations (*juntas de vecinos*), inspired by the "community based voluntary organization for disaster risk reduction" in Kobe called bōsai fukushi community or BOKOMI. Thus, the work of the DGIRD generally resonates with the bōsai focus on self-help and mutual help from Japan, specifically Kobe.

However, gestión del riesgo in Chile has an additional connotation that differs from bōsai in Japan. The Chilean National Office for Emergency (Oficina Nacional de Emergencia del Ministerio del Interior y Seguridad Pública, ONEMI) oversees all disaster-related policies at the national level, and its overarching mission is to "coordinate the national system of civil protection," which addresses largely natural disasters but also includes other emergencies.[60] Although the focus on "self-help" (autocuidado) in ONEMI's policies is similar to the emphases in bōsai, in Chile it exists in the context of a highly neoliberal society, wherein the individualization of public welfare has been promoted as a way to cut state expenditures.[61] Furthermore, with the 2018 reelection of the conservative billionaire president, Sebastián Piñera, questions of security (seguridad)—delinquency, drug trafficking, terrorism, and so on—have been foregrounded in national as well as local policies.[62] The mayor of Talcahuano, Henry Campos, who was elected to his post in 2016, was the first conservative politician to assume the role in Talcahuano in the postdictatorship era, and he is a member of the Unión Demócrata Independiente (UDI), the right-wing political party associated with Piñera's coalition government. The recent protests in 2019 have added to this public concern with security. Tellingly, in early 2018 the DGIRD in Talcahuano was reorganized from being under the mayor's office to being subsumed within the new Directorate of Public Security and Operations (Dirección de Seguridad Pública y Operaciones).

This outline of the different terms that circulate in my field sites illustrate how DRR, bōsai, and gestión del riesgo de desastres are loose translations of each other. Like the Turkish interpreter in Bulut and Kurultay's study, obfuscations or labors of half-translation are necessary to make relationships work.[63] Yet in these half-translations, certain messages came through across societies: the importance of self-help and mutual help, for example. What decisions do particular actors make in the labor of half-translations, in ways that convey certain meanings and leave others untranslated? What are the consequences of these selective translations? In the next section, I show ethnographically how Japanese DRR experts impressed upon JICA participants the idea of bōsai as a methodological approach to community participation, setting aside certain socioeconomic and political details.

Bōsai as Method

In January and February 2018, I took part in one of the month-long training courses that the DRLC organizes. Titled Raising Awareness of Disaster Risk Reduction, the course had been in place for about six years. This time, there were twelve participants from twelve countries, ranging from Niue in the Pacific Ocean to Afghanistan. A young official from a regional ministry of education from Chile was also participating. All courses are organized by a JICA official, designed and implemented by a partner institution, and managed on an everyday level by a training coordinator who acts as the translator and "tour guide."

Through no fault of the training coordinator, the translation of the content of the JICA course units was often fragmentary. Early in the Raising Awareness course that I observed, the training participants did a hazard-mapping exercise called "town watching" with a senior staff member and researcher at the Asian Disaster Reduction Center (ADRC). ADRC researchers had been using town watching as a method since 1993. Town watching is a form of community-based hazard-mapping exercise that derives from a participatory method that was used in urban development projects across Japan in the 1970s.[64] Citizens walk around a neighborhood to identify areas that might pose a threat, such as tangled electric cables that could cause a fire during an earthquake, as well as areas that might be a resource, such as open spaces where people could gather to evacuate. It is a way to encourage citizens to recognize historical traces of disaster in their neighborhoods and develop preparedness measures by becoming aware of local dangers and resources.

On the morning of January 18, 2018, the twelve JICA training participants from the Raising Awareness course and a dozen more from another course, the training coordinator, the JICA official in charge of the course, the staffer from the implementing organization, and I met with Hirata-san from ADRC to learn about town watching. Hirata-san divided the participants into three groups: A, B, and C. Each group of about six to seven participants sat around a cluster of tables, where a large blank map of the neighborhood we were going to that day was placed. Each participant also received copies of Hirata-san's slides and an A4-sized version of the blank map. Hirata-san explained that we would be walking around Nada ward, a central district of Kobe. The task of each group was to "make notes about the 'good' and 'bad' points in times of disaster, places that might be advantageous during disasters and those that would be dangerous."[65] Each group had to select a team leader, who would present findings; a photographer, who would take fifteen pictures of the good and bad points; and a notetaker, who would record the group's path and reasoning for selecting each of the good and bad points.

After the introductory meeting, we all climbed onto a minibus and rode quietly for twenty minutes to our destination. We arrived at a fire station, where two police officers and a firefighter were waiting for us. The firefighter joined the group that I was following, group B. After brief introductions, Hirata-san asked each group leader to select a path to start with. There were three possible directions, and our group leader, Martin from Chile, suggested the path in the middle. We turned right at the first corner and began to climb a hilly, narrow street. As we went up the hill, the houses started to appear dilapidated. They looked like row houses with makeshift extensions made of corrugated metal sheets that were rusting. We stood in front of a compact, two-story building with vines climbing up its walls, which seemed abandoned. "What do you think of these apartments? What is the threat here?" asked Hirata-san in English. Martin answered that they are probably empty, so if they caught fire, no one would notice. It can be a hazard for the entire community. He asked Hirata-san why the government had not done anything about them. Apparently, the city officials had tried to contact the owners, but they could not get a reply. In the end, the city decided to take control of the buildings, but there were still many steps left to get to that stage. Karen, from Niue, commented that someone must be cleaning the buildings from time to time because, despite the vines, they were not completely covered by plants. She also noticed the power lines that could easily catch on fire. Hirata-san added: "This shows the problem of ageing populations in Japan, [leading to] abandoned houses."

We turned left at the top of the hill and followed the street, which was now going downhill. Participants noticed that the houses looked different now: quite large, modern, and new. Hirata-san explained that the valley and the nonvalley areas of the neighborhood had different types of houses. He did not elaborate further. Karen noticed that on our right was a high wall of stones and concrete, on top of which stood some apartments. It looked like a retaining wall, often used when building houses on uneven and hilly areas. The wall was so tall that it looked like it was leaning in toward the street. "This would collapse during an earthquake!" exclaimed Karen, alarmed. She told Martin and noted the place as a dangerous "bad" spot. Hirata-san was listening but did not say anything.

We eventually arrived back at the fire station. Karen and Martin asked me if the neighborhood was wealthy since most of the houses looked big, and they knew that land was not cheap in Japan. I did not know the answer, so I asked the firefighter. He laughed, looking embarrassed by the question, and replied that some people in this area might be well off. It was a relatively desirable neighborhood because it had the mountains in the back where people could take walks, and also views of the ocean. He was not sure, however, and fell silent. Karen and Martin moved on to ask him about the work of firefighters in Kobe.

After lunch, everyone returned to the meeting room in the DRLC building to work on the maps. Hirata-san had printed the photographs from each group's camera during lunch break. The blank maps were still on each table, along with bags with various crafting tools. The members of each group gathered around their respective tables. Hirata-san asked everyone to mark the route that they had taken and, using stickers, put on the map a red dot for the bad points and a blue dot for the good points that they had identified during the walk.

After a short break, the groups had to create a matrix of problems and solutions. Our group started by discussing the problem of fires, then moved on to address landslides, floods, and earthquakes. The required costs of each solution differed—measures against landslides and floods called for infrastructural investments that would cost more—but for all solutions they wrote "immediate and ongoing" for the timeline. Martin stated: "With disasters we have to always think that an emergency can happen at any time, so we have to implement measures immediately and all the time." Everyone agreed.

In the final hour, the groups presented their maps and mitigation strategies on the matrix. When all three presentations were finished, Hirata-san placed the white board with group C's map under the projector screen and put up an image of the official hazard map of Nada ward. He pointed out that the two maps looked different because the one from the city showed risk zones for floods and landslides over a period of one hundred years or longer. A town-watching exercise would only capture about fifty years based on the experiences of residents. He explained that ADRC recommends people do the town watching with their neighbors, local authorities, and DRR experts when they return home, then create a matrix of the problems and solutions together. They could then produce a shared list of activities. A participant raised his hand and asked how they should interpret the difference between the official and local hazard maps. Hirata-san replied: "The city provides a hardcopy of the official hazard map to all houses every year, but most residents would not pay attention to it and probably put it to one side. But if you conduct a town watching workshop with the community, all people will remember and pay attention. So it is a tool of public awareness." Having a relatively accurate hazard map was important to make appropriate plans, but the message that Hirata-san wanted to underline was that the process in this activity was as important as, if not more than, the map at the end. Bōsai was a set of methods, not a package of information. Thus, there were some shared understandings, but there was much that was left unsaid. For instance, although Karen and Martin asked about the socioeconomic composition of the neighborhood in Nada ward, this was left unexplained. Karen had been alarmed by the tall retaining wall, and Hirata-san did not correct or agree with her.

At the time, I was perplexed by this lack of explanation and worried that participants would return to their countries with only partial understanding. It was only after speaking with Nicolás in Chile a few months later that I saw how my concerns were misplaced. I came to understand that the incomplete understandings were not a problem but an important aspect of the translation process in Talcahuano.

The Art of Incompleteness

In Talcahuano, I observed that Nicolás appeared to purposefully make both the planning process and execution of the caravanas incomplete, thereby inviting others to contribute. Nicolás had cultivated relationships with other departments in the municipality and external organizations, whose staffers planned and put on booths at the caravanas. But these collaborators were not consistent, and he was always looking for new partners. In late 2017, he approached a group within the health service department of the municipality to see if they would be interested in participating in the caravana the following year. The staffers of this department invited him to meet with a team working on mental health services in a national community-based program called Vida Chile, which has existed since the late 1990s.[66] The five team members were enthusiastic about the prospect of developing an activity to teach children how to care for the mental health of others during a disaster and promised Nicolás their assistance.

On April 18, 2018, I sat in one of the meetings that Nicolás and the JOCV volunteer had with the Vida Chile team. Nicolás had asked them to come up with an idea for their booth, and after having some tea and biscuits, one of the team members, Rafael, began to explain their proposal. The idea was to have a puppet show. They would first give an introductory explanation about the various emotional and physical effects of a disaster. Then they would have five scenarios in which a puppet is shown in crisis and another puppet is the "helper." Based on the situation portrayed, the children would need to guess the appropriate and inappropriate actions that they saw. After listening to their ideas, Nicolás offered a few suggestions for making the show participatory.

At one point, one of the women from the team commented that the Iza! Kaeru Caravan in Japan must be very modern, with touchscreens and technological devices. Nicolás shook his head. "They do have more resources, but it's not modern at all. All of their activities are very much hands-on and handmade, like how to make a poncho out of a plastic bag and decorate it with flower patterns made of paper." The team members were surprised. I had actually brought from Japan some of the pamphlets and a bandana that Plus Arts created for an Iza! Kaeru Caravan that I had attended in Japan. The JOCV volunteer handed out some samples of this to the team members. They were impressed by the quality of the paper and the cotton for the bandana, as well as the use of many colors on the pamphlets. They discussed how difficult it was to make things the same quality as in Japan given the constraints on resources.

Despite the differences, the materials from Japan showed the importance of making the event aesthetically attractive as well as informative. Nicolás told the team that presenting the booths in pretty and colorful ways was also an important part of the activity to appeal to children, and one of the women suggested that, in their case, they could use pastel colors to give a calming effect. They began to discuss how they could design the various parts of the puppet show. As we were wrapping up the meeting, Rafael told Nicolás that this was an important activity because most psychological programs were by adults for adults. A program that focused on children as actors in psychosocial care, not simply as recipients, was innovative, and he wanted to continue this line of work with Nicolás beyond the caravana.

There were aspects of these ideas that were the same as in Japan, such as the importance of aesthetics, but others that differed, such as having children provide mental health care in disasters. People in Talcahuano were constantly making partial connections between their world and what they imagined to be Japan. Moreover, just as the translation of Iza! Kaeru Caravan had been incomplete for Nicolás and required him to invent things, the event itself was an empty shell without the input from collaborators who needed to be enrolled in the project.[67] Translations create partial connections, temporary alliances that work in the interests of differently positioned actors that nevertheless share a specific problematization, in this case, around disaster preparedness.

What Remains

The labor of half-translations requires people to determine what to translate and what to leave behind. I do not think that this is intentional work; neither Hirata-san nor Nicolás explicitly explained that he left translations incomplete on purpose. But the inevitable partialness of the JICA trainings had required Nicolás to fill in the blanks in innovative ways. As such, there is a case to be made for practitioners and scholars alike to attend to particular ways of holding back that enable participation by diverse actors. The required specificity of the half-translations would depend on each context. But the fundamental observation here is that bringing "local" knowledge into conversation with "global" knowledge is not just a matter of making them commensurable. It is also about determining what kinds of incompleteness create room for different realities to coexist.

Yet there are nagging questions. In Michel Callon's famous recounting of French researchers' consolidation of knowledge about scallops in St. Brieuc Bay, the roles of Japanese scientists and their scallops, from which the French scientists took their inspiration, disappear from view.[68] Scientists, fishermen, and scallops form part of Callon's "sociology of translation," but not the Japanese. Translations—and theorizations of translation—always omit something to create their "matters of concern."[69] In the case of Callon's scientists and scallops, the omission of the Japanese probably enabled a science that seemed culture-less and universal. If so, what or who does the labor of half-translations in the case of the Japan-Chile disaster cooperation omit, and to what effect? In the hazard-mapping exercise that I observed at JICA, the socioeconomic and political context of the neighborhood we walked in remained unexplained. Is this depoliticization necessary for effective international cooperation and transnational communication? What would happen if political factors were inserted into these interactions?

Despite such questions, an attention to incompleteness promises a new epistemological paradigm. It shifts away from assumptions of fixity in DRR and improves understandings of how different contexts of disaster preparedness can speak to each other. A concern with "filling the gaps" and eliminating uncertainties to make risk assessments more accurate or mitigation measures more secure only leads to further efforts of the same, since there will always be further uncertainties and problems to fix.[70] This unending cycle of interventions would be even more acute in disaster cooperation, where varying cultures come into contact, producing additional unknown factors. Neither a response based on standardization nor "local/indigenous knowledge" would help here, because both assume a dichotomy that makes professional and lay knowledge mutually exclusive and hierarchically positioned against each other. What is needed now more than ever is a framework for DRR that enables a serious consideration of efforts emerging from the ground up, without its being essentialized as a "local" practice that is simply pitted against or integrated into existing approaches, and from cross-cultural interactions, without its being reduced through standardization. An attention to the generative potential of incompleteness can be the way forward.

"Acts of Men"

Disasters Neglected, Preventable, and Moral

Kenneth Hewitt

> The calamities . . . do not simply happen, nor are they sent; they proceed mainly from actions, and those the actions of men.
> —Andrew C. Bradley, *Shakespearean Tragedy: Lectures on Hamlet, Othello, King Lear, and Macbeth*

A volume devoted to critical thinking about disasters seems timely. Few who study or respond to disasters can avoid the sense of a global watershed in dangers and destructive events, and in contested ways of addressing them.[1] The incidence and costs of disasters continue to grow, as do the number of people exposed to dangerous conditions with inadequate protections. Death tolls have tended to decline, but they remain high. At the same time, there have been huge increases in disaster-related funding, new and expanded institutions, and companies seeking to profit from disaster. It is hard to keep up with the meetings, publications, institutes, and centers of excellence. As disaster preparedness merges with national ("homeland") security, it enjoys ever-expanding resources and scope.[2] The question I want to raise here, then, is: Why have these measures not even slowed the losses and adverse trends?

In particular, I want to call attention to three categories of disaster: famines, large accidents, and disasters of war. They all are primarily caused or compounded by human action or inaction, and their impacts are distributed unequally.[3] Since the 1980s, they all also have been increasingly displaced or absent from the field. They are absent from the Sendai Accords, the websites of the United Nations Office for Disaster Risk Reduction, and published disaster lists like those maintained by Munich Re and Swiss Re.[4] A sample of recent, notable, state-of-the-art work largely ignores them.[5] They therefore demand the attention of critical disaster studies.

Dearth and Famine

Famine was once pivotal in disaster studies. Since the 1980s, however, it has been increasingly neglected to the point that, in 1998, E. L. Quarantelli observed a "remarkable professional distance from" famine. He pondered treating it together with epidemics and droughts, or "FEDs," as "older type diffuse happenings." John Hannigan concurs and finds "valid conceptual reasons for excluding FEDs from the disaster rubric."[6]

Yet famine mortality still dwarfs most other disaster categories. Between the 1870s and 1970s, annual famine deaths averaged about 900,000. In each of some seventeen events, more than 2 million people died.[7] The Holodomor in 1930s Ukraine caused 7 to 10 million deaths, second only to the 1960s Great Leap Forward famine in China, with at least 15 million—and possibly as many as 45 million—deaths.[8] The mid-twentieth century did bring singular successes in prevention and relief, notably in South and East Asia, and there were hopes of ending hunger globally. Even so, Jeanne Kasperson and Robert Kates pronounced the 1980s a lost decade in these efforts.[9] And famines have returned in the twenty-first century, largely in sub-Saharan Africa. In 2017, those facing starvation included some 100,000 in South Sudan; about 400,000 in Nigeria, out of 5 million "in food crisis"; and some 10 million people in Yemen, a crisis that continues in 2020.[10] A recent report from my country, Canada—a wealthy G8 state and a huge exporter and donor of food—found that more than 4 million Canadians lack food security and experience hunger daily. Many more are malnourished or obese. This comprises a silent catastrophe for some 1.2 million children of poor families, single mothers, and impoverished elderly, disproportionately from racial and ethnic minorities—much like the vulnerability story for the COVID-19 pandemic of 2020.

Hunger is almost universal among Canada's Indigenous people, including 70 percent of preschool Inuit children. It is bound up with low incomes, the lack of jobs, unreliable services, and poor health and housing, a paternalistic, colonial system of government, the "usual suspects" of disaster risk generally.[11]

In 1983, I edited a collection of work on disaster entitled *Interpretations of Calamity*.[12] Most contributors addressed food security and hunger, which was not so unusual then. At the time, scholars tended to treat famine as a natural disaster, linking it to environmental causes of crop failure, mainly drought.[13] They commonly tied starvation to impersonal Malthusian limits or "overpopulation."[14] *Interpretations* rejected those ideas. The contributors' research showed that most famines originated in the deliberate or indirect results of commercial strategies, the actions of governments or land-owning oligarchs, forces of occupation, or imperial administrations.[15] Analyzing Ireland's "Great Hunger" in the 1840s, Bengal's 3 million dead in 1943, a possible 2 million civilian deaths in Biafra's 1967–1970 war, and other major disasters, none proved to be a *subsistence* famine—which is to say, none was precipitated by absolute food insufficiency.[16] In every case, even as people starved, adequate supplies of food were available in the economic world to which they belonged. In fact, exports of agricultural products typically continued from the famine-stricken regions. These were, first and foremost, man-made political disasters.

And who were most likely to starve to death, suffer permanent harm from malnutrition, or succumb to diseases responsible for most "famine deaths"? Who, in these famines, got displaced, ended up as permanent migrants and refugees, or were trafficked? For each case, the short answer was *the already hungry*. The famines all arose in, and for, particular subpopulations experiencing chronic or recurrent shortages—dearth—within given regions. Deaths and losses were concentrated in subpopulations among impoverished people who lacked a "voice" in their own critical survival issues and were perennially subject to social discrimination and hardship.[17] Thus, modern famines at least turn out to be moral and legal disasters. They represent failures to prevent or mitigate eminently preventable harm.

Scholars outside the disaster risk reduction (DRR) community largely came to similar conclusions. As Robert Bolin, Martina Jackson, and Allison Crist observed, "The famine literature . . . was perhaps the first to focus on social process rather than the environment as the disaster agent."[18] The irony is that as these insights gained acceptance, scholars, planners, and diplomats of DRR came to exclude famine from their attention altogether.

Large Accident Disasters

Large accident disasters include a diverse set of crises, some as old as humanity, others novel and sources of special modern impacts.[19] They are associated with the ever-greater prominence of urban and industrial activity since the mid-nineteenth century. In particular, they mark the "great acceleration" of the Anthropocene since 1945, with its technoscientific innovations and globalized organizations, dealing with high-volume, high-energy, and high-risk enterprises.[20] Charles Perrow connects accidents with modern trends toward ever-more-complex systems.[21] Ulrich Beck cites various examples among the "big risks" definitive of his "risk society."[22] Paul Virilio cites a growing peril of the accident in the modern world, emphasizing speed or "dromology" in modern communications and warfare, such that "in the course of the twentieth century the accident became a heavy industry."[23] Recent examples of large accidents include the 2017 Grenfell Tower fire in London; the Tianjin port explosion in China in 2014; and the train derailment, oil spill, and fire at Lac-Mégantic, Quebec, in 2013. Some of the worst catastrophes are involved— Bhopal, Chernobyl, *Deepwater Horizon*—as are innumerable unplanned explosions and releases of toxic chemicals. Large public gatherings that become death traps belong here, such as the Hillsborough football stadium crush in 1989, with 96 deaths, or the Mecca tunnel crush in 1990, with 1,426 deaths.[24] Accident disasters also represent a growing share of catastrophic loss claims, amounting to billions of dollars annually. And while studies have emphasized accident disasters in wealthier nations, globalization has carried novel threats to the poorest countries, too.

Large accidents were, however, largely missing from the International Decade for Natural Disaster Reduction and the Sendai Accords, individually and as a class. They are absent, too, from Ben Wisner, J. C. Gaillard, and Ilan Kelman's mammoth *Handbook of Hazards and Disaster Risk Reduction*, and from other texts otherwise central to the field of DRR. One reason has to do with professional or disciplinary "turf." Large accidents tend to be adopted by specialist fields, consultants, or businesses. They adopt an agent- or sector-specific view—as with aviation safety, for example—while supporting a technocratic view that rejects the notion of "the accident."

Apparently, the accident has no place in "acts of God." Few religions conceive of God as "accident prone," rather than all-knowing and all-seeing. In the natural sciences, the "real world" is seen as governed by natural laws. There may be randomness, even chaos, but not accidents.[25] Nevertheless, accidents are an everyday human experience, and they have been debated in Western culture since ancient times.

Calling something an "accident" does imply a contradiction. If truly accidental, what happens is spontaneous, unintended, not wanted by those involved. Deliberate or targeted harm is called something else: sabotage, criminal damage, terrorism, or the disasters of war addressed in the next section.[26] On the other hand, technical investigations have shown that accidents follow basic patterns in form, frequency, and severity; these patterns are sufficient to reward vigilance and improve safety. Formal inquiries into major events typically identify cause(s) and conclude they could have been prevented.[27] Commonly, narrow but critical decisions are found to have sacrificed safety to protect earnings.[28]

Further confusion can arise when "the accident" is misidentified as, or with, the damaging forces the accident released. The explosion, collapse, fire, or toxic spill is quite distinct from the process and accidental moment. "Big accidents almost always have very small beginnings," as Charles Perrow wrote. "The initiating event is often, taken by itself, seemingly quite trivial."[29] Consider the relatively minor signaling and navigational errors in Halifax Harbor, the morning of December 6, 1917, that led two ships to collide; compare them to the unprecedented damage and death when the munitions on one of the ships exploded and wrecked a quarter of the city.[30] Often, innovations have transformed key parts of everyday life and the planet's ecology unintentionally and before anything like full awareness of potential downsides is recognized. Technologies like TNT, ozone-depleting CFCs, and synthetic opioids—behavior-transforming items at the heart of modernity—went global in a few years. They were turned into large-scale, live social experiments. The crises they precipitated did not crop up until much later, and in unanticipated areas.[31]

Large accidents in novel and high-risk ventures are thus as much a revelation as an annihilating event.[32] They uncover dimensions missed in the rush to exploit consumer goods, synthetic materials, and artificial environments.[33] Inadequate safeguards prefigure accident-prone outcomes. And yet, large accidents are usually ignored in DRR studies.

Disasters of War

Older views placed war among the great forms of calamity.[34] Today, the disasters community largely ignores it.[35] Nevertheless, militarism and armed violence intrude into all aspects of disaster work and are among the greatest sources of disastrous death and destruction.[36] The exponential growth of war and military budgets has made them the "elephant in the room," not least in influencing the ideas and practices of disaster management.

My phrase "disasters of war" intentionally echoes the title of Francisco Goya's etchings from the 1808–1814 Peninsula War. In one bleak scene after another, Goya depicts terrified, uprooted, and massacred civilians, the cartloads of their dead tipped into mass graves. Those still alive are starving, wounded, imprisoned, or waiting for the executioner's bullet. Where soldiers appear, it is for hangings or firing squads. They rape, torture, and murder citizens; mutilate prisoners of war; or as captives themselves, are mutilated by other soldiers. Combat—the fighting war—is entirely absent.

Goya's "disasters" are far from warfare as normally understood. However bloody and ruinous, fighting is expected of armies. The fighting forces, their battles and losses, are generally viewed as heroic and brave, the highest and most selfless sacrifices, saviors of the nation. They are paid and ordered to kill and destroy. Goya's disasters, on the other hand, not only violate military rules of engagement; they have widely come to be seen as *crimes of war* and *crimes against humanity*.[37] They summon a deeper sense of "violence," one linked to *violation*: "to desecrate, dishonour, profane, defile ... corrupt or spoil."[38] They involve crimes and calamities of domicide, gendercide, urbicide, ethnic cleansing, and genocide, and, I suggest, if violence is central for critical disaster studies, they foreground legal and moral issues.[39]

Armed assaults on or involving civilians invariably create disasters. Civilian majorities are militarily defenseless, "noncombatants" by definition. Rarely are they adequately protected. Most of them experience war in their peacetime domestic and community settings; they are likely to witness vulnerable loved ones being attacked and maimed. The two world wars dominate modern totals of noncombatant as well as military casualties. But since 1945, the civilian share of casualties has kept rising.[40]

Consider the aerial bombing of British, German, and Japanese cities in World War II.[41] Civilian air raid casualties in the three countries exceeded 1.5 million killed, and 2.3 million more had major injuries.[42] More than 17 million city dwellers lost their homes. Air war histories rarely say much about those on the "receiving end." Yet governments paid careful attention to civilians in bombed cities, and assessments of their "morale" left remarkable troves of home front testimonies. These "views from below" of the civilian realities reveal the disasters of air power.[43]

Military authorities preferred incendiary and night raids because they minimized air force losses. But they were more indiscriminate and horrific for civilians, especially mothers and children. Urban households were predominantly woman headed, their menfolk at the front or drafted into war industries. The largest occupational category of raid victim was "housewife." Ten times more women civilians died than airmen sent against them. You might call it a gendered conflict: men above did most of the killing, women below the dying.

While the whole urban area campaigns seem a "man-made disaster," a smaller but decisive set of attacks caused unparalleled devastation.[44] Most cities experienced just one attack. Among these were Coventry in November 1940 (568 civilian deaths); Hamburg in July 1943 (40,000 civilian deaths), and Dresden in February 1945 (35,000 civilian deaths). The most destructive and lethal attack was on Tokyo on March 9, 1945, with over 100,000 dead and 25 percent of the city area burned out.[45] But hundreds of cities were virtually wiped out—the concentration and spread of destruction went far beyond, for example, current projections of climate change losses to the end of the twenty-first century—and each disaster raid remains inscribed in its city's history and survivors' memory as "*the* catastrophe."[46]

For urban dwellers, the disasters did not begin when the bombs started falling, nor did they end when the fires were out. The threat of annihilation lay over all the cities from the beginning to the end of the war, or until their "disaster raid" had occurred. There were thousands of raid alarms, most of them "false" but all terrorizing residents. For a decade or more after the attacks, survivors lived in ruined districts and makeshift shelters, surrounded by rubble, dust, and unexploded bombs; war remembrance was given over to reminders of unprecedented moral and humanitarian catastrophes.[47]

After 1945, air attacks continued the annihilation of cities: Pyonyang, Hanoi, Sarajevo, Grozny, Baghdad, Falluja, Sana'h, Mogadishu, Aleppo. And the majorities worst affected have been the "protected persons" of the Geneva Conventions of 1949: children, mothers of young children, the elderly, and the sick or disabled.[48] Raids in the Korean and Second Indo-China wars from the 1950s though the 1970s infamously favored napalm, responsible for terrible burn and carbon monoxide deaths among civilians. Recent wars have involved a greater deployment of high explosives, presumably reflecting arid land conditions and less flammable property in the greater Middle East and North Africa. In 2017 alone, almost 43,000 casualties and 24,848 deaths were reported due to explosive weapons.[49] Some 74 percent of the dead were civilians, rising to 97 percent for attacks on markets and places of worship. Refugees surveyed in Europe reported 85 percent were fleeing the threat of explosive violence. From Afghanistan, 92 percent were directly impacted by explosive violence, and 90 percent from Iraq were thus impacted.[50] Forcibly displaced populations have returned to levels not seen since the world wars.

Arguably, modern weapons and strategies have rendered cities, noncombatants, and nonmilitary items absolutely vulnerable. The huge investments in arms and armies coincide with the greatest destruction aimed at habitat and civilian casualties—and an extraordinary dearth of civilian protection, not least of peacemaking.

Disaster work also has deep roots in wartime civil defense, and the long shadow of the world wars hangs over the disasters field.[51] To a point. Nuclear war is the largest single threat to human and planetary survival but receives no attention in the disasters community.[52] Meanwhile, armed forces play an ever-greater role in disaster responses. Policing is increasingly heavily armed.[53] The lack of awareness, let alone pursuit, of conflict resolution, or peace research and advocacy, may explain the failure of DRR more generally.

Conclusion

The disasters field and its proposed actions seem awash in technocratic forms and formulae that still prevail, convenient for centralized administration and management, official if not neocolonial: "risk governance," "national platforms," "strategic frameworks," "stakeholders and their roles," "policies and management strategies," "modalities of cooperation," "inclusive risk-informed decision-making," "technology transfer and capacity," and "planning and implementation of local disaster risk management." Professional contributions highlight "conceptual frameworks," "Complex Systems," "multidisciplinarity," "multi-sectoral initiatives," "social construction of risk," "forensic investigations of disaster," and "underlying root causes and dynamic processes."[54] No doubt these matters appear relevant for responsible agencies and large institutions. They lie in wait for anyone wishing to contribute to their agendas, and appear as an emerging "dominant consensus."[55] It is doubtful they make much sense for the majorities of those at risk, other than as potential further threats. They fail to reflect an adequate view of disaster phenomena, risk, or experience. Meanwhile, they hide almost every danger discussed in this chapter, if not explaining why they are neglected.

Famines, large accidents, and disasters of war continue to occur. In each, a majority of those at risk and harmed are struggling against "packages" of adverse societal preconditions: debilitating mixes of racialized poverty and precarious work, chronic health problems and gendered violence, and chronic indebtedness and corrupt practices.[56] They are not "natural" disasters.[57] The same may be remarked for crises of debt and epidemics or "plagues."[58] They seem more likely to be sidelined by "inclusive risk-informed decision-making" and the like.

Such seemingly different disasters of famine, accident, and war do raise common issues and are sometimes intertwined. Disasters of war and related violence warrant attention in part because major actors continue to invest in armed conflict as the "threat of choice" and in militarized responses to disasters and other crises.[59] The rapid expansion of homeland security "disasterizes" attendant state conditions and obsessions: borders, migration and prison systems, "conflict minerals," and clandestine surveillance. Civil defense, originally focused on bombing threats to cities in the world wars, served as a basis for disaster management throughout the Cold War.[60] This helps perpetuate a "logic-of-war" or "patterns of war approach" that distorts the language, priorities, and performance of the disaster field.[61] It also makes the contrary case for putting conflict resolution, peacekeeping, peacebuilding, and principles at the heart of disaster reduction.[62]

Dismal as these conditions are, many of the unfavorable man-made preconditions and outcomes can be unmade—if that were the aim. Where safer priorities are adopted, the worst can be averted.[63] Detailed reports, walking the ground, and reassessing losses and casualties usually reveal that most destruction, if not all, could have been avoided. Technical assessments and inquiries into accident disasters may uncover carelessness, failures, and indifference but also typically also show they could have been avoided or prevented. Dearth can be countered by public services and social and environmental justice. Modern technoscientific developments can be made much safer, in enterprises that accept the need for, and adopt, precautionary measures and a commitment to safety cultures.[64] Over and against the anthropogenic indifference, the missteps, and the indifference revealed in disasters, there is massive evidence of remarkable care and public spirit, of humanitarian values outside as well as in disasters.[65] Societies should do better, and they can.

NOTES

Introduction

1. Phil O'Keefe, Ken Westgate, and Ben Wisner, "Taking the Naturalness out of Natural Disasters," *Nature* 260 (1976): 566–67; J. C. Gaillard et al., "Taking the 'Naturalness' out of Natural Disaster (Again)," *Natural Hazards Observer* 38, no. 3 (2014): 1, 14–16; Anthony Oliver-Smith, "What Is a Disaster? Anthropological Perspectives on a Persistent Question," in *The Angry Earth: Disasters in Anthropological Context*, ed. Anthony Oliver-Smith and Susanna M. Hoffman (New York: Routledge, 1999), 18–34; Ted Steinberg, *Acts of God: The Unnatural History of Natural Disasters in America*, 2nd ed. (Oxford: Oxford University Press, 2006); Ksenia Chmutina and Jason von Melding, "A Dilemma of Language: 'Natural Disasters' in Academic Literature," *International Journal of Disaster Risk Science* 10 (2019): 283–92; and Andy Horowitz, *Katrina: A History, 1915–2015* (Cambridge, MA: Harvard University Press, 2020).

2. For examples of influential popular attention to disaster, see Naomi Klein, *Shock Doctrine: The Rise of Disaster Capitalism* (New York: Picador, 2007); Rebecca Solnit, *Paradise Built in Hell: The Extraordinary Communities That Arise in Disaster* (New York: Penguin, 2009); Kathryn Schultz, "The Really Big One," *New Yorker*, July 20, 2015, 52–59; and Richard Lloyd Parry, *Ghosts of the Tsunami: Death and Life in Japan's Disaster Zone* (New York: MCD/Farrar, Straus, and Giroux, 2017).

3. To be sure, disaster risk reduction scholars have also questioned what constitutes a disaster, most notably in E. L. Quarantelli, ed., *What Is a Disaster? Perspectives on the Question* (London: Routledge, 1998).

4. On vulnerability, see Ben Wisner et al., *At Risk: Natural Hazards, People's Vulnerability and Disasters*, 2nd ed. (London: Routledge, 2004); on risk, see Ulrich Beck, *Risk Society: Towards a New Modernity*, trans. Mark Ritter (London: Sage, 1992); and Anthony Giddens, "Risk Society: The Context of British Politics," in *The Politics of Risk Society*, ed. Jane Franklin (Cambridge, UK: Polity Press, 1998), 23–34. For resilience, see note 8 and the related text.

5. Classic texts on these topics not cited elsewhere in this chapter include Gilbert Fowler White, "Human Adjustment to Floods: A Geographical Approach to the Flood Problem in the United States" (PhD diss., University of Chicago, 1942); Anthony F. C. Wallace, *Tornado in Worcester: An Exploratory Study of Individual and Community Behavior in an Extreme Situation* (Washington, DC: National Academy of Sciences, National Research Council, 1956); Russell R. Dynes, *Organized Behavior in Crisis* (Lexington, MA: Heath, 1970); Kai Erikson, *A New Species of Trouble: The Human Experience of Modern Disasters* (New York: Norton, 1994); and Lawrence J. Vale and Thomas J. Campanella, eds., *The Resilient City: How Modern Cities Recover from Disaster* (New York: Oxford University Press, 2005).

6. Scott Gabriel Knowles, *The Disaster Experts: Mastering Risk in Modern America* (Philadelphia: University of Pennsylvania Press, 2011); Roberto Barrios, *Governing Affect: Neoliberalism and Disaster Reconstruction* (Lincoln: University of Nebraska Press, 2017); and Jacob A. C. Remes, "'Committed as Near Neighbors': The Halifax Explosion and Border-Crossing People and Ideas," *American Review of Canadian Studies* 45, no. 1 (2015): 32–38. Beyond disaster, see James C. Scott, *Seeing Like a State: How Certain Schemes to Improve the Human Condition Have Failed* (New Haven, CT: Yale University Press, 1998); and Mari Armstrong-Hough, *Biomedicalization and the Practice of Culture: Globalization and Type 2 Diabetes in the United States and Japan* (Chapel Hill: University of North Carolina Press, 2018), 75–109.

7. On solutionism, see Evgeny Morozov, *To Save Everything, Click Here: The Folly of Technological Solutionism* (New York: Public Affairs, 2013).

8. Siambabala Bernard Manyena, "The Concept of Resilience Revisited," *Disasters* 30, no. 4 (2006): 433–50; D. E. Alexander, "Resilience and Disaster Risk Reduction: An Etymological Journey," *Natural Hazards Earth Systems Science* 13 (2013): 2707–16; Steven M. Southwick et al., "Resilience Definitions, Theory, and Challenges: Interdisciplinary Perspectives," *European Journal of Psychotraumatology* 5, no. 1 (2014), doi:10.3402/ejpt.v5.25338. For critiques of "resilience," see Mark Neocleous, "Resisting Resilience," *Radical Philosophy* 178 (March/April 2013): 2–7; John Pat Leary, "Keywords for the Age of Austerity 19: Resilience," Keywords: The New Language of Capitalism, June 23, 2015, https://keywordsforcapitalism.com/2015/06/23/keywords-for-the-age-of-austerity-19-resilience; Shelenda H. Baker, "Anti-Resistance: A Roadmap for Transformational Justice Within the Energy System," *Harvard Civil Rights-Civil Liberties Law Review* 54 (2019): 1–48; and Robin James, *Resilience and Melancholy: Pop Music, Feminism, Neoliberalism* (Arlesford, Hants, UK: Zero Books, 2015).

9. For examples of works that take seriously the lived experience of disasters and its political ramifications, see Kai T. Erikson, *Everything in Its Path: Destruction of Community in the Buffalo Creek Flood* (New York: Simon and Schuster, 1978); Karen Sawislak, *Smoldering City: Chicagoans and the Great Fire, 1871–1874* (Chicago: University of Chicago Press, 1995); Eric Klinenberg, *Heat Wave: A Social Autopsy of Disaster in Chicago*, 2nd ed. (Chicago: University of Chicago Press, 2015); Daniel P. Aldrich, *Building Resilience: Social Capital in Post-Disaster Recovery* (Chicago: University of Chicago Press, 2012); and Jacob A. C. Remes, *Disaster Citizenship: Survivors, Solidarity, and Power in the Progressive Era* (Urbana: University of Illinois Press, 2016).

10. We are grateful to Kenneth Hewitt for sharing the phrase "resilience must be resistance" with us.

11. For an early critique of the technocratic gaze of disaster studies, see Kenneth Hewitt, "The Idea of Calamity in a Technocratic Age," in *Interpretations of Calamity from the Viewpoint of Human Ecology*, ed. Kenneth Hewitt (Boston: Allen and Unwin, 1983), 3–32.

12. "If men define situations as real, they are real in their consequences," as William I. Thomas and Dorothy Swaine Thomas wrote long ago in *The Child in America: Behavior Problems and Programs* (New York: Alfred Knopf, 1928), 572.

13. Elizabeth Angell, "Assembling Disaster: Earthquakes and Urban Politics in Istanbul," *City* 18, no. 6 (2014): 667–78; Max Page, *The City's End: Two Centuries of Fantasies, Fears, and Premonitions of New York's Destruction* (New Haven, CT: Yale University Press, 2008); Lee Clarke, *Mission Improbable: Using Fantasy Documents to Tame Disaster* (Chicago: University of Chicago Press, 1999); Kevin Rozario, *The Culture of Calamity: Disaster and the Making of Modern America* (Chicago: University of Chicago Press, 2007); and Matthew Schneider-Mayerson, "Disaster

Movies and the 'Peak Oil' Movement: Does Popular Culture Encourage Eco-Apocalyptic Beliefs in the United States?," *Journal for the Study of Religion, Nature and Culture* 7, no. 3 (2013): 289–314. For an account of how the category "national calamity" was invented through anticipation and politics in the United States and exported via the American Red Cross, see Marian Moser Jones, *The American Red Cross from Clara Barton to the New Deal* (Baltimore, MD: Johns Hopkins University Press, 2013), esp. 28–29.

14. Kevin A. Gould, M. Magdalena Garcia, and Jacob A. C. Remes, "Beyond 'Natural-Disasters-Are-Not-Natural': The Work of State and Nature after the 2010 Earthquake in Chile," *Journal of Political Ecology* 23 (2016): 93–114; and Raymond Williams, "Ideas of Nature," in *Problems in Materialism and Culture* (London: Verso, 1980), 67–85.

15. Paul Crutzen and Eugene Stoermer, "The Anthropocene," *Global Change Newsletter* 41 (2000): 17–18; Will Steffen et al., "The Anthropocene: Conceptual and Historical Perspectives," *Philosophical Transactions of the Royal Society* 369 (2011): 842–67; Andreas Malm, "The Origins of Fossil Capital: From Water to Steam in the British Cotton Industry," *Historical Materialism* 21, no. 1 (2013): 15–68; Will Steffen et al., "The Trajectory of the Anthropocene: The Great Acceleration," *Anthropocene Review* 2, no. 1 (2015): 81–98; Donna Haraway and Martha Kenney, "Anthropocene, Capitalocene, Chthulhocene," in *Art in the Anthropocene: Encounters Among Aesthetics, Politics, Environments and Epistemologies*, ed. Heather Davis and Etienne Turpin (London: Open Humanities Press, 2015), 255–70; and Heather Davis and Zoe Todd, "On the Importance of a Date, or, Decolonizing the Anthropocene," *ACME: An International Journal for Critical Geographies* 16, no. 4 (2017): 761–80.

16. Horowitz, *Katrina*, 15; Andy Horowitz, "Hurricane Betsy and the Politics of Disaster in New Orleans's Lower Ninth Ward, 1965–1967," *Journal of Southern History* 80, no. 4 (November 2014): 893–934; Superstorm Research Lab, *A Tale of Two Sandys*, white paper, December 2013, https://superstormresearchlab.org/white-paper; Antonio Vázquez-Arroyo, "How Not to Learn from Catastrophe: Habermas, Critical Theory and the Catastrophization of Political Life," *Political Theory* 41 (October 2013): 738–65; and Antonio Vázquez-Arroyo, "The Antinomies of Violence and Catastrophe: Orders, Structures, and Agents," *New Political Science* 34 (June 2012): 211–21.

17. Klinenberg, *Heat Wave*; see also Bryant Simon, *The Hamlet Fire: A Tragic Story of Cheap Food, Cheap Government, and Cheap Lives* (New York: New Press, 2017); and Remes, *Disaster Citizenship*, 4.

18. Andy Horowitz, "Pre-Existing Conditions: Pandemics as History," *SSRC Items* (blog), July 9, 2020, https://items.ssrc.org/covid-19-and-the-social-sciences/disaster-studies/pre-existing -conditions-pandemics-as-history/.

19. Jacob A. C. Remes, "Covid-19 in a Border Nation," *SSRC Items* (blog), July 23, 2020, https://items.ssrc.org/covid-19-and-the-social-sciences/disaster-studies/covid-19-in-a-border -nation/.

20. Horowitz, *Katrina*, 15.

Chapter 1

1. Suzanne Hemann, "Marine Safety Engineers Add Value and Expertise to Coast Guard's Hurricane Response," *Marine Safety Engineering*, August 2018, 2.

2. "Fast Facts: Hurricane Costs," Office for Coastal Management, National Oceanic and Atmospheric Administration, n.d., https://coast.noaa.gov/states/fast-facts/hurricane-costs .html; and Giulia Afiune, "In Harvey's Wake: State Says Harvey's Death Toll Has Reached 88,"

Texan Tribune, October 13, 2017, https://www.texastribune.org/2017/10/13/harveys-death-toll
-reaches-93-people/.

3. Walter Benjamin, *Illuminations: Essays and Reflections* (New York: Schocken, 1968),
257; and Theodor Adorno and Max Horkheimer, *Towards a New Manifesto* (London: Verso,
2011), 39.

4. See Stephen Eric Bonner, *Of Critical Theory and Its Theorists* (New York: Routledge,
2002); Susan Buck-Morss, *Dreamworld and Catastrophe: The Passing of Mass Utopia in East
and West* (Cambridge, MA: MIT Press, 2002); Detlev Claussen, *Theodor Adorno: One Last
Genius* (Cambridge, MA: Belknap Press of Harvard University, 2008); Jack Jacobs, *The Frankfurt School, Jewish Lives, and Antisemitism* (Cambridge: Cambridge University Press, 2015);
Russell Jacoby, *Picture Imperfect: Utopian Thought for an Anti-Utopian Age* (New York: Colum-
bia University Press, 2005); Martin Jay, *The Dialectical Imagination: A History of the Frank-
furt School and the Institute of Social Research, 1923–1950* (Berkeley: University of California
Press, 1996); Leo Lowenthal, *Critical Theory and Frankfurt Theorists: Lectures-Correspondence-
Conversations* (New Brunswick, NJ: Transaction Publishers, 1989); Michael Löwy, *Redemption
& Utopia: Jewish Libertarian Thought in Central Europe, a Study in Elective Affinity* (Stanford,
CA: Stanford University Press, 1992); Michael Löwy, *Fire Alarm: Reading Walter Benjamin's
"On the Concept of History"* (London: Verso, 2005); Enzo Traverso, *Left-Wing Melancholia:
Marxism, History, and Memory* (New York: Columbia University Press, 2016); Thomas Wheat-
land, *The Frankfurt School in Exile* (Minneapolis: University of Minnesota Press, 2009); and
Rolf Wiggershaus, *The Frankfurt School: Its History, Theories, and Political Significance* (Cam-
bridge, MA: MIT Press, 1994).

5. Theodor Adorno, *Minima Moralia: Reflections from Damaged Life* (London: Verso,
2005), 122.

6. See Daniel P. Aldrich, *Building Resilience: Social Capital in Post-Disaster Recovery* (Chi-
cago: University of Chicago Press, 2012); Ulrich Beck, *Risk Society: Towards a New Modernity*
(Los Angeles: Sage, 1986); Ulrich Beck, *World at Risk* (Cambridge, UK: Polity Press, 2009); Mary
Douglas and Aaron Wildavsky, *Risk and Culture* (Berkeley: University of California Press, 1982);
Anique Hommels, Jessica Mesman, and Wiebe E. Bijker, eds., *Vulnerability in Technological
Cultures: New Directions in Research Governance* (Cambridge, MA: MIT Press, 2014); Sheila
Jasanoff, *Learning from Disaster: Risk Management After Bhopal* (Philadelphia: University of
Pennsylvania Press, 1994); Dennis Mileti, *Disasters by Design: A Reassessment of Natural Haz-
ards in the United States* (Washington, DC: Joseph Henry Press, 1999); and Kathleen Tierney,
The Social Roots of Risk: Producing Disasters, Promoting Resilience (Stanford, CA: Stanford Uni-
versity Press, 2014).

7. Gabrielle Hecht, "Interscalar Vehicles for an African Anthropocene: On Waste, Temporality, and Violence," *Cultural Anthropology* 33, no. 1 (2018): 109–41, 115.

8. Casey Conley, "Tugs Sink, Drillship Grounds as Hurricane Harvey Slams Texas," *Professional Mariner*, December 1, 2017, http://www.professionalmariner.com/December-January
-2018/Tugs-sink-drillship-grounds-as-Hurricane-Harvey-slams-Texas/.

9. "Coast Guard Rescued 15 People Near Port Aransas, Texas," United States Coast Guard,
news release, August 29, 2017, https://content.govdelivery.com/accounts/USDHSCG/bulletins
/1b3db25.

10. "Harvey Wrecked Three Towboats at Port Aransas," Maritime Executive, August 31,
2017, https://www.maritime-executive.com/article/harvey-grounded-or-sank-three-towboats
-at-port-aransas.

11. "Remarks at Briefing on Hurricane Harvey Relief Efforts in Corpus Christi, Texas," Public Papers of the Presidents, August 29, 2017, https://www.whitehouse.gov/briefings-statements/remarks-president-trump-briefing-hurricane-harvey-relief-efforts/.

12. "Ships Enter the Reopened Port of Corpus Christi," United States Coast Guard, news release, September 1, 2017, https://content.govdelivery.com/accounts/USDHSCG/bulletins/1b488b0.

13. "Coast Guard Monitors Recovery of Grounded Drill Ship Near Corpus Christi," United States Coast Guard, photo release, September 4, 2017, https://content.govdelivery.com/accounts/USDHSCG/bulletins/1b4f7e9.

14. "Ships Enter the Reopened Port of Corpus Christi."

15. Eric Yep, "Strong Currents Hamper Corpus Christi Drillship Salvage Operations," Lloyd's List Maritime Intelligence, August 31, 2017, https://lloydslist.maritimeintelligence.informa.com/LL111164/Strong-currents-hamper-Corpus-Christi-drillship-salvage-operations.

16. "Coast Guard Monitors Recovery of Grounded Drill Ship Near Corpus Christi."

17. "Cooper Rides Along in Dramatic Chopper Rescue," CNN, August 31, 2017, https://www.cnn.com/videos/weather/2017/08/31/texas-harvey-chopper-rescue-anderson-cooper.cnn.

18. Rye Druzin, "Port of Corpus Christi Remains Closed After Drilling Ship Breaks from Dock, Sinks Tugboat," *San Antonio Express News*, August 28, 2017, https://www.expressnews.com/business/eagle-ford-energy/article/Port-of-Corpus-Christi-closed-after-drilling-ship-12061558.php; and Jennifer Hiller, "Harvey Halts 20 Percent U.S. Refining Operations." *Houston Chronicle*, August 30, 2017.

19. Conley, "Tugs Sink, Drillship Grounds as Hurricane Harvey Slams Texas"; and Rich Miller, "Hurricane Heroes, Ferry Rescue Crew, Mooring System Win Plimsolls," *Professional Mariner*, November 30, 2018, http://www.professionalmariner.com/December-January-2019/Hurricane-heroes-ferry-rescue-crew-mooring-system-win-Plimsolls/.

20. "Drillship Aground in Aransas Pass," G Captain, August 30, 2017, https://forum.gcaptain.com/t/drillship-aground-in-aransas-pass/45965.

21. Josh Greenberg and T. Joseph Scanlon, "Old Media, New Media, and the Complex Story of Disasters," in *Oxford Research Encyclopedia of Natural Hazard Science* (July 2016), https://oxfordre.com/naturalhazardscience/view/10.1093/acrefore/9780199389407.001.0001/acrefore-9780199389407-e-21.

22. Russell R. Dynes, *Organized Behavior in Disaster* (Lexington, MA: D. C. Heath, 1970); Charles Fritz, *Disasters and Mental Health: Therapeutic Principles Drawn from Disaster Studies* (Newark: University of Delaware Disaster Research Center, 1961); and Enrico Louis Quarantelli, *What Is a Disaster? A Dozen Perspectives on the Question* (New York: Routledge, 2005). See also Scott Knowles, *The Disaster Experts* (Philadelphia: University of Pennsylvania Press, 2011).

23. James Kendra and Tricia Wachtendorf, *American Dunkirk: The Waterborne Evacuation of Manhattan on 9/11* (Philadelphia: Temple University Press, 2016); and Alice Fothergill and Lori Peek, *Children of Katrina* (Austin: University of Texas Press, 2015). On the ethics of event-scale disaster research, see Jennifer Henderson and Max Liboiron, "Compromise and Action: Tactics for Doing Ethical Research in Disaster Zones," in *Disaster Research and the Second Environmental Crisis*, ed. James Kendra, Scott G. Knowles, and Tricia Wachtendorf (Cham, Switzerland: Springer, 2019), 295–318; and James Kendra and Sarah Gregory, "Ethics in Disaster Research: A New Declaration," in Kendra, Knowles, and Wachtendorf, *Disaster Research and the Second Environmental Crisis*, 319–41.

24. *Emergency Response and Recovery: Central Takeaways from the Unprecedented 2017 Hurricane Season: Hearing Before the House Comm. on Transportation and Infrastructure*, 115th Cong. (November 2, 2017).

25. *Emergency Response and Recovery*, 83–92.

26. Angela Fritz, "Texas Governor Urges People to Evacuate, Even If It's Not 'Mandatory,'" *Washington Post*, August 25, 2017, https://www.washingtonpost.com/national/2017/live-updates/weather/hurricane-harvey-updates-preparation-evacuations-forecast-storm-latest/texas-governor-asks-people-to-evacuate-even-if-its-not-mandatory/?utm_term=.990a45dedb64.

27. "Major Hurricane Harvey—August 25–29, 2017," National Weather Service, n.d., https://www.weather.gov/crp/hurricane_harvey; and "Fast Facts: Hurricane Costs."

28. "Major Hurricane Harvey—August 25–29, 2017"; and "Fast Facts: Hurricane Costs."

29. For risk and disaster science, see Russell R. Dynes, "The Dialogue Between Voltaire and Rousseau on the Social Science View," *International Journal of Mass Emergencies and Disasters* 18, no. 1 (2000): 97–115; Theodore M. Porter, *Trust in Numbers: The Pursuit of Objectivity in Science and Public Life* (Princeton, NJ: Princeton University Press, 1995); and Carl-Henry Geschwind, *California Earthquakes: Science, Risk, and the Politics of Hazard Mitigation* (Baltimore, MD: Johns Hopkins University Press, 2008).

30. See Greg Bankoff, Georg Frerks, and Dorothea Hilhorst, eds., *Mapping Vulnerability: Disasters, Development and People* (London: Earthscan, 2003); Kenneth Hewitt, ed., *Interpretations of Calamity from the Viewpoint of Human Ecology* (Boston: Allen and Unwin, 1983); Kai Eriskon, *A New Species of Trouble: The Human Experience of Modern Disasters* (New York: Norton, 1994); Stephen Hilgartner, "Overflow and Containment in the Aftermath of Disaster," *Social Studies of Science* 37, no. 1 (February 2007), 153–58; Stephen Hilgartner, *Science on Stage: Expert Advice as Public Drama* (Stanford, CA: Stanford University Press, 2000); Jasanoff, *Learning from Disaster*; Ann Larabee, *Decade of Disaster* (Urbana: University of Illinois Press, 1999); Charles Perrow, *Normal Accidents: Living with High-Risk Technologies* (Princeton, NJ: Princeton University Press, 2011); Diane Vaughan, *The Challenger Launch Decision: Risky Technology, Culture, and Deviance at NASA* (Chicago: University of Chicago Press, 1997); Paul Susman, Phil O'Keefe, and Ben Wisner, "Global Disasters: A Radical Interpretation," in *Interpretations of Calamity from the Viewpoint of Human Ecology*, ed. Kenneth Hewitt (Boston: Allen and Unwin, 1983), 263–83; and Langdon Winner, *The Whale and the Reactor: A Search for Limits in an Age of High Technology* (Chicago: University of Chicago Press, 1986).

31. Ted Steinberg, *Acts of God: The Unnatural History of Natural Disaster in the United States*, 2nd ed. (New York: Oxford University Press, 2006); Mike Davis, *Ecology of Fear: Los Angeles and the Imagination of Disaster* (New York: Metropolitan, 1998); Mike Davis, *Late Victorian Holocausts: El Niño Famines and the Making of the Third World* (London: Verso, 2001); Carl Smith, *Urban Disorder and the Shape of Belief: The Great Chicago Fire, the Haymarket Bomb, and the Model Town of Pullman* (Chicago: University of Chicago Press, 1995); and Christine Meisner Rosen, *Limits of Power: Great Fires and the Process of City Growth in America* (New York: Cambridge University Press, 1986).

32. "Aranasas County Texas Multi-Jurisdictional Hazard Mitigation Action Plan," LAN—Lockwood, Andrews, & Newman, Inc., October 12, 2017, https://www.aransaspasstx.gov/DocumentCenter/View/646/Aransas-County-Texas-Multi-Jurisdictional-Hazard-Mitigation-Action-Plan.

33. Dan Parker, "Conservancy Meeting Draws 200+," *Port Aransas South Jetty*, January 23, 2019, https://www.portasouthjetty.com/articles/conservancy-meeting-draws-200/.

34. "Top 20 Concerns with a Harbor Island VLCC Terminal," Port Aransas Conservancy, 2018/2019, https://portaransasconservancy.com/top-20-concerns.

Chapter 2

1. "The Railway Calamity," *Saturday Review of Politics, Literature, Science and Art* 26, no. 670 (1868): 281.

2. Roger Cooter, "The Moment of the Accident: Culture, Militarism and Modernity in Late-Victorian Britain," in *Accidents in History: Injuries, Fatalities and Social Relations*, ed. Roger Cooter and Bill Luckin (Atlanta, GA: Rodopi, 1997), 107.

3. Ian Hacking, *The Taming of Chance* (Cambridge: Cambridge University Press, 1990).

4. Similar traumas were being experienced in the United States in this period on its railways and particularly on its waterways, where boiler explosions aboard steamships regularly inflicted horrific injuries from steam and shrapnel on unsuspecting travelers. The worst of these disasters occurred in April 1865, when two boilers on the steamboat *Sultana* exploded on the Mississippi river just north of Memphis, Tennessee, killing nearly one thousand people. In the national discourse the incident was subsumed within the larger tumult around President Abraham Lincoln's assassination, which had occurred barely two weeks earlier and, the day before the *Sultana* explosion, the killing of his assassin, John Wilkes Booth. See Gene Salecker, *Disaster on the Mississippi: The* Sultana *Explosion, April 27, 1865* (Annapolis, MD: Naval Institute Press, 1996).

5. "Railway Calamity," 281–82.

6. John Eric Erichsen, *On Railway and Other Injuries of the Nervous System* (Philadelphia: Henry C. Lea, 1867); and Ian Hacking, *Rewriting the Soul: Multiple Personality and the Sciences of Memory* (Princeton, NJ: Princeton University Press, 1995).

7. Cooter, "Moment of the Accident."

8. Anthony Giddens, *A Contemporary Critique of Historical Materialism*, vol. 1, *Power, Property and the State* (London: Macmillan, 1981), 92.

9. By the late years of the Victorian period this crisis of confidence had generalized to anxiety over imperial decline. In this era, the literary scholar Judith Wilt writes, British literature became preoccupied with "anxieties about the future consequences of present actions . . . fears connected with the demands of progress," and especially anxieties over counterattacks by subjugated peoples. See Judith Wilt, "The Imperial Mouth: Imperialism, the Gothic and Science Fiction," *Journal of Popular Culture* 14, no. 4 (1981): 624. These counterattack narratives articulated fears of reverse colonization. In both popular and literary novels of the period, the reverse-colonial threat was transmitted through the infrastructure and technology of empire, whether that infrastructure was turned against its masters (as in Bram Stoker's *Dracula* or Joseph Conrad's *Heart of Darkness*) or whether, as in H. G. Wells's *War of the Worlds*, the imperial core was besieged by an even more technologically advanced adversary. In all of these works, "a terrifying reversal has occurred: the colonizer finds himself in the position of the colonized, the exploiter becomes exploited, the victimizer victimized." Stephen D. Arata, "The Occidental Tourist: 'Dracula' and the Anxiety of Reverse Colonization," *Victorian Studies* 33, no. 4 (1990): 623.

10. "Railway Calamity," 281.

11. Charles Perrow, *Normal Accidents: Living with High Risk Technologies*, updated ed. (Princeton, NJ: Princeton University Press, 2011).

12. Ulrich Beck, *Risk Society: Towards a New Modernity* (New York: Sage, 1992).

13. Susan Neiman, *Evil in Modern Thought: An Alternative History of Philosophy* (Princeton, NJ: Princeton University Press, 2002).

14. Neiman, *Evil in Modern Thought*, 2.

15. Kathleen J. Tierney, "From the Margins to the Mainstream? Disaster Research at the Crossroads," *Annual Review of Sociology* 33 (2007): 503–25.

16. Eric Klinenberg, "When a Dissertation Chooses You," *Sociologica* 12, no. 1 (2019): 41–43.

17. Rebecca Elliott, "The Sociology of Climate Change as a Sociology of Loss," *European Journal of Sociology* 59, no. 3 (2018): 302.

18. Russell R. Dynes, "The Dialogue Between Voltaire and Rousseau on the Social Science View," *International Journal of Mass Emergencies and Disasters* 18, no. 1 (2000): 97–115.

19. Ana Cristina Araújo, "The Lisbon Earthquake of 1755: Public Distress and Political Propaganda," *e-Journal of Portuguese History* 4, no. 1 (2006): 2.

20. Araújo, "Lisbon Earthquake of 1755," 2.

21. Jürgen Wilke, "Historical Perspectives on Media Events: A Comparison of the Lisbon Earthquake in 1755 and the Tsunami Catastrophe in 2004," in *Media Events in a Global Age*, ed. Nick Couldry, Andreas Hepp, and Friedrich Krotz (London: Routledge, 2009), 45–60.

22. Neiman, *Evil in Modern Thought*, 244.

23. Gerrit Jasper Schenk, "'Human Security' in the Renaissance? 'Securitas', Infrastructure, Collective Goods and Natural Hazards in Tuscany and the Upper Rhine Valley," *Historical Social Research* 35, no. 4 (2010): 209–33.

24. Wolfgang Behringer, "Climatic Change and Witch-Hunting: The Impact of the Little Ice Age on Mentalities," *Climatic Change* 43 (1999): 335–51.

25. Johann Wolfgang von Goethe, *Truth and Fiction Relating to My Life*, trans. John Oxenford (Boston: Simonds and Co., 1902), 25.

26. T. D. Kendrick, *The Lisbon Earthquake* (New York: J. B. Lippincott, 1957), 185.

27. Neiman, *Evil in Modern Thought*, 248.

28. Kendrick, *Lisbon Earthquake*, 135–41.

29. Neiman, *Evil in Modern Thought*, 249–50.

30. Gerard Passannante, *The Lucretian Renaissance: Philology and the Afterlife of Tradition* (Chicago: University of Chicago Press, 2011), 35.

31. Gerard Passannante, *Catastrophizing: Materialism and the Making of Disaster* (Chicago: University of Chicago Press, 2019).

32. Deborah R. Coen, *The Earthquake Observers: Disaster Science from Lisbon to Richter* (Chicago: University of Chicago Press, 2013), 107.

33. William Farr, *Report of the Proceedings of the Fourth Session of the International Statistical Congress: Held in London July 16th, 1860, and the Following Five Days* (London: Her Majesty's Stationery Office, 1861).

34. Bruno Latour, *The Pasteurization of France*, trans. Alan Sheridan and John Law (Cambridge, MA: Harvard University Press, 1993), 62.

35. Latour, *Pasteurization of France*, 74.

36. Scott Gabriel Knowles, *The Disaster Experts: Mastering Risk in Modern America* (Philadelphia: University of Pennsylvania Press, 2011), 21.

37. Samuel Henry Prince, *Catastrophe and Social Change: Based upon a Sociological Study of the Halifax Disaster* (New York: Columbia University, 1920), 28.

38. Prince, *Catastrophe and Social Change*, 13.

39. Michele Landis Dauber, *The Sympathetic State: Disaster Relief and the Origins of the American Welfare State* (Chicago: University of Chicago Press, 2013).

40. Lowell Juilliard Carr, "Disaster and the Sequence-Pattern Concept of Social Change," *American Journal of Sociology* 38, no. 2 (1932): 211.

41. Gilbert Fowler White, "Human Adjustment to Floods: A Geographical Approach to the Flood Problem in the United States" (PhD diss., University of Chicago, 1942), 2.

42. Kenneth Hewitt, "The Idea of Calamity in a Technocratic Age," in *Interpretations of Calamity from the Viewpoint of Human Ecology*, ed. Kenneth Hewitt (Boston: Allen and Unwin, 1983), 3–32; and N. D. Macdonald et al., "The Significance of Gilbert F. White's 1945 Paper 'Human Adjustment to Floods' in the Development of Risk and Hazard Management," *Progress in Physical Geography: Earth and Environment* 36, no. 1 (2012): 125–33.

43. Lewis Mumford, *The City in History* (New York: Harcourt, 1961), 542.

44. Jacob A. C. Remes, "'Committed as Near Neighbors': The Halifax Explosion and Border-Crossing People and Ideas," *American Review of Canadian Studies* 45, no. 1 (March 2015): 26–43.

45. Prince, *Catastrophe and Social Change*, 26.

46. Jacob A. C. Remes, *Disaster Citizenship: Survivors, Solidarity, and Power in the Progressive Era* (Urbana: University of Illinois Press, 2016), 197.

47. Beck, *Risk Society*.

48. Peter Washer, *Emerging Infectious Diseases and Society* (New York: Palgrave Macmillan, 2014).

49. US Federal Emergency Management Agency, *2017 Hurricane Season FEMA After-Action Report* (Washington, DC, 2018).

50. Nishant Kishore et al., "Mortality in Puerto Rico after Hurricane Maria," *New England Journal of Medicine* 379, no. 2 (2018): 162–70.

51. Aninidta Issa et al., "Deaths Related to Hurricane Irma—Florida, Georgia, and North Carolina, September 4–October 10, 2017," *Morbidity and Mortality Weekly Report* 67, no. 30 (2018): 829–32.

52. Sebastiaan N. Jonkman et al., "Brief Communication: Loss of Life Due to Hurricane Harvey," *Natural Hazards and Earth System Sciences* 18, no. 4 (2018): 1073–78.

53. Edward N. Rappaport and B. Wayne Blanchard, "Fatalities in the United States Indirectly Associated with Atlantic Tropical Cyclones," *Bulletin of the American Meteorological Society* 97, no. 7 (2016): 1139–48.

54. Bruno Latour, "How Better to Register the Agency of Things: Ontology" (presentation at Yale Tanner Lecture Series, March 27, 2014), http://www.bruno-latour.fr/node/563.

55. Beck, *Risk Society*.

56. Paul N. Edwards, *A Vast Machine: Computer Models, Climate Data, and the Politics of Global Warming* (Cambridge, MA: MIT Press, 2010).

57. P. K. Haff, "Technology as a Geological Phenomenon: Implications for Human Well-Being," *Geological Society, London, Special Publications* 395, no. 1 (2014): 302.

58. A 2017 study estimated the physical mass of the technosphere at thirty trillion tons, approximately five orders of magnitude more than the total of human biomass . Put in starker terms by the environmental law scholar Jedediah Purdy, that translates to "approximately four

thousand tons of transformed earth per human being, or twenty-seven tons of technosphere for each pound of a 150-pound person." Jan Zalasiewicz et al., "Scale and Diversity of the Physical Technosphere: A Geological Perspective," *Anthropocene Review* 4, no. 1 (2017): 9–22; and Jedediah Purdy, "The World We've Built," *Dissent Magazine*, July 3, 2018.

59. Paul J. Crutzen, "The 'Anthropocene,'" *Journal de Physique IV (Proceedings)* 12, no. 10 (2002): 1–5; Simon L. Lewis and Mark A. Maslin, "Defining the Anthropocene," *Nature* 519, no. 7542 (2015): 171–80; Jamie Lorimer, "The Anthropo-scene: A Guide for the Perplexed," *Social Studies of Science* 47, no. 1 (2017): 117–42; and William H. McNeill and Charles P. Kindleberger, "Control and Catastrophe in Human Affairs," *Daedalus* 118, no. 1 (1989): 1–15.

60. McNeill and Kindleberger, "Control and Catastrophe in Human Affairs," 1.

61. B. Wayne Blanchard, *Guide to Emergency Management and Related Terms, Definitions, Concepts, Acronyms, Organizations, Programs, Guidance, Executive Orders & Legislation* (Washington, DC: Federal Emergency Management Agency, Emergency Management Institute, 2008).

62. Stephen J. Collier, "Enacting Catastrophe: Preparedness, Insurance, Budgetary Rationalization," *Economy and Society* 37, no. 2 (2008): 224–50; Stephen J. Collier and Andrew Lakoff, "Distributed Preparedness: The Spatial Logic of Domestic Security in the United States," *Environment and Planning D: Society and Space* 26, no. 1 (2008):7–28; Stephen J. Collier and Andrew Lakoff, "The Vulnerability of Vital Systems: How 'Critical Infrastructure' Became a Security Problem," in *Securing "the Homeland": Critical Infrastructure, Risk and (In)security*, ed. Myriam Dunn Cavelty and Kristian Søby Kristensen (London and New York: Routledge, 2008):17–39; Stephen J. Collier and Andrew Lakoff, "Vital Systems Security: Reflexive Biopolitics and the Government of Emergency," *Theory, Culture & Society* 32 no. 2 (2015):19–51; and Andrew Lakoff, *Unprepared: Global Health in a Time of Emergency* (Oakland: University of California Press, 2017).

63. The apotheosis of this practice was the *Bombing Encyclopedia of the World*, compiled by the Strategic Vulnerability Branch of the US Air Force beginning in 1946, with the "ultimate goal" of having "information on every potential target in every country" in the world, chosen for their strategic importance within a network of "larger target systems." Lynn Eden, *Whole World on Fire: Organizations, Knowledge, and Nuclear Weapons Devastation* (Ithaca, NY: Cornell University Press 2004), 107–9.

64. Collier and Lakoff, "Vulnerability of Vital Systems," 26.

65. Lakoff, *Unprepared*, 38.

66. Keith Bea, "The Formative Years: 1950–1978," in *Emergency Management: The American Experience 1900–2010*, ed. Claire B. Rubin (Boca Raton, FL: CRC Press, 2012): 83–114.

67. Exec. Order No. 13010, 61 Fed. Reg. 138 (July 17, 1996), 37345–50.

68. United States, President's Commission on Critical Infrastructure Protection, *Critical Foundations: Protecting America's Infrastructures* (Washington, DC, 1997), 3 (emphasis in original).

69. United States, *Critical Foundations*, 10.

70. United States, *Critical Foundations*, 3.

71. United States, *Critical Foundations*, ix.

72. Sean Gardiner, "The Dawn of 2000/Officials Hunker Down in 'Bunker' for Transition," *Newsday*, January 2, 2000.

73. Julie Fields, "N.Y. Command Center," *The Record*, January 1, 2000.

74. Marie-Hélène Huet, *The Culture of Disaster* (Chicago: University of Chicago Press, 2012), 3.

Chapter 3

1. "Rahm Emanuel on the Opportunities of Crisis," *Wall Street Journal*, November 19, 2008, https://www.youtube.com/watch?v=_mzcbXi1Tkk.

2. Neil deMause, "The Recession and the 'Deserving Poor': Poverty Finally on Media Radar but Only When It Hits the Middle Class," FAIR, February 9, 2009, https://fair.org/extra /the-recession-and-the-deserving-poor/; Lani Guinier and Gerald Torres, *The Miner's Canary: Enlisting Race, Resisting Power, Transforming Democracy* (Cambridge, MA: Harvard University Press, 2002); and John Kingdon, *Agendas, Alternatives, and Public Policies* (New York: Harper-Collins, 1995).

3. Amy Castro Baker, "Eroding the Wealth of Women: Gender and the Subprime Foreclosure Crisis," *Social Science Review* 88, no. 1 (2014): 59–91; Robert Cotterman, "New Evidence on the Relationship Between Race and Mortgage Default: The Importance of Credit History Data," Unicon Research Corporation, May 23, 2002, https://www.huduser.gov/Publications /PDF/crhistory.pdf; and Joint Center for Housing Studies of Harvard University, "The State of the Nation's Housing 2009," 2009, www.jchs.harvard.edu/publications/markets/son2009 /index.htm.

4. E. E. Schattschneider, *The Semisovereign People* (New York: Holt, Rinehart and Winston, 1960); Frank Baumgartner and Bryan Jones, *Agendas and Instability in American Politics* (Chicago: University of Chicago Press, 1993); and John W. Kingdon, *Agendas, Alternatives, and Public Policies* (New York: HarperCollins, 1995).

5. Antonio Vàzquez-Arroyo, "How Not to Learn from Catastrophe: Critical Theory and the Catastrophization of Political Life," *Political Theory* 4 (2013): 738–65.

6. Dara Z. Strolovitch, *When Bad Things Happen to Privileged People: Race, Gender, and the Political Construction of Crisis & Non-Crisis* (Chicago: University of Chicago Press, forthcoming).

7. Raymond Williams, *Keywords* (New York: Oxford University Press, 1976).

8. Daniel Immergluck, "Too Little, Too Late, and Too Timid: The Federal Response to the Foreclosure Crisis at the Five-Year Mark," *Housing Policy Debate* 23 (2013): 202–4.

9. US Department of Housing and Urban Development, Office of Policy Development and Research, *Report to Congress on the Root Causes of the Foreclosure Crisis* (Washington, DC, 2010).

10. Jeff Crump et al., "Cities Destroyed (Again) for Cash: Forum on the U.S. Foreclosure Crisis," *Urban Geography* 29 (2008): 745–84

11. Crump et al., "Cities Destroyed (Again) for Cash," 756.

12. Consumer Financial Protection Bureau, "What Is a Subprime Mortgage?," 2017, consumerfinance.gov/ask-cfpb/what-is-a-subprime-mortgage-en-110/.

13. Daniel Immergluck, *Foreclosed: High-Risk Lending, Deregulation, and the Undermining of America's Mortgage Market* (Ithaca, NY: Cornell University Press, 2009), 136.

14. Among the key changes were those enabled by the 1980 Depository Institutions Deregulation and Monetary Control Act, 1982 Alternative Mortgage Transaction Parity Act, 1984 Secondary Mortgage Market Enhancement Act, and 1986 Tax Reform Act (TRA); see Souphala Chomsisengphet and Anthony Pennington-Cross, "The Evolution of the Subprime Mortgage Market," *Federal Reserve Bank of St. Louis Review* (January/Februry 2006): 38. Also important was the 1978 Supreme Court decision in *Marquette National Bank of Minneapolis v. First of Omaha Service Corp.*, which allowed national banks to establish headquarters in states with high or no usury limits and to charge those rates to borrowers located in any state. Patricia McCoy

and Elizabeth Renuart, "The Legal Infrastructure of Subprime and Nontraditional Home Mortgages," in *Borrowing to Live: The Legal Infrastructure of Subprime and Nontraditional Homes Mortgages*, ed. Nicolas P. Retsinas and Eric S. Belsky (Washington, DC: Brookings Institution Press, 2008), 113.

15. Among the these laws were the 1968 Fair Housing Act, which prohibited discrimination in the sale, rental, and financing of housing based on race, religion, and national origin, and which was extended to include gender in 1974 and to people with disabilities and families with children in 1988; the 1974 Equal Credit Opportunity Act, which prohibited creditors from discrimination based on race, sex, age, national origin, or marital status, or because one receives public assistance; the 1977 Community Reinvestment Act, which encouraged banks and savings associations to lend to borrowers hoping to buy houses in low- and moderate-income neighborhoods in order to reduce "redlining," the practice whereby lenders denied mortgages to homeowners and would-be homeowners in neighborhoods deemed "unfit for investment"; and the 1975 Home Mortgage Disclosure Act, which required financial institutions to provide information to determine whether they are serving the housing credit needs of the neighborhoods and communities in which they are located and to aid public officials in targeting public investments from the private sector. Amendments to the HMDA that were passed in 1989 in the wake of the failure in the savings and loan sector further required the collection and disclosure of data about applicant and borrower characteristics to help identify discriminatory lending patterns and enforce antidiscrimination statutes.

16. Baker, "Eroding the Wealth of Women"; Greta Krippner, "Democracy of Credit: Ownership and the Politics of Credit Access in Late Twentieth Century America," *American Journal of Sociology* 123 (2017): 1–47; and Chloe Thurston, *At the Boundaries of Homeownership* (New York: Cambridge University Press, 2018).

17. For a full discussion of specific legislative steps taken by the state to promote financialization, see Kathe Newman, "The Perfect Storm: Contextualizing the Foreclosure Crisis," *Urban Geography* 29 (2008): 750–54; and Jamie Peck and Adam Tickell, "Neoliberalizing Space," *Antipode* 34 (2002): 380–404.

18. Baker, "Eroding the Wealth of Women"; and James Greer, "The Better Homes Movement and the Origins of Mortgage Redlining in the United States," in *Statebuilding from the Margins: Between Reconstruction and the New Deal*, ed. Julie Novkov and Carol Nackenoff (Philadelphia: University of Pennsylvania Press, 2014), 202–36.

19. Baker, "Eroding the Wealth of Women," 74–77.

20. Louise Seamster and Raphaël Charron-Chénier, "Predatory Inclusion and Education Debt: A New Approach to the Growing Racial Wealth Gap," *Social Currents* 4 (2017): 199–207; Keeanga-Yamahtta Taylor, *Race for Profit: How Banks and the Real Estate Industry Undermined Black Homeownership* (Chapel Hill: University of North Carolina Press, 2019); see also Baker, "Eroding the Wealth of Women"; Daniel Immergluck, *Credit to the Community: Community Reinvestment and Fair Lending Policy in the United States* (New York: Routledge 2004); and William Apgar, Amal Bendimerad, and Ren Essene, *Mortgage Market Channels and Fair Lending: An Analysis of HMDA Data* (Cambridge, MA: Joint Center for Housing Studies of Harvard University, 2007).

21. Consumer Financial Protection Bureau, "2013 Home Ownership and Equality Protection Act (HOEPA) Rule: Small Entity Compliance Guide," 2013, tinyurl.com/ya2ma5c6. HOEPA is Title I, subtitle B, of the Community Development and Regulatory Improvement Act of 1994, which "amends the Truth in Lending Act to prohibit certain terms and require

additional disclosures of the terms of home equity loans and second mortgages with certain interest rates or origination fees."

22. McCoy and Renuart, "Legal Infrastructure of Subprime and Nontraditional Home Mortgages," 119. "High-cost mortgages" were defined to include only ones in which the annual percentage rate (APR) at closing exceeded the yield on comparable Treasury security plus 8 percent for first-lien loans and plus 10 percent for junior-lien loans or in which the total points and fees exceeded "the greater of eight percent of the total loan amount or $400" (119).

23. US Department of Housing and Urban Development, Office of Policy Development and Research, *Report to Congress on the Root Causes of the Foreclosure Crisis* (Washington, DC, 2010), ix. See E. M. Gramlich, "Booms and Busts: The Case of Subprime Mortgages," *Economic Review* 92 (2007): 105–13; Ren S. Essene and William C. Apgar, *Understanding Mortgage Market Behavior: Creating Good Mortgage Options for All Americans* (Cambridge, MA: Joint Center for Housing Studies of Harvard University, 2007); and McCoy and Renaurt, "Legal Infrastructure of Subprime and Nontraditional Home Mortgages."

24. Chomsisengphet and Pennington-Cross, "Evolution of the Subprime Mortgage Market," 37.

25. Baker, "Eroding the Wealth of Women," 79.

26. National Training and Information Center, *Preying on Neighborhoods: Subprime Mortgage Lenders and Chicago Land Foreclosures* (Chicago, 1999).

27. Baker, "Eroding the Wealth of Women," 77. See also Allen Fishbein and Patrick Woodall, *Women Are Prime Targets for Subprime Lending: Women Are Disproportionately in High-Cost Mortgage Market* (Consumer Federation of America, 2006); and Kathleen Keest, "The Way Ahead: A Framework for Policy Responses" (presentation at Subprime Housing Crisis Symposium, University of Iowa, 2008), www.responsiblelending.org/sites/default/files/nodes/files/research-publication/Iowa-Subprime-Symposium.pdf.

28. Fishbein and Woodall, *Women Are Prime Targets*, 3.

29. Fishbein and Woodall, *Women Are Prime Targets*, 3.

30. Fishbein and Woodall, *Women Are Prime Targets*, 3; and Sandra Phillips, "The Subprime Mortgage Calamity and the African American Woman," *Review of Black Political Economy* 39 (2012): 227–37.

31. US Department of Housing and Urban Development, *Subprime Lending Report: Unequal Burden in Baltimore: Income and Racial Disparities in Subprime Lending*, 2000, https://www.huduser.gov/Publications/pdf/baltimore.pdf.

32. Debbie Gruenstein Bocian, Wie Li, and Keith S. Ernst, *Foreclosures by Race and Ethnicity* (Center for Responsible Lending, 2010), 3.

33. Bocian, Li, and Ernst, *Foreclosures by Race and Ethnicity*.

34. Baker, "Eroding the Wealth of Women," 76.

35. Cotterman, "New Evidence on the Relationship Between Race and Mortgage Default."

36. National Training and Information Center, *Preying on Neighborhoods*.

37. *Problem Surrounding the Mortgage Origination Process, Joint Hearings Before the Senate Subcommittee on Financial Institutions and Regulatory Relief and the Subcommittee on Housing Opportunity and Community Development of the Committee on Banking, Housing, and Urban Affairs*. 105th Cong., 1st sess. (1997), 77–79.

38. *Field Hearing on Community Solutions for the Prevention and Management of Foreclosures, House Committee on Financial Services, Subcommittee on Housing and Community Opportunity*, 109th Cong., 2nd sess. (August 23, 2006), 51.

39. Jonathan McCarthy and Richard W. Peach, "Are Home Prices the Next 'Bubble'?," *FRBNY Economic Policy Review* 10, no. 3 (2004): 2.

40. Rick Brooks and Ruth Simon, "Subprime Debacle Traps Even Very Credit-Worthy as Housing Boomed, Industry Pushed Loans to a Broader Market," *Wall Street Journal*, December 4, 2007, 3.

41. Jonathan Karp, "How the Mortgage Bar Keeps Moving Higher Home Buyers with Good Credit Confront Increased Scrutiny and Fewer Choices as Lenders React to Subprime Debacle," *Wall Street Journal*, August 14, 2007, D1.

42. Julie Creswell and Vikas Bajajmarch, "Mortgage Crisis Spirals, and Casualties Mount," *New York Times*, March 5, 2007, C1.

43. Bob Tedeschi, "Why Women Pay Higher Interest," *New York Times*, January 21, 2007, https://www.nytimes.com/2007/01/21/21mort.html

44. Peter Dreier et al., *Underwater America: How the So-Called Housing "Recovery" Is Bypassing Many American Communities* (Berkeley, CA: Haas Institute for a Fair and Inclusive Society, 2014); Baker, "Eroding the Wealth of Women"; and Daniel Immergluck, *Preventing the Next Mortgage Crisis: The Meltdown, the Federal Response, and the Future of Housing in America* (New York: Rowman & Littlefield, 2015).

45. Baker, "Eroding the Wealth of Women"; Vanesa Estrada Correa, "Blueprint for the American Dream? A Critical Discourse Analysis of Presidential Remakes on Minority Home-ownership," *Social Justice* 40 (2014): 16–27; Immgergluck, *Preventing the Next Mortgage Crisis*; and Elvin Wyly and C. S. Ponder, "Gender, Age, and Race in Subprime American," *Housing Policy Debate* 21 (2011): 529–64.

46. Immergluck, *Preventing the Next Mortgage Crisis*, 60.

47. Immergluck, *Preventing the Next Mortgage Crisis*, 60.

48. Dara Z. Strolovitch, "Of Mancessions and Hecoveries: Race, Gender, and the Political Construction of Economic Crisis and Recovery," *Perspectives on Politics* 11 (2013): 167–76; Dreier et al., *Underwater America*; and Baker, "Eroding the Wealth of Women."

49. Richard Fry and Anna Brown, "In a Recovering Market, Homeownership Rates Are Down Sharply for Blacks, Young Adults," Pew Research Center, 2016, www.pewsocialtrends.org/2016/12/15/in-a-recovering-market-homeownership-rates-are-down-sharply-for-blacks-young-adults/. The same was true among Latinos, among whom rates of homeownership saw a net gain from 41.2 percent in 1994 to 47 percent in 2016, although this rate was still lower than it was at its peak of 49.7 percent in 2007.

50. Jacob Faber, "Segregation and the Geography of Creditworthiness: Racial Inequality in a Recovered Mortgage Market," *Housing Policy Debate* 28 (2018): 215–47. See also Elizabeth Korver Glenn, "Compounding Inequalities: How Racial Stereotypes and Discrimination Accumulate Across the Stages of Housing Exchange," *American Sociological Review* 83 (2018): 627–56; and Douglas S. Massey et al., "Riding the Stagecoach to Hell: A Qualitative Analysis of Racial Discrimination in Mortgage Lending," *City & Community* 15 (2016): 118–36.

51. Daniel Immergluck, "Old Wine in Private Equity Bottles? The Resurgence of Contract-for-Deed Home Sales in US Urban Neighborhoods," *International Journal of Urban and Regional Research* 42 (2018): 651–65.

52. Immergluck, *Foreclosed*, 11.

53. "Remarks by President Trump, Vice President Pence, and Members of the Coronavirus Task Force in Press Briefing," April 7, 2020, www.whitehouse.gov/briefings-statements/remarks-president-trump-vice-president-pence-members-coronavirus-task-force-press-briefing-april-7-2020/ (emphasis added).

Chapter 4

1. Joel F. Audefroy, "Haiti: Post-Earthquake Lessons Learned from Traditional Construction," *Environment and Urbanization* 23, no. 2 (2011): 447–62; Eduardo Fierro and Cynthia Perry, *Preliminary Reconnaissance Report: 12 January 2010 Haiti Earthquake* (The Pacific Earthquake Engineering Research Center, 2010); L. Holliday, C. Ramseyer, and F. H. Grant, "Masonry Block Construction in Haiti," *WIT Transactions on the Built Environment* 120 (2011): 299–307; H. McWilliams and C. T. Griffin, "A Critical Assessment of Concrete and Masonry Structures for Reconstruction After Seismic Events in Developing Countries," in *Structures and Architecture: New Concepts, Applications and Challenges*, ed. Paulo J. S. Cruz (Leiden: CRC Press, 2013), 857–64.

2. Patrick Bellegarde-Smith, "A Man-Made Disaster: The Earthquake of January 12, 2010—A Haitian Perspective," *Journal of Black Studies* 42, no. 2 (March 2011): 264–75; Laurent Dubois, *Haiti: The Aftershocks of History* (New York: Metropolitan Books, 2012); Alex Dupuy, "Disaster Capitalism to the Rescue: The International Community and Haiti After the Earthquake," *NACLA Report on the Americas* 43, no. 4 (2010): 14–19; Anthony Oliver-Smith, "Haiti's 500 Year Earthquake," in *Tectonic Shifts: Haiti Since the Earthquake*, ed. Mark Schuller and Pablo Morales (Sterling, VA: Kumarian Press, 2012), 18–23; and Mark Schuller, *Humanitarian Aftershocks in Haiti* (New Brunswick, N.J.: Rutgers University Press, 2016).

3. Oliver-Smith, "Haiti's 500 Year Earthquake."

4. Anthony Oliver-Smith, "Theorizing Disasters: Nature, Power and Culture," in *Catastrophe and Culture: The Anthropology of Disaster*, ed. Susan H. Hoffman and Anthony Oliver-Smith (Santa Fe, NM: School of American Research Press, 2002), 23–47.

5. Howard Davis, *The Culture of Building* (Oxford: Oxford University Press, 2000).

6. Both of these buildings would collapse in the 2010 earthquake.

7. Regine O. Jackson, "The Failure of Categories: Haitians in the United Nations Organization in the Congo, 1960–64," *Journal of Haitian Studies* 20, no. 1 (2014): 34–64.

8. Henry Godard, "Transferts de captiaux et mutations urbaines à Port-au-Prince," in *Villes et migrations internationales de travail dans le Tiers-Monde: Actes de la Table Ronde Transferts de revenus et projets immobiliers des travailleurs migrants dans les pays en developpement* (Poitiers, France: Centre Interuniversitaires d'Etudes Mediterraneennes, Université de Poitiers, 1984), 311.

9. Bernard Dorin to Michel Jobert, "No. 17/AM," January 11, 1974, 524 PO/B box 266, Centre des Archives diplomatiques de Nantes, Nantes, France.

10. United Nations, CONADEP, and DTPTC, Plan de développement de Port-Au-Prince et de sa région métropolitiane, phase II, vol. 2, Les secteurs economiques et sociaux, UNCHBP, May 1975, 33.

11. Roger Gaillard, "Port-au-Prince en passe de devenir un monstre: Une interview d'Albert Mangonès," *Conjonction*, no. 119 (March 1973): 11.

12. Audefroy, "Haiti: Post-Earthquake Lessons Learned from Traditional Construction," 451.

13. Godard, "Transferts de captiaux et mutations urbaines à Port-au-Prince," 322.

14. "Port-Au-Prince, Haiti: History with Tropical Systems," Hurricane City, n.d., accessed July 28, 2018, http://www.hurricanecity.com/city/portauprince.htm.

15. Simon M. Fass, *Political Economy in Haiti: The Drama of Survival* (New Brunswick, NJ: Transaction Books, 1988), 189–235.

16. United Nations, CONADEP, and DTPTC, Plan de développement de Port-au-Prince et de sa région métropolitiane, vol. 1, HAI/ 74 R. 40, UNCHBP, August 1976, S-1075-0553, UNARMS.

17. American Concrete Institute 318 Standard (section 5.1.1).

18. Holliday, Ramseyer, and Grant, "Masonry Block Construction in Haiti," 207.

19. Robert Courland, *Concrete Planet: The Strange and Fascinating Story of the World's Most Common Man-Made Material* (Amherst, NY: Prometheus Books, 2011).

20. UNESCO, "Haiti: Training Brings Concrete Contribution to Reconstruction—Haiti," ReliefWeb, May 20, 2010, https://reliefweb.int/report/haiti/haiti-training-brings-concrete-con tribution-reconstruction.

21. Herbert Gold, *Haiti: Best Nightmare on Earth* (New Brunswick, NJ: Routledge, 2001), 65.

22. "Autour Du Problème Du Logement," *Le Nouvelliste*, June 28, 1973.

23. Jean Germain Gros, "Anatomy of a Haitian Tragedy: When the Fury of Nature Meets the Debility of the State," *Journal of Black Studies* 42, no. 2 (January 2011): 131–57.

24. Heyward Isham to Secretary of State, "Review of Issues Affecting US-Haitian Bilateral Relations," February 2, 1976, case no. F-2015-01847, doc. no. C05790538, US Department of State Freedom of Information Act, https://foia.state.gov/DOCUMENTS/Oct2016/F-2015 -01847/DOC_0C05790538/C05790538.pdf.

25. International Monetary Fund (IMF), *Haiti-Recent Economic Developments* (International Monetary Fund, June 2, 1970), 20.

26. McWilliams and Griffin, "Critical Assessment of Concrete and Masonry Structures," 2.1.

27. European Commission, Joint Research Center, "Haiti Earthquake January 2010 Damage Assessment Map," European Commission, February 21, 2013, https://ec.europa.eu/jrc/en /news/haiti-earthquake-first-damage-assessment-support-relief-efforts-7206, text.

Chapter 5

1. "In Pictures: Sierra Leone Slum," BBC, 2007, http://news.bbc.co.uk/2/shared/spl/hi /picture_gallery/07/africa_sierra_leone_slum/html/1.stm.

2. Windi Adriani et al., *Understanding Urban Risk Traps in Freetown Policy Brief No. 1: Water and Sanitation Related Diseases* (SLURC/DPU Action-Learning Alliance, 2018).

3. Aaron Clark-Ginsberg, "Participatory Risk Network Analysis: A Tool for Disaster Reduction Practitioners," *International Journal of Disaster Risk Reduction* 21 (2017): 430–37.

4. Andrew Maskrey, "Revisiting Community-Based Disaster Risk Management," *Environmental Hazards* 10, no. 1 (2011): 42–52; and Annelies, Heijmans, "The Social Life of Community-Based Disaster Risk Reduction: Origins, Politics and Framing" (paper presented at World Conference of Humanitarian Studies, Groningen, February 4–7, 2009).

5. Adriani et al., "Understanding Urban Risk Traps in Freetown Policy Brief No. 1"; Clark-Ginsberg, "Participatory Risk Network Analysis"; Fenda A. Akiwumi, "Global Incorporation and Local Conflict: Sierra Leonean Mining Regions," *Antipode* 44, no. 3 (2012): 581–600; and Megha Mukim, *Freetown Urban Sector Review: Options for Growth and Resilience* (Washington, DC: World Bank Group, 2018).

6. Clark-Ginsberg, "Participatory Risk Network Analysis."

7. Mukim, *Freetown Urban Sector Review*.

8. James Lewis and Ilan Kelman, "The Good, the Bad and the Ugly: Disaster Risk Reduction (DRR) Versus Disaster Risk Creation (DRC)," *PLOS Currents* 4 (2012), doi:10.1371/4f8d4eaec6af8.

9. Phil O'Keefe, Ken Westgate, and Ben Wisner, "Taking the Naturalness out of Natural Disasters," *Nature* 260 (1976): 566–67.

10. United Nations, Sendai Framework for Disaster Risk Reduction 2015–2030 (2015), https://www.unisdr.org/files/43291_sendaiframeworkfordrren.pdf.

11. Maskrey, "Revisiting Community-Based Disaster Risk Management."

12. During this project I also found many examples of Concern improving the lives of individuals and communities using a CBDRM approach. While this chapter focuses on a case in which CBDRM was not successful, other more positive examples of CBDRM can be found at https://www.preventionweb.net/search/pw#query=clark-ginsberg&hits=20&sortby =default&view=pw&filter=unisdrcontenttype%3A%5E%22Documents+%26+Publications %22%24.

13. Gabrielle Hecht, *The Radiance of France: Nuclear Power and National Identity After World War II* (Cambridge, MA: MIT Press, 1998.)

14. Hecht, *Radiance of France.*

15. Danny Marks and Eli Elinoff, "Splintering Disaster: Relocating Harm and Remaking Nature After the 2011 Floods in Bangkok," *International Development Planning Review* (May 2019): 273–94.

16. Lewis and Kelman, "The Good, the Bad and the Ugly"; Rob Nixon, *Slow Violence and the Environmentalism of the Poor* (Cambridge, MA: Harvard University Press, 2011); Anthony Oliver-Smith, "Haiti's 500 Year Earthquake," in *Tectonic Shifts: Haiti Since the Earthquake*, ed. Mark Schuller and Pablo Morales (Sterling, VA: Kumarian Press, 2012), 18–23; and Ben Wisner et al., *At Risk: Natural Hazards, People's Vulnerability and Disasters*, 2nd ed. (London: Routledge, 2004).

17. Lewis and Kelman. "The Good, the Bad and the Ugly."

18. Kenneth Hewitt, "The Idea of Calamity in a Technocratic Age," in *Interpretations of Calamity from the Viewpoint of Human Ecology*, ed. Kenneth Hewitt (Boston: Allen and Unwin, 1983), 3–32; John Hannigan, *Disasters Without Borders: The International Politics of Natural Disasters* (Cambridge, UK: Polity, 2012); and Cecile De Milliano et al., "Resilience: The Holy Grail or Yet Another Hype?," in *The Humanitarian Challenge: 20 Years European Network on Humanitarian Action (NOHA)*, ed. Pat Gibbons and Hans-Joachim Heintze (Heidelberg: Springer Cham, 2015), 17–30.

19. Greg Bankoff and Dorothea Hilhorst, "The Politics of Risk in the Philippines: Comparing State and NGO Perceptions of Disaster Management," *Disasters* 33, no. 4 (2009): 686–704.

20. Thomas Parke Hughes, *Networks of Power: Electrification in Western Society, 1880–1930* (Baltimore, MD: Johns Hopkins University Press, 1983).

21. UNISDR, "What Is Disaster Risk Reduction?," 2018, https://www.unisdr.org/who-we -are/what-is-drr.

22. David Chandler, *Resilience: The Governance of Complexity* (London: Routledge, 2014); and Aaron Clark-Ginsberg, "Disaster Risk Reduction Is Not 'Everyone's Business': Evidence from Three Countries," *International Journal of Disaster Risk Reduction* 43 (February 2020). doi:10.1016/j.ijdrr.2019.101375.

23. Manuel Tironi and Tania Manríquez, "Lateral Knowledge: Shifting Expertise for Disaster Management in Chile," *Disasters* 43, no. 2 (2019): 372–89.

24. Tina Wallace with Lisa Bornstein and Jennifer Chapman, *The Aid Chain: Coercion and Commitment in Development NGOs* (Bourton on Dunsmore, Rugby, Warwickshire: Practical Action Publishing, 2007).

25. Maskrey, "Revisiting Community-Based Disaster Risk Management."

26. Lilliana Abarca and Verele de Vreede, *Waste Management Situational Analysis in Urban WASH Consortium Areas in Freetown* (Urban WASH Consortium, 2013).

27. Clark-Ginsberg, "Disaster Risk Reduction Is Not 'Everyone's Business.'"

28. Office of National Security-Disaster Management Bureau (ONS-DMB), *National Progress Report on the Implementation of the Hyogo Framework for Action (2009–2011)* (Freetown, Sierra Leone, 2009).

29. Concern Worldwide, *Report on Fire Disaster in Susan's Bay* (n.p., 2011).

30. Maria Kaika, "'Don't Call Me Resilient Again!': The New Urban Agenda as Immunology . . . or . . . What Happens When Communities Refuse to Be Vaccinated with 'Smart Cities' and Indicators," *Environment and Urbanization* 29, no. 1 (2017): 89–102; and Colin Walch, "Typhoon Haiyan: Pushing the Limits of Resilience? The Effect of Land Inequality on Resilience and Disaster Risk Reduction Policies in the Philippines," *Critical Asian Studies* 50, no. 1 (2018): 122–35.

Chapter 6

1. Gautam Bhan, "This Is No Longer the City I Once Knew: Evictions, the Urban Poor and the Right to the City in Millennial Delhi," *Environment and Urbanization* 21, no. 1 (2009): 127–42.

2. Amita Baviskar, "What the Eye Does Not See: The Yamuna in the Imagination of Delhi," *Economic and Political Weekly* 46, no. 50 (2011): 45–53.

3. Usha Ramanathan, "Illegality and the Urban Poor," *Economic and Political Weekly* 41, no. 29 (2005): 3193–97.

4. Asher Ghertner, "Analysis of New Legal Discourse Behind Delhi's Slum Demolitions," *Economic and Political Weekly* 43, no. 20 (2008): 57–66.

5. Solomon Benjamin, "Governance, Economic Settings and Poverty in Bangalore," *Environment and Urbanization* 12, no. 1 (2000): 35–56; Bhan, "This Is No Longer the City I Once Knew"; Baviskar "What the Eye Does Not See"; and Liza Weinstein, *The Durable Slum: Dharavi and the Right to Stay Put in Globalizing Mumbai* (Minneapolis: University of Minnesota Press, 2014).

6. Weinstein, *Durable Slum*.

7. Ananya Roy, "Why India Cannot Plan Its Cities: Informality, Insurgence and the Idiom of Urbanization," *Planning Theory* 8, no. 1 (2009): 79.

8. Mary Hancock, *The Politics of Heritage from Madras to Chennai* (Bloomington: Indiana University Press, 2008).

9. Ghertner, "Analysis of New Legal Discourse."

10. Government of India, The Slum Areas (Improvement and Clearance) Act (Chennai, 1956).

11. Government of Tamil Nadu, Tamil Nadu Slum Areas (Improvement and Clearance) Act (Chennai, 1956).

12. Gopal Bhargava, *Pilot Programme of Slum Clearance for Madras City: An Unique Experiment* (New Delhi/Chennai: Government, Town and Country Planning Organization, National Seminar on Slums and Slum Clearance Schemes 1975), 109–11.

13. Government of Tamil Nadu, Tamil Nadu Slum Areas (Improvement and Clearance) Act (Chennai, 1971), 843.

14. Government of Tamil Nadu, Tamil Nadu Slum Areas (Improvement and Clearance) Act (Chennai, 1971).

15. K. S. Logavinayagam, *Why This Seminar on Slum Clearance?* (Chennai: Tamil Nadu Slum Clearance Board, National Seminar on Slums and Slum Clearance, 1975), 5.

16. S. Mariappan, *Remunerative Enterprises Schemes in Slum Clearance Board* (Madras: Tamil Nadu Slum Clearance Board, National Seminar on Slums and Slum Clearance Schemes, 1975), 93–100.

17. World Bank, *Project Performance Audit Report: India, First Madras Urban Development Project* (Washington, DC: World Bank, 1986).

18. S. Anandhi, *Contending Identities: Dalits and Secular Politics in Madras Slums* (New Delhi: Indian Social Institute, 1995).

19. Karen Coelho and Nithya V. Raman, "Salvaging and Scapegoating: Slum Evictions on Chennai's Waterways," *Economic and Political Weekly* 45, no. 21 (2010): 19–21, 23.

20. Coelho, and Raman, "Salvaging and Scapegoating," 23.

21. World Bank, *Project Performance Audit Report*; and Tamil Nadu Slum Clearance Board, *Project Implementation Plan for World Bank Aided Emergency Tsunami Reconstruction Project* (Chennai: TNSCB, 2005).

22. Karen Coelho and T. Venkat, "The Politics of Civil Society: Neighborhood Association-ism in Chennai," *Economic and Political Weekly* 44, nos. 26, 27 (2009): 358–67.

23. Pushpa Arabindoo, "Falling Apart at the Margins: Neighbourhood Transformations in Peri-Urban Chennai," *Development and Change* 40, no. 5 (2009): 879–91.

24. Joop W. de Wit, *Poverty, Policy and Politics in Madras Slums: Dynamics of Survival, Gender and Leadership* (New Delhi: Sage, 1996).

25. Coelho and Venkat, "Politics of Civil Society," 358–67.

26. People's Union for Civil Liberties, Tamil Nadu and Puducherry (PUCL-TN), *Report of Fact Finding Team on Forced Eviction and Rehabilitation in Chennai* (Chennai: PUCL, 2010).

27. Edwin Wilson v. The State of Tamil Nadu, "Memorandum of Application before the National Green Tribunal (SZ) Chennai," Chennai, 2014.

28. LKS India Pvt. Ltd., *Social Assessment Report: Integrated Cooum River Eco-Restoration Plan* (Chennai: TNUIFSL, CRRT, 2014).

29. Government of Tamil Nadu, Revenue Department, *Government Order* (Chennai, 2015).

30. Coelho and Raman, "Salvaging and Scapegoating," 21.

31. Government of Tamil Nadu, *Vision 2023: Strategic Plan for Infrastructure Development in Tamil Nadu* (Chennai, 2012).

32. De Wit, *Poverty, Policy and Politics in Madras Slums*.

33. Margaret Arnold, "Disaster Reconstruction and Risk Management for Poverty Reduc-tion," *Journal of International Affairs* 59, no. 2 (2006): 269–79.

34. Tamil Nadu State Disaster Management Agency (TNSDMA), *Tamil Nadu State Disas-ter Management Policy* (Chennai: Government of Tamil Nadu, 2014), 749.

35. Chennai Metropolitan Development Authority (CMDA), *Second Master Plan for Chen-nai Metropolitan Area, 2026*, vol. 1, *Vision, Strategies and Action Plans* (Chennai, 2008).

36. Arnold, "Disaster Reconstruction and Risk Management for Poverty Reduction."

37. World Bank, *Tamil Nadu and Puducherry Coastal Disaster Risk Reduction Project: Implementation Status & Results Report* (World Bank, 2016).

38. Government of Tamil Nadu, Revenue Department, *Government Order 172* (Chennai, 2005).

39. Government of Tamil Nadu, Revenue Department, *Government Order 371* (Chennai, 2008).

40. Government of Tamil Nadu, Revenue Department, *Government Order 326* (Chennai, 2005).

41. PUCL-TN, *Report of Fact Finding Team*.

42. Government of Tamil Nadu, Revenue Department, *Government Order 261* (Chennai, 2008).

43. PUCL-TN, *Report of Fact Finding Team.*

44. Comptroller and Auditor General of India, *Report of the Comptroller and Auditor General of India (General and Social)* (New Delhi: Government of India, 2005).

Chapter 7

1. Ike Brannan and Ari Blask, "The Government's Hidden Housing Subsidy for the Rich," The Cato Institute, August 8, 2017, https://www.politico.com/agenda/story/2017/08/08/hidden -subsidy-rich-flood-Insurance-000495.

2. Caroline Kousky et al., *The Emerging Private Residential Flood Insurance Market in the United States* (University of Pennsylvania, Wharton Risk Management and Decision Processes Center, 2018).

3. Rebecca Elliott, *Underwater: Loss, Flood Insurance, and the Moral Economy of Climate Change in the United States* (New York: Columbia University Press, 2020), ch. 3.

4. Stephen J. Collier and Savannah Cox, "Insurance and Urban Resilience" (working paper, 2020).

5. Emmy Bergsma, "Geographers Versus Managers: Expert Influence on the Construction of Values Underlying Flood Insurance in the United States," *Environmental Values* 25, no. 6 (2016): 687–705; and Robert E. Hinshaw, *Living with Nature's Extremes: The Life of Gilbert Fowler White* (Boulder, CO: Johnson Books, 2006).

6. Stephen J. Collier, "Neoliberalism and Natural Disaster: Insurance as a Political Technology of Catastrophe," *Journal of Cultural Economy* 7, no. 3 (2014): 273–90.

7. David Moss, *When All Else Fails: Government as the Ultimate Risk Manager* (Cambridge, MA: Harvard University Press, 2004); Scott Gabriel Knowles and Howard C. Kunreuther, "Troubled Waters: The National Flood Insurance Program in Historical Perspective," *Journal of Policy History* 26, no. 3 (2014): 327–53; and Erwann O. Michel-Kerjan and Carolyn Kousky, "Come Rain or Shine: Evidence on Flood Insurance Purchases in Florida," *Journal of Risk and Insurance* 77, no. 2 (2010): 369–97.

8. US Department of Housing and Urban Development (HUD), *Insurance and Other Programs for Financial Assistance to Flood Victims* (Washington, DC: Department of Housing and Urban Development, 1966), 39.

9. HUD, *Insurance and Other Programs for Financial Assistance to Flood Victims*, 8.

10. HUD, *Insurance and Other Programs for Financial Assistance to Flood Victims*, 102.

11. HUD, *Insurance and Other Programs for Financial Assistance to Flood Victims*, 11.

12. HUD, *Insurance and Other Programs for Financial Assistance to Flood Victims*, 11.

13. HUD, *Insurance and Other Programs for Financial Assistance to Flood Victims*, 99.

14. HUD, *Insurance and Other Programs for Financial Assistance to Flood Victims*, 119.

15. HUD, *Insurance and Other Programs for Financial Assistance to Flood Victims*, 9.

16. In June 1967, the legislation was submitted to Congress as an administration proposal was and introduced as H.R. 11197 in the House and as S. 1985 in the Senate.

17. 113 Cong. Rec. S13201 (September 14, 1967).

18. 113 Cong. Rec. S8736 (June 23, 1967).

19. 113 Cong. Rec. S13022 (September 14, 1967).

20. 113 Cong. Rec. S13023 (September 14, 1967).

21. 113 Cong. Rec. S13022 (September 14, 1967).

22. 113 Cong. Rec. S13023 (September 14, 1967).

23. 113 Cong. Rec. H14321 (November 1, 1967).

24. 113 Cong. Rec. S13023 (September 14, 1967).

25. 113 Cong. Rec. S13027 (September 14, 1967).

26. 113 Cong. Rec. S13036 (September 14, 1967).

27. 113 Cong. Rec. S13040–13041 (September 14, 1967).

28. 113 Cong. Rec. S13042 (September 14, 1967).

29. 113 Cong. Rec. S13038 (September 14, 1967).

30. Knowles and Kunreuther, "Troubled Waters."

31. US Federal Emergency Management Agency (FEMA), *A Chronology of Major Events Affecting the National Flood Insurance Program* (Washington, DC: FEMA, 2005).

32. Ernest B. Abbott, "Floods, Flood Insurance, Litigation, Politics—and Catastrophe: The National Flood Insurance Program," *Sea Grant Law and Policy Journal* 1, no. 1 (2008): 129–55.

33. Dan R. Anderson, "The National Flood Insurance Program: Problems and Potential," *Journal of Risk and Insurance* 41, no. 4 (1974): 588.

34. Anderson, "National Flood Insurance Program: Problems and Potential," 579–99.

35. *Hearing Before the Subcommittee on Government Efficiency and the District of Columbia, Senate Comm. on Governmental Affairs, on Loss of Financial Control over the National Flood Insurance Program*, 95th Cong. (April 11, 1977), 3 (statement of Henry Eschwege, Director Community and Economic Development Division).

36. *Hearing Before the Senate Comm. on Banking, Housing, and Urban Affairs Regarding Oversight of the National Flood Insurance Program*, 109th Cong. (October 18, 2005), 3 (testimony of J. Robert Hunter, Director of Insurance, Consumer Federation of America); and US Government Accountability Office (GAO), *HUD's Determination to Convert from Industry to Government Operation of the National Flood Insurance Program*, CED-78-122 (Washington, DC: Government Accountability Office, 1978).

37. *Hearing . . . Regarding Oversight of the National Flood Insurance Program*, 3 (Hunter).

38. Fred B. Power and E. Warren Shows, "A Status Report on the National Flood Insurance Program—Mid-1978," *Journal of Risk and Insurance* 46, no. 2 (1979): 61–76.

39. FEMA, *Chronology of Major Events Affecting the National Flood Insurance Program*.

40. Power and Shows, "Status Report on the National Flood Insurance Program," 68.

41. Abbott, "Floods, Flood Insurance, Litigation, Politics," 143.

42. FEMA, *Chronology of Major Events Affecting the National Flood Insurance Program*; and US Government Accountability Office (GAO), *Flood Insurance: Opportunities Exist to Improve Oversight of the WYO Program*, GAO-09-455 (Washington, DC: Government Accountability Office, 2009).

43. Michel-Kerjan and Kousky, "Come Rain or Shine."

44. Abbott, "Floods, Flood Insurance, Litigation, Politics," 144.

45. Michel-Kerjan and Kousky, "Come Rain or Shine."

46. GAO, *Flood Insurance: Opportunities Exist to Improve Oversight*, 10; US Government Accountability Office (GAO), *Flood Insurance: FEMA's Rate-Setting Process Warrants Attention*, GAO-09-12 (Washington, DC: Government Accountability Office, 2008); US Government Accountability Office (GAO), *Financial Management: Improvements Needed in National Flood Insurance Program's Financial Controls and Oversight*, GAO-10-66 (Washington, DC: Government Accountability Office, 2010).

47. Leigh Johnson, "Catastrophic Fixes: Cyclical Devaluation and Accumulation Through Climate Change Impacts," *Environment and Planning A* 47 (2015): 2503–21.

48. Peter Evans, *Embedded Autonomy: States and Industrial Transformation* (Princeton, NJ: Princeton University Press, 1995); and Neil Fligstein, *The Architecture of Markets* (Princeton, NJ: Princeton University Press, 2001).

Chapter 8

1. Jesmyn Ward, *Salvage the Bones* (New York: Bloomsbury, 2011), 135.

2. Bruno Latour, *Science in Action: How to Follow Scientists and Engineers Through Society* (Cambridge, MA: Harvard University Press, 1987), 239.

3. Because the duration of the reader's immersion in a mimetic (or apparently real) representation is crucial, it would be interesting for future scholars to consider—though beyond my scope here—whether other kinds of protracted narrative forms, be they in fictional or documentary television, radio, or podcast form, could achieve the epistemic effects I claim for the novel.

4. Lars Clausen, "Social Differentiation and the Long-Term Origin of Disasters," *Natural Hazards* 6 (1992): 182.

5. Claude Gilbert, "Studying Disaster: Changes in the Main Conceptual Tools," in *What Is a Disaster? Perspectives on the Question*, ed. E. L. Quarantelli (London: Routledge, 1998), 14, 16.

6. J. C. Gaillard, "The Climate Gap" *Climate and Development* 4, no. 4 (2012): 261–64, 261.

7. R. Dean Hardy et al., "Racial Coastal Formation: The Environmental Injustice of Color-blind Adaptation Planning for Sea-level Rise," *Geoforum* 87 (2017): 62–72, 69, 66, 70.

8. I mean to distinguish my use of the term to describe communication gaps during and about disasters from the way it is used by the reinsurance market to refer to the gap between the escalating value of insured properties in peak peril zones (and thus payout owed) and the "pool of capital available to backstop insurance companies." See John Seo, "Insuring Natural Disasters: Mind the (Disaster) Gap," G A M Investments, December 11, 2018, https://www.gam.com/en/our-thinking/investment-opinions/insuring-natural-disasters-mind-the disaster-gap.

9. See Rachel Morello-Frosch et al., "Environmental Justice and Southern California's 'Riskscape': The Distribution of Air Toxics Exposures and Health Risks Among Diverse Communities," *Urban Affairs Review* 36, no. 4 (March 2001), 551–78; see 553 for use of term. In terms of linking issues of exposure to environmental harm and reproductive health inequity, see also Morello-Frosch and Edmond D. Shenassa, "The Environmental 'Riskscape' and Social Inequality: Implications for Explaining Maternal and Child Health Disparities," *Environmental Health Perspectives* 114, no. 8 (August 2006): 1150–53.

10. Mervi Katriina Pantti and Karin Wahl-Jorgensen, "'Not an Act of God': Anger and Citizenship in Press Coverage of British Man-Made Disasters," *Media, Culture & Society* 33, no. 1 (January 2011): 118.

11. Jürgen Habermas, *The Structural Transformation of the Public Sphere: An Inquiry into a Category of Bourgeois Society*, trans. Thomas Burger with the assistance of Frederick Lawrence (1962; Cambridge, MA: MIT Press, 1989), 140, 178, 206, 170. See also Daniel Bell, *The Cultural Contradictions of Capitalism* (1976; New York: Basic Books, 1996), 108.

12. See Benedict Anderson, *Imagined Communities: Reflections on the Origin and Spread of Nationalism* (London: Verso, 1983).

13. Rob Nixon, *Slow Violence and the Environmentalism of the Poor* (Cambridge, MA: Harvard University Press, 2013).

14. Timothy Morton, *Hyperobjects: Philosophy and Ecology After the End of the World* (Minneapolis: University of Minnesota Press, 2013), 36, 16, 15.

15. Amitav Ghosh, *The Great Derangement: Climate Change and the Unthinkable* (Chicago: University of Chicago Press, 2016), 7, 20, 17. One could argue that the boundaries between "serious" and genre fiction that Ghosh insists upon have always been blurred; for a recent example, think of Cormack McCarthy's *The Road*, which is a futurist dark fantasy nevertheless told in the diurnal tempo, sobriety, and rich detail typical of realism—and is considered "serious fiction."

16. Many historians have outlined this eighteenth- and nineteenth-century shift away from a world of divine unpredictability to a modern world overseen by a rational God and managed on large scales by sciences of prediction and hence financial and municipal procedures that distributed risk across populations. See, for example, Keith Thomas, *Religion and the Decline of Magic* (New York: Scribner, 1971). Also, Michel Foucault argues for the rise of the biopolitical function of governments, which addressed subjects on a mass scale to "control the random element in biological processes" by maintaining an "overall equilibrium" through "complex systems of coordination"; see *Society Must Be Defended: Lectures at the College de France, 1975–1976*, trans. David Macey, ed. Mauro Bertani and Alessandro Fontana (Basingstoke, UK: Macmillan, 2003), 259, 249–50. As Timothy Campbell and Adam Sitze put it: "Death's slight withdrawal for living opens up the space for a knowledge of life that is irreducibly probabilistic in form.... [C]ollective life assumed the form of a massive bet." Introduction to *Biopolitics: A Reader* (Durham, NC: Duke University Press, 2013), 12.

17. Ghosh, *Great Derangement*, 36.

18. On this tradition of ideological critique, see Lauren Goodlad, who holds that the definition of realism this stance depends upon presumes a set of "generic or formal conventions that have never existed" (190); she points to many scholars who recognize "realism's centuries-long plurality and vitality ... , [its strenuous responses] to capitalist permutations across space and time" and believe in contemporary realism as "a transnational medium shot through with aesthetic possibility" (183). "Introduction: Worlding Realisms Now," *Novel: A Forum on Fiction* 49, no. 2 (2016): 183–201.

19. Victor Shklovsky, "From 'Art as Technique' 1917," in *Modernism: An Anthology of Sources and Documents*, ed. Vassiliki Kolocotroni, Jane Goldman, and Olga Taxidou (Chicago: University of Chicago Press, 1998), 217–21.

20. *Oxford English Dictionary*, s.v. "catastrophe," accessed February 4, 2013, https://www.oed.com/view/Entry/28794.

21. Lennard J. Davis, *Factual Fictions: The Origins of the English Novel* (Philadelphia: University of Pennsylvania Press, 1983), 46, 47.

22. Davis, *Factual Fictions*, 144.

23. As Cathy Gallagher puts it in "The Rise of Fictionality," in *The Novel*, vol. 1, *History, Geography, and Culture*, ed. Franco Moretti (Princeton, NJ: Princeton University Press, 2007): "Almost all of the developments we associate with modernity—from greater religious toleration to scientific discourse—required the kind of cognitive provisionality one practices in reading fiction, a competence in investing contingent and temporary credit" (347).

24. Daniel Defoe, *A Journal of the Plague Year*, ed. George Carpenter (London, 1722; New York: Longmans, Green, & Company, 1896), digitized by HathiTrust, https://catalog.hathitrust.org/Record/100761695), 20.

25. Defoe, *Journal of the Plague Year*, 18.

26. Cynthia Wall, "Novel Streets: The Rebuilding of London and Defoe's *A Journal of the Plague Year*," *Studies in the Novel* 30, no. 2 (Summer 1998): 174.

27. Defoe, *Journal of the Plague Year*, 94, 162.

28. Elizabeth Hoover, "Jesmyn Ward on *Salvage the Bones*," *Paris Review*, August 30, 2011, https://www.theparisreview.org/blog/2011/08/30/jesmyn-ward-on-salvage-the-bones/.

29. National Hurricane Center, *Tropical Cyclone Report: Hurricane Katrina* (2005; Miami, FL: National Hurricane Center, 2011), 1, 2, 12, https://www.nhc.noaa.gov/data/tcr/AL122005_Katrina.pdf.

30. For the meaning of "social" here, I am relying on Bruno Latour's broad definition of "*any thing* that does modify a state of affairs by making a difference" (71), no matter its category (human/nonhuman); see his *Reassembling the Social: An Introduction to Actor-Network-Theory* (Oxford: Oxford University Press, 2005) and its insistence that nonhumans "have to be *actors . . .* and not simply the hapless bearers of symbolic projection" (10).

31. Ward, *Salvage the Bones*, 89, 129–30, 132.

32. Ward, *Salvage the Bones*, 6–7.

33. Ward, *Salvage the Bones*, 226–27.

34. Hoover, "Jesmyn Ward on *Salvage the Bones*."

35. Pantti and Wahl-Jorgensen, "'Not an Act of God,'" 105–22.

Chapter 9

1. The Tōkai region, which includes Aiichi, Shizuoka, Mie, and Gifu prefectures, was key to the functioning of early modern Japan's political structures and economy and has been at the center of many of the networks and industries that shaped twentieth-century Japan as well. Approximately thirteen million people lived in the district in the mid-1970s.

2. Robert J. Geller, seismologist and professor emeritus of the University of Tokyo, explains his critiques of Japan's earthquake prediction regime in general and its effects on research funding in particular in *Nihonjin wa shiranai "jishin yochi" no shōtai* (Tokyo: Futabasha, 2011). See also Gregory Smits, *When the Earth Roars: Lessons from the History of Earthquakes in Japan* (Lanham, MD: Rowman & Littlefield, 2014), 121–43.

3. Susan Elizabeth Hough, *Predicting the Unpredictable: The Tumultuous Science of Earthquake Prediction* (Princeton, NJ: Princeton University Press, 2010), 108–24.

4. Unless otherwise indicated, "earthquake prediction" as used here refers to short-term earthquake prediction, which seeks to specify the location, magnitude, and time of occurrence of an event. Short-term in this context refers to an event that is at most several weeks away. Long-term, probabilistic forecasting operates on a different timescale, has its own problems, and is not our focus here.

5. *Mainichi shinbun*, September 8, 2017, morning ed., 21. For an early example of Geller's criticism of the Japanese program, see Robert J. Geller, "Shake-Up for Earthquake Prediction," *Nature* 352, no. 6333 (July 25, 1991): 275–76.

6. Deborah Lupton, *Risk*, 2nd ed. (London: Routledge, 2013), 28.

7. Lee Clarke, *Mission Improbable: Using Fantasy Documents to Tame Disaster* (Chicago: University of Chicago Press, 1999); and Scott Gabriel Knowles, *The Disaster Experts: Mastering Risk in Modern America* (Philadelphia: University of Pennsylvania Press, 2011).

8. This is not to say that there weren't concerns. See Mogi Kiyō, "Yochi sareta Surugawan Enshūnada chōōgata jishin no zenbō," *Shūkan Gendai* 11, no. 50 (December 18, 1969): 138–42.

9. References are to moment magnitude scale.

10. There were exceptions; for a fascinating analysis of the politics of resistance to plate tectonics theory in Japan, see Tomari Jirō, *Purēto tekutonikusu no kyozetsu to juyō: Sengo Nihon no chikyū kagakushi*, Shohan ed. (Tokyo: Tokyo Daigaku Shuppankai, 2008).

11. Masataka Andō, "Source Mechanisms and Tectonic Significance of Historical Earthquakes along the Nankai Trough, Japan," *Tectonophysics* 27, no. 2 (1975): 119–40.

12. Masataka Andō, "Possibility of a Major Earthquake in the Tokai District, Japan and Its Pre-estimated Seismotectonic Effects," *Tectonophysics* 25 (1975): 70.

13. For earlier discussion of seismic gaps in the Japanese context, see Andō, "Possibility of a Major Earthquake in the Tokai District, Japan," 70; Utsu Tokuji, "Hokkaido shūhen ni okeru Daijishin no katsudo to Nemuro minamihooki jishin ni tsuite," *Jishin yochi renrakukai no kaiho* 7 (March 1972): 7–13; and Rikitake Tsuneji, "Daijishin wa tsune ni yochi sarete iru," *Chūō Kōron* 88, no. 9 (September 1973): 176–82.

14. Andō, "Possibility of a Major Earthquake in the Tokai District, Japan," 81.

15. See Ishibashi Katsuhiko, "Surugawan jishinsetsu koshi," *Kagaku* 73, no. 9 (September 2003): 1060.

16. Ishibashi, "Surugawan jishinsetsu koshi," 1061. A summary of the key findings was published in the committee's in-house newsletter several months later as "Re-examination of a Great Earthquake Expected in the Tokai District, Central Japan—Possibility of the 'Suruga Bay Earthquake.'" Ishibashi Katsuhiko, "Tōkai chihō ni yosō sareru daijishin no saikentō—Surugawan jishin no kanosei," *Jishin yochi renrakukai kaihō* 17, nos. 4–13 (February 1977): 126–32.

17. *Mainichi shinbun*, September 4, 1976, 17. For an account by a journalist in the audience, see Kawabata Nobumasa, "Daikibo jishin taisaku tokubetsu sochihō seitei tōji no naibu jijyō," *Kagaku* 73, no. 9 (September 2003): 1047.

18. *Asahi shinbun*, November 6, 1976, evening ed., 8.

19. Ishibashi, "Surugawan jishinsetsu koshi," 1062.

20. *Asahi shinbun*, October 5, 1976, 22.

21. See Kerry Smith, "Earthquake Prediction in Occupied Japan," *Historical Social Research* 40, no. 2 (2015): 105-133.

22. Ando, "Possibility of a Major Earthquake in the Tokai District, Japan."

23. See for example Tokyo Shōbōcho kasai yobō taisaku iinkai, *Tokyo-to no daishin kasai higai no kentō: Taisaku ni taisuru shiryō* (Tokyo: Tokyo Shōbōcho, 1967).

24. Saigai taisaku tokubetsu iinkai, session 4, February 16, 1978, 84th Diet, Lower House, 18. Shizuoka released its first official damage and casualty estimates for a Tōkai earthquake in November 1978; as Yamamoto had anticipated, the report concluded that in the absence of a successful prediction, the earthquake would take 10,927 lives. That figure would rise if deaths due to secondary hazards were taken into account, but the report also concluded that if scientists successfully predicted the earthquake and warned people ahead of time, the number of fatalities would fall to zero. *Asahi shinbun*, January 12, 1994, Shizuoka morning ed. Shizuoka continued to adjust its methods and categories in the three earthquake disaster damage studies that followed, in 1993, 2001, and 2013, respectively.

25. *Yomiuri shinbun*, September 1, 1970, morning ed., 5.

26. NHK Shakaibu, *Jishin ni sonaeru: Anata no bōsai taisaku* (Tokyo: Nihon hōso shuppan kyōkai, 1971).

27. The first articles in the *Asahi*'s "Magunichūdo (Magnitude) 8" series appeared in mid-October 1976, just as Ishibashi's warnings were making the news.

28. A remake came out in 2006.

29. Kawasumi Hiroshi, "San Furunando (Rosanzerusu) Jishin to sono kunren," *Soil Mechanics and Foundation Engineering* 19, no. 8 (August 25, 1971): 34–40. Similar claims of

superior Japanese construction practices followed the 1994 Northridge earthquake but were proven inaccurate the following year in Kobe.

30. *Asahi shinbun*, March 6, 1971, morning ed., 1.

31. Rikitake Tsuneji, *Earthquake Forecasting and Warning* (Tokyo: Center for Academic Publications Japan, 1982), 99.

32. Rikitake, *Earthquake Forecasting and Warning*, 273.

33. Jirō Tomari, *Nihon no jishin yochi kenkyū 130-nenshi* (Tokyo: Tokyo Daigaku Shuppankai, 2015).

34. Jishin yochi keikaku kenkyū gurupu, "Jishin yochi: Genjō to sono suishin keikaku" (1962).

35. Hough, *Predicting the Unpredictable*, 108–24; Kelin Wang et al., "Predicting the 1975 Haicheng Earthquake," *Bulletin of the Seismological Society of America* 96, no. 3 (June 2006): 757–95; and Fa-ti Fan, "'Collective Monitoring, Collective Defense': Science, Earthquakes, and Politics in Communist China," *Science in Context* 25, no. 1 (March 2012): 127–54.

36. Jishin yochi renrakukai, *Jishin Yochi Renrakukai 10-nen no ayumi*, Yatabe-machi (Ibaraki-ken) (Tokyo: Kankōsha Kokudo Chiriin Nihon Sokuryō Kyōkai, 1979), 38.

37. Saigai taisaku tokubetsu iinkai, session 10, April 19, 1978, 84th Diet, Lower House, 38.

38. Mogi Kiyō, *Jishin yochi o kangaeru* (Tokyo: Iwanami Shoten, 1998), 167–72, 177.

39. *Mainichi shinbun*, September 8, 2017, morning ed., 21.

40. See Morris Low, *Science and the Building of a New Japan* (New York: Palgrave Macmillan, 2005) for an analysis of the rise of Japan's nuclear energy industry and the scientists caught up in it.

41. Project Vela Uniform, for example, solicited seismologists' help in the early 1960s to monitor Soviet nuclear weapons tests and transformed the field in the process. Something similar happened to seismology in Japan, but there it was the pursuit of earthquake prediction that changed the field's trajectory. See, for example, Kai-Henrik Barth, "The Politics of Seismology: Nuclear Testing, Arms Control, and the Transformation of a Discipline," *Social Studies of Science* 33 (2003): 743–81.

42. Knowles, *Disaster Experts*.

43. Clarke, *Mission Improbable*, 13. Thanks to Fa-ti Fan for bringing Clarke's work to my attention.

44. Clarke, *Mission Improbable*, 4.

Chapter 10

1. Mara Benadusi, "Pedagogies of the Unknown: Unpacking 'Culture' in Disaster Risk Reduction Education," *Journal of Contingencies and Crisis Management* 22, no. 3 (2014): 174–83; Rajib Shaw, Koichi Shiwaku, and Yukiko Takeuchi., *Disaster Education* (Bingley, UK: Emerald Group Publishing, 2011); UNISDR, Sendai Framework for Disaster Risk Reduction 2015–2030 (2015), https://www.unisdr.org/files/43291_sendaiframeworkfordrren.pdf, 15; and Ben Wisner, "Let Our Children Teach Us! A Review of the Role of Education and Knowledge in Disaster Risk Reduction," ISDR System Thematic Cluster/Platform on Knowledge and Education, 2006, http://www.unisdr.org/files/609_10030.pdf.

2. Cabinet Office, Government of Japan, *Disaster Management in Japan*, white paper, 2015, http://www.bousai.go.jp/kaigirep/hakusho/pdf/WP2015_DM_Full_Version.pdf, 16.

3. Japan International Cooperation Agency (JICA), "DRLC Tenth Anniversary: Memorial for the 10th Anniversary of the Disaster Reduction Learning Center," 2017, https://www.jica.go .jp/kansai/drlc/ku57pq000005kh18-att/drlc_10th_en.pdf.

4. Ministry of Foreign Affairs (MOFA), *Country Assistance Profile for Chile* (Tokyo: MOFA, 2012).

5. Anna Lowenhaupt Tsing, "Transitions as Translations," in *Transitions, Environments, Translations: Feminisms in International Politics*, ed. Joan W. Scott, Cora Kaplan, and Debra Keates (New York: Routledge, 1997), 253–72.

6. Brian Wynne, "Uncertainty and Environmental Learning: Reconceiving Science and Policy in the Preventive Paradigm," *Global Environmental Change* 2, no. 2 (1992): 116.

7. Wynne, "Uncertainty and Environmental Learning," 116.

8. Antonella Cavallo and Vernon Ireland, "Preparing for Complex Interdependent Risks: A System of Systems Approach to Building Disaster Resilience," *International Journal of Disaster Risk Reduction* 9 (2014): 182; and Elizabeth Gasiorowski-Denis, "Mainstreaming Disaster Management," ISO, July 8, 2015, https://www.iso.org/news/2015/07/Ref1982.html.

9. Matthew Leitch, "ISO 31000:2009—The New International Standard on Risk Management," *Risk Analysis* 30, no. 6 (2010): 888; and Ilan Kelman, "Lost for Words Amongst Disaster Risk Science Vocabulary?," *International Journal of Disaster Risk Science* 9 (2018): 281–91.

10. K. Poljanšek et al., *Science for Disaster Risk Management 2017: Knowing Better and Losing Less*, EUR 28034 EN (Luxemburg: Publications Office of the European Union, 2017), 113.

11. Daniel P. Aldrich, "Challenges to Coordination: Understanding Intergovernmental Friction During Disasters," *International Journal of Disaster Risk Science* 10 (2019): 307.

12. Aldrich, "Challenges to Coordination," 314.

13. Wynne, "Uncertainty and Environmental Learning," 119.

14. Victoria Sword-Daniels et al., "Embodied Uncertainty: Living with Complexity and Natural Hazards," *Journal of Risk Research* 21, no. 3 (2018): 290–307.

15. Graham Haughton et al., "In Search of 'Lost' Knowledge and Outsourced Expertise in Flood Risk Management," *Transactions of the Institute of British Geographers* 40 (2015): 375–86.

16. All names are pseudonyms unless otherwise stated.

17. I use the term "disaster preparedness" loosely to refer to a wide range of logics and activities that have to do with interventions aimed at mitigating potential harms caused by disasters.

18. I use the suffix "-san" for the Japanese names of people I know from fieldwork. Nagata-san's name has not been changed because he is mentioned in this chapter in his role as Plus Arts' representative, and no confidential information is disclosed.

19. For an overview of Iza! Kaeru Caravan, see http://kaeru-caravan.jp/en.html.

20. Interview with author, April 3, 2017.

21. Conversation with author, April 23, 2018.

22. I thank David Rojas for alerting me to this.

23. Marie Chatel, "Spotlight: Alejandro Aravena," *Arch Daily*, June 22, 2018.

24. Clara Han, *Life in Debt: Times of Care and Violence in Neoliberal Chile* (Berkeley: University of California Press, 2012), 15–16; and Bruce Ferguson and Jesus Navarrete, "New Approaches to Progressive Housing in Latin America: A Key to Habitat Programs and Policy," *Habitat International* 27 (2003): 309–23.

25. Marilyn Strathern, *Partial Connections*, updated ed.(1991; Walnut Creek, CA: Altamira Press, 2004).

26. I thank Scotti Parrish for this insight.

27. UNISDR, Issue Brief: International Cooperation in Support of a Post-2015 Framework for Disaster Risk Reduction, Ministerial Roundtable, 2015, 2.

28. Benadusi, "Pedagogies of the Unknown," 174.

29. Maia Green, "Globalizing Development in Tanzania: Policy Franchising Through Participatory Project Management," *Critique of Anthropology* 23, no. 2 (2003): 123–43; and Britt Halvorson, "Woven Worlds: Material Things, Bureaucratization, and Dilemmas of Caregiving in Lutheran Humanitarianism," *American Ethnologist* 39, no. 1 (2012): 122–37.

30. Greg Bankoff, *Cultures of Disaster: Society and Natural Hazards in the Philippines* (London: RoutledgeCurzon, 2003); and Norio Maki, "Hajimeni: Ajia to saigai/bōsai" [Introduction: Disasters and disaster risk reduction and Asia], in *Kokusai kyōryoku to bōsai: Tsukuru, yorisou, kitaeru* [International cooperation and disaster risk reduction: Create, accompany, strengthen] (Kyoto: Kyoto daigaku gakujutsu shuppan ka, 2015).

31. Shūhei Kimura, "Jinruigaku ni okeru saigai kenkyū: Koremade to korekara" [Disaster research in anthropology: Past and future], in *Saigai bunka no keishō to sōzō* [Inheritance and creation of disaster cultures], ed. Hashimoto Hiroyuki and Hayashi Isao (Kyoto: Rinsen Books, 2016), 34; and F. Krüger et al., *Cultures and Disasters: Understanding Cultural Framings in Disaster Risk Reduction* (Oxford: Routledge, 2015).

32. US Federal Emergency Management Agency (FEMA), *Building Cultures of Preparedness: A Report for the Emergency Management Higher Education Community* (Washington, DC, 2019); and International Federation of the Red Cross, *World Disasters Report: Focus on Culture and Risk*, 2014, https://www.ifrc.org/Global/Documents/Secretariat/201410/WDR%202014.pdf.

33. Jake Rom D. Cadag and J. C. Gaillard, "Integrating Knowledge and Actions in Disaster Risk Reduction: The Contribution of Participatory Mapping," *Area* 44, no. 1 (2012): 100–109.

34. Samantha Jones et al., "Governance Struggles and Policy Processes in Disaster Risk Reduction: A Case Study from Nepal," *Geoforum* 57 (2014): 78–90.

35. Alev Bulut and Turgay Kurultay, "Interpreters-in-Aid at Disasters," *Translator* 7, no. 2 (2001): 249–63.

36. Bulut and Kurultay, "Interpreters-in-Aid at Disasters," 256.

37. Sadrine Revet, "A Small World: Ethnography of a Natural Disaster Simulation in Lima, Peru," *Social Anthropology* 21, no. 1 (2013): 45.

38. Michel Callon, "Some Elements of a Sociology of Translation: Domestication of the Scallops and the Fishermen of St. Brieuc Bay," in *Power, Action and Belief: A New Sociology of Knowledge?*, ed. John Law (London: Routledge & Kegan Paul, 1986); Bruno Latour, "The Powers of Association," in *Power, Action, and Belief: A New Sociology of Knowledge?*, ed. John Law (London: Routledge & Kegan Paul, 1986), 264–80; and Susan Leigh Star and James R. Griesemer, "Institutional Ecology, 'Translations' and Boundary Objects: Amateurs and Professionals in Berkeley's Museum of Vertebrate Zoology, 1907–39," *Social Studies of Science* 19, no. 3 (1989): 387–420.

39. Anna Lowenhaupt Tsing, "Worlding the Matsutake Diaspora; or, Can Actor-Network Theory Experiment with Holism?," in *Experiments in Holism: Theory and Practice in Contemporary Anthropology*, ed. Ton Otto and Nils Bubandt (London: Blackwell Publishing, 2010), 48; and Daena Funahashi, "Rule by Good People: Health Governance and the Violence of Moral Authority in Thailand," *Cultural Anthropology* 31, no. 1 (2016): 107–30.

40. Tsing, "Transitions as Translations," 253.

41. Walter Benjamin, "The Task of the Translator," in *Walter Benjamin: Selected Writings*, vol. 1, *1913–1926*, ed. Marcus Bullock and Michael W. Jennings (1923; Cambridge, MA: Harvard University Press, 1996), 260.

42. Benjamin, "Task of the Translator," 262.

43. Andrea Ballestero, "What Is in a Percentage?: Calculation as the Poetic Translation of Human Rights," *Indiana Journal of Global Legal Studies* 21, no. 1 (2014): 34; and Kregg Hetherington, "Regular Soybeans: Translation and Framing in the Ontological Politics of a Coup," *Indiana Journal of Global Legal Studies* 21, no. 1 (2014): 55–78.

44. Strathern, *Partial Connections*, 54.

45. Donna J. Haraway, "A Cyborg Manifesto: Science, Technology, and Socialist-Feminism in the Late Twentieth Century," in *Simians, Cyborgs, and Women: The Reinvention of Nature* (New York: Routledge, 1991), 177; and Marisol de la Cadena, *Earth Beings: Ecologies of Practice Across Andean Worlds* (Durham, NC: Duke University Press, 2015).

46. Interview with author, September 2, 2016.

47. Ulrich Beck, *Risk Society: Towards a New Modernity* (New York: Sage, 1992).

48. Lee Clarke, *Mission Improbable: Using Fantasy Documents to Tame Disaster* (Chicago: University of Chicago Press, 1999), 11.

49. Joe Deville and Michael Guggenheim, "From Preparedness to Risk: From the Singular Risk of Nuclear War to the Plurality of all Hazards," *British Journal of Sociology* 69, no. 3 (2017): 803.

50. Kasia Paprocki, "All That Is Solid Melts into the Bay: Anticipatory Ruination and Climate Change Adaptation," *Antipode* 51, no. 1 (2018): 295–315; and Austin Zeiderman, *Endangered City: The Politics of Security and Risk in Bogotá* (Durham, NC: Duke University Press, 2016).

51. Greg Bankoff and Dorothea Hilhorst, "The Politics of Risk in the Philippines: Comparing State and NGO Perceptions of Disaster Management," *Disasters* 33, no. 4 (2009): 686–704; and J. C. Gaillard and Jessica Mercer, "From Knowledge to Action: Bridging Gaps in Disaster Risk Reduction," *Progress in Human Geography* 37, no. 1 (2013): 93–114.

52. Cabinet Office, Government of Japan, foreword to *Disaster Management in Japan*.

53. Shūhei Kimura, "Mirai no jishin wo meguru risuku: Nihon ni okeru jishin no 'risuku-ka' purosesu no sobyō" [Risks relating to future earthquakes: A sketch of the process of "risk-alization" of disasters in Japan], in *Risuku no jinruigaku: Fukakujitsu na sekai wo ikiru* [The anthropology of risk: Living in an indeterminate world], ed. Azuma Kentarō, Ichinoawa Junpei, I'ida Taku, and Kimura Shūhei (Kyoto: Sekai Shisō sha, 2014).

54. Joe Deville et al., "Concrete Governmentality: Shelters and the Transformations of Preparedness," *Sociological Review* 62, S1 (2014): 183–210; and Patrick Roberts, "Private Choices, Public Harms: The Evolution of National Disaster Organizations in the United States," in *Disaster and the Politics of Intervention*, ed. Andrew Lakoff (New York: Columbia University Press, 2010), 42–69.

55. Cabinet Office, Government of Japan, "Chi'iki seikatsu kiso shūdan no soshikika—jichitai gyōsei to jichi soshiki to shiteno chōnaikai" [Institutionalization of community basic livelihood collectives—the community councils as local government bodies and self-governing organizations], in *1923 Kantō Daishinsai (dai sanpen)* [1923 Great Kanto earthquake (vol. 3)], *Saigai kyōkun no keishō ni kansuru senmon chōsakai hōkokusho* [Expert report on the transmission of lessons learned from disasters], March 2008.

56. Robert Bajek, Yoko Matsuda, and Norio Okada, "Japan's Jishu-bosai-soshiki Community Activities: Analysis of Its Role in Participatory Community Disaster Risk Management," *Natural Hazards* 44, no. 2 (2008): 281–92.

57. Interview with author, September 2, 2016.

58. UNISDR, "Chile Still Living with Quake Effects," News Archive, February 27, 2012, https://www.unisdr.org/archive/25366.

59. Mauricio Torres Méndez et al.,"Resilencia comunitaria y sentido de comunidad durante la respuesta y recuperación al Terremoto-tsunami del Año 2010, Talcahuano-Chile," *Revista de Estudios Latinoamericanos sobre Reducción del Riesgo de Desastres* (REDER) 2, no. 1 (2018): 21–23.

60. Oficina Nacional de Emergencia del Ministerio del Interior y Seguridad Pública. N.d. "Presentación" [Introduction], accessed on October 13, 2018, http://www.onemi.cl/presentacion/.

61. Neoliberalization is not absent in Japan either, but the context and history of *bōsai* is slightly different. Julia Paley, *Marketing Democracy: Power and Social Movements in Post-Dictatorship Chile* (Berkeley: University of California Press, 2001), 147.

62. "Piñera Proposes Five Major National Agreements on His First Day as President," *Santiago Times*, March 12, 2018.

63. Bulut and Kurultay, "Interpreters-in-Aid at Disasters."

64. Taun wocchingu tebiki sakusei i'inkai [Town Watching Guide Drafting Committee], *Bōsai taun wocchingu jissen tebiki* [Practical guide for disaster risk reduction town watching] (Saijō City, 2008), 46.

65. Author's fieldnotes, January 18, 2018.

66. Judith Salinas et al., "Vida Chile 1998–2006: Resultados y desafíos de la política de promoción de la salud en Chile," *Revista Panamericana de Salud Pública* 23, nos. 2/3 (2007): 136–44.

67. Star and Griesemer, "Institutional Ecology, 'Translations' and Boundary Objects."

68. Callon, "Some Elements of a Sociology of Translation," 6, 9; and Tsing, "Worlding the Matsutake Diaspora."

69. Bruno Latour, "Why Has Critique Run out of Steam? From Matters of Fact to Matters of Concern," *Critical Inquiry* 30, no. 2 (2004): 225–248.

70. Limor Samimian-Darash, "Practicing Uncertainty: Scenario-Based Preparedness Exercises in Israel," *Cultural Anthropology* 31, no. 3 (2016): 381–82.

Afterword

1. Dorothea Hilhorst, ed., *Disaster, Conflict and Society in Crisis* (London: Routledge, 2013); Anthony Oliver-Smith et al., *Forensic Investigations of Disasters (FORIN): A Conceptual Framework and Guide to Research*, IRDR FORIN Publications no. 2 (Beijing: Integrated Research on Disaster Risk, 2016); and Karen Sudmeier-Rieux et al., eds., *Emerging Issues in Disaster Risk Reduction, Migration, Climate Change and Sustainable Development* (Heidelberg: Springer International, 2017).

2. Kenneth Hewitt, "Disaster Risk Reduction (DRR) in the Era of 'Homeland Security': The Struggle for Preventive, Non-Violent, and Transformative Approaches," in *Emerging Issues in Disaster Risk Reduction, Migration, Climate Change and Sustainable Development*, ed. Karen Sudmeier-Rieux et al. (Heidelberg: Springer International, 2017), 35–52.

3. Mainly they are called "man-made," a more gender-accurate term. Women play important roles in disaster and are disproportionately affected in many of them. In an overwhelmingly patriarchal world, however, they rarely control or have much say about the sources of risk. They are more likely to experience violence and to be silenced in and beyond disasters. See Elaine Enarson and Bob Pease, eds., *Men, Masculinities and Disaster* (New York: Routledge, 2016).

4. UNISDR, "Natural Hazards, Unnatural Disasters: The Economics of Effective Prevention," 2010, https://www.unisdr.org/we/inform/publications/15136.

5. Ben Wisner, J. C. Gaillard, and Ilan Kelman, eds., *The Routledge Handbook of Hazards and Disaster Risk Reduction* (London: Routledge, 2012); John Hannigan, *Disasters Without Borders: The International Politics of Natural Disasters* (Cambridge: Polity Press, 2012); Jörn Birkmann, ed., *Measuring Vulnerability to Natural Hazards: Towards Disaster Resilient Societies* (Tokyo: United Nations University Press, 2006); Patrick Pigeon and Julien Rebotier, *Disaster Prevention Policies: A Challenging and Critical Outlook* (London: Elsevier, 2016); Ali Faraz-amand, *Global Cases in Best and Worst Practice in Crisis and Emergency Management* (Boca Raton, FL: CRC Press, 2016); Oliver-Smith et al., *Forensic Investigations of Disasters*; Enarson and Pease, *Men, Masculinities and Disaster*; UNISDR, Sendai Framework for Disaster Risk Reduction 2015–2030 (2015), https://www.unisdr.org/files/43291_sendaiframeworkfordrren.pdf; and Sudmeier-Rieux et al., *Emerging Issues in Disaster Risk Reduction*.

6. Cornelius Walford, *The Famines of the World: Past and Present* (London: Edward Stanford, 1879); Pitirim A. Sorokin, *Man and Society in Calamity* (New Brunswick, NJ: Transaction Publishers, 1946); E. L. Quarantelli, "Epilogue: Where We Have Been and Where Might We Go," in *What Is a Disaster? Perspectives on the Question*, ed. E. L. Quarantelli (London: Routledge, 1998), 260; and Hannigan, *Disasters Without Borders*, 1.

7. Cormac Ó Gráda, *Famine: A Short History* (Princeton, NJ: Princeton University Press, 2009), 95.

8. Jasper Becker, *Hungry Ghosts: Mao's Secret Famine* (New York: Henry Holt, 1996).

9. Jeanne X. Kasperson and Robert W. Kates, eds., "Overcoming Hunger in the 1990s," special issue, *Food Policy* 15, no. 4 (August 1990).

10. Famine Early Warning System Network, USAID, *Acute Food Insecurity: May* (Washington, DC, 2017).

11. V. Tarasuk and A. Mitchell, *Household Food Insecurity in Canada, 2017–18*, Report of PROOF (University of Toronto, 2020).

12. Kenneth Hewitt, ed., *Interpretations of Calamity from the Viewpoint of Human Ecology* (Boston: Allen and Unwin, 1983). See especially "The Idea of Calamity in a Technocratic Age," 3–32.

13. Reid A. Bryson and Thomas J. Murray, *Climates of Hunger: Mankind and the World's Changing Weather* (Madison: University of Wisconsin Press, 1979); and Lester Brown and Hal Kane, *Full House: Reassessing the Earth's Population Carrying Capacity* (New York: Norton, 1994).

14. Paul R. Ehrlich [and Anne Ehrlich], *The Population Bomb* (New York: Ballantine, 1968); cf. Betsy Hartmann, *Reproductive Rights: The Global Politic of Population Control* (Boston: South End Press, 1995).

15. See especially Jean Copans, "The Sahelian Drought: Social Sciences and the Political Economy of Underdevelopment," in *Interpretations of Calamity from the Viewpoint of Human Ecology*, ed. Kenneth Hewitt (Boston: Allen and Unwin, 1983), 84–97.

16. On the Bengal famine, see also B. M. Bhatia, *Famines in India: A Study in Some Aspects of the Economic History of India, 1860–1965* (Bombay: Asia Publishing House, 1967).

17. M. J. Watts, *Silent Violence: Food, Famine, and Peasantry in Northern Nigeria* (Berkeley: University of California Press, 1983).

18. Robert Bolin, Martina Jackson, and Allison Crist, "Gender Inequality, Vulnerability and Disaster: Issues in Theory and Research," in *The Gendered Terrain of Disaster: Through Women's Eyes*, ed. Elaine Enarson and Betty H. Morrow (Westport, CT: Praeger, 1998), 38. One notable strand of this thought descends from Michel Foucault's 1977–1978 lectures at the Collège de France, the second of which specifically addressed famine. Foucault understood famine not primarily as

a rare disaster, but rather as a constant concern of government. Abundance and dearth, Foucault argued, were pivotal in policies and statemaking. See Michel Foucault, *Society Must Be Defended: Lectures at the College de France, 1975–1976*, trans. David Macey, ed. Mauro Bertani and Alessandro Fontana (Basingstoke, UK: Macmillan, 2003), 30, 31. A second crucial thread descends from economist Amartya Sen, who noted that "starvation is the characteristic of some people not having enough food to eat . . . not the characteristic of there being not enough food." Amartya Sen, *Poverty and Famines: An Essay on Entitlement and Deprivation* (Oxford: Clarendon Press of Oxford University Press, 1982), 1; see also Becker, *Hungry Ghosts*. Also influential have been C. Woodham-Smith, *The Great Hunger* (London: Hamish Hamilton, 1962); Susan George, *How the Other Half Dies: The Real Reasons for World Hunger* (Montclair, NJ: Allanheld, Osmun, 1977); Frances Moore Lappe and Joseph Collins, *World Hunger: Ten Myths*, 4th ed. (San Francisco: Institute for Food and Development Policy, 1979); and Hartmann, *Reproductive Rights*.

19. Barry Turner referred to "man-made disasters" interchangeably with "large scale accidents." Barry A. Turner and Nick F. Pidgeon, *Man-Made Disasters*, 2nd ed. (Oxford: Butterworth-Heinemann, 1997). This relates to Cutter's work differentiating "living with" technological hazards from confronting technological disasters or "incidents." Susan L. Cutter, *Living with Risk: The Geography of Technological Hazards* (London: Edward Arnold, 1993).

20. Paul J. Crutzen, "The 'Anthropocene,'" *Journal de Physique IV (Proceedings)* 12, no. 10 (2002): 1–5; H. Macdonald, *Commentary: The Security-Industrial Complex* (New York: Manhattan Institute for Policy Research, 2006); Scott D. Sagan, *The Limits of Safety: Organizations, Accidents and Nuclear Weapons* (Princeton, NJ: Princeton University Press 1993); and K. E. Weick and K. H. Roberts, "Collective Mind in Organizations: Heedful Interrelating on Flight Decks," *Administrative Science Quarterly* 38 (1993): 357–81.

21. Charles Perrow, *Normal Accidents: Living with High Risk Technologies*, updated ed. (Princeton, NJ: Princeton University Press, 2011).

22. Ulrich Beck, "Politics of Risk Society," in *The Politics of Risk Society*, ed. Jane Franklin (London: Polity Press, 1998), 9–22.

23. Paul Virilio, *The Original Accident* (Cambridge, UK: Polity Press, 2005), 12.

24. Phil Scraton, *Hillsborough: The Truth* (Liverpool, UK: Mainstream Publishing 1999).

25. This neglect or refusal is not without precedent. According to Jane Green, "Classical social theorists were silent about accidents, and other disciplines claimed that accidents were not really accidents." Jane Green, *Risk and Misfortune: The Social Construction of Accidents* (London: University College London Press, 1997), 41. For a fuller discussion and historical perspective, see chapter 2 in this volume.

26. According to Virilio, "The word 'accident' signifies what arises unexpectedly—in a device, or systems or product . . . the surprise of failure or destruction." Virilio, *Original Accident*, 70.

27. Herbert W. Heinrich, *Industrial Accident Prevention: A Scientific Approach* (New York: McGraw-Hill, 1931); Turner and Pidgeon, *Man-Made Disasters*; and Kenneth Hewitt, "Environmental Disasters in Social Context: Toward a Preventive and Precautionary Approach," *Natural Hazards* 66 (2012): 3–14.

28. In a study of "industrial accidents," chemical engineer Trevor Kletz showed the same or similar disasters recur in the same industries, even the same place, a decade or two apart. His conclusion was that "organizations have no memory, at least as far as safety is concerned." Trevor A. Kletz, *Lessons from Disaster: How Organizations Have No Memory and Accidents Recur* (Rugby, UK: Institution of Chemical Engineers, 1993), 173.

29. Perrow, *Normal Accidents*, 5.

30. Jacob A. C. Remes, *Disaster Citizenship: Survivors, Solidary, and Power in the Progressive Era* (Urbana: University of Illinois Press, 2016); and Janet F. Kitz, *Shattered City: The Halifax Explosion and the Road to Recovery* (Halifax, NS: Nimbus, 2010).

31. An influential notion, "normal accidents" in high-risk industries is a deliberate oxymoron, as the inevitable shock seems the very opposite of "normal" life. Perrow, *Normal Accidents*.

32. A late modern problem, expressed by Scott Sagan, is: "How does one even begin to study something that has never occurred?" Sagan, *Limits of Safety*, 1.

33. Novel threats and inadequate safeguards prefigure Beck's assertion that "as nature becomes permeated by industrialization and tradition is dissolved, *new types of incalculability emerge . . . the production of risks is the consequence of scientific and political efforts to control them.*" Beck, "Politics of Risk Society," 12 (emphasis added).

34. Sorokin, *Man and Society in Calamity*; and Kenneth Hewitt, *Regions of Risk: A Geographical Introduction to Disasters* (Harlow, UK: Addison Wesly Longman, 1997), ch. 5.

35. Armed force is not the focus in any of my reference set, listed in note 6. Exceptions that address the matter include Hilhorst, *Disaster, Conflict and Society in Crisis*; and Kenneth Hewitt, "Total War Meets Totalitarian Planning: Some Reflections on Königsberg/Kaliningrad," in *A Blessing in Disguise: War and Town Planning in Europe 1940–1945*, ed. J. Düwel and N. Gutschow (Berlin: Dom Publishers, 2013), 88–103.

36. Kenneth Hewitt, "Place Annihilation: Area Bombing and the Fate of Urban Places," *Annals of the Association of American Geographers* 73 (1983): 257–84; and Hewitt, "Disaster Risk Reduction (DRR) in the Era of 'Homeland Security.'"

37. Roy Gutman, David Reiff, and Anthony Dworkin, eds., *Crimes of War 2.0: What the Public Should Know* (New York: Norton, 2007).

38. *Oxford English Dictionary*, s.v. "violate," https://www.oed.com /view/Entry/223627.

39. J. Douglas Porteous and S. E. Smith, *Domicide: The Global Destruction of Home* (Montreal and Kingston: McGill-Queen's University Press, 2002); Stephen Graham, ed., *Cites, War and Terrorism: Towards an Urban Geopolitics* (Oxford: Blackwell, 2004); Derek Gregory and Allan Pred, eds., *Violent Geographies: Fear, Terror, and Political Violence* (London: Routledge, 2006); and Hewitt, "Total War Meets Totalitarian Planning."

40. R. J. Rummell, *Death by Government* (New Brunswick, NJ: Transaction Publishers, 1994); and Hewitt, *Regions of Risk*.

41. Hewitt, "Place Annihilation"; and Hewitt, "Total War Meets Totalitarian Planning."

42. Kenneth Hewitt, "'When the Great Planes Came and Made Ashes of Our City . . .': Towards an Oral Geography of the Disasters of War," *Antipode* 26, no. 1 (1994): 1–34.

43. The US Strategic Bombing Survey, especially its Morale Division, interviewed thousands of bombing raid survivors in Germany and Japan; see *The Effect of Bombing on Medical and Health Care in Germany*, report no. 65 (Washington, DC: United States Strategic Bombing, Morale Division, Medical Branch, 1945) and *The Effects of Strategic Bombing on Japanese Morale* (Washington, DC: Pacific Survey, Morale Division, 1947). For the UK there are the Mass Observation archives; see Tom Harrisson, *Living Through the Blitz* (London: Penguin, 1976).

44. Hewitt, "Place Annihilation."

45. Kenneth Hewitt, "Proving Grounds of Urbicide: Civilian Perspectives on the Bombing of Capital Cities," *ACME: An International E-journal for Critical Geographies* 8, no. 2 (2009): 340–75.

46. Kenneth Hewitt, "Reign of Fire: The Civilian Experience and Urban Consequences of the Destruction of German Cities, 1942–1945," in *Kriegzerstörung und Wiederaufbau deutscher Städte*, ed. J. Nipper and M. Mutz (Cologne: Geographische Arbeiten Hft, 1993), 57:25–45; Hewitt, *Regions of Risk*; and Hewitt, "Total War Meets Totalitarian Planning."

47. Robert Jay Lifton and Eric Markusen, *The Genocidal Mentality: Nazi Holocaust and Nuclear Threat* (New York: Basic Books, 1990).

48. Airwars, "Our Monitoring of Civilian Harm," 2020, airwars.org.

49. Jennifer Dathan, *When the Bombs Fall Silent: The Reverberating Effects of Explosive Weapons*, Report of Action on Armed Violence, May 2018, https://aoav.org.uk/wp-content/uploads/2018/06/Reverberating-effects-v5.pdf.

50. Jennifer Dathan, Hauke Waszkewitz, and Michael Hart, *The Refugee Explosion: How Europe Treats Refuges Feeling Explosive Violence*, Report of Action on Armed Violence, 2017.

51. Terence H. O'Brien, *Civil Defence* (London: H.M.S.O., 1955). See also chapter 2 in this volume.

52. Exceptions include Hilhorst, *Disaster, Conflict and Society in Crisis*; and Hewitt, "Disaster Risk Reduction (DRR) in the Era of 'Homeland Security.'"

53. This entanglement can be referred to as the "Security Industrial Complex." Hewitt, "Disaster Risk Reduction (DRR) in the Era of 'Homeland Security'"; and *NATO's Role in Disaster Assistance* (Euro-Atlantic Disaster Response Coordination Centre, Civil Emergency Planning, North Atlantic Treaty Organization, November 2001).

54. UNISDR, *United Nations Office for Disaster Risk Reduction: Annual Report 1918* (Geneva: UN Office for the Coordination of Humanitarian Affairs, 2019); and Oliver-Smith et al., *Forensic Investigations of Disasters*.

55. Hewitt, "Idea of Calamity."

56. A. Lavell, *Viviendo en riesgo: Comunidades vulnerables y prevencion de desas tres en America Latina* (Bogota: LA RED/FLACSO, 1994); Ted Steinberg, *Acts of God: The Unnatural History of Natural Disaster in America*, 2nd ed. (New York: Oxford University Press, 2006); Kenneth Hewitt, "Disasters in 'Development' Contexts: Contradictions and Options for a Preventive Approach," *Jàmbá: Journal of Disaster Risk Studies* 5, no. 2 (2013): 1–9; and Hewitt, "Disaster Risk Reduction in the Era of 'Homeland Security.'"

57. Phil O'Keefe, Ken Westgate, and Ben Wisner, "Taking the Naturalness out of Natural Disasters," *Nature* 260 (1976): 566–67; J. Lewis, "The Susceptibility of the Vulnerable: Some Realities Reassessed," *Disaster Prevention and Management* 23, no. 1 (2014): 2–11; Patrick Bellegarde-Smith, "A Man-Made Disaster: The Earthquake of January 12, 2010—A Haitian Perspective," *Journal of Black Studies* 42, no. 2 (2011): 264–75; and Juliana Svistova and Loretta Pyles, *Production of Disaster and Recovery in Post-Earthquake Haiti: Disaster Industrial Complex* (Abingdon, Oxon: Routledge, 2018).

58. On debt, see chapter 3 in this volume; on epidemics, see Paul Farmer, *Infections and Inequities: The Modern Plagues*, 2nd ed. (Berkeley: University of California Press, 1999).

59. Graham, *Cities, War, and Terrorism*; and Carolyn Nordstrom, *Shadows of War: Violence, Power and International Profiteering in the 21st Century* (Berkeley: University of California Press, 2004).

60. R. W. Mack and George Baker, *The Occasion Instant: The Structure of Social Responses to Unanticipated Air Raid Warnings* (Washington, DC: National Academy of Sciences-National Research Council, 1961).

61. Kenneth Hewitt, "The Social Space of Terror: Towards a Civil Interpretation of Total War," *Environment and Planning D: Society and Space* 5, no. 4 (December 1987): 445–74; David E. Alexander, "From Civil Defense to Civil Protection and Back Again," *Disaster Prevention and Management* 11, no. 3 (2002): 209–13; P. Amacher, "You're on Your Own Again," *Bulletin of the Atomic Scientists* 59 (May 2003): 34–43. For "logic of war," see B. Buzan, O. Waever, and J. de Wilde, *Security: A New Framework* (London: Lynne Rienner, 1998); on "patterns of war" see Claude Gilbert, "Studying Disasters: Changes in the Main Conceptual Tools," in *What Is a Disaster? Perspectives on the Question*, ed. E. L. Quarantelli (New York: Routledge, 1998), 11–18.

62. Hilhorst, *Disaster, Conflict and Society in Crisis*.

63. A. Maskrey, *Disaster Mitigation: A Community Based Approach* (Oxford: Oxfam, 1989); Louise Comfort et al., "Reframing Disaster Policy: The Global Evolution of Vulnerable Communities," *Environmental Hazards: Human and Policy Dimensions* 1, no. 1 (1999): 39–44; and Greg Bankoff, Georg Frerks, and Dorothea Hilhorst, *Mapping Vulnerability: Disasters, Development, and People* (London: Earthscan, 2004).

64. Sagan, *Limits of Safety*.

65. All of this speaks to Alicia Sliwinski's argument for the "moral economy" of response to disasters. Alicia Sliwinski, *A House of One's Own: The Moral Economy of Post-Disaster Aid in El Salvador* (Montreal and Kingston: McGill-Queen's University Press, 2018).

BIBLIOGRAPHY

Abarca, Lilliana, and Verele de Vreede. *Waste Management Situational Analysis in Urban WASH Consortium Areas in Freetown*. Urban WASH Consortium, 2013.

Abbott, Andrew. *Time Matters: On Theory and Method*. Chicago: University of Chicago Press, 2001.

Abbott, Ernest B. "Floods, Flood Insurance, Litigation, Politics—and Catastrophe: The National Flood Insurance Program." *Sea Grant Law and Policy Journal* 1, no. 1 (2008): 129–55.

Adorno, Theodor. *Minima Moralia: Reflections from Damaged Life*. London: Verso, 2005.

Adorno, Theodor, and Max Horkheimer. *Towards a New Manifesto*. London: Verso, 2011.

Adriani, Windi, Carolina Campos, Yaakoub El Hage, Yu-Te Lee, Ana Maria Rodriguez, Jorge Roman, Shattyk Tastemirova, and Jiahui Wang. "*Understanding Urban Risk Traps in Freetown Policy Brief No. 1: Water and Sanitation Related Diseases.*" SLURC/DPU Action-Learning Alliance, 2018.

Akiwumi, Fenda A. "Global Incorporation and Local Conflict: Sierra Leonean Mining Regions." *Antipode* 44, no. 3 (2012): 581–600.

Aldrich, Daniel P. *Building Resilience: Social Capital in Post-disaster Recovery*. Chicago: University of Chicago Press, 2012.

———. "Challenges to Coordination: Understanding Intergovernmental Friction During Disasters." *International Journal of Disaster Risk Science* 10 (2019): 306–16.

Alexander, D. E. "Resilience and Disaster Risk Reduction: An Etymological Journey." *Natural Hazards Earth Systems Science* 13 (2013): 2707–16.

Alexander, David E. "From Civil Defense to Civil Protection and Back Again." *Disaster Prevention and Management* 11, no. 3 (2002): 209–13.

Allen, Barbara, and Rachel A. Dowty Beech. *Dynamics of Disaster: Lessons on Risk, Response and Recovery*. New York: Routledge, 2013.

Allen, Barbara L. *Uneasy Alchemy: Citizens and Experts in Louisiana's Chemical Corridor Disputes*. Cambridge, MA: MIT Press, 2003.

Amacher, P. "You're on Your Own Again." *Bulletin of the Atomic Scientists* 59 (May 2003): 34–43.

Anandhi, S. *Contending Identities: Dalits and Secular Politics in Madras Slums*. New Delhi: Indian Social Institute, 1995.

Anderson, Benedict. *Imagined Communities: Reflections on the Origin and Spread of Nationalism*. London: Verso, 1983.

Anderson, Dan R. "The National Flood Insurance Program: Problems and Potential." *Journal of Risk and Insurance* 41, no. 4 (1974): 579–99.

Ando, Masataka. "Possibility of a Major Earthquake in the Tokai District, Japan and Its Pre-estimated Seismotectonic Effects." *Tectonophysics* 25, nos. 1–2 (1975): 69–85.

———. "Source Mechanisms and Tectonic Significance of Historical Earthquakes Along the Nankai Trough, Japan." *Tectonophysics* 27, no. 2 (1975): 119–40.

Angell, Elizabeth. "Assembling Disaster: Earthquakes and Urban Politics in Istanbul." *City* 18, no. 6 (2014): 667–78.

Angus, Ian. *Facing the Anthropocene: Fossil Capitalism and the Crisis of the Earth System.* New York: Monthly Review Press, 2016.

Apgar, William, Amal Bendimerad, and Ren Essene. *Mortgage Market Channels and Fair Lending: An Analysis of HMDA Data.* Cambridge, MA: Joint Center for Housing Studies of Harvard University, 2007.

Arabindoo, Pushpa. "'City of Sand': Stately Re-imagination of Marina Beach in Chennai." *International Journal of Urban and Regional Research* 35, no. 2 (2011): 379–401.

———. "Falling Apart at the Margins? Neighborhood Transformations in Peri-urban Chennai." *Development and Change* 40, no. 5 (2009): 879–901.

———. "Rhetoric of the 'Slum.'" *City* 15, no. 6 (2011): 636–46.

Arata, Stephen D. "The Occidental Tourist: 'Dracula' and the Anxiety of Reverse Colonization." *Victorian Studies* 33, no. 4 (1990): 621–45.

Araújo, Ana Cristina. "The Lisbon Earthquake of 1755: Public Distress and Political Propaganda." *e-Journal of Portuguese History* 4, no. 1 (2006): 1–11.

Armstrong-Hough, Mari. *Biomedicalization and the Practice of Culture: Globalization and Type 2 Diabetes in the United States and Japan.* Chapel Hill: University of North Carolina Press, 2018.

Arnold, Jorg. "'The Death of Sympathy': Coal Mining, Workplace Hazards, and the Politics of Risk in Britain, ca. 1970–1990." *Historical Social Research* 41, no. 1 (2016): 91–110.

Arnold, Margaret. "Disaster Reconstruction and Risk Management for Poverty Reduction." *Journal of International Affairs* 59, no. 2 (2006): 269–79.

Arya, A., and L. Srivastava. "Application of Research Findings in Earthquake Disaster Preparedness Planning Management." *Regional Development Dialogue* 9, no. 1 (1988): 13–35.

Audefroy, Joel F. "Haiti: Post-Earthquake Lessons Learned from Traditional Construction." *Environment and Urbanization* 23, no. 2 (2011): 447–62.

"Autour du problème du logement." *Le Nouvelliste*, June 28, 1973.

Auyero, Javier, and Debora Swistun. "The Social Production of Toxic Uncertainty." *American Sociological Review* 73, no. 3 (2008): 357–79.

Bajek, Robert, Yoko Matsuda, and Norio Okada. "Japan's Jishu-bosai-soshiki Community Activities: Analysis of Its Role in Participatory Community Disaster Risk Management." *Natural Hazards* 44, no. 2 (2008): 281–92.

Baker, Amy Castro. "Eroding the Wealth of Women: Gender and the Subprime Foreclosure Crisis." *Social Science Review* 88, no. 1 (2014): 59–91.

Baker, Leslie. "'A Visitation of Providence': Public Health and Eugenic Reform in the Wake of the Halifax Disaster." *Canadian Bulletin of Medical History* 31, no. 1 (2014): 99–122.

Baker, Shalanda H. "Anti-Resistance: A Roadmap for Transformational Justice Within the Energy System." *Harvard Civil Rights-Civil Liberties Law Review* 54 (2019): 1–48.

Ballestero, Andrea. "What Is in a Percentage? Calculation as the Poetic Translation of Human Rights." *Indiana Journal of Global Legal Studies* 21, no. 1 (2014): 27–53.

Bankoff, Greg. *Cultures of Disaster: Society and Natural Hazards in the Philippines.* London: RoutledgeCurzon, 2003.

———. "No Such Thing as Natural Disasters." *Harvard International Review* (online). August 23, 2010. http://hir.harvard.edu/no-such-thing-as-natural-disasters.

Bankoff, Greg, Georg Frerks, and Dorothea Hilhorst. *Mapping Vulnerability: Disasters, Development, and People*. London: Earthscan, 2003.

Bankoff, Greg, and Dorothea Hilhorst. "The Politics of Risk in the Philippines: Comparing State and NGO Perceptions of Disaster Management." *Disasters* 33, no. 4 (2009): 686–704.

Barrios, Roberto. *Governing Affect: Neoliberalism and Disaster Reconstruction*. Lincoln: University of Nebraska Press, 2017.

Barry, John M. *Rising Tide: The Great Mississippi Flood of 1927 and How It Changed America*. New York: Simon and Schuster, 2007.

Barth, Kai-Henrik. "The Politics of Seismology: Nuclear Testing, Arms Control, and the Transformation of a Discipline." *Social Studies of Science* 33 (2003): 743–81.

Barton, Allen H. *Communities in Disaster: A Sociological Analysis of Collective Stress Situations*. Garden City, NY: Doubleday, 1969.

Baumgartner, Frank, and Bryan Jones. *Agendas and Instability in American Politics*. Chicago: University of Chicago Press, 1993.

Baviskar, Amita. "What the Eye Does Not See: The Yamuna in the Imagination of Delhi." *Economic and Political Weekly* 46, no. 50 (2011): 45–53.

Bea, Keith. "The Formative Years: 1950–1978." In *Emergency Management: The American Experience 1900–2010*, edited by Claire B. Rubin, 83–114. Boca Raton, FL: CRC Press, 2012.

Beck, Ulrich. "Politics of Risk Society." In *The Politics of Risk Society*, edited by Jane Franklin, 9–22. London: Polity Press, 1998.

———. *Risk Society: Towards a New Modernity*. Translated by Mark Ritter. London: Sage, 1992.

———. *World at Risk*. Malden, MA: Polity Press, 2009.

Becker, Jasper. *Hungry Ghosts: Mao's Secret Famine*. New York: Henry Holt, 1996.

Behringer, Wolfgang. "Climatic Change and Witch-Hunting: The Impact of the Little Ice Age on Mentalities." *Climatic Change* 43 (1999): 335–51.

Bell, Daniel. *The Cultural Contradictions of Capitalism*. New York: Basic Books, 1996. First published 1976.

Bellegarde-Smith, Patrick. "A Man-Made Disaster: The Earthquake of January 12, 2010—A Haitian Perspective." *Journal of Black Studies* 42, no. 2 (2011): 264–75.

Benadusi, Mara. "Pedagogies of the Unknown: Unpacking 'Culture' in Disaster Risk Reduction Education." *Journal of Contingencies and Crisis Management* 22, no. 3 (2014): 174–83.

Benjamin, Solomon. "Governance, Economic Settings and Poverty in Bangalore." *Environment and Urbanization* 12, no. 1 (2000): 35–56.

Benjamin, Walter. *Illuminations: Essays and Reflections*. New York: Schocken, 1968.

———. "The Task of the Translator." In *Walter Benjamin: Selected Writings*. Vol. 1, *1913–1926*, edited by Marcus Bullock and Michael W. Jennings, 253–63. Cambridge, MA: Harvard University Press, 1996. First published 1923.

Berger, John. *Portraits: John Berger on Artists*. London: Verso, 2015.

Bergsma, Emmy. "Geographers Versus Managers: Expert Influence on the Construction of Values Underlying Flood Insurance in the United States." *Environmental Values* 25, no. 6 (2016): 687–705.

Bhan, Gautam. "This Is No Longer the City I Once Knew: Evictions, the Urban Poor and the Right to the City in Millennial Delhi." *Environment and Urbanization* 21, no. 1 (2009): 127–42.

Bhargava, Gopal. *Pilot Programme of Slum Clearance for Madras City: An Unique Experiment*. New Delhi/Chennai: Government, Town and Country Planning Organization, National Seminar on Slums and Slum Clearance Schemes, 1975.

Bhatia, B. M. *Famines in India: A Study in Some Aspects of the Economic History of India, 1860–1965*. Bombay: Asia Publishing House, 1967.

Birkmann, Jörn, ed. *Measuring Vulnerability to Natural Hazards: Towards Disaster Resilient Societies*. Tokyo: United Nations University Press, 2006.

Bjorkman, Lisa. "Becoming a Slum: From Municipal Colony to Illegal Settlement in Liberalization Era Mumbai." *International Journal of Urban and Regional Research* 38, no. 1 (2013): 36–59.

Blaikie, Piers, Terry Cannon, Ian Davis, and Ben Wisner. *At Risk: Natural Hazards, People's Vulnerability and Disasters*. 1st ed. New York: Routledge, 1994.

Blanchard, B. Wayne. *Guide to Emergency Management and Related Terms, Definitions, Concepts, Acronyms, Organizations, Programs, Guidance, Executive Orders & Legislation*. Washington, DC: Federal Emergency Management Agency, Emergency Management Institute, 2008.

Blanchot, Maurice. *The Writing of the Disaster*. Lincoln: University of Nebraska Press, 2015.

Blumenberg, Hans. *Shipwreck with Spectator: Paradigm of a Metaphor for Existence*. Cambridge, MA: MIT Press, 1997.

Bocian, Debbie Gruenstein, Wei Li, and Keith S. Ernst. *Foreclosures by Race and Ethnicity*. Center for Responsible Lending, 2010.

Boli, J., and G. M. Thomas. "World Culture in the World Polity: A Century of International Non-governmental Organization." *American Sociological Review* 62, no. 2 (1997): 171–90.

Bolin, Robert, Martina Jackson, and Allison Crist. "Gender Inequality, Vulnerability and Disaster: Issues in Theory and Research." In *The Gendered Terrain of Disaster: Through Women's Eyes*, edited by Elaine Enarson and Betty H. Morrow, 27–44. Westport, CT: Praeger, 1998.

Bond, David. "Governing Disaster: The Political Life of the Environment during the BP Oil Spill." *Cultural Anthropology* 28, no. 4 (2013): 694–715.

Bonner, Stephen Eric. *Of Critical Theory and Its Theorists*. New York: Routledge, 2002.

Bonneuil, Christophe, and Jean-Baptiste Fressoz. *The Shock of the Anthropocene*. New York: Verso Books, 2013.

Bradley, Andrew C. *Shakespearean Tragedy: Lectures on Hamlet, Othello, King Lear, and Macbeth*. London: Macmillan, 1906.

Brannan, Ike, and Ari Blask. "The Government's Hidden Housing Subsidy for the Rich." The Cato Institute, August 8, 2017. https://www.politico.com/agenda/story/2017/08/08/hidden-subsidy-rich-flood-Insurance-000495.

Brian Lehrer Show. "Governor Cuomo: Blackout, ICE Raids and MTA Shakeup" episode. Aired on WNYC-FM, July 15, 2019.

Brooks, Rick, and Ruth Simon. "Subprime Debacle Traps Even Very Credit-Worthy as Housing Boomed, Industry Pushed Loans to a Broader Market." *Wall Street Journal*, December 4, 2007, 3.

Brown, Kathryn L. *Plutopia: Nuclear Families, Atomic Cities, and the Great Soviet and American Plutonium Disasters*. New York: Oxford University Press, 2013.

Brown, Lester, and Hal Kane. *Full House: Reassessing the Earth's Population Carrying Capacity*. New York: Norton, 1994.

Bryson, Reid A., and Thomas J. Murray. *Climates of Hunger: Mankind and the World's Changing Weather*. Madison: University of Wisconsin Press, 1979.

Buck-Morss, Susan. *Dreamworld and Catastrophe: The Passing of Mass Utopia in East and West*. Cambridge, MA: MIT Press, 2002.

Bullard, Robert D. *Dumping in Dixie: Race, Class, and Environmental Quality.* 3rd ed. New York: Routledge, 2018.

Bulut, Alev, and Turgay Kurultay. "Interpreters-in-Aid at Disasters." *Translator* 7, no. 2 (2001): 249–63.

Burton, Ian, Robert W. Kates, and Gilbert F. White. *The Environment as Hazard.* 2nd ed. New York: Guilford Press, 1993.

Button, Gregory. *Disaster Culture: Knowledge and Uncertainty in the Wake of Human and Environmental Catastrophe.* New York: Routledge, 2016. First published 2010.

Buzan, B., O. Waever, and J. de Wilde. *Security: A New Framework.* London: Lynne Rienner, 1998.

Cabinet Office, Government of Japan. "Chi'iki seikatsu kiso shūdan no soshikika—jichitai gyōsei to jichi soshiki to shiteno chōnaikai" [Institutionalization of community basic livelihood collectives—the community councils as local government bodies and self-governing organizations], in *1923 Kantō Daishinsai (dai sanpen)* [1923 Great Kanto earthquake (vol. 3)], *Saigai kyōkun no keishō ni kansuru senmon chōsakai hōkokusho* [Expert report on the transmission of lessons learned from disasters]. March 2008.

Cabinet Office, Government of Japan. *Disaster Management in Japan.* White paper. 2015. http://www.bousai.go.jp/kaigirep/hakusho/pdf/WP2015_DM_Full_Version.pdf.

Cadag, Jake, Rom D., and J. C. Gaillard. "Integrating Knowledge and Actions in Disaster Risk Reduction: The Contribution of Participatory Mapping." *Area* 44, no. 1 (2012): 100–109.

Callon, Michel. "Some Elements of a Sociology of Translation: Domestication of the Scallops and the Fishermen of St. Brieuc Bay." In *Power, Action and Belief: A New Sociology of Knowledge?*, edited by John Law, 196–223. London: Routledge, 1986.

Campbell, J. L. "Mechanisms of Evolutionary Change in Economic Governance: Interaction, Interpretation, and Bricolage." In *Evolutionary Economics and Path Dependence*, edited by L. Magnusson and J. Ottosson, 10–-32. Cheltenham, UK: Edward Elgar, 1997.

Campbell, Timothy, and Adam Sitze. *Biopolitics: A Reader.* Durham, NC: Duke University Press, 2013.

Carr, Lowell Juilliard. "Disaster and the Sequence-Pattern Concept of Social Change." *American Journal of Sociology* 38, no. 2 (1932): 207–18.

Carson, Rachel. *Silent Spring.* Boston: Houghton Mifflin Harcourt, 2002.

Cavallo, Antonella, and Vernon Ireland. "Preparing for Complex Interdependent Risks: A System of Systems Approach to Building Disaster Resilience." *International Journal of Disaster Risk Reduction* 9 (2014): 181–93.

Centeno, Miguel, Manish Nag, Thayer S. Patterson, Andrew Shaver, and A. Jason Windawi. "The Emergence of Global Systemic Risk." *Annual Review of Sociology* 41 (2015): 65–85.

Chandler, David. *Resilience: The Governance of Complexity.* London: Routledge, 2014.

Chatel, Marie. "Spotlight: Alejandro Aravena." *ArchDaily*, June 22, 2018. https://www.archdaily.com/789618/spotlight-alejandro-aravena.

Chmutina, Ksenia, and Jason von Melding. "A Dilemma of Language: 'Natural Disasters' in Academic Literature." *International Journal of Disaster Risk Science* 10 (2019): 283–92.

Choi, Vivian Y. "Anticipatory States: Tsunami, War, and Insecurity in Sri Lanka." *Cultural Anthropology* 30, no. 2 (2015): 286–309.

Chomsisengphet, Souphala, and Anthony Pennington-Cross. "The Evolution of the Subprime Mortgage Market." *Federal Reserve Bank of St. Louis Review* 88, no. 1 (2006):31–56.

Clancey, Greg. *Earthquake Nation: The Cultural Politics of Japanese Seismicity, 1868-1930.* Berkeley: University of California Press, 2006.

Clarke, Lee. *Acceptable Risk? Making Decisions in a Toxic Environment*. Berkeley: University of California Press, 1991.

———. *Mission Improbable: Using Fantasy Documents to Tame Disaster*. Chicago: University of Chicago Press, 1999.

Clark-Ginsberg, Aaron. "Disaster Risk Reduction Is Not 'Everyone's Business': Evidence from Three Countries." *International Journal of Disaster Risk Reduction* 43 (February 2020). doi:10.1016/j.ijdrr.2019.101375.

———. "Participatory Risk Network Analysis: A Tool for Disaster Reduction Practitioners." *International Journal of Disaster Risk Reduction* 21 (2017): 430–37.

Clausen, Lars. "Social Differentiation and the Long-Term Origin of Disasters." *Natural Hazards* 6, no. 2 (September 1992): 181–90.

Claussen, Detlev. *Theodor Adorno: One Last Genius*. Cambridge, MA: The Belknap Press of Harvard University, 2008.

Coelho, Karen. "Placing the Poor in the Flood Path: Post-disaster Slum Resettlement in Chennai." *Caravan*, January 4, 2016.

Coelho, Karen, and Nithya V. Raman. "Salvaging and Scapegoating: Slum Evictions on Chennai's Waterways." *Economic and Political Weekly* 45, no. 21 (2010): 19–21, 23.

Coelho, Karen, and T. Venkat. "The Politics of Civil Society: Neighborhood Associationism in Chennai." *Economic and Political Weekly* 44, nos. 26, 27 (2009): 358–67.

Cohen, Deborah R. *The Earthquake Observers: Disaster Science from Lisbon to Richter*. Chicago: University of Chicago Press, 2013.

Collier, Stephen J. "Enacting Catastrophe: Preparedness, Insurance, Budgetary Rationalization." *Economy and Society* 37, no. 2 (2008): 224–50.

———. "Neoliberalism and Natural Disaster: Insurance as a Political Technology of Catastrophe." *Journal of Cultural Economy* 7, no. 3 (2014): 273–90.

Collier, Stephen J., and Savannah Cox. "Insurance and Urban Resilience." Working paper, 2020.

Collier, Stephen J., and Andrew Lakoff. "Distributed Preparedness: The Spatial Logic of Domestic Security in the United States." *Environment and Planning D: Society and Space* 26, no. 1 (2008): 7–28.

———. "Vital Systems Security: Reflexive Biopolitics and the Government of Emergency." *Theory, Culture & Society* 32, no. 2 (2015): 19–51.

———. "The Vulnerability of Vital Systems: How 'Critical Infrastructure' Became a Security Problem." In *Securing "the Homeland": Critical Infrastructure, Risk and (In)security*, edited by Myriam Dunn Cavelty and Kristian Søby Kristensen, 17–39. London: Routledge, 2008.

Comfort, Louise, Ben Wisner, Susan L. Cutter, Roger S. Pulwarty, Kenneth Hewitt, Anthony Oliver-Smith, John D. Wiener, Maureen Fordham, Walter G. Peacock, and Fred Krimgold. "Reframing Disaster Policy: The Global Evolution of Vulnerable Communities." *Environmental Hazards: Human and Policy Dimensions* 1, no. 1 (1999): 39–44.

Concern Worldwide. *Report on Fire Disaster in Susan's Bay*. n.p., 2011.

Consumer Financial Protection Bureau (CFPB). "2013 Home Ownership and Equity Protection Act (HOEPA) Rule: Small Entity Compliance Guide." 2013. tinyurl.com/ya2ma5c6.

———. "What Is a Subprime Mortgage?" 2017. consumerfinance.gov/ask-cfpb/what-is-a- sub prime-mortgage-en-110/.

Cooter, Roger. "The Moment of the Accident: Culture, Militarism and Modernity in Late-Victorian Britain." In *Accidents in History: Injuries, Fatalities and Social Relations*, edited by Roger Cooter and Bill Luckin, 41:107–57. Atlanta, GA: Rodopi, 1997.

Copans, Jean. "The Sahelian Drought: Social Sciences and the Political Economy of Underdevelopment." In *Interpretations of Calamity from the Viewpoint of Human Ecology*, edited by Kenneth Hewitt, 84–97. Boston: Allen and Unwin, 1983.

Correa, Vanesa Estrada. "Blueprint for the American Dream? A Critical Discourse Analysis of Presidential Remarks on Minority Homeownership." *Social Justice* 40 (2014): 16–27.

Costain, Anne N. *Inviting Women's Rebellion*. Baltimore, MD: Johns Hopkins University Press, 1992.

Cotterman, Robert F. "New Evidence on the Relationship Between Race and Mortgage Default: The Importance of Credit History Data." Unicon Research Corporation. May 23, 2002. https://www.huduser.gov/Publications/PDF/crhistory.pdf.

Courland, Robert. *Concrete Planet: The Strange and Fascinating Story of the World's Most Common Man-Made Material*. Amherst, NY: Prometheus Books, 2011.

Crenshaw, Kimberlé. "Demarginalizing the Intersection of Race and Sex." *University of Chicago Legal Forum* 39 (1989): 139–67.

Creswell, Julie, and Vikas Bajajmarch. "Mortgage Crisis Spirals, and Casualties Mount." *New York Times*, March 5, 2007, C1.

Crump, Jeff, Kathe Newman, Eric S. Belsky, Phil Ashton, David H. Kaplan, Daniel J. Hammel, and Elvin Wyly. "Cities Destroyed (Again) for Cash: Forum on the US Foreclosure Crisis." *Urban Geography* 29 (2008): 745–84.

Crutzen, Paul, and Eugene Stoermer. "The Anthropocene." *Global Change Newsletter* 41 (2000): 17–18.

Crutzen, Paul J. "The 'Anthropocene.'" *Journal de Physique IV (Proceedings)* 12, no. 10 (2002): 1–5.

———. "Geology of Mankind." *Nature* 415 (January 3, 2002): 23.

Cutter, Susan L. *American Hazardscapes: The Regionalization of Hazards and Disasters*. Washington, DC: Joseph Henry Press, 2002.

———. *Living with Risk: The Geography of Technological Hazards*. London: Edward Arnold, 1993.

Dathan, Jennifer. *When the Bombs Fall Silent: The Reverberating Effects of Explosive Weapons*. Report of Action on Armed Violence. May 2018.

Dathan, Jennifer, Hauke Waszkewitz, and Michael Hart. *The Refugee Explosion: How Europe Treats Refuges Feeling Explosive Violence*. Report of Action on Armed Violence. 2017.

Dauber, Michele Landis. *The Sympathetic State: Disaster Relief and the Origins of the American Welfare State*. Chicago: University of Chicago Press, 2013.

Davis, Heather, and Zoe Todd. "On the Importance of a Date, or, Decolonizing the Anthropocene." *ACME: An International Journal for Critical Geographies* 16, no. 4 (2017): 761–80.

Davis, Howard. *The Culture of Building*. New York: Oxford University Press, 2000.

Davis, Lennard J. *Factual Fictions: The Origins of the English Novel*. Philadelphia: University of Pennsylvania Press, 1983.

Davis, Mike. *Ecology of Fear: Los Angeles and the Imagination of Disaster*. New York: Metropolitan, 1998.

———. *Late Victorian Holocausts: El Niño Famines and the Making of the Third World*. London: Verso, 2001.

De la Cadena, Marisol. *Earth Beings: Ecologies of Practice Across Andean Worlds*. Durham, NC: Duke University Press, 2015.

De Milliano, Cecile, Marijn Faling, Aaron Clark-Ginsberg, Dominic Crowley, and Pat Gibbons. "Resilience: The Holy Grail or Yet Another Hype?" In *The Humanitarian Challenge: 20 Years*

European Network on Humanitarian Action (NOHA), edited by Pat Gibbons and Hans-Joachim Heintze, 17–30. Heidelberg: Springer Cham, 2015.

De Wit, Joop W. *Poverty, Policy and Politics in Madras Slums: Dynamics of Survival, Gender and Leadership*. New Delhi: Sage, 1996.

Defoe, Daniel. *A Journal of the Plague Year*. Edited by George Carpenter. New York: Longmans, Green, 1896. First published 1722. https://catalog.hathitrust.org/Record/100761695.

DeMause, Neil. "The Recession and the 'Deserving Poor': Poverty Finally on Media Radar—But Only When It Hits the Middle Class." *Extra!* March 2009. https://fair.org/extra/the-recession-and-the-deserving-poor/.

Desai, Renu. "Governing the Urban Poor: Riverfront Development, Slum Resettlement and the Politics of Inclusion in Ahmedabad." *Economic and Political Weekly* 47, no. 2 (2012): 49–56.

Deville, Joe, and Michael Guggenheim. "From Preparedness to Risk: From the Singular Risk of Nuclear War to the Plurality of all Hazards." *British Journal of Sociology* 69, no. 3 (2017): 799–824.

Deville, Joe, Michael Guggenheim, and Zuzana Hrdličková. "Concrete Governmentality: Shelters and the Transformations of Preparedness." *Sociological Review* 62, S1 (2014): 183–210.

DiMaggio, Paul. "Interest and Agency in Institutional Theory." In *Institutional Patterns and Organizations: Culture and Environment*, edited by L. G. Zucker, 3–21. Cambridge, MA: Ballinger, 1988.

DiMaggio, Paul, and W. W. Powell. "The Iron Cage Revisited: Institutional Isomorphism and Collective Rationality in Organizational Fields." *American Sociological Review* 48, no. 2 (1983): 147–60.

Diwakar, Pranathi. "A Recipe for Disaster: Framing Risk and Vulnerability in Slum Relocation Policies in Chennai, India." *City & Community* 18, no. 4 (December 2019): 1314–37.

Doherty, Gareth, and Moises Lino E. Silva. "Formally Informal: Daily Life and the Shock of Order in a Brazilian Favela." *Built Environment* 37, no. 1 (2011): 30–41.

Douglas, Mary, and Aaron Wildavsky. *Risk and Culture: An Essay on the Selection of Technological and Environmental Dangers*. Berkeley: University of California Press, 1982.

Dreier, Peter, Saqib Bhatti, Rob Call, Alex Schwartz, and Gregory Squires. *Underwater America: How the So-Called Housing "Recovery" Is Bypassing Many American Communities*. Berkeley, CA: Haas Institute for a Fair and Inclusive Society, 2014.

Dubois, Laurent. *Haiti: The Aftershocks of History*. New York: Metropolitan Books, 2012.

Dupuy, Alex. "Disaster Capitalism to the Rescue: The International Community and Haiti after the Earthquake." *NACLA Report on the Americas* 43, no. 4 (2010): 14–19.

Dynes, Russell R. "The Dialogue Between Voltaire and Rousseau on the Social Science View." *International Journal of Mass Emergencies and Disasters* 18, no. 1 (2000): 97–115.

———. "The Lisbon Earthquake in 1755: The First Modern Disaster." Disaster Research Center Preliminary Papers no. 333. University of Delaware, Newark, 2003.

———. *Organized Behavior in Disaster*. Lexington, MA: D. C. Heath, 1970.

Dyson, Michael Eric. *Come Hell or High Water: Hurricane Katrina and the Color of Disaster*. New York: Civitas Books, 2007.

Edelman, Murray. *Political Language: Words That Succeed and Policies That Fail*. New York: Academic Press, 1977.

———. *The Symbolic Uses of Politics*. Urbana: University of Illinois, 1964.

Eden, Lynn. *Whole World on Fire: Organizations, Knowledge, and Nuclear Weapons Devastation*. Ithaca, NY: Cornell University Press, 2004.

Edwards, Paul N. *A Vast Machine: Computer Models, Climate Data, and the Politics of Global Warming*. Cambridge, MA: MIT Press, 2010.

Ehrlich, Paul R., [and Anne Ehrlich]. *The Population Bomb*. New York: Ballantine, 1968.

Elliott, Rebecca. "Old Program, New Threats: Accounting for Climate Change in U.S. Flood Insurance." Working paper, 2019.

———. "The Sociology of Climate Change as a Sociology of Loss." *European Journal of Sociology* 59, no. 3 (2018): 301–37.

———. *Underwater: Loss, Flood Insurance, and the Moral Economy of Climate Change in the United States*. New York: Columbia University Press, 2020.

Enarson, Elaine, and Bob Pease, eds. *Men, Masculinities and Disaster*. New York: Routledge, 2016.

Erichsen, John Eric. *On Railway and Other Injuries of the Nervous System*. Philadelphia: Henry C. Lea, 1867.

Eriksen, Christine, Nicholas Gill, and Lesley Head. "The Gendered Dimensions of Bushfire in Changing Rural Landscapes in Australia." *Journal of Rural Studies* 26, no. 4 (2010): 332–42.

Erikson, Kai. *A New Species of Trouble: The Human Experience of Modern Disasters*. New York: Norton, 1994.

Erikson, Kai T. *Everything in Its Path: Destruction of Community in the Buffalo Creek Flood*. New York: Simon and Schuster, 1978.

Essene, Ren S., and William C. Apgar. *Understanding Mortgage Market Behavior: Creating Good Mortgage Options for All Americans*. Cambridge, MA: Joint Center for Housing Studies of Harvard University, 2007.

European Commission's Joint Research Center. "Haiti Earthquake January 2010 Damage Assessment Map." European Commission. February 21, 2013. https://ec.europa.eu/jrc/en/news/haiti-earthquake-first-damage-assessment-support-relief-efforts-7206.

Evans, Peter. *Embedded Autonomy: States and Industrial Transformation*. Princeton, NJ: Princeton University Press, 1995.

Faber, Jacob. "Racial Dynamics of Subprime Mortgage Lending at the Peak." *Housing Policy Debate* 23 (2013): 328–49.

———. "Segregation and the Geography of Creditworthiness: Racial Inequality in a Recovered Mortgage Market." *Housing Policy Debate* 28 (2018): 215–47.

Fainstein, Norman I., and Susan S. Fainstein. *Regime Strategies, Communal Resistance, and Economic Forces*. New York: Longman, 1983.

Famine Early Warning System Network, USAID. *Acute Food Insecurity: May*. Washington, DC, 2017.

Fan, Fa-ti. "'Collective Monitoring, Collective Defense': Science, Earthquakes, and Politics in Communist China." *Science in Context* 25, no. 1 (2012): 127–54.

Farazamand, Ali. *Global Cases in Best and Worst Practice in Crisis and Emergency Management*. Boca Raton, FL: CRC Press, 2016.

Farmer, Paul. *Infections and Inequities: The Modern Plagues*. 2nd ed. Berkeley: University of California Press, 1999.

Farr, William. *Report of the Proceedings of the Fourth Session of the International Statistical Congress: Held in London July 16th, 1860, and the Following Five Days*. London: Her Majesty's Stationery Office, 1861.

Fass, Simon M. *Political Economy in Haiti: The Drama of Survival*. New Brunswick, NJ: Transaction Books, 1988.

Feldman, Martha S. "Resources in Emerging Structures and Processes of Change." *Organization Science* 15, no. 3 (2004): 295–309.

Ferguson, Bruce, and Navarrete, Jesus. "New Approaches to Progressive Housing in Latin America: A Key to Habitat Programs and Policy." *Habitat International* 27 (2003): 309–23.

Field Hearing on Community Solutions for the Prevention and Management of Foreclosures, House Committee on Financial Services, Subcommittee on Housing and Community Opportunity, 109th Cong. (August 23, 2006).

Fields, Julie. "N.Y. Command Center." *The Record,* January 1, 2000.

Fierro, Eduardo, and Cynthia Perry. *Preliminary Reconnaissance Report: 12 January 2010 Haiti Earthquake.* The Pacific Earthquake Engineering Research Center (PEER), 2010.

Finn, Megan. "Information Infrastructure and Descriptions of the 1857 Fort Tejon Earthquake." *Information & Culture* 48, no. 2 (2013): 194–221.

Fischer, Henry W. *Response to Disaster: Fact Versus Fiction and Its Perpetuation: The Sociology of Disaster.* Lanham, MD: University Press of America, 1998.

———. *The Sociology of Disaster: Definitions, Research Questions and Measurements in a Post-September 11, 2001 Environment.* Atlanta, GA: American Sociological Association, 2003.

Fishbein, Allen, and Patrick Woodall. *Women Are Prime Targets for Subprime Lending: Women Are Disproportionately in High-Cost Mortgage Market.* Consumer Federation of America, 2006.

Fligstein, Neil. *The Architecture of Markets.* Princeton, NJ: Princeton University Press, 2001.

Fortun, Kim. *Advocacy After Bhopal: Environmentalism, Disaster, New Global Orders.* Chicago: University of Chicago Press, 2009.

Fortun, Kim, Scott Gabriel Knowles, Vivian Choi, Paul Jobin, Miwao Matsumoto, Pedro De la Torre III, Max Liboiron, and Luis Felipe R. Murillo. "Researching Disaster from an STS Perspective." In *The Handbook of Science and Technology Studies,* 4th ed., edited by Ulrike Felt, Rayvon Fouché, Clark A. Miller, and Laurel Smith-Doerr, 1003–28. Cambridge, MA: MIT Press, 2016.

Fothergill, Alice. *Heads Above Water: Gender, Class, and Family in the Grand Forks Flood.* Albany: SUNY Press, 2012.

Fothergill, Alice, and Lori Peek. *Children of Katrina.* Austin: University of Texas Press, 2015.

Foucault, Michel. *Society Must Be Defended: Lectures at the College de France, 1975–1976.* Translated by David Macey. Edited by Mauro Bertani and Alessandro Fontana. Basingstoke, UK: Macmillan, 2003.

Fradkin, Philip L. *The Great Earthquake and Firestorms of 1906: How San Francisco Nearly Destroyed Itself.* Berkeley: University of California Press, 2005.

Francis, Megan Ming. *Civil Rights and the Making of the Modern American State.* New York: Cambridge University Press, 2014.

Fraser, Nancy and Linda Gordon. "'Dependency' Demystified: Inscriptions of Power in a Keyword of the Welfare State." *Social Politics: International Studies in Gender, State & Society* 1, no. 1 (1994): 4–31.

———. "A Genealogy of Dependency: Tracing a Keyword of the U.S. Welfare State." *Signs: Journal of Women in Culture and Society* 19 (1994): 309–36.

Frickel, Scott, and M. Bess Vincent. "Hurricane Katrina, Contamination, and the Unintended Organization of Ignorance." *Technology in Society* 29, no. 2 (2007): 181–88.

Fritz, Charles. *Disasters and Mental Health: Therapeutic Principles Drawn from Disaster Studies.* University of Delaware Disaster Research Center, 1961.

Fry, Richard, and Anna Brown. "In a Recovering Market, Homeownership Rates Are Down Sharply for Blacks, Young Adults." Pew Research Center. 2016. www.pewsocialtrends.org /2016/12/15/in-a-recovering-market-homeownership-rates-are-down-sharply-for-blacks -young-adults/.

Funahashi, Daena. "Rule by Good People: Health Governance and the Violence of Moral Authority in Thailand." *Cultural Anthropology* 31, no. 1 (2016): 107–30.

Gadgil, Madhav, and Ramachandra Guha. *Ecology and Equity: The Use and Abuse of Nature in Contemporary India*. London: Routledge, 2013.

Gagliardone, Iginio. "'A Country in Order': Technopolitics, Nation Building, and the Development of ICT in Ethiopia." *Information Technologies & International Development* 10, no. 1 (2014): 3–19.

Gaillard, J. C. "The Climate Gap." *Climate and Development* 4, no. 4 (2012): 261–64.

Gaillard, J. C., Michael Glantz, Ilan Kelman, Ben Wisner, Zenaida Delica-Willison, and Mark Keim. "Taking the 'Naturalness' out of Natural Disaster (Again)." *Natural Hazards Observer* 38, no. 3 (2014): 1, 14–16.

Gaillard, J. C., and Jessica Mercer. "From Knowledge to Action: Bridging Gaps in Disaster Risk Reduction." *Progress in Human Geography* 37, no. 1 (2013): 93–114.

Gaillard, Roger. "Port-au-Prince en passe de devenir un monstre: Une interview d'Albert Mangonès." *Conjonction*, no. 119 (1973): 11–17.

Gallagher, Catherine. "The Rise of Fictionality." In *The Novel*, Vol. 1, *History, Geography, and Culture*, edited by Franco Moretti, 336–63. Princeton, NJ: Princeton University Press, 2007.

Gardiner, Sean. "The Dawn of 2000/Officials Hunker Down in 'Bunker' for Transition." *Newsday*, January 2, 2000.

Gasiorowski-Denis, Elizabeth. "Mainstreaming Disaster Management." *News* (blog), International Organization for Standardization, July 8, 2015. https://www.iso.org/news/2015/07 /Ref1982.html.

Geller, Robert J. *Nihonjin wa shiranai "jishin yochi" no shōtai*. Tokyo: Futabasha, 2011.

———. "Shake-Up for Earthquake Prediction." *Nature* 352, no. 6333 (1991): 275–76.

George, Susan. *How the Other Half Dies: The Real Reasons for World Hunger*. Montclair, NJ: Allanheld, Osmun, 1977.

Geschwind, Carl-Henry. *California Earthquakes: Science, Risk, and the Politics of Hazard Mitigation*. Baltimore, MD: Johns Hopkins University Press, 2008.

Ghertner, Asher. "Analysis of New Legal Discourse Behind Delhi's Slum Demolitions." *Economic and Political Weekly* 43, no. 20 (2008): 57–66.

Ghosh, Amitav. *The Great Derangement: Climate Change and the Unthinkable*. Chicago: University of Chicago Press, 2016.

Giddens, Anthony. *The Consequences of Modernity*. Stanford, CA: Stanford University Press, 1990.

———. *A Contemporary Critique of Historical Materialism*. Vol. 1, *Power, Property and the State*. London: Macmillan, 1981.

———. "Risk Society: The Context of British Politics." In *The Politics of Risk Society*, edited by Jane Franklin, 23–34. Cambridge, UK: Polity Press, 1998.

Gilbert, Claude. "Studying Disaster: Changes in the Main Conceptual Tools." In *What Is a Disaster? Perspectives on the Question*, edited by E. L. Quarantelli, 11–18. London: Routledge, 1998.

Glenn, Elizabeth Korver. "Compounding Inequalities: How Racial Stereotypes and Discrimination Accumulate Across the Stages of Housing Exchange." *American Sociological Review* 83 (2018): 627–56.

Godard, Henry. "Transferts de captiaux et mutations urbaines à Port-au-Prince." In *Villes et migrations internationales de travail dans le Tiers-Monde: Actes de la Table Ronde Transferts de revenus et projets immobiliers des travailleurs migrants dans les pays en developpement*, 301–28. Poitiers, France: Centre Interuniversitaires d'Etudes Mediterraneennes, Université de Poitiers, 1984.

Gold, Herbert. *Haiti: Best Nightmare on Earth*. New Brunswick, NJ: Routledge, 2001.

Goodlad, Lauren. "Introduction: Worlding Realisms Now." *Novel: A Forum on Fiction* 49, no. 2 (2016): 183–201.

Goethe, Johann Wolfgang von. *Truth and Fiction Relating to My Life*. Translated by John Oxenford. Boston: Simonds, 1902.

Gouda, Frances, Remco Raben, Henk Schulte Nordholt, and Ann Laura Stoler. "Ann Laura Stoler, Along the Archival Grain: Epistemic Anxieties and Colonial Common Sense." *Bijdragen Tot de Taal-, Land-En Volkenkunde/Journal of the Humanities and Social Sciences of Southeast Asia* 165, no. 4 (2009): 551–67.

Gould, Kevin A., M. Magdalena Garcia, and Jacob A. C. Remes. "Beyond 'Natural-Disasters-Are-Not-Natural': The Work of State and Nature After the 2010 Earthquake in Chile." *Journal of Political Ecology* 23, no. 1 (2016): 93–114.

Graham, Kevin Fox. "Critical Theory and Katrina: Disaster, Spectacle, and Imminent Critique." *City* 11 (2007): 81–99.

Graham, Stephen, ed. *Cites, War and Terrorism: Towards an Urban Geopolitics*. Oxford: Blackwell, 2004.

Gramlich, E. M. "Booms and Busts: The Case of Subprime Mortgages." *Economic Review* 92, (2007): 105–13.

Green, Jane. *Risk and Misfortune: The Social Construction of Accidents*. London: University College London Press, 1997.

Green, Maia. "Globalizing Development in Tanzania: Policy Franchising Through Participatory Project Management." *Critique of Anthropology* 23, no. 2 (2003): 123–43.

Greenberg, Josh, and T. Joseph Scanlon. "Old Media, New Media, and the Complex Story of Disasters." In *Oxford Research Encyclopedia of Natural Hazard Science*. July 2016. https://doi.org/10.1093/acrefore/9780199389407.013.21.

Greer, James. "The Better Homes Movement and the Origins of Mortgage Redlining in the United States." In *Statebuilding from the Margins: Between Reconstruction and the New Deal*, edited by Julie Novkov and Carol Nackenoff, 203–36. Philadelphia: University of Pennsylvania Press, 2014.

Gregory, Derek, and Allan Pred, eds. *Violent Geographies: Fear, Terror, and Political Violence*. London: Routledge, 2006.

Gros, Jean Germain. "Anatomy of a Haitian Tragedy: When the Fury of Nature Meets the Debility of the State." *Journal of Black Studies* 42, no. 2 (2011): 131–57.

Guinier, Lani, and Gerald Torres. *The Miner's Canary: Enlisting Race, Resisting Power, Transforming Democracy*. Cambridge, MA: Harvard University Press, 2002.

Gutman, Roy, David Reiff, and Anthony Dworkin, eds. *Crimes of War 2.0: What the Public Should Know*. New York: Norton, 2007.

Habermas, Jürgen. *The Structural Transformation of the Public Sphere*. Translated by Thomas Burger with the assistance of Frederick Lawrence. Cambridge, MA: MIT Press, 1989. First published 1962.

Hacking, Ian. *Rewriting the Soul: Multiple Personality and the Sciences of Memory*. Princeton, NJ: Princeton University Press, 1995.

———. *The Taming of Chance*. Cambridge: Cambridge University Press, 1990.

Haff, P. K. "Technology as a Geological Phenomenon: Implications for Human Well-Being." *Geological Society, London, Special Publications* 395, no. 1 (2014): 301–9.

Hagen, Ryan. "The Constant Metropolis: Disaster Risk Managers and the Production of Stability in New York City." PhD diss., Columbia University, 2019.

Halvorson, Britt. "Woven Worlds: Material Things, Bureaucratization, and Dilemmas of Care-giving in Lutheran Humanitarianism." *American Ethnologist* 39, no. 1 (2012): 122–37.

Han, Clara. *Life in Debt: Times of Care and Violence in Neoliberal Chile*. Berkeley: University of California Press, 2012.

Hancock, Mary. *The Politics of Heritage from Madras to Chennai*. Bloomington: Indiana University Press, 2008.

Hannigan, John. *Disasters Without Borders: The International Politics of Natural Disasters*. Cambridge: Polity, 2012.

Haraway, Donna, and Martha Kenney. "Anthropocene, Capitalocene, Chthulhocene." In *Art in the Anthropocene: Encounters Among Aesthetics, Politics, Environments and Epistemologies*, edited by Heather Davis and Etienne Turpin, 255–70. London: Open Humanities Press, 2015.

Haraway, Donna J. "A Cyborg Manifesto: Science, Technology, and Socialist-Feminism in the Late Twentieth Century." In *Simians, Cyborgs, and Women: The Reinvention of Nature*, 149–81. New York: Routledge, 1991.

———. *Staying with the Trouble: Making Kin in the Chthulucene*. Durham, NC: Duke University Press, 2016.

Hardy, R. Dean, et al., "Racial Coastal Formation: The Environmental Injustice of Colorblind Adaptation Planning for Sea-Level Rise." *Geoforum* 87 (2017): 62–72.

Harrisson, Tom. *Living Through the Blitz*. London: Penguin, 1976.

Hartmann, Betsy. *Reproductive Rights: The Global Politic of Population Control*. Boston: South End Press, 1995.

Haughton, Graham, Greg Bankoff, and Tom J. Coulthard. "In Search of 'Lost' Knowledge and Outsourced Expertise in Flood Risk Management." *Transactions of the Institute of British Geographers* 40 (2015): 375–86.

Hearing Before the Senate Comm. on Banking, Housing, and Urban Affairs Regarding Oversight of the National Flood Insurance Program. 109th Cong. (October 18, 2005) (testimony of J. Robert Hunter, Director of Insurance, Consumer Federation of America).

Hearing Before the Subcommittee on Government Efficiency and the District of Columbia, Senate Comm. on Governmental Affairs, on Loss of Financial Control over the National Flood Insurance Program. 95th Cong. (April 11, 1977) (statement of Henry Eschwege, Director Community and Economic Development Division).

Hecht, Gabrielle. *Being Nuclear: Africans and the Global Uranium Trade*. Cambridge, MA: MIT Press, 2012.

———. "Interscalar Vehicles for an African Anthropocene: On Waste, Temporality, and Violence." *Cultural Anthropology* 33, no. 1 (2018): 109–41.

———. *The Radiance of France: Nuclear Power and National Identity After World War II*. Cambridge, MA: MIT Press, 1998.

Heijmans, Annelies. "The Social Life of Community-Based Disaster Risk Reduction: Origins, Politics and Framing." Paper presented at World Conference of Humanitarian Studies, Groningen, February 4–8, 2009.

Heinrich, Herbert W. *Industrial Accident Prevention: A Scientific Approach*. New York: McGraw-Hill, 1931.

Hemann, Suzanne. "Marine Safety Engineers Add Value and Expertise to Coast Guard's Hurricane Response." *Marine Safety Engineering*, August 2018, 2.

Henderson, Jennifer, and Max Liboiron. "Compromise and Action: Tactics for Doing Ethical Research in Disaster Zones." In *Disaster Research and the Second Environmental Crisis*, edited by James Kendra, Scott G. Knowles, and Tricia Wachtendorf, 295–318. Cham, Switzerland: Springer, 2019.

Hetherington, Kregg. "Regular Soybeans: Translation and Framing in the Ontological Politics of a Coup." *Indiana Journal of Global Legal Studies* 21, no. 1 (2014): 55–78.

Hewitt, Kenneth. "Disaster Risk Reduction (DRR) in the Era of 'Homeland Security': The Struggle for Preventive, Non-violent, and Transformative Approaches." In *Emerging Issues in Disaster Risk Reduction, Migration, Climate Change and Sustainable Development*, edited by Karen Sudmeier-Rieux et al., 35–52. Heidelberg: Springer International, 2017.

———. "Disasters in 'Development' Contexts: Contradictions and Options for a Preventive Approach." *Jàmbá: Journal of Disaster Risk Studies* 5, no. 2 (2013): 1–9.

———. "Environmental Disasters in Social Context: Toward a Preventive and Precautionary Approach." *Natural Hazards* 66 (2012): 3–14.

———. "The Idea of Calamity in a Technocratic Age." In *Interpretations of Calamity from the Viewpoint of Human Ecology*, edited by Kenneth Hewitt, 3–32. Boston: Allen and Unwin, 1983.

———, ed. *Interpretations of Calamity from the Viewpoint of Human Ecology*. Boston: Allen and Unwin, 1983.

———. "Place Annihilation: Area Bombing and the Fate of Urban Places." *Annals of the Association of American Geographers* 73 (1983): 257–84.

———. "Proving Grounds of Urbicide: Civilian Perspectives on the Bombing of Capital Cities." *ACME: An International E-journal for Critical Geographies* 8, no. 2 (2009): 340–75.

———. "Reign of Fire: The Civilian Experience and Urban Consequences of the Destruction of German Cities, 1942–1945." In *Kriegzerstörung und Wiederaufbau deutscher Städte*, edited by J. Nipper and M. Mutz, , 57:25–45. Cologne: Geographische Arbeiten Hft, 1993.

———. *Regions of Risk: A Geographical Introduction to Disasters*. Harlow, UK: Addison Wesley Longman, 1997.

———. "The Social Space of Terror: Towards a Civil Interpretation of Total War." *Environment and Planning D: Society and Space* 5, no. 4 (December 1987): 445–74.

———. "Total War Meets Totalitarian Planning: Some Reflections on Königsberg/Kaliningrad." In *A Blessing in Disguise: War and Town Planning in Europe 1940–1945*, edited by J. Düwel and N. Gutschow, 88–103. Berlin: Dom Publishers, 2013.

———. "'When the Great Planes Came and Made Ashes of Our City . . .': Towards an Oral Geography of the Disasters of War." *Antipode* 26, no. 1 (1994): 1–34.

Hilgartner, Stephen. "Overflow and Containment in the Aftermath of Disaster." *Social Studies of Science* 37, no. 1 (February 2007): 153–58.

———. *Science on Stage: Expert Advice as Public Drama*. Stanford, CA: Stanford University Press, 2000.

Hilhorst, Dorothea, ed. *Disaster, Conflict and Society in Crisis*. London: Routledge, 2013.

Hinshaw, Robert E. *Living with Nature's Extremes: The Life of Gilbert Fowler White*. Boulder, CO: Johnson Books, 2006.

Hodges, Brian David, Ayelet Kuper, and Scott Reeves. "Qualitative Research: Discourse Analysis." *British Medical Journal* 337, no. 7669 (2008): 570–72.

Holliday, L., C. Ramseyer, and F. H. Grant. "Masonry Block Construction in Haiti." *WIT Transactions on the Built Environment* 120 (2011): 299–307.

Hommels, Anique, Jessica Mesman, and Wiebe E. Bijker, eds. *Vulnerability in Technological Cultures: New Directions in Research Governance*. Cambridge, MA: MIT Press, 2014.

Hoover, Elizabeth. "Jesmyn Ward on Salvage the Bones." *Paris Review*, August 30, 2011. https://www.theparisreview.org/blog/2011/08/30/jesmyn-ward-on-salvage-the-bones.

Horowitz, Andy. "Hurricane Betsy and the Politics of Disaster in New Orleans's Lower Ninth Ward, 1965–1967." *Journal of Southern History* 80, no. 4 (November 2014): 893–934.

———. *Katrina: A History, 1915–2015*. Cambridge, MA: Harvard University Press, 2020.

———. "Pre-Existing Conditions: Pandemics as History," *SSRC Items* (blog), July 9, 2020. https://items.ssrc.org/covid-19-and-the-social-sciences/disaster-studies/pre-existing-conditions-pandemics-as-history/.

Hough, Susan Elizabeth. *Predicting the Unpredictable: The Tumultuous Science of Earthquake Prediction*. Princeton:, NJ Princeton University Press, 2010.

Huet, Marie-Hélène. *The Culture of Disaster*. Chicago: University of Chicago Press, 2012.

Hughes, Thomas Parke. *Networks of Power: Electrification in Western Society, 1880–1930*. Baltimore, MD: Johns Hopkins University Press,1983.

Immergluck, Daniel. *Credit to the Community: Community Reinvestment and Fair Lending Policy in the United States*. New York: Routledge 2004.

———. *Foreclosed: High-Risk Lending, Deregulation, and the Undermining of America's Mortgage Market*. Ithaca, NY: Cornell University Press, 2009.

———. "Old Wine in Private Equity Bottles? The Resurgence of Contract-for-Deed Home Sales in US Urban Neighborhoods." *International Journal of Urban and Regional Research* 42 (2018): 651–65.

———. *Preventing the Next Mortgage Crisis: The Meltdown, the Federal Response, and the Future of Housing in America*. Lanham, MD: Rowman & Littlefield, 2015.

———."Too Little, Too Late, and Too Timid: The Federal Response to the Foreclosure Crisis at the Five-Year Mark." *Housing Policy Debate* 23 (2013): 199–232.

"In Pictures: Sierra Leone Slum." BBC. 2017. http://news.bbc.co.uk/2/shared/spl/hi/picture_gallery/07/africa_sierra_leone_slum/html/1.stm.

International Federation of the Red Cross. "World Disasters Report: Focus on Culture and Risk." 2014. https://www.ifrc.org/Global/Documents/Secretariat/201410/WDR%202014.pdf.

International Monetary Fund (IMF). *Haiti—Recent Economic Developments*. International Monetary Fund, June 2, 1970. https://archivescatalog.imf.org/Details/ArchiveExecutive/125035177.

Isham, Heyward, to Secretary of State. "Review of Issues Affecting US-Haitian Bilateral Relations." February 2, 1976. Case no. F-2015-01847, doc. no. C05790538. US Department of State Freedom of Information Act. https://foia.state.gov/DOCUMENTS/Oct2016/F-2015-01847/DOC_0C05790538/C05790538.pdf.

Ishibashi Katsuhiko. "Surugawan jishinsetsu koshi." *Kagaku* 73, no. 9 (2003): 1057–64.

———. "Tōkai chihō ni yosō sareru daijishin no saikentō—Surugawan jishin no kanosei." *Jishin yochi renrakukai kaihō* 17, nos. 4–13 (1977): 126–32.

Issa, Anindita, Kirtana Ramadugu, Prakash Mulay, Janet Hamilton, Vivi Siegel, Chris Harrison, Christine M. Campbell, Carina Blackmore, Tesfaye Bayleyegn, and Tegan Boehmer. "Deaths Related to Hurricane Irma—Florida, Georgia, and North Carolina, September 4–October 10, 2017." *Morbidity and Mortality Weekly Report* 67, no. 30 (2018): 829–32.

Jackson, Regine O. "The Failure of Categories: Haitians in the United Nations Organization in the Congo, 1960–64." *Journal of Haitian Studies* 20, no. 1 (2014): 34–64.

Jacobs, Jack. *The Frankfurt School, Jewish Lives, and Antisemitism*. Cambridge: Cambridge University Press, 2015.

Jacoby, Russell. *Picture Imperfect: Utopian Thought for an Anti-Utopian Age*. New York: Columbia University Press, 2005.

James, Robin. *Resilience and Melancholy: Pop Music, Feminism, Neoliberalism*. Arlesford, Hants, UK: Zero Books, 2015.

Jameson, Fredric. "The Dialectics of Disaster." *South Atlantic Quarterly* 101 (2002): 297–304.

Japan International Cooperation Agency (JICA). "DRLC Tenth Anniversary: Memorial for the 10th Anniversary of the Disaster Reduction Learning Center." 2017. https://www.jica.go.jp/kansai/drlc/ku57pq000005kh18-att/drlc_10th_en.pdf.

Jasanoff, Sheila. "Bhopal's Trials of Knowledge and Ignorance." *Isis* 98, no. 2 (2007): 344–50.

———. *Learning from Disaster: Risk Management After Bhopal*. Philadelphia: University of Pennsylvania Press, 1994.

Jay, Martin. *The Dialectical Imagination: A History of the Frankfurt School and the Institute of Social Research, 1923–1950*. Berkeley: University of California Press, 1996.

Jigyasu, Rohit. "Disaster: A 'Reality' or 'Construct'? Perspective from the 'East.'" In *What Is a Disaster? New Answers to Old Questions*, edited by Ronald W. Perry and E. L. Quarantelli, 49–60. London: Routledge, 2005.

Jishin yochi keikaku kenkyū gurupu. "Jishin yochi: Genjō to sono suishin keikaku" (1962).

Jishin yochi renrakukai. *Jishin Yochi Renrakukai 10-nen no ayumi*. Yatabe-machi (Ibaraki-ken). Tokyo: Kankōsha Kokudo Chiriin Nihon Sokuryō Kyōkai, 1979.

Johnson, Leigh. "Catastrophic Fixes: Cyclical Devaluation and Accumulation Through Climate Change Impacts." *Environment and Planning A* 47 (2015): 2503–21.

Joint Center for Housing Studies of Harvard University. "The State of the Nation's Housing 2009." 2009. http://www.jchs.harvard.edu/publications/markets/son2009/index.htm.

Jones, Marian Moser. *The American Red Cross from Clara Barton to the New Deal*. Baltimore, MD: Johns Hopkins University Press, 2013.

Jones, Samantha, Katie J. Oven, Bernard Manyena, and Komal Aryal. "Governance Struggles and Policy Processes in Disaster Risk Reduction: A Case Study from Nepal." *Geoforum* 57 (2014): 78–90.

Jonkman, Sebastiaan N., Maartje Godfroy, Antonia Sebastian, and Bas Kolen. "Brief Communication: Loss of Life Due to Hurricane Harvey." *Natural Hazards and Earth System Sciences* 18, no. 4 (2018):1073–78.

Junn, Jane. "Dynamic Categories and the Context of Power." In *The Future of Political Science: 100 Perspectives*, edited by Gary King, Kay L. Schlozman, and Norman Nie, 25–27.-New York: Routledge, 2009.

——. "Square Pegs and Round Holes: Challenges of Fitting Individual-Level Analysis to a Theory of Politicized Context of Gender." *Politics & Gender* 3 (2007): 124–34.

Kaika, Maria. "'Don't Call Me Resilient Again!' The New Urban Agenda as Immunology . . . or . . . What Happens When Communities Refuse to Be Vaccinated with 'Smart Cities' and Indicators." *Environment and Urbanization* 29, no. 1 (2017): 89–102.

Kamath, Lalitha. "New Policy Paradigms and Actual Practices in Slum Housing: The Case of Housing Projects in Bengaluru." *Economic and Political Weekly* 47, nos. 47/48 (2012): 76–86.

Karp, Jonathan. "How the Mortgage Bar Keeps Moving Higher: Home Buyers with Good Credit Confront Increased Scrutiny and Fewer Choices as Lenders React to Subprime Debacle," *Wall Street Journal*, August 14, 2007, D1.

Kasperson, Jeanne X., and Robert W. Kates, eds. "Overcoming Hunger in the 1990s." Special issue, *Food Policy* 15, no. 4 (August 1990).

Kawabata Nobumasa. "Daikibo jishin taisaku tokubetsu sochihō seitei tōji no naibu jijyō." *Kagaku* 73, no. 9 (2003): 1044–50.

Kawasumi Hiroshi. "San Furunando (Rosanzerusu) Jishin to sono kunren." *Soil Mechanics and Foundation Engineering* 19, no. 8 (1971): 34–40.

Keest, Kathleen. "The Way Ahead: A Framework for Policy Responses." Presentation at Subprime Housing Crisis Symposium, University of Iowa, October 10–11, 2008. www.respon siblelending.org/sites/default/files/nodes/files/research-publication/Iowa-Subprime -Symposium.pdf.

Kelman, Ilan. "Lost for Words Amongst Disaster Risk Science Vocabulary?" *International Journal of Disaster Risk Science* 9 (2018): 281–91.

Kendra, James, and Sarah Gregory. "Ethics in Disaster Research: A New Declaration." In *Disaster Research and the Second Environmental Crisis*, edited by James Kendra, Scott G. Knowles, and Tricia Wachtendorf, 319–41. Cham, Switzerland: Springer, 2019.

Kendra, James, and Tricia Wachtendorf. *American Dunkirk: The Waterborne Evacuation of Manhattan on 9/11*. Philadelphia: Temple University Press, 2016.

Kendrick, T. D. *The Lisbon Earthquake*. New York: J. B. Lippincott, 1957.

Kimura Shūhei. "Jinruigaku ni okeru saigai kenkyū: Koremade to korekara" [Disaster research in anthropology: Past and future]. In *Saigai bunka no keishō to sōzō* [Inheritance and creation of disaster cultures], edited by Hashimoto Hiroyuki and Hayashi Isao, 29–43. Kyoto: Rinsen Books, 2016.

——. "Mirai no jishin wo meguru risuku: Nihon ni okeru jishin no 'risuku-ka' purosesu no sobyō" [Risks relating to future earthquakes: A sketch of the process of "risk-alization" of disasters in Japan]. In *Risuku no jinruigaku: Fukakujitsu na sekai wo ikiru* [The anthropology of risk: Living in an indeterminate world], edited by Azuma Kentarō, Ichinoawa Junpei, I'ida Taku, and Kimura Shūhei, 83–103. Kyoto: Sekai Shisō sha, 2014.

Kingdon, John W. *Agendas, Alternatives, and Public Policies*. New York: HarperCollins, 1995.

Kishore, Nishant, D. Marqués, A. Mahmud, M. V. Kiang, I. Rodriguez, A. Fuller, P. Ebner, C. Sorensen, F. Racy, J. Lemery, et al. "Mortality in Puerto Rico after Hurricane Maria." *New England Journal of Medicine* 379, no. 2 (2018): 162–70.

Kitz, Janet F. *Shattered City: The Halifax Explosion and the Road to Recovery*. Halifax, NS: Nimbus, 2010.

Klein, Naomi. *Shock Doctrine: The Rise of Disaster Capitalism*. New York: Picador, 2007.

Kletz, Trevor A. *Lessons from Disaster: How Organizations Have No Memory and Accidents Recur*. Rugby, UK: Institution of Chemical Engineers, 1993.

Klinenberg, Eric. *Heat Wave: A Social Autopsy of Disaster in Chicago*. 2nd ed. Chicago: University of Chicago Press, 2015.

———. "When a Dissertation Chooses You." *Sociologica* 12, no. 1 (2019): 41–43.

Knowles, Scott Gabriel. *The Disaster Experts: Mastering Risk in Modern America*. Philadelphia: University of Pennsylvania Press, 2011.

Knowles, Scott Gabriel, and Howard C. Kunreuther. "Troubled Waters: The National Flood Insurance Program in Historical Perspective." *Journal of Policy History* 26, no. 3 (2014): 327–53.

Kousky, Caroline, Howard C. Kunreuther, Brett Lingle, and Leonard Shabman. *The Emerging Private Residential Flood Insurance Market in the United States*. University of Pennsylvania, Wharton Risk Management and Decision Processes Center, 2018.

Krippner, Greta. *Capitalizing on Crisis: The Political Origins of the Rise of Finance*. Cambridge, MA: Harvard University Press, 2011.

———. "Democracy of Credit: Ownership and the Politics of Credit Access in Late Twentieth-Century America." *American Journal of Sociology* 123 (2017): 1–47.

Kroll-Smith, J. Stephen, and Stephen Robert Couch. *The Real Disaster Is Above Ground: A Mine Fire and Social Conflict*. Lexington: University Press of Kentucky, 2015.

Krüger, F., G. Bankoff, T. Cannon, B. Orlowski, and L.F. Schipper. *Cultures and Disasters: Understanding Cultural Framings in Disaster Risk Reduction*. Oxford: Routledge, 2015.

Kuchinskaya, Olga. *The Politics of Invisibility: Public Knowledge about Radiation Health Effects After Chernobyl*. Cambridge, MA: MIT Press, 2014.

Kumaran, T. Vasantha, and Elizabeth Negi. "Experiences of Rural and Urban Communities in Tamil Nadu in the Aftermath of the 2004 Tsunami." *Built Environment* 32, no. 4 (2006): 375–86.

Lakoff, Andrew. *Unprepared: Global Health in a Time of Emergency*. Oakland: University of California Press, 2017.

Lakoff, Andrew, and Eric Klinenberg. "Of Risk and Pork: Urban Security and the Politics of Objectivity." *Theory and Society* 39, no. 5 (2010): 503–25.

Lappe, Frances Moore, and Joseph Collins. *World Hunger: Ten Myths*. 4th ed. San Francisco: Institute for Food and Development Policy, 1979.

Larabee, Ann. *Decade of Disaster*. Urbana: University of Illinois Press, 1999.

Latour, Bruno. "How Better to Register the Agency of Things: Ontology." Presentation in Yale Tanner Lecture Series. March 27, 2014. http://www.bruno-latour.fr/node/563.

———. *The Pasteurization of France*. Translated by Alan Sheridan and John Law. Cambridge, MA: Harvard University Press, 1993.

———. "The Powers of Association." In *Power, Action, and Belief: A New Sociology of Knowledge*, edited by John Law, 264–80. London: Routledge & Kegan Paul, 1986.

———. *Reassembling the Social: An Introduction to Actor-Network-Theory*. Oxford: Oxford University Press, 2005.

———. *Science in Action: How to Follow Scientists and Engineers Through Society*. Cambridge, MA: Harvard University Press, 1987.

———. "Technology Is Society Made Durable." *Sociological Review Monograph* 38 (1991): 103–31.

———. "Where Are the Missing Masses? The Sociology of a Few Mundane Artifacts." In *Shaping Technology/Building Society: Studies in Sociotechnical Change*, edited by Wiebe Bijker and John Law, 225–58. Cambridge, MA: MIT Press, 1992.

———. "Why Has Critique Run out of Steam? From Matters of Fact to Matters of Concern." *Critical Inquiry* 30, no. 2 (2004): 225–48.

Lavell, A. *Viviendo en riesgo: Comunidades vulnerables y prevencion de desas tres en America Latina.* Bogota: LA RED/FLACSO, 1994.

Law, John. "Notes on the Theory of the Actor-Network: Ordering, Strategy and Heterogeneity." *Systems Practice* 5 (1992): 379–93.

Leary, John Pat. "Keywords for the Age of Austerity 19: Resilience." Keywords: The New Language of Capitalism. June 23, 2015. https://keywordsforcapitalism.com/2015/06/23/keywords-for-the-age-of-austerity-19-resilience.

Leitch, Matthew. "ISO 31000:2009—The New International Standard on Risk Management." *Risk Analysis* 30, no. 6 (2010): 887–92.

Lewis, J. "The Susceptibility of the Vulnerable: Some Realities Reassessed." *Disaster Prevention and Management* 23, no. 1 (2014): 2–11.

Lewis, James, and Ilan Kelman. "The Good, the Bad and the Ugly: Disaster Risk Reduction (DRR) Versus Disaster Risk Creation (DRC)." *PLOS Currents* 4 (2012): 22919564. https://pubmed.ncbi.nlm.nih.gov/22919564.

Lewis, Simon L., and Mark A. Maslin. "Defining the Anthropocene." *Nature* 519, no. 7542 (2015): 171–80.

Liboiron, Max. "Disaster Data, Data Activism: Grassroots Responses to Representing Superstorm Sandy." In *Extreme Weather and Global Media*, edited by Julia Leyda and Diane Negra, 152–70. New York: Routledge, 2015.

Lifton, Robert Jay, and Eric Markusen. *The Genocidal Mentality: Nazi Holocaust and Nuclear Threat.* New York: Basic Books, 1990.

Lindee, M. Susan. *Suffering Made Real: American Science and the Survivors at Hiroshima.* Chicago: University of Chicago Press, 2008.

Lloyd Parry, Richard. *Ghosts of the Tsunami: Death and Life in Japan's Disaster Zone.* New York: MCD/Farrar, Straus, and Giroux, 2017.

Lorimer, Jamie. "The Anthropo-scene: A Guide for the Perplexed." *Social Studies of Science* 47, no. 1 (2017): 117–42.

Low, Morris. *Science and the Building of a New Japan.* New York: Palgrave Macmillan, 2005.

Lowenthal, Leo. *Critical Theory and Frankfurt Theorists: Lectures-Correspondence-Conversations.* New Brunswick, NJ: Transaction Publishers, 1989.

Löwy, Michael. *Fire Alarm: Reading Walter Benjamin's "On the Concept of History".* London: Verso, 2005.

———. *Redemption & Utopia: Jewish Libertarian Thought in Central Europe, a Study in Elective Affinity.* Stanford, CA: Stanford University Press, 1992.

Lupton, Deborah. *Risk.* 2nd ed. New York: Routledge, 2013.

Macdonald, H. *Commentary: The Security-Industrial Complex.* New York: Manhattan Institute for Policy Research, 2006.

Macdonald, N. D., Dave Chester, Heather Sangster, Beverly Todd, and Janet Hooke. "The Significance of Gilbert F. White's 1945 Paper 'Human Adjustment to Floods' in the Development of Risk and Hazard Management." *Progress in Physical Geography: Earth and Environment* 36, no. 1 (2012): 125–33.

Mack, R. W., and George Baker. *The Occasion Instant: The Structure of Social Responses to Unanticipated Air Raid Warnings.* Washington, DC: National Academy of Sciences-National Research Council, 1961.

MacKenzie, Donald. "Material Signals: A Historical Sociology of High-Frequency Trading." *American Journal of Sociology* 123, no. 6 (2018): 1635–83.

Makhijani, Arjun, Howard Hu, and Katherine Yih. *Nuclear Wastelands: A Global Guide to Nuclear Weapons Production and Its Health and Environmental Effects*. Cambridge, MA: MIT Press, 2000.

Maki Norio. "Hajimeni: Ajia to saigai/bōsai" [Introduction: Disasters and disaster risk reduction and Asia]. In *Kokusai kyōryoku to bōsai: Tsukuru, yorisou, kitaeru* [International cooperation and disaster risk reduction: Create, accompany, strengthen], 1–16, Kyoto: Kyoto daigaku gakujutsu shuppan ka, 2015.

Malm, Andreas. "The Origins of Fossil Capital: From Water to Steam in the British Cotton Industry." *Historical Materialism* 21, no. 1 (2013): 15–68.

Manecksha, Freny. "Pushing the Poor to the Periphery in Mumbai." *Economic and Political Weekly* 46, no. 51 (2011): 26–28.

Manyena, Siambabala Bernard. "The Concept of Resilience Revisited." *Disasters* 30, no. 4 (2006): 433–50.

Markowitz, Gerald, and David Rosner. *Deceit and Denial: The Deadly Politics of Industrial Pollution*. Berkeley: University of California Press, 2013.

Marks, Danny, and Eli Elinoff. "Splintering Disaster: Relocating Harm and Remaking Nature After the 2011 Floods in Bangkok." *International Development Planning Review* (May 2019): 273–94.

Martland, Samuel. "Reconstructing the City, Constructing the State: Government in Valparaíso after the Earthquake of 1906." *Hispanic American Historical Review* 87, no. 2 (2007): 221–54.

Maskrey, Andrew. *Disaster Mitigation: A Community Based Approach*. Oxford: Oxfam, 1989.

———. "Revisiting Community-Based Disaster Risk Management." *Environmental Hazards* 10, no. 1 (2011): 42–52.

Massey, Douglas S., Jacob S. Rugh, Justin P. Steil, and Len Albright. "Riding the Stagecoach to Hell: A Qualitative Analysis of Racial Discrimination in Mortgage Lending." *City & Community* 15 (2016): 118–36.

Mauch, Christof, and Christian Pfister. *Natural Disasters, Cultural Responses: Case Studies Toward a Global Environmental History*. Lanham, MD: Lexington Books, 2009.

Mayhew, David. "Wars and American Politics." *Perspectives on Politics* 3 (2005):473–93.

McCall, Leslie. *The Undeserving Rich: American Beliefs About Inequality, Opportunity, and Redistribution*. New York: Cambridge University Press, 2013.

McCarthy, Cormack. *The Road*. New York: Alfred A. Knopf, 2006.

McCarthy, Jonathan, and Richard W. Peach. "Are Home Prices the Next 'Bubble'?" *FRBNY Economic Policy Review* 10, no. 3 (2004): 1–17.

McCoy, Patricia, and Elizabeth Renuart. "The Legal Infrastructure of Subprime and Nontraditional Home Mortgages." In *Borrowing to Live: The Legal Infrastructure of Subprime and Nontraditional Homes Mortgages*, edited by Nicolas P. Retsinas and Eric S. Belsky. Washington, DC: Brookings Institution Press, 2008.

McCulloch, Jock. *Asbestos Blues: Labour, Capital, Physicians & the State in South Africa*. Oxford: James Currey, 2002.

———. "Counting the Cost: Gold Mining and Occupational Disease in Contemporary South Africa." *African Affairs* 108, no. 431 (2009): 221–40.

McNeill, J. R., and Peter Engelke. *The Great Acceleration: An Environmental History of the Anthropocene Since 1945*. Cambridge, MA: Harvard University Press, 2014.

McNeill, William H., and Charles P. Kindleberger. "Control and Catastrophe in Human Affairs." *Daedalus* 118, no. 1 (1989): 1–15.

McWilliams, H., and C. T. Griffin. "A Critical Assessment of Concrete and Masonry Structures for Reconstruction after Seismic Events in Developing Countries." In *Structures and Architecture: New Concepts, Applications and Challenges*, edited by Paulo J. S. Cruz, 857–64. Leiden: CRC Press, 2013.

Melville, Herman. "The Lightning-Rod Man." In *Herman Melville: Pierre, Israel Potter, The Piazza Tales, The Confidence-Man, Uncollected Prose, & Billy Budd*, 756–63. New York: Library of America, 1984. First published 1854.

Meyer, J. W., J. Boli, G. M. Thomas, and F. O. Ramirez. "World Society and the Nation-State." *American Journal of Sociology* 103 (1994): 144–81.

Meyer, J. W., W. R. Scott, and T. E. Deal. "Institutional and Technical Sources of Organizational Structure: Explaining the Structure of Educational Organization." In *Organizational Environments: Ritual and Rationality*, edited by J. W. Meyer and W. R. Scott, 45–67. Beverly Hills, CA: Sage, 1983.

Michel-Kerjan, Erwann O. "Catastrophe Economics: The National Flood Insurance Program." *Journal of Economic Perspectives* 24, no. 4 (2010): 165–86.

Michel-Kerjan, Erwann O., and Carolyn Kousky. "Come Rain or Shine: Evidence on Flood Insurance Purchases in Florida." *Journal of Risk and Insurance* 77, no. 2 (2010): 369–97.

Mileti, Dennis. *Disasters by Design: A Reassessment of Natural Hazards in the United States.* Washington, DC: Joseph Henry Press, 1999.

Ministry of Foreign Affairs (MOFA). *Country Assistance Profile for Chile.* Tokyo: MOFA, 2012.

Mitchell, Timothy. *Carbon Democracy: Political Power in the Age of Oil.* New York: Verso, 2011.

———. "The Limits of the State: Beyond Statist Approaches and Their Critics." *American Political Science Review* 85, no. 1 (1991): 77–96.

———. "State, Economy, and the State Effect." In *State/Culture: State Formation after the Cultural Turn*, edited by George Steinmetz, 76–97. Ithaca, NY: Cornell University Press, 1999.

Mitman, Gregg, Michelle Murphy, and Christopher Sellers. *Landscapes of Exposure: Knowledge and Illness in Modern Environments. Osiris* vol. 19. Chicago: University of Chicago Press, 2004.

Mogi Kiyō. *Jishin yochi o kangaeru.* Tokyo: Iwanami Shoten, 1998.

———. "Yochi sareta Surugawan Enshūnada chōōgata jishin no zenbō." *Shūkan Gendai* 11, no. 50 (1969): 138–42.

Moore, Jason W., ed. *Anthropocene or Capitalocene? Nature, History, and the Crisis of Capitalism.* Oakland, CA: PM Press, 2016.

———. *Capitalism in the Web of Life: Ecology and the Accumulation of Capital.* New York: Verso Books, 2015.

Morello-Frosch, Rachel, Manuel Pastor, and James Sadd. "Environmental Justice and Southern California's 'Riskscape': The Distribution of Air Toxics Exposures and Health Risks among Diverse Communities." *Urban Affairs Review* 36, no. 4 (March 2001): 551–78.

Morello-Frosch, Rachel, and Edmond D. Shenassa, "The Environmental 'Riskscape' and Social Inequality: Implications for Explaining Maternal and Child Health Disparities." *Environmental Health Perspectives* 114, no. 8 (August 2006): 1150–53.

Morozov, Evgeny. *To Save Everything, Click Here: The Folly of Technological Solutionism.* New York: Public Affairs, 2013.

Morton, Timothy. *Hyperobjects: Philosophy and Ecology After the End of the World.* Minneapolis: University of Minnesota Press, 2013.

Moss, David. *When All Else Fails: Government as the Ultimate Risk Manager.* Cambridge, MA: Harvard University Press, 2004.

Mukim, Megha. *Freetown Urban Sector Review: Options for Growth and Resilience.* Washington, DC: World Bank Group, 2018.

Mumford, Lewis. *The City in History.* New York: Harcourt, 1961.

Murphy, Michelle. *Sick Building Syndrome and the Problem of Uncertainty: Environmental Politics, Technoscience, and Women Workers.* Durham, NC: Duke University Press, 2006.

Mythen, Gabe. "Reappraising the Risk Society Thesis: Telescopic Sight Or Myopic Vision?" *Current Sociology* 55 (2007): 793–813.

National Hurricane Center. *Tropical Cyclone Report.* National Hurricane Center, 2011.

National Training and Information Center. *Preying on Neighborhoods: Subprime Mortgage Lenders and Chicago Land Foreclosures.* Chicago, 1999.

NATO's Role in Disaster Assistance. Euro-Atlantic Disaster Response Coordination Centre, Civil Emergency Planning, North Atlantic Treaty Organization, November 2001.

Neiman, Susan. *Evil in Modern Thought: An Alternative History of Philosophy.* Princeton, NJ: Princeton University Press, 2002.

Neocleous, Mark. "Resisting Resilience." *Radical Philosophy* 178 (March/April 2013): 2–7.

Newman, Kathe. "The Perfect Storm: Contextualizing the Foreclosure Crisis." *Urban Geography* 29 (2008): 750–54.

NHK Shakaibu. *Jishin ni sonaeru: Anata no bōsai taisaku.* Tokyo: Nihon hōso shuppan kyōkai, 1971.

Nixon, Rob. *Slow Violence and the Environmentalism of the Poor.* Cambridge, MA: Harvard University Press, 2013.

Nordstrom, Carolyn. *Shadows of War: Violence, Power and International Profiteering in the 21st Century.* Berkeley: University of California Press, 2004.

Ó Gráda, Cormac. *Famine: A Short History.* Princeton, NJ: Princeton University Press, 2009.

O'Brien, Terence H., *Civil Defence.* London: H.M.S.O., 1955.

Office of National Security-Disaster Management Bureau (ONS-DMB). *National Progress Report on the Implementation of the Hyogo Framework for Action (2009–2011).* Freetown, Sierra Leone, 2009.

Oficina Nacional de Emergencia del Ministerio del Interior y Seguridad Pública. N.d. "Presentación" [Introduction]. http://www.onemi.cl/presentacion/.

O'Keefe, Phil, Ken Westgate, and Ben Wisner. "Taking the Naturalness out of Natural Disasters." *Nature* 260 (1976): 566–67.

Oliver-Smith, Anthony. "Haiti's 500 Year Earthquake." In *Tectonic Shifts: Haiti Since the Earthquake,* edited by Mark Schuller and Pablo Morales, 18–23. Sterling, VA: Kumarian Press, 2012.

———. *The Martyred City: Death and Rebirth in the Andes.* Albuquerque: University of New Mexico Press, 1986.

———. "Peru's Five-Hundred-Year Earthquake: Vulnerability in Historical Context." In *The Angry Earth Disasters in Anthropological Context,* edited by Anthony Oliver-Smith and Susanna M. Hoffman, 88–102. New York: Routledge, 2012.

———. "Theorizing Disasters: Nature, Power and Culture." In *Catastrophe and Culture: The Anthropology of Disaster,* edited by Susan H. Hoffman and Anthony Oliver-Smith, 23–47. Santa Fe, NM: School of American Research Press, 2002.

———. "What Is a Disaster? Anthropological Perspectives on a Persistent Question." In *The Angry Earth: Disasters in Anthropological Context,* edited by Anthony Oliver-Smith and Susanna M. Hoffman, 18–34. New York: Routledge, 1999.

Oliver-Smith, Anthony, Irasema Alcantara-Ayala, Ian Burton, and Allan M. Lavell. *Forensic Investigations of Disasters (FORIN): A Conceptual Framework and Guide to Research*. IRDR FORIN Publications no. 2. Beijing: Integrated Research on Disaster Risk, 2016.

Oreskes, Naomi, and Erik M. Conway. *The Collapse of Western Civilization: A View from the Future*. New York: Columbia University Press, 2014.

———. *Merchants of Doubt: How a Handful of Scientists Obscured the Truth on Issues from Tobacco to Global Warming*. New York: Bloomsbury Press, 2011.

Page, Max. *The City's End: Two Centuries of Fantasies, Fears, and Premonitions of New York's Destruction*. New Haven, CT: Yale University Press, 2008.

Paley, Julia. *Marketing Democracy: Power and Social Movements in Post-Dictatorship Chile*. Berkeley: University of California Press, 2001.

Pantti, Mervi Katriina, and Karin Wahl-Jorgensen. "'Not an Act of God': Anger and Citizenship in Press Coverage of British Man-Made Disasters." *Media, Culture & Society* 33, no. 1 (January 2011): 105–22.

Paprocki, Kasia. "All That Is Solid Melts into the Bay: Anticipatory Ruination and Climate Change Adaptation." *Antipode* 51, no. 1 (2018): 295–315.

Parikka, Jussi. *The Anthrobscene*. Minneapolis: University of Minnesota Press, 2014.

Passannante, Gerard. *Catastrophizing: Materialism and the Making of Disaster*. Chicago: University of Chicago Press, 2019.

———. *The Lucretian Renaissance: Philosophy and the Aftermath of Tradition*. Chicago: University of Chicago Press, 2011.

Peck, Jamie, and Adam Tickell. "Neoliberalizing Space." *Antipode* 34 (2002): 380–404.

Pelling, Mark. *Natural Disasters and Development in a Globalizing World*. London: Routledge, 2003.

———. *The Vulnerability of Cities: Natural Disasters and Social Resilience*. London: Earthscan, 2003.

Pereira, Alvaro S. "The Opportunity of a Disaster: The Economic Impact of the 1755 Lisbon Earthquake." *Journal of Economic History* 69, no. 2 (2009): 466–99.

Perrow, Charles. *Normal Accidents: Living with High Risk Technologies*. Updated ed. Princeton, NJ: Princeton University Press, 2011.

Perry, Ronald W. "What Is a Disaster?" In *Handbook of Disaster Research*, edited by Havidán Rodríguez, Enrico L. Quarantelli, and Russell R. Dynes, 1–15. New York: Springer, 2007.

Perry, Ronald W., Michael K. Lindell, and Kathleen J. Tierney. *Facing the Unexpected: Disaster Preparedness and Response in the United States*. Washington, DC: Joseph Henry Press, 2001.

Petryna, Adriana. *Life Exposed: Biological Citizens after Chernobyl*. Princeton, NJ: Princeton University Press, 2013.

Phillips, Sandra. "The Subprime Mortgage Calamity and the African American Woman." *Review of Black Political Economy* 39 (2012): 227–37.

Pigeon, Patrick, and Julien Rebotier. *Disaster Prevention Policies: A Challenging and Critical Outlook*. London: Elsevier, 2016.

Poljanšek, Karmen, Montserrat M. Ferrer, Tom De Groeve, and Ian Clark.*Science for Disaster Risk Management 2017: Knowing Better and Losing Less*. EUR 28034 EN. Luxembourg: Publications Office of the European Union, 2017.

"Port-Au-Prince, Haiti: History with Tropical Systems." Hurricane City. N.d. Accessed July 28, 2018. http://www.hurricanecity.com/city/portauprince.htm.

Porteous, J. Douglas, and S. E. Smith. *Domicide: The Global Destruction of Home*. Montreal and Kingston: McGill-Queen's University Press, 2002.

Porter, Theodore M. *Trust in Numbers: The Pursuit of Objectivity in Science and Public Life.* Princeton, NJ: Princeton University Press, 1995.

Powell, Lawrence N. "What Does American History Tell Us about Katrina and Vice Versa?" *Journal of American History* 94, no. 3 (2007): 863–76.

Power, Fred B., and E. Warren Shows. "A Status Report on the National Flood Insurance Program—Mid-1978." *Journal of Risk and Insurance* 46, no. 2 (1979): 61–76.

Prince, Samuel Henry. *Catastrophe and Social Change: Based upon a Sociological Study of the Halifax Disaster.* New York: Columbia University, 1920.

Pritchard, Sara B. "An Envirotechnical Disaster: Nature, Technology, and Politics at Fukushima." *Environmental History* 17, no. 2 (2012): 219–43.

Problem Surrounding the Mortgage Origination Process, Joint Hearings Before the Senate Subcommittee on Financial Institutions and Regulatory Relief and the Subcommittee on Housing Opportunity and Community Development of the Committee on Banking, Housing, and Urban Affairs. 105th Cong. (July 9 and 15, 1997), 77–79.

Purdy, Jedediah. *After Nature: A Politics for the Anthropocene.* Cambridge, MA: Harvard University Press, 2015.

——. "The World We've Built." *Dissent Magazine*, July 3, 2018.

Quarantelli, E. L. "Epilogue: Where We Have Been and Where Might We Go." In *What Is a Disaster? Perspectives on the Question*, edited by E. L. Quarantelli, 234–73. London: Routledge, 1998.

——, ed. *What Is a Disaster? A Dozen Perspectives on the Question.* New York: Routledge, 2005.

——, ed. *What Is a Disaster? Perspectives on the Question.* London: Routledge, 1998.

Quarantelli, Enrico. "What Is a Disaster? The Need for Clarification in Definition and Conceptualization in Research." In *Disasters and Mental Health: Selected Contemporary Perspectives*, edited by S. Solomon, 41–73. Washington, DC: US Government Printing Office, 1985.

Quinn, Sarah L. "Government Policy, Housing, and the Origins of Securitization, 1780–1968." PhD diss., Department of Sociology, University of California, Berkeley, 2010.

Raboy, Marc, and Bernard Degenais. *Media, Crisis, and Democracy.* Thousand Oaks, CA: Sage, 1992.

"The Railway Calamity." *Saturday Review of Politics, Literature, Science and Art* 26, no. 670 (1868): 281–82.

Raman, Nithya V., and Priti Narayan. *Access to Finance for Incremental Construction: A Study from Three Low-Income Settlements in Chennai.* Transparent Chennai (CDF, IFMR), Chennai: Rajeev Awaz Yojana (RAY), Government of India, 2012.

Ramanathan, Usha. "Illegality and the Urban Poor." *Economic and Political Weekly* 41, no. 29 (2005): 3193–97.

Rappaport, Edward N., and B. Wayne Blanchard. "Fatalities in the United States Indirectly Associated with Atlantic Tropical Cyclones." *Bulletin of the American Meteorological Society* 97, no. 7 (2016): 1139–48.

Remes, Jacob A. C. "'Committed as Near Neighbors': The Halifax Explosion and Border-Crossing People and Ideas." *American Review of Canadian Studies* 45, no. 1 (March 2015): 26–43.

——. "Covid-19 in a Border Nation." *SSRC Items* (blog), July 23, 2020. https://items.ssrc.org/covid-19-and-the-social-sciences/disaster-studies/covid-19-in-a-border-nation/.

——. *Disaster Citizenship: Survivors, Solidarity, and Power in the Progressive Era.* Urbana: University of Illinois Press, 2016.

Renn, Ortwin. *Risk Governance: Coping with Uncertainty in a Complex World*. Abingdon, UK: Routledge, 2017.

Revet, Sadrine. "A Small World: Ethnography of a Natural Disaster Simulation in Lima, Peru." *Social Anthropology* 21, no. 1 (2013): 38–53.

Rikitake Tsuneji. "Daijishin wa tsune ni yochi sarete iru." *Chūō Kōron* 88, no. 9 (1973): 176–82.

———. *Earthquake Forecasting and Warning*. Tokyo: Center for Academic Publications Japan, 1982.

Rodríguez, Havidán, William Donner, and Joseph E. Trainor, eds. *Handbook of Disaster Research*. 2nd ed. New York: Springer International Publishing, 2018.

Roberts, Patrick. "Private Choices, Public Harms: The Evolution of National Disaster Organizations in the United States." In *Disaster and the Politics of Intervention*, edited by Andrew Lakoff, 42–69. New York: Columbia University Press, 2010.

Rosen, Christine Meisner. *Limits of Power: Great Fires and the Process of City Growth in America*. New York: Cambridge University Press, 1986.

Roy, Ananya. "Why India Cannot Plan Its Cities: Informality, Insurgence and the Idiom of Urbanization." *Planning Theory* 8, no. 1 (2009): 76–87.

Rozario, Kevin. *The Culture of Calamity: Disaster and the Making of Modern America*. Chicago: University of Chicago Press, 2007.

Rugh, Jacob, and Douglas Massey. "Racial Segregation and the American Foreclosure Crisis." *American Sociological Review* 75 (2010): 629–51.

Rummell, R. J. *Death by Government*. New Brunswick, NJ: Transaction Publishers, 1994.

Sagan, Scott D. *The Limits of Safety: Organizations, Accidents and Nuclear Weapons*. Princeton, NJ: Princeton University Press, 1993.

Salecker, Gene. *Disaster on the Mississippi: The* Sultana *Explosion, April 27, 1865*. Annapolis, MD: Naval Institute Press, 1996.

Salinas, Judith, Anselmo Cancino, Sergio Pezoa, Fernando Salamanca, and Marina Soto. "Vida Chile 1998-2006: Resultados y desafíos de la política de promoción de la salud en Chile." *Revista Panamericana de Salud Pública* 23, nos. 2/3 (2007): 136–44.

Samimian-Darash, Limor. "Practicing Uncertainty: Scenario-Based Preparedness Exercises in Israel." *Cultural Anthropology* 31, no. 3 (2016): 381–82.

Sawislak, Karen. *Smoldering City: Chicagoans and the Great Fire, 1871-1874*. Chicago: University of Chicago Press, 1995.

Schattschneider, E. E. *The Semisovereign People*. New York: Holt, Rinehart and Winston, 1960.

Schenk, Gerrit Jasper. "'Human Security' in the Renaissance? 'Securitas', Infrastructure, Collective Goods and Natural Hazards in Tuscany and the Upper Rhine Valley." *Historical Social Research* 35, no. 4 (2010): 209–33.

Schneiberg, Marc, and Elisabeth S. Clemens. "The Typical Tools for the Job: Research Strategies in Institutional Analysis." *Sociological Theory* 24, no. 3 (2006): 195–227.

Schneider-Mayerson, Matthew. "Disaster Movies and the 'Peak Oil' Movement: Does Popular Culture Encourage Eco-Apocalyptic Beliefs in the United States?" *Journal for the Study of Religion, Nature and Culture* 7, no. 3 (2013): 289–314.

Schuller, Mark. *Humanitarian Aftershocks in Haiti*. New Brunswick, NJ: Rutgers University Press, 2016.

Schultz, Kathryn. "The Really Big One." *New Yorker* July 20, 2015, 52–59.

Scott, James C. *Seeing Like a State: How Certain Schemes to Improve the Human Condition Have Failed*. New Haven, CT: Yale University Press, 1998.

Scraton, Phil. *Hillsborough: The Truth*. Liverpool, UK: Mainstream Publishing, 1999.

Seamster, Louise, and Raphaël Charron-Chénier. "Predatory Inclusion and Education Debt: A New Approach to the Growing Racial Wealth Gap." *Social Currents* 4 (2017): 199–207.

Sen, Amartya. *Poverty and Famines: An Essay on Entitlement and Deprivation*. Oxford: Clarendon Press of Oxford University Press, 1982.

Seo, John. "Insuring Natural Disasters: Mind the (Disaster) Gap." GAM Investments. December 11, 2018. https://www.gam.com/en/our-thinking/investment-opinions/insuring-natural-disasters-mind-the-disaster-gap.

Sewell, William H. "Historical Events as Transformations of Structures: Inventing Revolution at the Bastille." *Theory and Society* 25, no. 6 (1995): 841–81.

———. "A Theory of Structure: Duality, Agency, and Transformation." *American Journal of Sociology* 98, no. 1 (1992): 1–29.

Shapin, Steven, and Simon Schaffer. *Leviathan and the Air-Pump: Hobbes, Boyle, and the Experimental Life*. Princeton, NJ: Princeton University Press, 2011.

Shaw, Rajib, Koichi Shiwaku, and Yukiko Takeuchi. *Disaster Education*. Bingley, UK: Emerald Group Publishing, 2011.

Shklovsky, Victor. "From 'Art as Technique' 1917." In *Modernism: An Anthology of Source and Documents*, edited by Vassiliki Kolocotroni, Jane Goldman, and Olga Taxidou, 217–21. Chicago: University of Chicago Press, 1998.

Shrivastava, Paul. *Bhopal: Anatomy of a Crisis*. Newbury Park, CA: Sage, 1992.

Simmel, Georg. "The Metropolis and Mental Life." In *The Sociology of Georg Simmel*, edited by Kurt H. Wolff, 409–24. New York: Free Press, 1950.

Simon, Bryant. *The Hamlet Fire: A Tragic Story of Cheap Food, Cheap Government, and Cheap Lives*. New York: New Press, 2017.

Sliwinski, Alicia. *A House of One's Own: The Moral Economy of Post-Disaster Aid in El Salvador*. Montreal and Kingston: McGill-Queen's University Press, 2018.

Smith, Carl. *Urban Disorder and the Shape of Belief: The Great Chicago Fire, the Haymarket Bomb, and the Model Town of Pullman*. Chicago: University of Chicago Press, 1995.

Smith, Keith. *Environmental Hazards: Assessing Risk and Reducing Disaster*. New York: Routledge, 2003.

Smith, Kerry. "Earthquake Prediction in Occupied Japan." *Historical Social Research* 40, no. 2 (2015): 105–33.

Smits, Gregory. *When the Earth Roars: Lessons from the History of Earthquakes in Japan*. Lanham, MD: Rowman & Littlefield, 2014.

Solnit, Rebecca. *Paradise Built in Hell: The Extraordinary Communities That Arise in Disaster*. New York: Penguin, 2009.

Sontag, Susan. "The Imagination of Disaster." *Commentary* 40, no. 4 (October 1965): 42–48.

Sorokin, Pitirim A. *Man and Society in Calamity*. New Brunswick, NJ: Transaction Publishers, 1946.

Southwick, Steven M., George A. Bonanno, Anne S. Masten, Catherine Panter-Brick, and Rachel Yehuda. "Resilience Definitions, Theory, and Challenges: Interdisciplinary Perspectives." *European Journal of Psychotraumatology* 5, no. 1 (2014), doi:10.3402/ejpt.v5.25338.

Squires, Gregory, and Chester Hartman. *There Is No Such Thing as a Natural Disaster: Race, Class, and Hurricane Katrina*. New York: Routledge, 2013.

Stallings, Robert. "Disaster and the Theory of Social Order." In *What Is a Disaster? A Dozen Perspectives on the Question*, edited by E. L. Quarantelli, 127–45. New York: Routledge, 1998.

Star, Susan Leigh, and James R. Griesemer. "Institutional Ecology, 'Translations' and Boundary Objects: Amateurs and Professionals in Berkeley's Museum of Vertebrate Zoology, 1907–39." *Social Studies of Science* 19, no. 3 (1989): 387–420.

Steffen, Will, Wendy Broadgate, Lisa Deutsch, Owen Gaffney, and Cornelia Ludwig. "The Trajectory of the Anthropocene: The Great Acceleration." *Anthropocene Review* 2, no. 1 (2015): 81–98.

Steffen, Will, Paul J. Crutzen, and John R. McNeill. "The Anthropocene: Are Humans Now Overwhelming the Great Forces of Nature?" *Ambio* 36, no. 8 (December 2007): 614–21.

Steffen, Will, Jacques Grinevald, Paul Crutzen, and John McNeill. "The Anthropocene: Conceptual and Historical Perspectives." *Philosophical Transactions of the Royal Society* 369 (2011): 842–67.

Steinberg, Ted. *Acts of God: The Unnatural History of Natural Disaster in America.* 2nd ed. Oxford: Oxford University Press, 2006.

Stengers, Isabelle. *In Catastrophic Times: Resisting the Coming Barbarism.* Translated by Andrew Goffey. London: Open Humanities Press, 2015. First published 2009. http://www .openhumanitiespress.org/books/titles/in-catastrophic-times/.

Strathern, Marilyn. *Partial Connections.* Updated ed. Walnut Creek, CA: Altamira Press, 2004.

Strolovitch, Dara Z. "Advocacy in Hard Times." In *Nonprofit Advocacy,* edited by Steven R. Smith, Yutaka Tsujinaka, and Robert Pekkanen, 137–69. Baltimore, MD: Johns Hopkins University Press, 2014.

———. *Affirmative Advocacy: Race, Class, and Gender in Interest Group Politics.* Chicago: University of Chicago Press, 2007.

———. "Of Mancessions and Hecoveries: Race, Gender, and the Political Construction of Economic Crises and Recoveries." *Perspectives on Politics* 11, no. 1 (2013): 167–76.

———. *When Bad Things Happen to Privileged People: Race, Gender, and the Political Construction of Crisis & Non-Crisis.* Chicago: University of Chicago Press, forthcoming.

Sudmeier-Rieux, Karen, Manuela Fernández, Ivanna M. Penna, Michel Jaboyedoff, and J. C. Gaillard, eds. *Emerging Issues in Disaster Risk Reduction, Migration, Climate Change and Sustainable Development.* Heidelberg: Springer International, 2017.

Sundstrom, William. "Last Hired, First Fired? Unemployment and Urban Black Workers during the Great Depression." *Journal of Economic History* 52 (1992): 415–29.

Superstorm Research Lab [Erin Bergren, Jessica Coffey, Daniel Aldana Cohen, Ned Crowley, Liz Koslov, Max Liboiron, Alexis Merdjanoff, Adam Murphree, and David Wachsmuth]. "A Tale of Two Sandys." White paper. December 2013. https://superstormresearchlab.org /white-paper/.

Susman, Paul, Phil O'Keefe, and Ben Wisner. "Global Disasters: A Radical Interpretation." In *Interpretations of Calamity from the Viewpoint of Human Ecology,* edited by Kenneth Hewitt, 263–83. Boston: Allen and Unwin, 1983.

Svistova, Juliana, and Loretta Pyles. *Production of Disaster and Recovery in Post-earthquake Haiti: Disaster Industrial Complex.* Abingdon, Oxon: Routledge, 2018.

Sword-Daniels, Victoria, Christine Eriksen, Emma E. Hudson-Doyle, Ryan Alaniz, Carolina Adler, Todd Schenk, and Suzanne Vallance. "Embodied Uncertainty: Living with Complexity and Natural Hazards." *Journal of Risk Research* 21, no. 3 (2018): 290–307.

Szasz, Andrew. *EcoPopulism: Toxic Waste and the Movement for Environmental Justice.* Minneapolis: University of Minnesota Press, 1994.

Tamil Nadu Slum Clearance Board and Darashaw and Co. Pvt. Ltd. *Rajiv Awas Yojana (RAY): Slum Free City Plan of Action—Chennai City Corporation*. Chennai: Chennai City Corporation, 2013.

Tarasuk, V., and A. Mitchell. *Household Food Insecurity in Canada, 2017–18*. Report of PROOF. University of Toronto, 2020.

Taun wocchingu tebiki sakusei i'inkai [Town Watching Guide Drafting Committee]. *Bōsai Taun wocchingu jissen tebiki* [Practical guide for disaster risk reduction town watching]. Saijō City, 2008. https://www.preventionweb.net/files/12062_townwatching.pdf.

Taylor, Keeanga-Yamahtta. *Race for Profit: How Banks and the Real Estate Industry Undermined Black Homeownership*. Chapel Hill: University of North Carolina Press, 2019.

Thomas, Keith. *Religion and the Decline of Magic*. New York: Scribner, 1971.

Thomas, William I., and Dorothy Swaine Thomas. *The Child in America: Behavior Problems and Programs*. New York: Alfred Knopf, 1928.

Thurston, Chloe. *At the Boundaries of Homeownership*. New York: Cambridge University Press, 2018.

Tierney, Kathleen. "Disaster Governance: Social, Political, and Economic Dimensions." *Annual Review of Environment and Resources* 37 (2012): 341–63.

———. *The Social Roots of Risk: Producing Disasters, Promoting Resilience*. Stanford, CA: Stanford University Press, 2014.

Tierney, Kathleen J. "From the Margins to the Mainstream? Disaster Research at the Crossroads." *Annual Review of Sociology* 33 (2007): 503–25.

Tironi, Manuel, and Tania Manríquez. 2019. "Lateral Knowledge: Shifting Expertise for Disaster Management in Chile." *Disasters* 43, no. 2 (2019): 372–89.

Tironi, Manuel, Israel Rodríguez-Giralt, and Michael Guggenheim. *Disasters and Politics: Materials, Experiments, Preparedness*. Chichester, West Sussex: Wiley, 2014.

Tokyo Shōbōcho kasai yobō taisaku iinkai. *Tokyo-to no daishin kasai higai no kentō: Taisaku ni taisuru shiryō*. Tokyo: Tokyo Shōbōcho, 1967.

Tolbert, Pamela S., and Lynne G. Zucker. "The Institutionalization of Institutional Theory." In *Studying Organization: Theory & Method*, edited by Stewart R. Clegg and Cynthia Hardy, 169–84. London: Sage, 1999.

Tomari, Jirō. *Nihon no jishin yochi kenkyū 130-nenshi: Meijiki kara Higashi Nihon Daishinsai made*. Tokyo: Tokyo Daigaku Shuppankai, 2015.

———. *Purēto tekutonikusu no kyozetsu to juyō: Sengo Nihon no chikyū kagakushi*. Shohan ed. Tokyo: Tokyo Daigaku Shuppankai, 2008.

Torres Méndez, Mauricio, Beatriz Cid Aguayo, María Teresa Bull, Jenny Moreno, Alejandro Lara, Carlos Gonzalez Aburto, and Bárbara Henríquez Arriagada. "Resilencia comunitaria y sentido de comunidad durante la respuesta y recuperación al Terremoto-tsunami del año 2010, Talcahuano-Chile." *Revista de Estudios Latinoamericanos sobre Reducción del Riesgo de Desastres* (REDER) 2, no. 1: 21–37.

Traverso, Enzo. *Left-Wing Melancholia: Marxism, History, and Memory*. New York: Columbia University Press, 2016.

Tsing, Anna Lowenhaupt. *The Mushroom at the End of the World: On the Possibility of Life in Capitalist Ruins*. Princeton, NJ: Princeton University Press, 2015.

———. "Transitions as Translations." In *Transitions, Environments, Translations: Feminisms in International Politics*, edited by Joan W. Scott, Cora Kaplan, and Debra Keates, 253–72. New York: Routledge, 1997.

———. "Worlding the Matsutake Diaspora; or, Can Actor-Network Theory Experiment with Holism?" In *Experiments in Holism: Theory and Practice in Contemporary Anthropology,* edited by Ton Otto and Nils Bubandt, 47–66. London: Blackwell, 2010.

Turner, Barry A., and Nick F. Pidgeon. *Man-Made Disasters.* 2nd ed. Oxford: Butterworth-Heinemann, 1997.

UNESCO. "Haiti: Training Brings Concrete Contribution to Reconstruction—Haiti." Relief-Web. May 20, 2010. https://reliefweb.int/report/haiti/haiti-training-brings-concrete-contribution-reconstruction.

United Nations, CONADEP, and DTPTC. Plan de développement de Port-Au-Prince et de sa région métropolitiane, phase II. Vol. 2, Les secteurs economiques et sociaux. UNCHBP. May 1975, 33.

———. Plan de développement de Port-au-Prince et de sa région métropolitiane. Vol. 1, HAI/ 74 R. 40, UNCHBP, August 1976, S-1075-0553, UNARMS.

United Nations Office for Disaster Risk Reduction (UNISDR). Issue Brief: International Cooperation in Support of a Post-2015 Framework for Disaster Risk Reduction. Ministerial Roundtable, 2015.

———. *Living with Risk: A Global Review of Disaster Reduction Initiatives.* Vol. 1. Geneva: UNISDR, 2014.

———. *Local Governments and Disaster Risk Reduction: Good Practices and Lessons Learned.* A contribution to the "Making Cities Resilient" Campaign. Geneva: UNISDR, 2010.

———. "Natural Hazards, Unnatural Disasters: The Economics of Effective Prevention." 2010. https://www.unisdr.org/we/inform/publications/15136.

———. Sendai Framework for Disaster Risk Reduction 2015–2030. 2015. https://www.unisdr.org/files/43291_sendaiframeworkfordrren.pdf.

———. *United Nations Office for Disaster Risk Reduction: Annual Report 2018.* Geneva: UN Office for the Coordination of Humanitarian Affairs, 2019.

———. "What Is Disaster Risk Reduction?" 2018. https://www.unisdr.org/who-we-are/what-is-drr.

United States. President's Commission on Critical Infrastructure Protection. *Critical Foundations: Protecting America's Infrastructures.* The Report of the President's Commission on Critical Infrastructure Protection. Washington, DC: The President's Commission on Critical Infrastructure Protection, 1997.

US Department of Housing and Urban Development. *Insurance and Other Programs for Financial Assistance to Flood Victims.* Washington, DC: Department of Housing and Urban Development, 1966.

———. *Subprime Lending Report: Unequal Burden in Baltimore; Income and Racial Disparities in Subprime Lending.* 2000. https://www.huduser.gov/Publications/pdf/baltimore.pdf.

US Department of Housing and Urban Development, Office of Policy Development and Research. *Report to Congress on the Root Causes of the Foreclosure Crisis.* Washington, DC, 2010.

US Federal Emergency Management Agency (FEMA). *2017 Hurricane Season FEMA After-Action Report.* Washington, DC, 2018.

———. *Building Cultures of Preparedness: A report for the emergency management higher education community.* Washington, DC, 2019.

———. *A Chronology of Major Events Affecting the National Flood Insurance Program.* Washington, DC, 2005.

US Government Accountability Office (GAO). *Financial Management: Improvements Needed in National Flood Insurance Program's Financial Controls and Oversight.* GAO-10-66. Washington, DC: Government Accountability Office, 2010.

———. *Flood Insurance: FEMA's Rate-Setting Process Warrants Attention.* GAO-09-12. Washington, DC: Government Accountability Office, 2008.

———. *Flood Insurance: Opportunities Exist to Improve Oversight of the WYO Program.* GAO-09-455. Washington, DC: Government Accountability Office, 2009.

———. *HUD's Determination to Convert from Industry to Government Operation of the National Flood Insurance Program.* CED-78-122. Washington, DC: Government Accountability Office, 1978.

US Strategic Bombing Survey. *The Effect of Bombing on Medical and Health Care in Germany.* Report no. 65. Washington, DC: United States Strategic Bombing, Morale Division, Medical Branch, 1945.

———. *The Effects of Strategic Bombing on Japanese Morale.* Washington, DC: Pacific Survey, Morale Division, 1947.

Utsu Tokuji. "Hokkaido shūhen ni okeru daijishin no katsudo to Nemuro nanpō oki jishin ni tsuite." *Jishin yochi renrakukai no kaihō* 7 (1972): 7–13.

Vale, Lawrence J., and Thomas J. Campanella, eds. *The Resilient City: How Modern Cities Recover from Disaster.* New York: Oxford University Press, 2005.

Vaughan, Diane. "The Dark Side of Organizations: Mistake, Misconduct, and Disaster." *Annual Review of Sociology* 25, no. 1 (1999): 271–305.

———. *The* Challenger *Launch Decision: Risky Technology, Culture, and Deviance at NASA.* Chicago: University of Chicago Press, 1997.

Vázquez-Arroyo, Antonio. "The Antinomies of Violence and Catastrophe: Orders, Structures, and Agents." *New Political Science* 34 (June 2012): 211–21.

———. "How Not to Learn from Catastrophe: Critical Theory and the Catastrophization of Political Life." *Political Theory* 41 (2013): 738–65.

Virilio, Paul. *The Original Accident.* Cambridge, UK: Polity Press, 2005.

Wachira, George. "Conflicts in Africa as Compound Disasters: Complex Crises Requiring Comprehensive Responses." *Journal of Contingencies and Crisis Management* 5, no. 2 (1997): 109–17.

Walch, Colin. "Typhoon Haiyan: Pushing the Limits of Resilience? The Effect of Land Inequality on Resilience and Disaster Risk Reduction Policies in the Philippines." *Critical Asian Studies* 50, no. 1 (2018): 122–35.

Walford, Cornelius. *The Famines of the World: Past and Present.* London: Edward Stanford, 1879.

Walker, Brett L. *Toxic Archipelago: A History of Industrial Disease in Japan.* Seattle: University of Washington Press, 2011.

Wall, Cynthia. "Novel Streets: The Rebuilding of London and Defoe's *A Journal of the Plague Year.*" *Studies in the Novel* 30, no. 2 (Summer 1998): 164–77.

Wallace, Anthony F. C. *Tornado in Worcester: An Exploratory Study of Individual and Community Behavior in an Extreme Situation.* Washington, DC: National Academy of Sciences, National Research Council, 1956

Wallace, Tina, with Lisa Bornstein and Jennifer Chapman. *The Aid Chain: Coercion and Commitment in Development NGOs.* Bourton on Dunsmore, Rugby, Warwickshire: Practical Action Publishing, 2007.

Wang, Kelin, Qi-Fu Chen, Shihong Sun, and Andong Wang. "Predicting the 1975 Haicheng Earthquake." *Bulletin of the Seismological Society of America* 96, no. 3 (2006): 757–95.

Ward, Jesmyn. *Salvage the Bones: A Novel.* New York: Bloomsbury, 2011.

Washer, Peter. *Emerging Infectious Diseases and Society.* New York: Palgrave Macmillan, 2014.

Watts, M. J. *Silent Violence: Food, Famine, and Peasantry in Northern Nigeria.* Berkeley: University of California Press, 1983.

Weick, Karl E. "The Collapse of Sensemaking in Organizations: The Mann Gulch Disaster." *Administrative Science Quarterly* 38, no. 4 (1993): 628–52.

Weick, K. E., and K. H. Roberts. "Collective Mind in Organizations: Heedful Interrelating on Flight Decks." *Administrative Science Quarterly* 38 (1993): 357–81.

Weinstein, Liza. *The Durable Slum: Dharavi and the Right to Stay Put in Globalizing Mumbai.* Minneapolis: University of Minnesota Press, 2014.

Wheatland, Thomas. *The Frankfurt School in Exile.* Minneapolis: University of Minnesota Press, 2009.

White, Gilbert Fowler. "Human Adjustment to Floods: A Geographical Approach to the Flood Problem in the United States." PhD diss., University of Chicago, 1942.

———. *Natural Hazards, Local, National, Global.* Oxford: Oxford University Press, 1974.

Wiggershaus, Rolf. *The Frankfurt School: Its History, Theories, and Political Significance.* Cambridge, MA: MIT Press, 1994.

Wilke, Jürgen. "Historical Perspectives on Media Events: A Comparison of the Lisbon Earthquake in 1755 and the Tsunami Catastrophe in 2004." In *Media Events in a Global Age,* edited by Nick Couldry, Andreas Hepp, and Friedrich Krotz, 45–60. New York: Routledge, 2009.

Williams, Raymond. "Ideas of Nature." In *Problems in Materialism and Culture,* 67–85. London: Verso, 1980.

———. *Keywords.* New York: Oxford University Press, 1976.

Wilt, Judith. "The Imperial Mouth: Imperialism, the Gothic and Science Fiction." *Journal of Popular Culture* 14, no. 4 (1981): 618–28.

Winkler, Allan M. *Life Under a Cloud: American Anxiety About the Atom.* Urbana: University of Illinois Press, 1999.

Winner, Langdon. *The Whale and the Reactor: A Search for Limits in an Age of High Technology.* Chicago: University of Chicago Press, 1986.

Wisner, Ben. "Let Our Children Teach Us! A Review of the Role of Education and Knowledge in Disaster Risk Reduction." ISDR System Thematic Cluster/Platform on Knowledge and Education. 2006. http://www.unisdr.org/files/609_10030.pdf.

Wisner, Ben, Piers Blaikie, Terry Cannon, and Ian Davis. *At Risk: Natural Hazards, People's Vulnerability and Disasters.* 2nd ed. London: Routledge, 2004.

Wisner, Ben, J. C. Gaillard, and Ilan Kelman, eds. *The Routledge Handbook of Hazards and Disaster Risk Reduction.* London: Routledge, 2012.

Wisner, Ben, and Henry Luce. "Disaster Vulnerability: Scale, Power and Daily Life." *GeoJournal* 30, no. 2 (1993): 127–40.

Wisner, Ben, Phil O'Keefe, and Ken Westgate. "Global Systems and Local Disasters: The Untapped Power of People's 'Science.'" *Disasters* 1, no. 1 (1977): 47–57.

Woodham-Smith, C. *The Great Hunger.* London: Hamish Hamilton, 1962.

World Bank. *Project Performance Audit Report: India, First Madras Urban Development Project.* Washington, DC: World Bank, 1986.

———. *Tamil Nadu and Puducherry Coastal Disaster Risk Reduction Project: Implementation Status & Results Report.* World Bank, 2016.

Wyly, Elvin, and C. S. Ponder. "Gender, Age, and Race in Subprime America." *Housing Policy Debate* 21 (2011): 529–64.

Wynne, Brian. "Uncertainty and Environmental Learning: Reconceiving Science and Policy in the Preventive Paradigm." *Global Environmental Change* 2, no. 2 (1992): 111–27.

Zalasiewicz, Jan, Mark Williams, Colin N. Waters, Anthony D. Barnosky, John Palmesino, Ann-Sofi Rönnskog, Matt Edgeworth, Cath Neal, Alejandro Cearreta, and Erle C. Ellis. "Scale and Diversity of the Physical Technosphere: A Geological Perspective." *Anthropocene Review* 4, no. 1 (2017): 9–22.

Zeiderman, Austin. *Endangered City: The Politics of Security and Risk in Bogotá.* Durham, NC: Duke University Press, 2016.

———. "On Shaky Ground: The Making of Risk in Bogotá." *Environment and Planning* 44, no. 7 (2012): 1570–88.

Zylinska, Joanna. *The End of Man: A Feminist Counterapocalypse.* Minneapolis: University of Minnesota Press, 2018.

INDEX

Aaron Clark-Ginsberg is a social scientist at the nonprofit and nonpartisan RAND Corporation. A disaster researcher by training, Dr. Clark-Ginsberg has topical expertise in disaster risk reduction, community resilience, critical infrastructure protection, and governance. Dr. Clark-Ginsberg has conducted disaster-related research for governmental and nongovernmental agencies in more than ten countries across Africa, Europe, Asia, and the Americas. His published research is about hazard management, especially where it can affect humans and their communities.

Pranathi Diwakar is a PhD candidate in sociology at the University of Chicago. Her research focuses on inequality, urban life, and cultural practice, and her writing has appeared in *City & Community* and *Economic & Political Weekly*.

Rebecca Elliott is assistant professor of sociology at the London School of Economics and Political Science. Her research examines the intersections of environmental change and economic life as they relate to climate change, US public policy, and everyday consumption practices. She is the author of *Underwater: Loss, Flood Insurance, and the Moral Economy of Climate Change in the United States* (Columbia University Press, 2020).

Ryan Hagen is a postdoctoral researcher in the Department of Sociology at Columbia University. His research is at the intersection of historical sociology, organizational sociology, and the sociology of science, knowledge, and technology.

Kenneth Hewitt is professor emeritus in geography and environmental studies and a research associate in the Cold Regions Research Centre, Wilfrid Laurier University. His academic career included tenured professorships at the University of Toronto and Rutgers University, New Jersey. His main teaching, research, and consulting fields are geomorphology and high mountain environments, environmental disasters, and peace research.

Andy Horowitz is assistant professor of history and the Paul and Debra Gibbons Professor in the School of Liberal Arts at Tulane University. He is the author of *Katrina: A History, 1915–2015* (Harvard University Press, 2020).

Scott Gabriel Knowles is professor in the Graduate School of Science and Technology Policy at the Korea Advanced Institute of Science and Technology (KAIST). Knowles is the author of *The Disaster Experts: Mastering Risk in Modern America* (University of Pennsylvania Press, 2011), editor of *Imagining Philadelphia: Edmund Bacon and the Future of the City* (University of Pennsylvania Press, 2009), and coeditor (with Richardson Dilworth) of *Building Drexel: The University and Its City, 1891–2016* (Temple University Press, 2016) and (with Art Molella) of *World's Fairs in the Cold War: Science, Technology, and the Culture of Progress* (University of Pittsburgh Press, 2019). He is series coeditor (with Kim Fortun) of Critical Studies in Risk and Disaster (University of Pennsylvania Press).

Zachary Loeb is a PhD candidate in the history and sociology of science department at the University of Pennsylvania. Loeb's research sits at the intersection of the history of technology and disaster studies, with a particular focus on prophecies of doom. Currently, Loeb is writing a dissertation on the year 2000 computing crisis (Y2K).

Susan Scott Parrish is Arthur F. Thurnau Professor at the University of Michigan, where she teaches in both the Program in the Environment and the Department of English. Her recent book, *The Flood Year 1927: A Cultural History* (Princeton University Press, 2017), examines how the most devastating, and publicly absorbing, US flood of the twentieth century—the Great Mississippi Flood—took on meaning as it moved across media platforms, across sectional divides, and across the color line.

Claire Antone Payton is a historian and postdoctoral fellow at the Carter G. Woodson Institute for African American and African Studies at the University of Virginia. Her research interests center on urbanization and disaster in the Caribbean, with a focus on the material and political history of twentieth-century Haiti.

Jacob A. C. Remes is clinical associate professor of history in New York University's Gallatin School of Individualized Study, where he directs the Initiative for Critical Disaster Studies. Trained as a labor and working-class historian of the United States and Canada, he is the author of *Disaster Citizenship: Survivors, Solidarity, and Power in the Progressive Era* (University of Illinois Press, 2016).

Kerry Smith is a historian of modern Japan in the Departments of East Asian Studies and History at Brown University. He is the author of *A Time of Crisis: Japan, the Great Depression, and Rural Revitalization* (Harvard University Asia Center, 2001) and a number of shorter works on topics including war memory, museums, and the history of earthquakes and earthquake science in Japan. He is completing a book manuscript on disaster as an ongoing condition in modern Japan and the role of scientists as mediators of the public's understanding of the hazards and risks the nation has faced.

Dara Z. Strolovitch is professor at Princeton University, where she holds appointments in gender and sexuality studies, African American studies, and politics. Beginning in fall 2021, she will be professor of women's, gender, and sexuality studies, American studies, and political science at Yale. Her research focuses on American politics, political representation, and the intersecting politics of race, class, gender, and sexuality. She is the author of the award-winning book *Affirmative Advocacy: Race, Class, and Gender in Interest Group Politics* (University of Chicago Press, 2007), and her next book, *When Bad Things Happen to Privileged People: Race, Gender, and the Political Construction of Crisis & Non-Crisis*, is forthcoming from the University of Chicago Press.

Chika Watanabe is lecturer (assistant professor) in social anthropology at the University of Manchester (UK). She is the author of *Becoming One: Religion, Development, and Environmentalism in a Japanese NGO in Myanmar* (University of Hawai'i Press, 2019) and several articles on development, religion/secularity, and NGOs in journals such as *American Ethnologist*, *American Anthropologist*, and *Cultural Anthropology*. She is currently working on a project examining international cooperation around disaster preparedness between Japan and Chile.

ACKNOWLEDGMENTS

This volume grew out of a conference held in September 2018 at New York University's Gallatin School of Individualized Study. We are grateful to Dean Susanne Wofford for her welcome and her intellectual and especially material support; to Associate Dean Linda Wheeler Reiss for administrative support; and to the special events office, including Michael Wess and especially Associate Director Theresa Anderson, without whom the conference would have been impossible. Four Gallatin colleagues, Marie Cruz Soto, Rosalind Fredericks, Karen Holmberg, and Eugenia Kisin, graciously chaired the conference sessions. We are grateful too for support from the Tulane University Department of History. Thanks also to research assistant extraordinaire Madison Kelts and to Anna-Morgan Leonards, who helped iron out the bibliography. Timothy Pearson created the index. We thank Robert Lockhart, our editor at the University of Pennsylvania Press, for his help and advice, and for shepherding this book through publication.

An earlier version of Pranathi Diwakar's chapter appeared as "A Recipe for Disaster: Framing Risk and Vulnerability in Slum Relocation Policies in Chennai, India," *City & Community* 18, no. 4 (December 2019): 1314–37, and we are grateful to the journal's editors for permission to include a substantially revised version in this volume.

Thanks are also due to the contributors to this volume and to Louis Gerdelan, who not only contributed their own ideas but generously and collegially workshopped all the other chapters. Finally, we gratefully acknowledge Elizabeth Angell, anthropologist of earthquakes, who was our partner in planning the initial conference, and who helped to select this roster of scholars and subjects from the hundreds of applicants who responded to our initial call to help chart the future of disaster studies. Though she did not participate in editing this volume, its table of contents reflects her vision as much as ours—and is better for it.